Pages 2/3: The first British rigid airship, the *Mayfly*, approaches the mooring pontoon in the centre of Barrow's Cavendish Dock shortly after first emerging from her shed on 22 May 1911.

# Airship Saga

The history of airships seen through the eyes of the men who designed, built and flew them

**LORD VENTRY** and **EUGÈNE M. KOLEŚNIK**

**BLANDFORD PRESS**

Poole          Dorset

*First published in the U.K. 1982 by Blandford Press,*
*Link House, West Street, Poole, Dorset, BH15 1LL*

*Copyright © 1982 Blandford Books Ltd*

*Distributed in the United States by*
*Sterling Publishing Co., Inc.,*
*2 Park Avenue, New York, N.Y. 10016*

**British Library Cataloguing in Publication Data**

Ventry, Arthur Frederick Daubeney Olav Eveleigh
  de Molyns Ventry, *Baron*
  An airship saga.
  1. Airships—History
  I. Title II. Koleśnik, Eugène M.
  629.133′24′0922        TL650

*ISBN 0 7137 1001 2*

*Typeset by Polyglot Pte Ltd, Singapore*

*Printed by Richard Clay Ltd., Bungay, Suffolk*

Pages 4/5: The rigid airship *Los Angeles* flying over
USS *Raleigh* during fleet manoeuvres, October 1930.

# Contents

# Preface

Years ago now I asked some of my airship friends if they would write of their experiences for a possible book; this is the result. Many of them have since passed away, but it is still possible to thank them all for their co-operation and patience. The fact that at long last the book can be published is due to a writer friend, Eugene M. Koleśnik, who, together with Blandford Press, created this volume based on some of my original material. As a result, Great Britain, France, Germany, Italy and Norway are represented by contributions from some of the best known airship men of their day; whom I am proud to have had among my friends.

*Ventry*

*This book is dedicated to the memory of the airship pioneers whose perseverance in the face of great odds, and in particular throughout two world wars, has bequeathed to us a record of remarkable courage and dedication to duty, all too little known today.*

# Acknowledgements

The bulk of this book is made up from the contributions of many fine old airship men, most of whom are, unfortunately, no longer alive, and to these pioneers who preserved their log books and service records for posterity, we extend our sincere gratitude. Those who provided special contributions and to whom, therefore, a special debt of gratitude is due are: Wing Commander J. N. Fletcher, AFC; Wing Commander T. R. Cave–Browne–Cave, CBE; Major J. Struthers, DSC, AFC; Air Vice-Marshal P. E. Maitland, CB, CBE, MVD, AFC; Engineer Général Etienne Joux; Colonel Tito Tombesi; Major General Hjalmar Riiser-Larsen, KCB; Captain Hans von Schiller; Squadron Leader T. P. York-Moore; and Roger Munck. Special mention should also be made of the editors of the *Wingfoot Lighter-than-Air Society Bulletin* for giving permission to use quotations from lectures given by: James F. Boyle; Ralph H. Upson; Lieutenant Commander Walter Bjerre; Captain Klein; Commander Herman G. Spahr; Commander Jack R. Hunt; and Commander Ernest W. Steffen. Special mention must also be made of J. Gordon Vaeth for all his kind help in the past. Thanks are also due to J. A. C. Aird, MVO, MBE, for translating Norwegian material, to Wing Commander J. N. Fletcher, AFC, for translating the Italian material, to Peter J. Walker for translating German material, and to Alex Vanags-Baginskis for translating Russian and German documents and providing material from his own archives, and to John Batchelor for executing the cutaway drawing of the *Hindenburg*. Mr Lyle Schwilling of the Goodyear Aerospace Corporation provided much useful material on the development of the Goodyear-built airships, and Mr Frank Kiernan of RAE Cardington provided valuable assistance with British rigid and non-rigid airships, and we extend our warmest gratitude to them also. We are most grateful to Kate Spells who gave considerable and invaluable assistance with the typing and general editing of the manuscript, and with French and Italian translations. Last, but by no means least, we wish to thank the publishers for making this book possible, and in particular Barry Gregory of Blandford Press whose sound advice and *almost* unlimited patience are appreciated deeply, and Michael Burns who co-ordinated the various stages of producing this book.

# Introduction

The past decade has seen a remarkable resurgence in the popularity of airships, and the growing interest in these machines has involved governments, financial institutions and international commercial organisations, as well as a few visionaries and some hard-headed technologists. But just as important have been the intrepid and generous men who were connected with rigid and non-rigid airships when these craft were in their heyday — almost half a century ago in Europe, and as late as 1962 in the United States of America — for these men have provided the new generation of airship constructors with the benefit of their skills and knowledge, which is based on first-hand experience. Inevitably, this so-called airship renaissance has brought with it a flood of books on the subject. Some of these works, such as those by Robin Higham and Douglas H. Robinson, are excellent studies based on original research and are now regarded as classics, but unfortunately many of the general histories consist of regurgitated inaccuracies, and some, like a recent book by a popular spy fiction writer, seem to revel in the cheap and sensational, concentrating on the horrors of the worst airship disasters. In some small measure it is hoped that the *Airship Saga* will do a little to counteract this type of journalism, for it contains something of the achievement of the airship in terms of the triumphs of technical skill, courage and human endurance.

It is absurd to talk of the airship's failure for, as this book will show, it was the politicians that failed the airship. Also, the airshipmen of the past were often accused of committing acts of blind faith in relying on their ungainly machines, but again this is an absurd contention and is only in part true of the earliest airship constructors. This accusation should not be levelled at the designers of the later airships or for that matter the men who flew them, for their convictions were based on sound principles of scientific fact and flying skills

## Airships versus Prejudice

achieved through rigorous training and practice. The endurance feats of the British and American anti-submarine airship pilots and the ingenious geodetic principle of design applied by the late Sir Barnes Wallis to the *R 100* are testament to the skills and ability doubted by the critics of the airship.

Even today, a technical innovation needs time for testing and even if a concept is proved over a number of years, accidents, due to mechanical or human failure, can still happen. For example, the accident rate for aeroplanes in the Western public transport system alone, despite all attempts at improvement, continues today at a depressing two fatal crashes for every million take-offs, which together with the concurrent toll on passengers' lives makes for a horrifying indictment of a supposedly well-tried means of transport. On the other hand, the airship has a remarkable safety record, particularly for a prototype air transport system, as the long life of the *Graf Zeppelin* illustrates so well. The first passenger casualties in the history of airships were in the *Hindenburg* when it perished over Lakehurst on 6 May 1937 killing 35 passengers and crewmen out of a total of 97; the number of fare-paying passengers killed was 13. In contrast, an air

crash involving a modern heavier-than-air machine, in other words an aeroplane, often results in 100 per cent fatalities! It is surprising then that the airship failed to survive as part of our modern transport system, but political expediency has no conscience, particularly when fired by the hysteria of a reporter like Herb Morrison of Station WLS in Chicago.

This concern for the sensational, compounded with conservatism, ignorance, blind prejudice and the vote-catching panderings of politicians, condemned the airship in the past. But despite some naïve and sceptical views, still in evidence today, the airship seems to have a better chance of a revival than it has since the last war.

Some small indication of the capabilities of airships can be found in the pages of this book. The flights of the *Norge* to the North Pole and the operational flights of American, British, French, German and Italian airship crews illustrates the remarkable endurance and range of the airship — and, indeed, the remarkable courage and tenacity of the airship crews in the face of all manner of dangers and difficulty. The information in this book mainly comes from old airship hands, directly and indirectly: Engineer Général Etienne Joux, Major J. Struthers and Wing Commander J. N. Fletcher, Wing Commander T. R. Cave-Browne-Cave, Air Vice-Marshal P. E. Maitland, Major General H. Riiser-Larsen, Colonel Tito Tombesi, Captain Hans von Schiller and Squadron Leader T. R. York-Moore.

Before continuing with a discussion of the operations of the British rigid airship and the German Zeppelins it is important to cover some of the technical points not explained in the body of the book. Reference to what is set out below, adapted from technical notes specially prepared by Wing Commander Fletcher, should help the reader to understand the principles of buoyant flight.

To understand any description of airship operations it is necessary to know something of the technical principles of aerostatics involved. An airship is in essence merely a controllable balloon, and the first thing to be grasped is the science of ballooning.

All matter is in one of three states, solid, liquid or gaseous. It is well known that substances lighter than water will float in water. It is equally true that substances lighter than air will float in air. If an object is totally submerged in a liquid or gas, it must obviously displace its own volume. If the object weighs more than the matter displaced the object will sink, but if it weighs less than the matter displaced the object will float and will rise until the matter displaced equals the weight of the object immersed. The object will float, and will neither rise nor fall until some change occurs in the relative weights of the floating object and the medium in which it floats.

If a bag of 1,000 cu ft capacity is inflated with air in the same medium, the weight of air in the bag must obviously equal the weight of the air displaced. The weight of the bag itself must be added to the weight of the air, and if such a contraption were to be raised a few feet off the ground and then let go, it would drop to the ground. If however, the bag were to be filled with superheated air the volume of such air would weigh less than the air it displaces and the contraption would rise. This device was, in fact, the first type of balloon, and was used by Montgolfier and many others to make exhibition ascents.

At normal temperature and pressure 1,000 cu ft of air weighs 75 lb (34 kg) and the same volume of hydrogen, 5 lb (2.26 kg). So if our bag is filled with hydrogen it will weigh 70 lb (31.75 kg) less than the air it displaces, less the actual weight of the bag. If this contraption is let go it will rise in free air until the rarefied air displaced at a greater height weighs the same as the bag full of hydrogen.

All sorts of complications creep in, however. The hydrogen bag, for example, will not stop at the height of equilibrium because of its momentum. It will continue to rise until the pull of its increasing 'heaviness' checks the rise and causes it to begin to fall again. Then, unless something is done about it, it will fall until it hits the ground, where it will bounce and rise to a new position of equilibrium

# Airship Theory

which it will again overshoot. This process will go on indefinitely.

Another complication is produced by changes of temperature. Warm air weighs less than cold air, so that the lift of a bag will vary with the temperature of the surrounding air. Warm gas weighs less than cold gas but it also expands as it warms. When it expands it must be allowed to escape, lest it should burst the bag. Then when the gas cools again there will be less of it, so that the lift of the original bag full of gas will be diminishing. Lift is the technical term used to express the difference between the gross weight of a bag full of gas and the gross weight of the air it displaces.

Every operation of an airship is governed by these considerations, subject to further complications caused by the use of engines to drive the airship through the air.

It is quite possible and indeed normal practice to drive an airship off the ground exactly as an aeroplane is driven off. This practice seems to have originated at Farnborough in 1913 with the military airship *Beta*. The swivelling propellers of the other army airships made it possible to handle them as helicopters. In this way use was made of dynamic lift, caused by the forward movement of the ship through the air. This dynamic lift was, of course, additional to the static lift derived from the gas. In other words, the negative lift of an airship that does not float can be overcome by the thrust of its engines and propellers. The reverse of

this operation is not so feasible, because of the enormous run in that would be required, though a strong steady wind would assist.

The simplest form of airship is an elongated bag or envelope, below which is slung a car in which crew, engines and fuel can be carried. The envelope itself will carry rudders and elevators, which are controlled from the car. Obviously, therefore, the envelope must be big enough to displace such an amount of air as will weigh more than the total weights involved. Take some simple, but imaginary figures:

| | | |
|---|---|---|
| **gas bag, control surfaces** | 1,000 lb | (453.60 kg) |
| **car, engines, propellers** | 1,500 lb | (680.40 kg) |
| **crew** | 300 lb | (136.00 kg) |
| **fuel** | 350 lb | (158.75 kg) |
| **useful load** | 350 lb | (158.75 kg) |
| | 3,500 lb | (1,587.50 kg) |

If the maximum lift of 1,000 cu ft of hydrogen is 70 lb (31.75 kg), the volume of hydrogen needed to lift such a ship would be 50,000 cu ft. In practice, to allow for a decrease in gas purity, lower barometer and higher temperatures, it would be wise to assume a lift of not more than 68 lb (31 kg), and 65 lb (29.5 kg) would be safer still. This would mean a larger envelope.

The US Airship Service used helium, a completely inert gas. Hydrogen has the great disadvantage of being explosive when mixed with air, and inflammable at all times. Helium, however, weighs about 15 lb (7 kg) per 1,000 cu ft so that the volume of helium gas needed to lift 3,500 lb (1,587.5 kg) would be about 60,000 cu ft.

There is no intention here of going into all the mathematical and physical details affecting the operation of an airship. Suffice it to say that exposure to sun, causing the gas in the envelope to superheat, can cause very large and very rapid variation of lift. If the ship is cooled in flight by the passage of air over the envelope, this may not be serious; but if the ship is stationary on the ground, or is moving slowly on coming in to land, rapid adjustments would have to be made. The colour of the envelope has an effect on this superheating process: black or dark blue as used on military airships was the worst colour to use, and these ships could hardly be flown at all in daytime, except early in the morning, or evening. Yellow was a common colour until about 1917, when an aluminium shade was adopted almost everywhere. The sun's rays could thus be reflected and this helped to reduce superheat.

Superheating, however, can be a help to the pilot. If for some reason the ship has lost gas and is heavy while flying at night, a landing after sunrise would mean a gain in lift, for by flying slowly the gas would heat up and, by expanding, displace a greater volume of air.

The shape of the envelope is designed to facilitate its passage through the air — in other words the streamlined shape is customary. When, however, airships began to be used for serious purposes and loads increased, it became necessary to depart from the simple elongated envelope with the car suspended below it.

The design of an envelope large enough to carry very great loads presents serious difficulties. When the shape of the envelope is maintained only by the pressure of the gas inside it, it is obvious that high pressure would call for very strong fabrics of considerable weight. At one time, a short car had to be suspended quite a long way below the envelope so that no serious longitudinal compression was exerted by the rigging on the envelope itself. In the days with which we are concerned this vertical distance was a serious matter. Airships were kept in their sheds, and the height of the roof necessarily limited the overall height of the ship.

A French design, the *Astra-Torres*, went a long way to overcome this difficulty by adopting an envelope of clover leaf shape in section, allowing the rigging wires to pass almost vertically to the car. The British Eta patch, designed for the airship *Eta*, was also a step forward. These patches were fan-shaped, and were placed on the envelope at such an angle that there was a direct pull, for there was one patch for each rigging leg. This reduced the load on the envelope, and so a short car could be slung quite close under it.

Today, sheds are mostly used for docking purposes, and the mooring mast, which originated in Britain, is in common use. Goodyear have solved the height problem by slinging the car from two or more curtains attached to the roof of the envelope and inside it, the suspension cables coming out of the bottom of the envelope via gas-tight glands. The car

is slung so close that a secondary, external suspension is faired in, so there is no drag from the rigging, the car and envelope forming one unit.

Due to improved load distribution, and to fabrics combining great strength with much lighter weight, non-rigid ships up to a million and a half cubic feet have been built, but there is a limit to the possible size of a non-rigid envelope. Because of this, two other types came into use more or less simultaneously, the semi-rigid which was largely used in Italy, and the rigid envelope developed by Count Zeppelin, the German designer and inventor. The semi-rigid airship used a framework attached to the envelope itself, extending over a considerable length of envelope. Engines, cars, fuel and useful load could be carried within this framework or suspended in cars close beneath it.

The rigid airship used a cylindrical framework with cigar-shaped bow and stern, with both ends slightly rounded or pointed. The framework was covered by an outer cover of waterproof fabric, and was subdivided inside from 15 to 18 bays, each containing a gas-bag. Within the framework was a passage way for the crew moving between their place of duty and their bunks and mess-room. Sometimes an extension of the gangway or keel provided a passenger saloon, and engine cars were slung from either side or below the gangway. The German design was amazingly successful in operation, but no one quite succeeded in imitating it. British designs on the same principle were only moderately successful.

It is desirable to give some idea of the size of these aircraft, for whether they performed a service or commercial role, all depended on the useful load which they could carry. If it was desirable to carry useful loads of the same weight as the gross weight of the ship itself, the non-rigid necessary for this fifty-fifty ratio would need a capacity of about 500,000 cu ft and the rigid would need about 2,000,000 cu ft. They could carry a hundred passengers in complete comfort, or an equal load of bombs. In their heyday they were *the* air transport of the day: they could fly round the world, across the Atlantic, from Italy to Alaska and over the North Pole, by night or in fog as comfortably as by day or in clear weather.

A point of interest arising out of the foregoing schedule of achievements is

that airship engines have to run satisfactorily for long periods. In the case of larger ships with two or more engines it is usually possible to stop one at a time. Engineers are carried who can carry out quite extensive repairs in flight, and so get an engine going again that has broken down. So far, this has never been possible in any aeroplane, and is one of the airship's great advantages.

The longest flight made by any aircraft, without refuelling, was made in 1958 by an American Naval Airship of the 'ZPG-2' class, which remained airborne for 264 hours, 14 minutes, when it cruised for 9,448 miles (15,205 km). This flight was no stunt; the ship carried its full equipment on board and full crew. No aeroplane carrying a worthwhile payload could equal or come anywhere near this performance. The ship in fact made a double crossing of the Atlantic without landing. Long flights have indeed always been commonplace with the airship, which probably has three or four times the duration of the aeroplane.

The research and development which made it possible for British aeroplanes to fly continuously for the long periods which are usual today owes a great deal to the design staff at the old Royal Airship Works at Cardington. However, a high safety factor in airships combined with high efficiency is a difficult standard to maintain, though it may prove possible with new materials and further experience.

Although many practical designs for airships had been developed in the nineteenth century, it was not until 1884 that *La France*, the first airship able to make a circular flight, was built at Chalais–Meudon in France and flown by Captain Charles Renard and Arthur Krebs. The original power unit for this airship was a cumbersome eight horse power Gramme electric motor weighing 211 lb (95.70 kg) and powered by banks of batteries weighing a staggering 900 lb (408 kg), which soon induced the operators to install a bipole dynamo to reduce weight. However, it was not until the internal combustion engine was developed and made light enough for airship propulsion that the true dirigible was able to fly in sustained flight with some measure of impunity against the elements.

Airships began to be regarded with more than passing interest only when Count Ferdinand von Zeppelin's dreams were formulated into a semblance of the future technology. In Germany in particular the rigid airship soon entered the country's consciousness and, as enthusiasm for Count Zeppelin began to grow, became a symbol of national pride and, to some degree, Teutonic 'supremacy'. Count Zeppelin was a far-sighted and intensely patriotic individual whose desire to provide Germany with an immense rigid aerial cruiser stemmed more from his conviction that such a vehicle was imperative to his country for military purposes, in the face of the French success with *La France*, than from any burning desire to develop a new technology for any altruistic reasons, though it is hard to believe that the novelty of his creation did not fire his imagination with visions of how the advancement of technology would affect the future of the airship. However, it is clear that Count Zeppelin was no great *polytechnos*, for this is evident from his lack of technical training, and the fact that he had to enlist the assistance of Theodor Kober, a young engineer, to help him develop his first design. The first design, embodied in a proposal to the Kaiser, was examined by a commission which advised against spending government money on the project, but with assistance from Professor Müller-Breslau, who can rightly be credited with producing the original Zeppelin design, the Count began construction of *Luftschiff Zeppelin I* (*LZ I*). The airship only made three ascents totalling

# Zeppelins and Other Early Airships

two hours, proving that it was underpowered, amongst other defects, and therefore was broken up in 1901.

The Count suffered many setbacks in his enterprise, including the destruction of his second and fourth airships, but with his fifth airship he flew a predetermined course during a 24-hour period and as a result the War Ministry purchased *LZ 3* and *LZ 5* for the army. *LZ 6*, however, built in expectance of further government orders remained unsold and was later taken over by the Deutsche Luftschiffahrts-Aktien-Gesellschaft (DELAG) and enlarged. She was burnt in her shed in 1910.

1▼

DELAG, which was formed by the Count in 1909, almost suffered bankruptcy when its first three airships were destroyed in accidents, but with the completion of *LZ 10*, the *Schwaben*, in 1911 came a reasonable amount of success. This airship, however, was destroyed, without loss of life on 28 June 1912, after making 218 flights and carrying 1,553 passengers. But at this time the *Viktoria Luise* was in operation, soon to be followed by the *Hansa* and the *Sachsen*. By mid-1914 over 10,000 passengers had been carried on these ships and 1,588 flights had been made. However, during the flights with passengers, and in between these flights, army and navy personnel were trained in airship handling in preparation for the war that, for the Germans, was regarded as inevitable.

*L I* (builder's number *LZ 14*) was the first naval Zeppelin to be ordered. She was completed in 1912, but did not have a long life, for she crashed in the North Sea on 9 September 1913. The navy's second Zeppelin, *L 2*, was burned in the air in the course of her tenth flight, during altitude tests. By this time Korvettenkapitän Peter Strasser, who was appointed as head of the Naval Airship Division in place of Korvettenkapitän Friedrich Metzing — who was killed in the *L I* disaster — had built up the airship organisation, carrying on with flight training in the commercial airship *Sachsen*. Grand Admiral von Tirpitz, his faith in airships now severely shaken,

1 The partly covered framework of *LZ 1* in the huge floating shed at Manzell in 1899. This, Count Zeppelin's first airship, was built with a capital of 800,000 marks, of which the Count contributed 300,000 and Carl Berg, the industrialist who produced and financed the Schwarz metalclad airship, supplied 100,000, and the rest was subscribed by other businessmen in smaller amounts. The reason for building the airship in the floating shed was that the Count believed that water would provide a softer landing ground for his ships than the hard and even terrain ashore, and because the hangar would always be capable of turning with the wind. The two Daimler engines had a total horse power of only 28.4 and each drove two aluminium four-bladed propellers, which gave the ship a speed of approximately 17 mph. The propellers looked very much like ships' screws.

reluctantly placed an order for *L 3* with the Zeppelin company, so that the Airship Division would at least have a ship of its own. *L 3*, however, did not meet naval specifications, being almost a replica of her predecessor, but nevertheless served well to illustrate some values of the military uses of rigid airships.

Since the foundation of the Luftschiffbau Schütte-Lanz in 1909 by Dr Ing E. H. Johann Schütte, with the financial backing of Dr Karl Lanz and August Röchling, two Mannheim industrialists, the Zeppelin organisation had strong competition. Dr Schütte was a trained naval architect and engineer whose skills were applied to producing designs far in advance of the Zeppelin and without many of its eccentricities, but his airships suffered from a weakness inherent in the choice of construction materials. Dr Schütte used a kind of plywood, made from thin layers of aspen held together with casein glue, to fabricate the girders, in order to assure the greatest possible lightness for his airships. This choice of material was unfortunate for despite the use of waterproofing materials the girders were softened and loosened by atmospheric dampness, and the girders were also of uneven strength and quality. Peter Strasser, after several years of war, commented that experience had demonstrated that the laminated wooden girders were unsuitable for airship construction, because they weakened and broke even under a moderate degree of humidity. It

2 Count Ferdinand von Zeppelin photographed in the control car of an early Zeppelin. Born on 8 July 1838, the Count, a provincial German soldier and nobleman, joined the army of his native state of Württemberg at the age of 15. In 1863 the Count took leave of absence from the army to go to America as an official observer of the Civil War. It was while in America that he made an ascent in a tethered balloon filled with coal gas which, together with a lecture, by Heinrich von Stephan on how mail might be carried around the world by air, fired his imagination and started him on, at first, a hobby that became the sole purpose of his life. The Count died on 8 March 1917, nearly 80 years old, having devoted his almost fanatical energy, and the greater part of his fortune, to developing the rigid airship, the embodiment of his dreams and a symbol, in its military and civil manifestations, of nationalism for the German people.

2▲

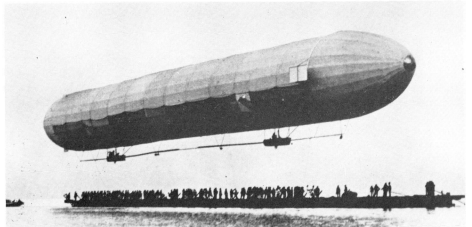

4▼                                             3▲

4 Count Zeppelin in the control car of *LZ 3* which was his first commercial success. It was sold to the army along with *LZ 5*, the airships becoming *Z I* and *Z II* respectively. This photograph appears to be one taken prior to the flight of the modified *LZ 3* on 26 September 1907 in which the ship flew back and forth several times across Lake Constance in three and a half hours. During this flight four passengers were carried including Dr Hugo Eckener and Count Zeppelin's daughter, Countess Hella. *LZ 3*'s predecessor *LZ 2* was an improvement on the original design, but through a series of misfortunes the ship was damaged on the second attempt to fly it, and was therefore dismantled. *LZ 3*, which made its first flight on 9 October 1906, with 11 people on board, had a gas volume of 403,600 cu ft, and was 414 ft (126.18 m) long and 38.5 ft (11.73 m) in diameter. Two Daimler engines provided the motive power, and a speed of 25 mph was reached on trials. The ship was lengthened in 1908 to 440.25 ft (134.18 m) and one more gas bag was inserted, bringing the total hydrogen volume at 100 per cent inflation to 430,800 cu ft. The total horse power of the Daimler engines on the lengthened ship was uprated from 170 to 210, and a new speed of 27.8 mph was reached on trials. Count Zeppelin was remarkably successful with *LZ 3*. She was finally dismantled at Metz in the autumn of 1913.

3 *LZ 1*, with Count Zeppelin in command, made its first flight at Manzell on 2 July 1900. The illustration shows the airship tethered to a barge on Lake Constance on the evening before its flight. The ship began its ascent at 2000 hours with five people on board, and flew for about 18 minutes. Two more flights took place in the same year, on 17 and 24 October, but the cost of financing them had exhausted the company's assets. A considerable number of improvements were made to *LZ 1* between its first and last flights but she was dismantled early in 1901 mainly because she lacked sufficient speed and control in flight. *LZ 1* was 420 ft (128 m) long and 38.5 ft (11.73 m) in diameter, and the total gas volume was 399,000 cu ft. The useful lift is calculated to have been 1,430 lb (648 kg). The airship had no control surfaces, except for a pair of crude rectangular rudders placed above and below the nose, and a smaller pair fitted aft, and a 220 lb (100 kg) lead weight, which was winched back and forth between the two cars, served instead of elevating planes. The longitudinal members and the transverse rings were fabricated from pure aluminium, but the structure offered little resistance to compression or lateral bending loads.

5▲    6▲    7▼

5 The ornate interior of the passenger coach of the *Deutschland, LZ 7*, the first passenger-carrying rigid airship. She made her first flight on 19 June 1910, but was wrecked on the 28th, when a gale forced her down in the Teutoberg Forest. She made 24 flights, carrying 436 passengers.

6 *LZ 5* made her first flight on 26 May 1909. She was almost identical to *LZ 4* from which a number of her components were salvaged. *LZ 5* is depicted with temporary repairs after she was damaged on a demonstration flight. After rebuilding, she was handed over to the German Army Airship Battalion, designated *Z 11*. She made 16 military flights and was wrecked in a storm on 25 April 1910.

7 A tail view of *LZ 3* in 1906 showing the multiple control surfaces, typical of pre-war Zeppelins. She became the army airship *Z I*. She made her maiden flight on 9 October 1906 and in lengthened form made her first flight on 21 October 1908.

8 The *Ersatz Deutschland* in 1911. The third passenger craft built for DELAG, she first flew on 19 June 1910. She had a gas volume of 683,000 cu ft, a length of 486 ft (148.13 m) and a diameter of 46 ft (14.02 m), and had 18 gas bags. Her useful lift was 11,000 lb (4,989.51 kg). Three 120 hp Daimler engines produced a speed of 37 mph on trials. She was practically identical to her predecessor, the *Deutschland*, being constructed from components from her. She was wrecked at Düsseldorf on 16 May 1911. A serious accident to her in April 1911 had one good outcome in that Dr Eckener prompted DELAG to overhaul safety aspects in airship and ground crews' training completely.

8▼

is also reported that humidity alone reduced the strength of the girders by as much as 50 per cent. For two years before the end of the war Dr Schütte experimented with duralumin tube girders, but no airships were constructed from this material before the close of hostilities.

Altogether, the Luftschiffbau Schütte-Lanz constructed 20 airships, of which 11 were for the army and nine for the navy. Two more on the stocks remained uncompleted.

During the early stages of the war the vulnerability of the army airships to ground fire confirmed the worst fears of the War Ministry. Also, the inadequacy of the airships as scouts whose task was to penetrate deep into the enemy's rear areas was proved, with high cost to the army service. It was, therefore, a series of disasters, culminating with the crash of *Z VIII* on the Vosges Mountains, that ended the reconnaissance role of the army airships. The army ships were now employed on ineffective night attacks, and, with serious consequences for the future role of airships, in bombing raids on armaments factories and important transportation links.

It was while the army was formulating an effective role for its airships, that the navy developed the Zeppelin as a scouting cruiser for the fleet. This was a job the airship was ideally suited for, providing rapid coverage of a wider area than had been possible with conventional surface scouting vessels.

Although three of the early primitive Zeppelins, *L 3*, *L 4* and *L 6*, carried out the first strategic bombing raid on Britain on 19/20 January 1915, and several more inconclusive raids were made up until *L 10* successfully raided the South Shields area on 15/16 June, causing considerable damage to factories on either side of the Tyne, no systematic assaults were carried out on London until the series of squadron raids beginning with the raid on the night of 9/10 August 1915. Numerous raids with varying degrees of 'success' were made on London, the North of England and as far up as Edinburgh, in an intensified attempt to disrupt industrial production and divert troops from the front. A peak in operations was reached with the raids on Edinburgh on 2 April 1916 which resulted in considerable loss of life and material damage. The damage to Britain's economy, however, was out of all proportion

to the effort in men and materials which the Germans put into the Zeppelin raids.

The campaign against Britain continued in May 1916 with the introduction into service of the *L 30*, the first of the so-called super-Zeppelins. Although ships of this type had a greater length and a much greater gas volume — 1,950,000 cu ft as opposed to 1,359,400 cu ft in *L 21* and 1,126,400 cu ft in *L 19* — and six engines instead of the four Maybachs in previous ships, the performance while on bombing missions was only slightly above that of previous designs.

The strategic bombing raids on Britain brought the reality that the war had ceased to be between armies and navies only, but rather that it was now a war of peoples. The Zeppelin raids that began in 1915 and decreased towards the end of the summer in 1916, were now being succeeded by aeroplane raids — an indication of the effect of the explosive bullet on the hydrogen-filled raiders. In this phase of the Zeppelin operations little material damage was done to Britain's industries and less than 2,000 casualties were caused, yet it is considered that at least a sixth of the production of munitions was lost through the disorganising effect of the raids.

Towards the end of 1916 Strasser ordered his airships to attack London repeatedly in a suicidal all-out assault that succeeded only in destroying his ships at an alarming rate, and with them his most experienced crews — he still had not come to terms with the explosive Brock and Pomeroy ammunition. Yet, in spite of the dreadful losses sustained by the Zeppelin crews, a new type of airship was developed, known to the British as a 'height-climber'. These were specially lightened ships that could carry out raids at altitudes of 16,000 to 20,000 ft, but the new technical developments failed to anticipate the considerable problems of altitude sickness on the crews when operating in the sub-stratosphere. However, the new Zeppelin raiders rendered the whole British anti-Zeppelin defence system obsolete, outclassing all the defensive aircraft and anti-aircraft guns developed for the defence of London and the rest of the country. But through a combination of ill-luck, bad weather, mechanical failure, and the dreaded explosive bullet the Zeppelin raids on Britain tailed off until the final raid on the British coast on 5/6 August 1918, on

which *L 53*, *L 46*, *L 65* and *L 70* were despatched. On this raid Peter Strasser, the beloved leader of the Airship Division, was killed when *L 70*, one of the most advanced wartime Zeppelins, was shot down by incendiary fire from aircraft off the Norfolk coast. Several days later *L 53* was brought down by accurate fire from Lieutenant S. D. Culley flying a Sopwith 2F1 Camel from a lighter towed by the destroyer HMS *Redoubt* of the Harwich Force.

The loss of these ships, and the death of the Naval Division leader, virtually emasculated the service, and ensured its end. Peter Strasser's enthusiasm for the airship service and his obsession with the strategic bombing of Britain, and particularly the bombing of London, brought about his own untimely death, but he is still regarded as being in the front rank of those who contributed to the development of airship technology, next only to Count Zeppelin and Dr Eckener. The last war patrol by the Airship Division took place on 13 October 1918 when *L 63* and *L 65* were ordered out with battleships and minesweepers of the High Seas Fleet, but the Zeppelins were unable to carry out their task because of a heavy cloud cover which restricted vision.

Mutiny broke out in the navy towards the end of October and the revolutionary fervour spread to the ground crews at the airship bases, resulting in the arrest of all the officers, who were sent home after several days in custody, and two days before the signing of the Armistice the remaining airships were hung up in their sheds and deflated. However, the Zeppelin flight crews remained loyal to the defeated regime and taking their cue from the scuttling of the German fleet at Scapa Flow, they entered the airship sheds and wrecked the ships in them on 23 June 1919. All five ships at Nordholz were destroyed, as were the two ships at Wittmundhaven, but at Alhorn *L 64* and *L 71* were untouched owing to treachery.

In the course of the war the Zeppelin had done minimal damage to the enemy at enormous cost to the Naval Airship Service; it had failed in its main task of bombing the enemies of Germany into submission, and in fact only served to strengthen the resolve of the populations of the cities attacked to fight back, just as in the Second World War the relentless bombing of London produced the opposite of the desired effect.

9▲      10▲                     11▼

9  Count Zeppelin photographed on board the *LZ 30* (builders' number LZ 62) on the ship's first flight on 28 May 1916. The officer standing next to the Count is Hauptmann (captain) Macher. On this flight the airship went down to a height of about 98 ft (30 m) between Heidelberg and Darmstadt, and overtook a goods train which was travelling at about 74 mph. This was the last flight Count Zeppelin made in an airship.

10  Dr Ludwig Dürr joined Count Zeppelin's organisation in 1899 when he was 21 years old and soon was adopted by the Count as chief engineer, and remained with the company to be responsible for the design and construction of 118 more rigid airships. Dr Dürr seems to have been uncomfortable with people from outside the Zeppelin organisation, and particularly non-Germans, for his dealings with the Americans after the Second World War proved to be somewhat strained — he was reported by the Americans to be 'a very difficult man to deal with'.

11  Dr Hugo Eckener, who proved to be the greatest supporter of Count Zeppelin despite his early technical criticisms of *LZ 1* and *LZ 2* in the *Frankfurter Zeitung*, also later took over the Zeppelin organisation and expanded it between the two world wars. Dr Douglas H. Robinson has stated that Dr Eckener was the greatest airship pilot of all time, and the records support this statement fully.

12  Fregatten-Kapitän Peter Strasser, the forceful and dynamic naval officer who became Chief of the Naval Airship Division just two weeks after his predecessor's death in *LZ 1*, which was forced down in the sea off Heligoland in a severe storm on 9 September 1913. Strasser rose in the estimation of his superiors and he was eventually promoted to the position of Leader of Airships on 23 November 1916, and during his time as Leader he vigorously campaigned for the expansion of the Airship Service, with considerable results. Strasser was killed when *LZ 70* was shot down by British aircraft off the Norfolk coast on 5 August 1918, which was the final demoralizing blow to the German Naval Airship Division as an effective fighting force. Now that the driving force behind the Zeppelin raids on England was gone, the raids ceased.

12▼

13 *SL 2*, the streamlined airship constructed from laminated plywood girders by the Luftschiffbau Schütte-Lanz of Mannheim-Rheinau for the German Army. Launched on 28 February 1914, she had a gas volume of 861,900 cu ft contained in 15 gas bags. The length was 474 ft (144.47 m) and the diameter was 59.7 ft (18.19 m). She was lengthened during May to August 1915 to 513.25 ft (156.43 m) and another gas bag was added bringing the gas volume up to 981,600 cu ft. Four 95 hp Maybach C-X engines drove the ship at just over 55 mph while on trials. *SL 2* was wrecked during a storm at Luckenwalde on 10 February 1916. Schütte-Lanz built 11 airships for the German Army and nine for the Navy.

14 *L 30* builders' number LZ 62, the first of the 'r'-type (1,949,600 cu ft class), made its maiden flight on 28 May 1916. She was flown from Friedrichshafen to the Naval Air Station at Nordholz on 29 May 1916. Just over 649.5 ft (197.96 m) in length and 78.4 ft (23.89 m) in diameter, she had 19 gas bags and her useful lift was 61,600 lb (27,942.29 kg). Six 240 hp Maybach HSLu engines drove her at a speed of 62 mph. She was dismantled at Seerappen in the summer of 1920.

15 *L 20*, the first of the lengthened 'q'-type Zeppelins, was wrecked off the Norwegian coast on 3 May 1916. *L 20* was one of a group of eight raiders that attempted to bomb the north of England on the night of 2 May. Weather reports indicated the approach of a low-pressure area, so all except *L 14* and *L 20* headed for the Midlands. *L 14* ran into heavy weather and after dropping some of its bomb load on a field near Arbroath returned to base. *L 20*, commanded by Kapitänleutnant Stabbert, kept to a more northerly course, intending to reach the Firth of Forth Bridge, and was blown as far as Loch Ness by a strong SE wind. Stabbert headed for the coast, and by 0600 hrs radio bearings were obtained from Nordholz, indicating that *L 20* was in the latitude of the Orkney Islands, Stabbert realised that there was insufficient fuel to reach Germany, and requested immediate assistance by radio. He was instructed that naval vessels would steam to his aid off Denmark. Only enough fuel for five hours remained and the freshening SSE wind indicated that at least ten hours would be required to reach the north of Denmark. Stabbert now had no choice but to make for Norway where he crash-landed in a fjord near Stavanger. Six of the crew were rescued by fishing vessels and under international law were repatriated as shipwrecked mariners, but Stabbert and 19 others were interned. Stabbert escaped to Germany seven months later.

13▲

14▼

15▼

16 The tail gun platform of a Zeppelin showing the gunner and his 7.92 mm Maxim aircraft machine gun. It became an efficient air defence weapon when it was synchronised and the gun lightened and air-cooled. (The German Army was equipped with the heavy, water-cooled '08 pattern Maxim initially and later with a lighter version known as the '08/15.)

16◀

18▼

17 A tail view of *L 53* being walked into her hangar by a ground crew of several hundred men. Handling the large Zeppelins was extremely labour-intensive, requiring three or four hundred men who would first haul a ship down by the three main long landing ropes and then take control of her by holding on to numerous short ropes attached along the keel. To prevent any lateral motion of the ship while entering or leaving the hangar, tackles, attached to trolleys, were fixed to her fore and aft. These trolleys ran on rails that went through the hangar, extending for 600 ft (182.88 m) on each side. *L 53* was a 'v'-type and had a volume of 1,977,360 cu ft. She was shot down off Terschelling by British aircraft on 20 October 1917.

18 *L 46*, builders' number *LZ 94*, was a 't'-type Zeppelin with a volume of 1,970,300 cu ft, and was the first Zeppelin to have streamlined midships cars. She was destroyed in the Ahlhorn explosion on 5 January 1918, in which *L 47*, *L 51*, *L 58* and *SL 20* were also destroyed. The airship sheds I and II were heavily damaged, and sheds III and IV were destroyed in this incident. There is no clear indication of how the fire and consequent explosion at Ahlhorn began, but it is theorised that a part of the roof of Shed I may have fallen through *L 51*, puncturing one of the fuel tanks, breaking some of the bracing wires, which in turn created sparks that ignited the leaking fuel. The burning *L 51* then caused the hydrogen in *L 47* to expand and discharge through the automatic valves, and an explosion followed that spread from shed to shed.

19 Following the loss of *L 57* on the evening of 7 October during a storm, the sponsors of the projected intercontinental flight from Jamboli, Bulgaria, to Khartoum designated the *L 59* to take supplies to General von Lettow-Vorbeck's hard-pressed forces in East Africa. Under the command of Kapitänleutnant Ludwig Bockholt *L 59* took off from Staaken on 3 November laden with 15 tons of ammunition, medical supplies and other necessary equipment, clearing the Balkan mountains early next morning, and landing at Jamboli after 28 hours of flying. Two abortive attempts were made to fly to Africa, but on 21 November, after a favourable weather forecast, *L 59* left Jamboli on her epic journey of over 4,200 miles (7,780 km), flying continously for nearly four days. Because of the worsening situation in the German colony the Colonial Office informed the Naval Staff that it would no longer take responsibility for the flight, so it was decided to abandon it. Radio contact with the Zeppelin was attempted from 21 to 23 November, but contact was only made at 1430 hours on the 23rd when she was just 125 miles (231.5 km) due west of her objective. *L 55* broke off the operation and returned to Jamboli on 25 November, her 22 crew members dejected at the failure of their mission. *L 59* was a 'w'-type Zeppelin with a volume of 2,418,700 cu ft and a length of 743 ft (226.46 m). She was rebuilt during December and February 1918, and was used for bombing raids on Naples and the Nile Delta, much against the wishes of Peter Strasser, who was overruled by the Kaiser. However, on an attempted raid on Malta on 7 April 1918, *L 59* burned in the air over the Straits of Otranto with 23 crew on board. This incident was witnessed by Oberleutnant zur See Sprenger aboard the submarine *UB 53*, who reported that from all appearances the Zeppelin was shot down. But as the Italians made no claims to have destroyed the ship the German authorities concluded that her loss was due to an accident.

20 *L 48*, builders' number LZ 95, was the first of the '*L 48*' class, of which five were built, all being of the 'n'-type. *L 48* made her first flight on 22 May 1917 and was commissioned the following day. She was shot down by British aircraft at Theberton, in Suffolk, on 17 June 1917 after making only eight flights for the German Naval Airship Division. Of the crew on board at the time when *L 48* was brought down, 14 were killed and three survived. The other ships in this class were *L 49*, *L 51*, *L 52* and *L 54*. The length of the ship was 644.66 ft (196.49 m) and her diameter was 78.5 ft (23.92 m). Five Maybach engines, totalling 1,200 hp drove the ship at 66.9 mph on trials.

17

19▼

20▼

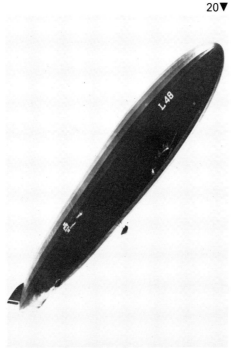

**21▲**

**22▲**

**23▼**

21 The observation car (sub-cloud car) of the army airship *LZ 90*, which fell from the Zeppelin and landed near Manningtree. The car fell, with about 5,000 ft of cable, when *LZ 90* came inland at Frinton, south of the Naze, at 23.05 hrs, stopped her engines and prepared to lower the car. The locking mechanism on the winch failed and the cable, with the car attached, ran out. The winch was then dropped and when examined by British Intelligence was found to bear marks which suggested that the crew had attempted to jam an iron bar into the gears to stop the cable unreeling. The car was made from duralumin and was 14 ft (4.26 m) long and 4 ft (1.21 m) deep. The observer lay on his stomach on a mattress, and a telephone connected him with the ship. Small celluloid windows provided fields of view on either side towards the front of the car. Smoking was permitted in the car, so there was a certain amount of competition for the post of observer amongst the crew.

22 *L 39*, the 'r'-type Zeppelin which was shot down by anti-aircraft fire at Compiègne in France with the loss of all 17 crew members on 17 March 1917. This ship had 19 gas bags with a total gas capacity of 1,949,600 cu ft. She was 644.6 ft (196.47 m) in length and 78.5 ft (23.92 m) in diameter. Power was supplied by six Maybach HSLu engines with a total of 1,440 hp. Trials speed was 63.5 mph.

23 One of the two 20 mm Becker guns carried in the control car of most Zeppelins after the summer of 1918. The machine cannon fired ball, tracer and explosive ammunition and had a rate of fire of 350 rounds per minute.

24 The control and forward engine car of what is probably a 'p'– or 'r'– type Zeppelin photographed in 1917. The large single propeller can be seen at the extreme rear of the car.

**24▼**

25 On 19 July 1918 the first aircraft carrier attack against a land target was made by seven Sopwith Camels flown off the deck of HMS *Furious*. The objective was the airship base at Tondern, and the 'Toska' shed housing *L 54* and *L 60* was successfully bombed, implanting in the Airship Division a fear of further attacks on the other bases.

25▲                                             26▼

26 *L 71*, builders' number LZ 113, was an 'x'-type Zeppelin with a volume of 2,195,800 cu ft. She was lengthened from 693.7 ft (211.44 m) to 743.17 ft (226.51 m), increasing her volume to 2,418,700 cu ft. The diameter was 78.4 ft (23.89 m). *L 71* made her maiden flight on 29 July 1918, and was commissioned into service on 10 August, making only eight flights before she was decommissioned on 9 November 1918. On 11 July 1920 she was surrendered to England at Pulham as part of Germany's war reparations.

Towards the end of the nineteenth century Britain and Germany began to compete for supremacy at sea; the German drive towards colonial imperialism, and the economic and political competition among European powers in Africa and Asia encouraged and made essential a larger and more powerful German naval force. German colonial aspirations, her earlier expansion overseas, and finally the series of Navy Laws authorising considerable expansion of the fleet exacerbated the situation to such an extent that the challenge was taken up in 1903 when Britain began her programme of naval rearmament and Parliament approved the formation of the North Sea Fleet. For the first time British naval policy was turned towards Germany rather than France or Russia. In 1905 the keel of the first Dreadnought was laid in Britain, and when Germany followed suit soon after with an unlimited policy of naval construction, the race for naval rearmament began in deadly earnest, leading Europe nearer to the brink of war.

The turn of the century also heralded a new era of technological change, in particular in the area of aviation and aeronautics. New weapons were being developed and, in the case of the aeroplane and the airship, were neither fully understood nor absorbed into the military structures. The airship in particular, which by 1914 had been developed in Germany to a considerable degree, had not yet been evaluated, and therefore its future role was as yet uncertain.

Britain, as much as Germany, needed an aerial force for the conflict that was to come, but Britain did not have any advocate of the airship at the time with the influence and fanatical driving force of Count Zeppelin. One reason why Britain was always so far behind the Germans in the construction and handling of rigid airships was because of the lack of continuous experience in this field. For example, up until 4 August 1914 no less than 23 Zeppelins had been launched, in addition to a couple of Schütte–Lanz airships, and all of these ships had been flown — although there were a large number of mishaps, there was little loss of life — resulting in a wealth of design and flying experience. On the other hand Britain had only launched one rigid airship, *Naval Airship No. 1* in 1911. Also known as the *Mayfly*, she was as short-lived as her name suggests, collapsing on leaving her shed at Barrow for the

# British Rigid Airships

second time in 1911. But although the *Mayfly* never flew, she was the very first airship to be moored out to a mast, surviving wind gusts of up to some 43 mph.

The first British rigid airship to fly was *No. 9*, on 27 November 1916, piloted by the then Wing Captain E. A. Masterman who was in charge of the rigid airship programme. *No. 9* proved to be so much overweight that the two 180 hp German Maybach engines in the after car had to be removed in favour of a lighter Maybach of 250 hp. The reduction in speed made *No. 9* of little operational value, but she was a useful school ship and experimental craft generally.

In contrast to Britain's slowness in developing rigid airships, the Germans by this time had launched some 50 Zeppelins and eight Schütte-Lanz airships, and so were naturally far ahead of the British designers in technical experience and know-how. The British firm of Vickers was also hampered by the small airship shed it was forced to use, and although it built *No. 23*, and *R 26* of the larger and improved '23' class, it was unable to contract for the '33' class airships. The '33' class were modelled on the German 'L 30' class and would have had a real operational value if only they could have been completed before November 1918. However, as a form of compensation, Vickers were allowed to build the *R 80* after the war.

The '23' class ships, the later '23X' class, *R 27* and *R 29*, were built by Beardmore at Inchinnan and Armstrong

at Barlow near Howden. These firms each had a single large shed, and had also built the '23' class airships *No. 24* and *No. 25* respectively.

The two '23X' class ships, *R 27* and *R 29*, proved to be the most useful of the British war time rigids. Weight in these ships was saved by removing the keel, but the swivelling propellers were retained aft as well as forward. All '23' class ships, as well as *No. 9*, had swivelling propellers forward, and found them of great assistance when taking off and landing. Wing Captain Masterman put all of these ships through their trials, with no mishaps, proving how important the experience gained previously with nonrigid ships had been. When the Royal Air Force was formed on 1 April 1918, Masterman left the Airship Service to take over a command in Scotland as a Brigadier General, and Wing Commander W. C. Hicks took over as trials pilot until the launching of *R 34*.

In addition to Vickers at Barrow, Beardmore, and Armstrong–Whitworth, Short Brothers became airship constructors, and in their shed at Cardington the company built *R 31* and *R 32*, airships of the Schütte–Lanz type with wooden frames and girders. *R 31* had girder trouble and had to land at Howden on her way north to East Fortune. The only shed available at Howden had been occupied by *R 27* which was destroyed by fire on 16 August 1918, and the building, which was damaged in the fire, still leaked badly when *R 31* was there, causing extensive water damage. Early in 1919 she was deleted from the effective list as damp had made her dangerous, rotting the wooden framework extensively. Conversely, *R 32*, launched in 1919, was a success, logging 260 hours' flying time before she was taken out of commission with the closing down of the Airship Service in 1921. It is thought that both ships could have been of great operational value had they been used with the fleet in the North Sea.

As has been already mentioned, the shed at Barrow was not large enough for the '33' class, so Vickers were allowed to build *R 80*, which was a fine ship, designed by the late Sir Barnes Wallis. She was launched on 19 June 1920, and being fully streamlined had a speed of 70 mph. With her disposable lift of 14.85 tons out of a total weight of 38.25 tons, she was the most efficient ship of British design at the time.

*R 33* and *R 34* were constructed to the same technical standards as the Zeppelins built in 1916, but were launched in 1919. *R 34* made the first ever double crossing of the Atlantic in July 1919, piloted by Major G. H. Scott, who was later killed at Beauvais in the *R 101* disaster. Major Scott was also in charge of a highly successful series of trials at Pulham in 1921, in which the *R 33* was employed, although *R 36* was also used for a short time, until she damaged her bows in a mooring mishap on 21 June 1921. Because of a lack of funds *R 36* never flew again, being scrapped with *R 80* in 1925 as an economy measure. The mooring trials showed that when landing to a mast only eight to ten men were needed, as opposed to landing to a ground crew, when a landing party of 300 or more men would be required. This made the operation of airships possible from an economic point of view.

In spite of the success at Pulham, early in 1921 the Air Ministry decided to close down the Airship Service, and by the end of the year British aviation was in a very bad state, the aeroplane side struggling along with temporary subsidies, while airships were placed in suspended animation. Rigid airship flying in Britain ceased until 1925, when the government and commercial organisations produced schemes for large commercial airships to link distant parts of the empire with Britain.

Cardington had been taken over by the State, and was now designated as the Royal Airship Works, and a new ship, the *R 38*, was launched on 23 June 1921. This ship was the largest yet built and was intended for operating over the North Sea at great heights, being very lightly constructed. However, she only flew on four flights — her girders had failed, and she was unstable at high speeds. The British airship experts had called for extensive trials of 100 to 150 hours before she was handed over to the US Navy, which had purchased her, but they were overruled by those in authority who had no experience of airships. On 24 August 1921 she broke in two when over Hull and fell in flames into the River Humber! Air Commander Maitland and a fine crew were killed, and Britain and America lost some of their best airship men. *R 38* had only about half the strength of previous British rigids, and as little was known of the dynamic forces she would be subjected to in flight, C. R.

Campbell, who was in charge of the Royal Airship Works, asked that *R 32* should be kept in commission long enough to find out what these stresses would be, but his request was turned down, so only static forces, doubled, were allowed for, which proved not to be enough. C. R. Campbell was among those who perished in *R 38*, and so when the new airship programme was embarked on in 1924, the staff at the Royal Airship Works at Cardington had more or less to start from scratch.

After the loss of the *R 38* an Airships Stressing Panel was belatedly set up, and to a certain extent the designers of future airships were forced to build their ships to such high safety factors that weights were increased. This high degree of caution, it would seem, was a natural reaction to the *R 38* tragedy.

The Labour Government at the time made a political decision to divide the available airship expertise between two competing organisations, Vickers and the state-run concern, so in 1924 airships were revived as part of the general aviation policy. As a start two airships *R 100* and *R 101* were to be built, one at Howden by the Airship Guarantee Company and the other at Cardington by the Royal Airship Works. Barnes Wallis, with his great design experience behind him, was in charge at Howden, and Colonel V. C. Richmond was placed in charge of the Cardington team. Colonel Richmond had little experience with rigid airships, but was an able engineer who had served with airships during the war on the development of fabrics, and was a good administrator. Among his staff was Squadron Leader F. M. Rope who had played an important part on the engineering side, with non-rigid airships, during the war, and the powerplant aspect was in the sole charge of Wing Commander T. R. Cave-Browne-Cave whose airship experience dated back to 1913.

From the very beginning the Howden team, although they lacked adequate finance, had far greater experience with airships, and were much less constrained when they wished to change their minds about any point of design, not being bound by the political shackles that hampered the Cardington team. The Howden team were also free to use lightweight aeroplane engines, while the Cardington party were forced to use heavy oil diesel engines, which were about twice the estimated weight. This factor largely

accounts for the reason why the *R 101*'s useful lift was about 38 tons and *R 100*'s 57 tons. Both airships were grossly overweight, and if a comparison with the efficiency ratio of the *Graf Zeppelin* is made, it can be seen that Britain still lagged sadly behind the Germans. The efficiency ratios were 39 per cent for the *R 100*, and 25 per cent for the *R 101* before she had an extra gas-bag fitted, and 48 per cent for the *Graf Zeppelin*!

It is of significance to note that in 1925 *R 33* was flown from Cardington to Pulham for research work for *R 101*. On 16 April she broke away from the Pulham mast in a full gale, and in spite of her smashed bows, made a safe landing back at Pulham on the next day, piloted by the then Flight Lieutenant R. S. Booth, later the captain of the *R 100*. The *R 33* was flown intermittently until 23 November 1926, after which she was taken out of commission because her hull was showing signs of weakening, and in any case by this time money was running short for work with airships. So it is clear that there was no flight training before *R 101* made her first flight on 29 October 1929, and *R 100* made hers on 16 December in the same year.

*R 100*, before setting out on her flight to Canada in July and August 1930, had completed her trials, but *R 101* on the other hand never had a chance to do so before she was forced to embark on the difficult route to India. *R 100* came back from her Canadian flight and landed at Cardington in safety, but *R 101* came down at Beauvais and caught fire, and tragically Richmond, Scott and nearly all the crew and passengers, including the Air Minister, Lord Thompson, perished. The last flight of the *R 101* was also the last flight made by a British rigid airship.

If, however, and it can only be conjecture, when *R 38*, *R 100* and *R 101*, were being constructed and tested, there had been an experienced airship officer of the calibre, for example, of Air Commander Masterman, in charge at the Air Ministry, the whole sad story might have ended differently. He could have supervised the work at Howden and Cardington, and there would not have been the so-called rivalry between them.

Eugène M. Koleśnik

23

29  The *Mayfly* made her shed trials before the Advisory Committee for Aeronautics on 13 February 1911, during which the engines were run and the controls were operated, but outdoor tests could not be conducted until the end of March, when the weather moderated. The photograph shows the *Mayfly* approaching the mooring pontoon in the centre of Cavendish Dock at Barrow on 22 May 1911, the day she was warped out of her shed for the first time. On the pontoon a 38 ft (11.59 m) high mast was fixed, inclined 23 degrees to windward, and attached to it was a cross yard with strips of canvas intended to serve as a wind-break. The wind-break caused the ship to yaw badly and so was removed, and she became more stable when attached to the mast, withstanding winds gusting up to 43 mph. *Mayfly* was the first airship to be moored to a mast. The ship was damaged when returning to her shed on 25 May and during the subsequent repairs the opportunity was taken to lighten her, as she was overweight by three tons and could not become airborne with all her equipment on board. The ship was lightened so much that she was weakened considerably, and when she emerged from her shed on 24 September she was struck by a squall which pushed her over on her beam ends. She then righted herself and broke in two. After the Court of Inquiry, the findings of which Churchill refused to have published, the naval airship section was disbanded, and *Mayfly's* remains were left to rot in her shed. *Mayfly* had cost £41,500 and the repairs and alterations were reputed to have raised the cost to almost £70,000. This may seem a lot of money to pay for an aircraft that never flew, but her brief career had supplied much valuable scientific data to British researchers. So the *Mayfly* was not quite the fiasco she was claimed to be.

28▼                                                                                       27▲

27  The Mayfly moored to the floating mast at Barrow. Note the wind-break on the mast.

28  A rare view of Britain's first rigid airship, His Majesty's Airship *No 1*, more widely known as the *Mayfly*, in her floating shed at Barrow. Work began on the ship and her shed in 1909, but actual erection of the ship only began when the shed was completed in mid-1910. The photograph shows the *Mayfly* from the after car, along the external keel to the forward car, on which one of the two four-bladed propellers can be seen. The *Mayfly* had a volume of 663,518 cu ft, and was 512 ft (156 m) long and had a diameter of 48 ft (14.63 m). Two Wolseley engines, each of 80 hp, were intended to provide the motive power.

29▲                    30▼                                    31▼

30 Colonel E.M. Maitland, Commanding Officer at
Pulham in 1916, became the head of the Airship
Service in the summer of 1917. As the Air Ministry's
Director of Airships Maitland became an Air
Commodore. He was a dedicated airshipman, greatly
respected by those in authority and much loved by
those who served under him. The photograph was
taken when Colonel Maitland was in attendance at
parachuting trials.

31 Commander E.A.D. Masterman (later General),
Officer Commanding the airship section, with Winston
Churchill, the First Sea Lord of the Admiralty, at
Farnborough in October 1913. Commander Masterman
was responsible, together with Barnes Wallis, for the
steel lattice-work tower constructed at Pulham in 1919
for mooring airships. This mast had enormous
advantages over earlier types in that the head rotated
around a vertical axis, and the ship could also be
serviced from it.

**32▲**

32 *No. 9*, the first British rigid airship to fly, made her first sortie into the open at Barrow on 16 November 1916 and her first flight on the 27th. She was unable to lift her contract weight of 3.1 tons, but was accepted by the Admiralty on condition that Vickers modified her, after which she was found to have a disposable lift of 3.8 tons, and was taken over by the navy on 4 April 1917. Construction began as early as autumn 1915, therefore her gestation was indeed a long one, mainly attributable to interminable discussions between the civilian engineers and the Admiralty officials, with resultant constant design changes. However, other causes of delay were the Irish rebellion, which halted the delivery of the gas bags nets, which were made of Irish flax, and an inter-union dispute over who should drill holes in the plywood panels. *No. 9* was delivered to Wing Commander Masterman's Rigid Airship Trial Flight at Howden, Yorkshire and spent most of her time in mooring and handling experiments. After only 198 hours, 16 minutes in the air, she was taken to Pulham and kept there from 29 October 1917 until June 1918 when she was dismantled. *No. 9* was 526 ft (160.32 m) long and had a volume of 889,300 cu ft. *No. 9* was obsolescent, if not obsolete by the time she flew. Four years elapsed between the first design work and entering service, putting British rigid airship technology far behind Germany's.

**33▼**

33 *No. 23* under construction at Vickers' Walney Island shed at Barrow. The partially inflated gas bags can be seen through the lattice-work of main-frames longitudinal girders, and mesh wiring. The midships engine can just be seen amongst the scaffolding under the keel. The lines to the left of the framework are part of the tackle used to lift the hull so that the keel could be attached.

34 The midships engine car of *No. 23*. When *No. 23* was first constructed she had four Wolseley 250 hp engines. One engine was placed in the forward car and one in the aft car, each driving a pair of swivelling propellers, and two engines were placed in the midships engine car, each driving a single fixed propeller. Later, the aft car was replaced by a wing car from the captured German *L 33*. Rolls-Royce 12-cyclinder 250 hp engines replaced the Wolseleys at a later date.

**34▼**

35 *No. 23* in flight. This rigid airship, built by Vickers, was the first of the '23' class, of which *No. 24* was built by Beardmore, *No. 25* by Armstrong Whitworth, and *R 26* completed by Vickers. The design of the '23' class was similar to that of *No. 9* except that an extra bag was inserted amidships and the ends enlarged to give the greater volume of 942,000 cu ft. Ten airships of this class were approved by the Treasury in April 1916, but the remainder were built as the '23X' class. *No. 23* was 535 ft (163 m) in length and 53 ft (16.15 m) in diameter. The tests of *No. 23*'s gas bags took place on 25 January 1917, and the lift and trim trials took place on 26 August that year, 12 months after the promised delivery date. *No. 23* finally made her first flight on 19 September and was accepted by the navy on the same day. The total flying time of *No. 23* before she was dismantled at Pulham in September 1919 was 321 hours, 30 minutes.

35▲

36▼

36 *No. 25* of the '23' class, built by Armstrong Whitworth at Selby and launched on 14 October 1917. On the flight she was found to have less lateral stability than *No. 23*, but she was much more stable in elevation and more easily controlled. During later flights her 18 gas bags surged badly causing marked changes in trim. Various modifications were made to the ship and she passed her official acceptance trials on 23 December 1917. The designation of *No. 25* had now been changed to *R 25*, and before she was dismantled at Cranwell in September 1919 she had completed 271 and a half hours flying time.

37▼

37 This photograph of the internal structure of a British rigid airship was identified by Sir Barnes Wallis as one of the early Vickers airships built in 1917, which indicates that the ship must be one of the '23' class. The hull of the ship, suspended from the roof of her shed, seems to be almost complete with all transverse frames, longitudinals, and most of the mesh-wire bracing in place. The outer cover has not yet been put on the hull, and the gas bags have not been inserted either. Extension ladders on either side of the keel, in the centre of the picture, give some idea of the scale. On the left the framework of another rigid under construction can just be seen, proving that the picture was taken inside the double-shed at Barrow.

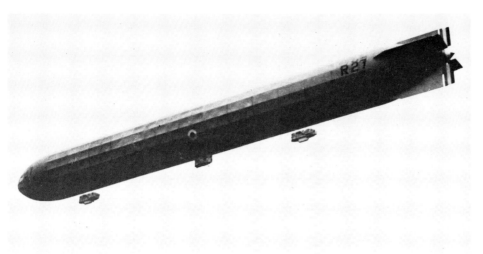

38 *R 27* was an improved '23' class design, designated the '23X' class. This design, a notable advance on earlier British designs, was chosen from a number of alternatives by the Rigid Airship Committee at a meeting held on 16 March 1917. Constructed by Beardmore at Inchinnan, she first flew in June 1918, and made 56 mph, powered by four Rolls-Royce engines. She was 539 ft (164.28 m) long and 53 ft (16.15 m) in diameter, and her 18 gas bags contained 990,000 cu ft of hydrogen. She logged 90 hours before she was burnt in her shed at Howden on 16 August 1918.

39 *R 29*, was almost identical to *R 27*. The first really useful British rigid airship, she was constructed by Armstrong Whitworth at Selby (Barlow), first flying in June 1918. *R 29*, like *R 27* had no external keel. Petrol, oil and ballast tanks, formerly kept in the keel, were suspended from the radial bracing wires. *R 29* was the only British rigid to enter into action with U-boats: the first escaped, the second struck a mine while being chased, and the third was hit by a 120 lb bomb and sunk by surface vessels. She logged 438 hours flight time, and was dismantled at East Fortune on 24 October 1919.

40 *R 31*, was launched in August 1918. She was 614 ft (187.14 m) long and 65.5 ft (19.96 m) in diameter. The number of gas bags was 21, and the cubic capacity 1,535,000. The useful lift was about 37,000 lb (16,782.91 kg). *R 31* spent only nine hours flying, last flying on 6 November 1918.

41 Major G.H. Scott, Squadron Leader F.M. Rope (left), and Flight Lieutenant H.C. Irwin, future captain of *R 101* (right), in *R 33*'s control car at Cardington in April 1925. All were killed in the *R 101*.

39▼

38▲

40▼

41▼

42▲

42 The '33' class ships *R 33* and *R 34* were copies of the captured Zeppelin *L 33. R 33* was built at Selby (Barlow) by Armstrong Whitworth and made her first flight on 6 March 1919, and *R 34* was built by Beardmore at Inchinnan and made her first flight on 14 March 1919. These ships had 19 gas bags having a total volume of 1,950,000 cu ft, and were 643 ft (195 m) in length and 78.75 ft (24 m) in diameter. Power was provided by five Sunbeam Maori engines, and each ship was capable of flying at 60 mph. *R 33* logged about 800 hours flying time, and although still in good flying condition was deleted from the effective list in 1927 for reasons of economy. She was eventually dismantled in 1928. *R 34* logged 500 hours flying time and was wrecked at Howden on 27 January 1921, because there was no mooring mast.

43 *R 34* made the first East-West Atlantic crossing by air. She set out from East Fortune at 0142 hrs on 2 July 1919 and 108 hours, 12 minutes later anded at Mineola airfield on Long Island on 6 July. The return trip was started on 20 July. Landfall was made over Ireland at 2000 hours on 12 July. The crew of *R 34* had received a tumultuous welcome from thousands of spectators when she reached America, and the hospitality was

almost overwhelming, yet her landing at Pulham on 13 July was an anti-climax after journey of 7,000 miles (12,964 km). Alcock and Brown only bridged the gap between Newfoundland and Ireland in their aeroplane flight, but *R 34* made the first aerial voyage from the United States to England, a remarkable achievement for which the crew received little reward.

43▼

29

44 *R 36* was begun by Beardmore before the end of the war, but at the close of hostilities work on her was suspended. She was completed as a civil ship, making her first flight on 1 April 1921, and was equipped with two forward cars from *L 71*, each containing a Maybach engine, and three Sunbeam Cossacks were placed in the rear cars. She was 672 ft (204.82 m) long and 78.75 ft (24 m) in diameter. She had a volume of 2,101,000 cu ft. *R 36* only made seven flights totalling 80 hours, and on 21 June 1921 she was damaged when she overshot the mooring mast at Pulham, and then was kept in her shed until she was dismantled in 1927.

44▲

45▼

45 A close up of the control car of *R 36*, taken during construction in Beardmore's shed at Inchinnan near Glasgow.

46 The unfinished and unfurnished passenger lounge aboard the *R 101*, during her construction at the Royal Airship Works at Cardington. At this stage the outer cover was being placed on the hull, and at the top right of the picture part of the shed can be seen through the, as yet, uncovered frameworth.

47 *R 101* nearing completion in her shed at Cardington, near Bedford. This ship was an expensive experimental airship and suffered from much official interference during construction, which resulted in many novelties being introduced into the design.

46▼

47▼

48▶

48 *R 80*, the first streamlined British airship, was designed by Barnes Wallis and built by Vickers at Barrow. The streamlined control car and wing engine can be seen clearly, as can the forward gun position on top of the envelope. There was also a tail gun position. She first flew on 19 July 1920, and with her four Wolseley-Maybach engines had a top speed of 70 mph. The volume was 1,200,000 cu ft, and her length was 535 ft (163 m), and she was 70 ft (21.33 m) in diameter. The ship flew a total of 73 hours and was used for training American crews. Her last flight was made on 20 September 1921. She was dismantled at Pulham, as an economy measure, in 1925. *R 80*, strangely, was never used for scientific flying trials.

49▲　　　　　50▼　51▼

49 An internal view of the *R 101* with the outer cover in place, showing the structure downship from the bows to the tail. The gaps between the sections of fabric on the outer cover have not yet been sealed. Fuel and ballast tanks can be seen along the structure of the ship, and the passengers' quarters can also be seen above the control car, which is visible through the uncovered keel.

50 *R 101* on the tower at Cardington. She could be serviced from this structure which also had a lift. She was 132 ft (40.29 m) in diameter and 732 ft (223.11 m) long before she was lengthened to 777 ft (236.83 m) by the insertion of another gas bag, increasing the number to 17, and her volume from 5,000,000 to 5,500,000 cu ft. Five Beardmore diesels enabled the *R 101* to fly at 72 mph.

51 *R 101* made her first flight on 14 October 1929. She set out on her twelfth flight on 4 September 1930 but crashed at Beauvais in France and burst into flames, *en route* for India, with the loss of 48 of those on board. This heralded the end of British rigid airship development.

52▲ 53▼

52 The framework of *R 100* in the shed at Howden before the application of the outer cover. Barnes Wallis's ingenious principles of geodetic design were first utilised in the construction of the *R 100*, but this system of construction was made famous during the Second World War when it was applied to aeroplanes, and the magnificent durability of the Vickers Wellington was attributable entirely to Wallis's geodetic construction. The lives of countless airmen were saved by an aircraft 'that could fly, so it seemed, so long as it had an engine'.

53 *R 100* under construction in her shed at Howden. This ship was designed by a team headed by Barnes Wallis, and built by the Airship Guarantee Company, of which Vickers held the majority of the shares.

54▲

54 *R 100* on the tower at Montreal in Canada in July 1930. *R 100* only made nine flights, logging 297 hours in the air, and spending a further 827 hours at the mast. She left for Canada on 29 July 1930 and arrived at Montreal on 1 August. The ship started out on the return journey on 13 August and landed at Cardington on the 16th. This was to be her last flight for she was taken into her shed the next day, only to emerge as £450 worth of scrap on 16 November 1931.

55▼

55 *R 100* on the tower at Cardington in 1930. The ship made her first flight on 16 December 1929, and was 709 ft (216.10 m) in length and 130 ft (39.62 m) in diameter. The total capacity of her 15 gas bags was 5,156,000 cu ft but she was generally kept at a volume of 5,000,000 of hydrogen. *R 100* was a remarkable piece of engineering work, and had a constructional advantage over *R 101* in that any girder could be replaced by simply unbolting its ends.

56  One of the wing engine cars on the *R 100*. Six
Rolls-Royce Condor IIIB engines, with a total horse
power of 4,200, drove the *R 100* at a maximum speed
of 83 mph. In contrast to *R 101*'s diesel engines, the
ones in the *R 100* were aeroplane engines running on
petrol. Each engine car had a Bristol gas starter to start
up the engines. Two AC six-cylinder engines in the
wing cars ran 15Kw generators that supplied the
electrical power for lighting, heating and cooking.

56▼

# Great Britain

This chapter is mainly concerned with the development and employment of non-rigid airships, from the formation of the Airship Service through the founding of the Air Battalion, the Royal Flying Corps, and the Royal Naval Air Service. The first part of the chapter, devoted to the beginnings of the Airship Service and operations at Cranwell Training Wing I, was contributed by Wing Commander J. N. Fletcher, AFC, who piloted some of the earliest service airships and did much to convince the authorities of the value of lighter-than-air craft.

The notes on Submarine Scout (SS) airships were contributed by Wing Commander T. R. Cave-Browne-Cave, CBE, and the information on airship operations 1914–18 and Mullion

## Beginnings of the British Airship Service

Air Station was written by Major J. Struthers, DSC, AFC. Squadron Leader T. P. York-Moore provided the piece concerned mainly with the operations of Airship Expeditionary Force No. 2, while the part on North Sea (NS) airships was contributed by Air Vice-Marshal P. E. Maitland. This collection of material is intended to give a clear picture of the technical and operational progress of British airships during the First World War and highlight the bravery and ingenuity of men on war patrols in all weathers, in, at the outset, unreliable machines.

The final section, contributed by Roger Munck, chief designer for Airship Developments, brings the chapter on British airships into the present.

The Air Battalion, Royal Engineers, was still recruiting its personnel from the Corps up to the time of the formation of the Royal Flying Corps (RFC). Two officers having been lost at sea in a free balloon in 1910, Col J. B. Capper, who was then just relinquishing command, came to Chatham and called for volunteers from the senior course of young officers. Of the two who volunteered, one was slightly short-sighted, and I, the other volunteer, was accepted. At the conclusion of the same course I was duly posted to the Air Battalion and joined very early in 1912.

The Air Battalion was still a horse-drawn unit in that part of the army designated as Army Troops. The first necessity for a new officer was, therefore, to take a Mounted Duty Course and so 'win one's spurs'. That formality completed, the new recruit was able to begin his new career.

One of the two companies in the Air Battalion, No. 1, was devoted to 'lighter than air' and was stationed at Farnborough alongside the Royal Aircraft Establishment, then the Army Aircraft Factory, where all its equipment was manufactured. Captain E. M. Maitland was its commanding officer and Lieutenant C. M. Waterlow acted as instructor. The No. 2 Company 'heavier than air'

lived on the Plain, but its officers were frequently with us at HQ with aircraft under test or repair.

Waterlow wasted no time: the day of my arrival was distinctly windy, but a captive balloon was taken out and up we went. At 400 ft (122 m) a gust caught us and smacked us down again to the ground. After the third grounding Waterlow looked pretty green, and declared he had had enough. I was still too green to be sea-sick but glad enough to fall in with his wishes. Apparently the more one did of this sort of thing, the worse was the effect upon one's tummy. The balloon was taken home, kites were brought out and the next lesson began.

The captive balloon of those days was a spherical balloon made of goldbeater's skin. It had no stabilising device whatever, and consequently could not be used in winds exceeding 20 mph. In winds above that speed the Cody kites could be used but although I mastered the art, I was too heavy for the job and rarely succeeded in getting higher than 50 ft (15.24 m).

In order to become an airship pilot one had first to graduate as a balloon pilot. Accordingly we would set off in suitable weather and go wherever the wind chanced to take us. The courses consisted of three or more runs under tuition, followed by at least one night run and one

solo run. There is quite an art in ballooning and one learns a lot about the vagaries of the atmosphere. If a balloon leaves the ground with a certain 'lift' it will rise until the diminishing density of the air neutralises the 'lift'. At that stage the balloon rises still further under its own impetus until its increasing 'heaviness' brings it to a halt. As it is then heavier than the air it displaces, it must begin to fall, and if nothing is done by the pilot, it will fall until it hits the ground. Then it will go up again and repeat the performance almost indefinitely. If however, ballast is released as soon as the balloon first begins to fall, it should be possible to check the fall at or near the position of equilibrium, which is the height at which the balloon weighs exactly as much as the air it displaces. Once, there, it may stay for hours, subject only to changes in temperature, from the sun going behind a cloud, or conversely, the release of ballast or of gas. Thus, the first object of the free balloon pilot is to find a suitable position of equilibrium.

Trained army airship pilots were in considerable demand at Hurlingham when balloon races were being organised. One very windy Saturday afternoon found me at Hurlingham with Captain E. M. Maitland of the Essex Regiment, my CO in the RFC. He was a keen amateur balloonist and parachutist, and he did me the honour of asking me to pilot his balloon for him. We were third to leave the ground. The first two went off low over the houses straight to the south coast, obviously limited to a mere 40 miles (64.37 km) or so, which, in a long distance race, held little prospect of success. Maitland agreed with me that there might be a more favourable wind higher up, so up we shot with lots of lift to 10,000 ft (3,048 m), and presently found ourselves drifting gently along the old London South West Railway past Basingstoke. We landed not very far from Southampton and felt we had done fairly well. The winning balloon and another which took the same line went much higher and ended up in County Durham.

Fortified by this amusing experience, I bought a huge ball of string on my next visit to Hurlingham. The father of Lieutenant T. G. Hetherington, 18th Hussars and RFC Airship Squadron, was a balloon enthusiast and I was detailed to pilot it for them. It was a very calm day indeed, and after hanging in the air over Dulwich for an hour, I fastened my key ring to the end of the string and began to pay out. When 2,000 ft (610 m) of string had gone we saw the markers belly out in a stream of air and promptly went down to catch the breeze, there to find a new position of equilibrium. That worked splendidly; we sailed off towards Dover feeling very pleased. However, the stream petered out and we landed near Horsham in the grounds of a convent where we were anything but welcome.

In order to understand what follows, going back to the period of tuition, a short technical dissertation is necessary. A free balloon is a more or less spherical container of gas surrounded by a network of string from which the basket is suspended. The container, known as the envelope, may be made of any gas-tight material and need have no strength at all. Early balloons were in fact made of paper. The bottom of the envelope is freely open to the air and gas can escape through a short canvas sleeve which is always quite open. At the top of the balloon there is a suitable disc-valve which can be opened by the pilot to let out gas from the top. When the balloon reaches its position of equilibrium it will be full of gas at exactly the same pressure as the surrounding atmosphere. When it falls below that position, for whatever

cause, the balloon ceases to be full and the bottom of the envelope begins to crinkle.

The time came when I was judged competent to take my last test: the night flight and solo flight. The night flight, solo, I believe, passed without incident and I landed near Cambridge, entranced by the slow drift in the early dawn across orchards and fields with the dawn chorus in full swing. The solo flight also passed without incident until the very end. It was a very calm day and I was stuck over a field near Aylesbury for a long time, so deciding that there was nothing to be gained by going on, pulled the gas valve to let out gas and come down. At that moment, however, a cumulus cloud of which I had not been aware took a hand in the proceedings and began to suck me up. Looking at my altimeter, which should have shown a steady fall, I saw instead a steady rise. Somewhat irritated by this, and being unwilling to risk a descent on to the chimney-pots of Aylesbury, which were only a few hundred yards away, I valved more gas. Unthinkingly, and very unwisely, I continued to valve until the altimeter showed 6,000 ft (1,820 m). Then I began to come down, still over the same quite small field. Landing without a bump I looked up and saw that my envelope was only about one-third full. I had in fact parachuted down. The balloon was so empty that when I stepped out of the basket it just stood there unable to lift even the light wicker basket.

In spite of my gaffe, I was passed out as a balloon pilot on 2 July 1912, with Aeronaut's Certificate No. 24.

One more ballooning story merits telling. I was now competent to instruct others, and when the RFC was formed, it fell to me to instruct the newly joined members of No. 1 Squadron. Lieutenant the Hon. J. Boyle and J. D. Mackworth were sent off with me on a run which nearly ended in disaster. Near Basingstoke it was pretty clear that a very high wind was getting up and I decided to land. There was a series of open stubble fields divided by very thick hedges, almost thickets, full of hazels and three or four yards in depth. We hit the ground in the middle of one field and the basket turned on its side as the balloon careered towards the hedge. We all hung on like grim death and the two pupils looked rather shocked. I had time to comfort them by assuring them that nothing more

frightful than a broken arm need be anticipated. Dragging through the hedge took several seconds in which I concluded that there was no means of handling the balloon after we had got out, and so I gave the order to abandon ship and followed my pupils as they went. Off went the balloon and we picked ourselves up quite unhurt. Afterwards it was made clear to me that I had been very naughty indeed — I should have gone off in the balloon and in failing to do so I merited a court-martial on a charge of hazarding War Department equipment or even of 'conduct unbecoming'! The balloon was recovered quite unharmed in the New Forest.

At a very early date, that is, well before the Royal Flying Corps was formed, the War Office announced a grant of £75 to any officer who learned to fly an aeroplane. Most people who went for this took their tuition at Brooklands, so having no ready money, I asked Colonel Cody whether he would teach me at Farnborough and wait for the grant to come through. This he agreed to do. Every possible evening after work I went off to his shed at the far end of Laffans Plain and very soon became sufficiently proficient to fix the date for my test.

Cody, who had no money either, was loath to let me fly unaccompanied and, up to the very last evening before the test, sat immediately behind me keeping a watchful, too watchful as it proved, eye upon me. I had just completed my figures of eight and was gliding down to land, still on a gentle turn. About 800 yards (730 m) away stood the little pavilion at the saluting base and, for a brief moment we were gliding directly towards it. Cody, fearing I was going to hit the pavilion, leaned over my shoulder and pushed the stick hard forward. We hit the ground at about 75 mph and both fell out. As he fell, Cody's foot touched the engine switch and the machine picked up at once. As I rolled over like a shot rabbit and sat up, I saw the machine bounce twice and then stagger into the air. I remember thinking it had just enough petrol in the tank to carry it to Lower Hale and was wondering what would happen then. However, the tip of a wing just caught a tree on the canal bank 500 yds away and the machine crashed. Cody got hit on the ankle as the machine surged past him. I was quite unhurt, but my test had to be delayed until he got another machine into the air.

During the waiting period I went to see Cody as often as I could, and one day, saw leaning up against the wall of the shed, four enormous 'kites'. To my question he replied, 'They are the rudders and elevators of my new monoplane, but I cannot see how to fix them to the nacelle.' Taking a square sheet of paper, I folded it into a four-winged pointed dart and snipped off the end. He saw at once that the rudders and elevators could be held in such a set-up and devised his tail accordingly. Some days later, as I stood with him in his shed, his carpenter came in with an enormous hickory spar, roughly 4 in × 4 in × 20 in and said, 'Mr Cody, where shall I cut the tenons?' Cody picked up the spar, balanced it on one hand, and taking a blue pencil from behind his ear marked the sites of the four tenons that would be needed. The spar was to be his landing skid.

The machine flew very well, but he crashed it by hitting a cow when landing. Cody was killed in August 1913, after winning the military trials with his biplane, *Cathedral*, which I had crashed.

**Non-rigid airships**

From January to August 1912 there were two military airships, *Gamma I* and *Beta I*, while a larger ship, *Delta*, was under construction. The envelopes of the two former ships were old and becoming porous, so it was decided that new and larger ones should be made.

Britain's only civilian contractor, E. T. Willows, built an envelope for *Gamma* with a volume of 101,000 cu ft. *Beta* was given a new envelope of 42,000 cu ft, which like the old one (33,000 cu ft) was made of gold-beater's skin. A new car was built for this ship with a 50 hp Clerget engine. These three ships all made their first flights in September 1912 and were ready just before the army manoeuvres. This gave too little time for proper trials and led to breakdowns.

*Beta* was a lovely thing to handle in the air. She carried a crew of three: pilot, passenger and engineer; she had one engine, driving two wooden propellers arranged on either side on tubular 'arms'. Lessons from earlier models had been so well assimilated that she was extremely well balanced. Flying usually started about 5 am and went on until breakfast time. The air was still, and the only snag was persistent ground mist which lay like a blanket over everything. However,

50 ft (15.24 m) up one was generally in bright sunshine and we could always, or nearly always, see the tops of tall buildings and Caesar's Camp.

To the best of my recollection the usual programme was a series of five-minute flips, changing passenger and/or pilot as the occasion demanded. One day, however, the mist was so deep that no landmarks were visible at all. After circling round for a few minutes, breakfast began to call. I should, of course, have sat up there and waited for the mist to clear but forgot to be cautious and, as I still knew pretty well where I was, I put the nose down and made for home. Almost at once there was a startled gasp from my passenger and I just caught a glimpse, as I turned to ask what was worrying him, of the golden cockerel which adorned the dome of the Cambridge Hospital, Aldershot. We had missed it by inches.

Non-rigid airships, unlike free balloons, had a totally enclosed gas container in which the pressure of the gas exceeded the pressure of the atmosphere. This was enough to keep the shape and provide adequate support for the control fins. On top of the envelope was a valve which would open automatically if the gas pressure exceeded prudent limits. It could also be opened by the pilot to let off gas, if that should ever be necessary. In every respect the gas behaved as has been described in the earlier passage about free balloons. Gas expanded and had to escape when one went up, and contracted when one came down.

To remedy the effect of contracting, and to keep the shape and rigidity of the envelope, one had to blow air into a ballonet which lay inside and on the lower surface of the envelope. This was simply effected by opening a valve in a rigid sleeve which scooped in the air, either from the propeller slip-stream or from the ship's own movement through the air. If one failed to do this the nose of the envelope would collapse and the ship would limp home barely under control. A suitable gas pressure gauge was provided to enable the pilot to watch this. The military ships, however, had a blower in the car, the air-scoop being a later development.

Our heavier-than-air friends lost no chance of pointing out that we were easy meat, a point we did not fail to take. We had, however, some advantages over them: we could fly at night, and often

did; we could fly in fog; we could fly very slowly and even drift like a balloon in perfect silence; and we thought that we could keep in the air for hours at a time and so, like the tortoise, defeat the hare. We also began to think we might be useful over the sea, especially if aeroplanes were not there.

Meanwhile, there was *Gamma* which had swivelling propellers, a much bigger ship than *Beta*, and normally carried a crew of four: pilot, coxswain, wireless operator observer and engineer. With her swivelling propellers she could pull herself down into a very restricted space and pull herself out again, as well as going astern if she wanted to stop in a hurry. Hers was the first envelope to be made of rubberised fabric. *Delta* was larger again but never seemed to have the same beautiful manoeuvrability.

We used *Gamma* extensively rather than *Beta* to seek out mooring places where an airship could lie secure against high wind, as *Gamma* could almost do without a landing party, but *Beta* never could, although in the open a very small handful of men sufficed. On one occasion I took Edward Maitland, my CO, to breakfast with St Loe Strachey, editor of the *Spectator*, at Newlands Corner. Mr Strachey and his butler acted as landing party and the ship was moored on the tennis lawn. On another occasion *Beta* 'attended the wedding' of Captain R. Pigot at Medenham and was moored overnight on the lawn.

Mooring-out places were needed for army manoeuvres and we had ships at Dunchurch near Rugby (*Delta* and *Eta* in 1913, and *Beta* at Thetford in 1912) moored out for a week or so between the futile reconnaissance flights which were made. Jesus College, Cambridge; Odiham chalk pits; Woodstock Park; Berkamstead Castle grounds, were all reconnoitred and used. The last named is an oval which just contains a quarter-mile running track. It is surrounded by high trees standing on the mounds of the old walls. Getting in presented no problem and we stayed overnight to give the school a chance to visit the ship, but heavy thunder and rain all night soaked the envelope and made it so heavy that all natural lift had vanished in the morning. We just pulled her out by sheer engine power.

To give some idea of the handiness of *Beta*, the following example will serve. We were moored out at Thetford in

Norfolk during the 1912 manoeuvres and were despatched on a reconnaissance in the very early dawn. Thetford was clear of fog but our area of search towards Cambridge was completely blanketed by a thick ground fog. From Cambridge itself the only ground feature visible was the twin tower of Ely Cathedral. Abandoning the reconnaissance, we set off for home using Ely as our guide. As we left the fog we found ourselves over a very substantial forest in which a broad ride pointed directly towards Thetford. We 'motored' along this ride at the height of nought feet for several miles, passing a keeper's cottage at an intersection as we flew. We often wondered what sort of animal the startled keeper thought we were.

These flights on manoeuvres were futile for a variety of reasons. The 'higher

58▼

57 *Nulli Secundus*, also known as *No. 1*, was Britain's first service airship, being built at the Balloon Factory at Farnborough in 1907 for the army. She was a semi-rigid airship and had a length of 122 ft (37.18 m) and a diameter of 25 ft (7.62 m). She was powered by an Antoinette 50 hp engine and flew at speeds ranging from 16 to 22 mph. Her original volume was 50,000 cu ft but she was reconstructed in 1908 and her capacity increased to 56,000 cu ft. Various stabilising arrangements were tried on her by Colonel John Capper and Samuel Cody who was instrumental in producing her. The photograph shows *Nulli Secundus* in 1908.

58 *Baby*, constructed at the Balloon Factory, Farnborough in 1909, was the first airship to have a ballonet. Her volume was 21,186 cu ft, and she was 83.75 ft (25.52 m) in length and had a maximum diameter of 24.75 ft (7.54 m). Later in 1909 her car and control surfaces were reconstructed, and in 1910 she was enlarged to 33,307 cu ft. She was modified and a 35 hp Green engine was installed, which gave her a maximum speed of 26 mph.

57▲

ARMY AIRSHIP 'BABY'

59◄

59 *Beta I* was the first non-rigid airship to be moored to a mast. The photograph was taken at Farnborough where *Beta I* was moored to the first 'high' mast on 19 and 20 February 1912. During the trials winds were recorded gusting up to 33 mph.

brass' had no experience of the use of aircraft and we had no experience of the art of air-reconnaissance. We were not told what to look for; we had no satisfactory means of communicating even if we found anything; we could not possibly distinguish friend from foe; we could hardly be expected to find a skeleton force which was the form usually taken by the 'enemy'; and the height at which we could fly made us an easy target for a firearm. The minimum requirement for a night reconnaissance would have been 7,000 ft (2,134 m). The maximum height attained by any airship in air service was attained by *Beta* on trials in 1913, when she reached 4,200 ft (1,280 m)

Once under way an airship, although heavy, can fly quite well but cannot manoeuvre easily. The aerofoil effect vanishes as soon as one begins to turn. This was well exemplified at the end of one long flight in which one of the naval contingent was acting as pilot under in-struction. For some unexplained reason, probably a leaky envelope, we reached base after a four- or five-hour circular flight to Tring and back, very heavy indeed. The captain passed the landing ground at 500 ft (152 m) and put the ship into a tight turn over Laffan's Plain. She began to fall very fast and I warned him to straighten out, but he was very senior to me and refused to do so. We hit the ground hard on a fringe of trees by Cody's shed. No damage was done, but it was an excellent lesson.

After that it became commonplace to fly off quite heavy, overloaded with fuel. As long as we kept a straight course it didn't matter at all; but I have known the lower tail plane at the stern of the envelope scratch along the ground at take-off. Owing to their greater speed and manoeuvrability, modern airships can turn when heavy. After a few hours' flying the surplus fuel is burnt up and the ship can then 'float' if necessary.

The War Office Military Aeroplane trials were held on Salisbury Plain during a spell of very inclement weather in August 1912. A courtesy visit by *Gamma* was planned but we had to wait for suitable weather. At last a possible day came and we flew down, landed and tied up at a mooring mast. After tea we began to fly home to Farnborough. A nasty head wind slowed us down badly and by the time we got to the Test Valley it was evident that we were going to be late for dinner, to say the least. A very high screen of elms near a village made us decide to moor out for the night. The ship was brought down to about 100 ft (30.5 m) and there we hovered and waited for help. A boy scout came first, read our message, and went off to collect a few men. The party hauled us down and we moored out behind the screen of trees, flying back to base next day after having been royally entertained by the residents.

60▼

Airship "Beta II".  MAYS. Aldershot.

61▲

62▲

63▲

64▼

60 *Beta II* became Naval Airship *No. 17* in 1914. The car of the ship is shown in the photograph and the 50 hp Clerget engine can be clearly seen. The ship was launched in 1912 and had a volume of 42,000 cu ft.

61 Naval Airship *No. 3* photographed in 1914. She was built by the Astra Company of Paris in 1913, and later modified a number of times before she was finally deflated in 1915 and put into storage. The envelope was 229,450 cu ft in capacity and was 248 ft long. She was powered by two 200 hp Chenu engines and had a top speed of just over 51 mph.

62 *Eta II*, Naval Airship *No. 10*, on trials at Kingsnorth on 5 January 1916. She was an experimental ship consisting of a spare envelope from *Eta I* and a car built by the French Astra Company for the envelope used for *Coastal No. I (CI)*. She only made three flights.

63 *Gamma II* leaving the moat at Fort Grange, Portsmouth, by using her swivelling propellers, in June 1914. *Gamma II* was constructed by the Royal Aircraft Factory and Willows & Company in 1912. At first she was used by the army but was taken over by the navy and became Naval Airship *No. 18*. She was powered by two Iris engines with a total of 80 hp and could reach a maximum speed of 30 mph.

64 The Parseval Naval Airship *No. 6* made her first flight trials at Barrow in 1915. In 1918 she was modified at Pulham, and had the same general specifications as *No. 7*. The volume was 364,000 cu ft, her length was 312 ft (55 m) and the diameter was 51 ft (15.54 m). The useful lift was 7,052 lb (3,198.73 kg).

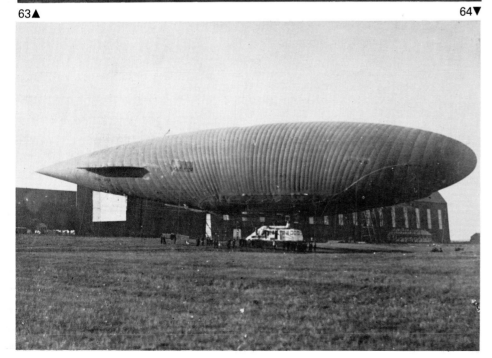

## The Royal Flying Corps and the Royal Naval Air Service

The Royal Flying Corps was formed on 13 May 1912 and the Air Battalion became part of it. A large number of new recruits arrived from other regiments and, after spending most of the summer in camp at Farnborough, were allotted to their respective squadrons. No. 1 Squadron, commanded by Major E. M. Maitland, was 'lighter-than-air' and newly-joined officers had to be trained. The brunt of this fell upon me. This was barely finished when yet another group of newcomers arrived, officers and men of the Airship Section of the Naval Wing, RFC. The whole of 1913 and most of 1914 was happily spent on this and as far as I can remember there were no untoward incidents.

Naturally enough everything was intensified. Two new airships were bought: one was *PL 18*, a Parseval of German origin, which became HMA *No. 4*; the other, an Astra-Torres of French origin, was HMA *No. 3*. Mr E. T. Willows, a Cardiff dentist, had also built himself a small airship, HMA *No. 2*, rather smaller than *Beta*, which he brought to Farnborough and the Admiralty bought it for experimental purposes. *Delta* was already in commission and *Eta* was under construction. The last named was, I think, a flop, largely owing to a defective chain drive and leaky envelope; *Delta* did not come up to expectations and was very little used. She proved capable, however, of leaving the ground vertically when 650 lb (295 kg) heavy and she did well on the 1913 manoeuvres.

In addition to my ordinary squadron duties, I was appointed an assistant experimental officer attached to HQ under Captain Musgrave, RE. The main emphasis for me lay on photography. The Sappers already had field photographic sections in being and their equipment included a sort of conjuror's box in which plates could be developed and prints made within a very few minutes of the arrival of the undeveloped plate.

Experimental navigation and communication from air to ground also formed part of my duties but nothing of real value emerged. Wireless telegraphy was still very much in its infancy, and that was in the very capable hands of Captain Lefroy, RE.

By the end of 1913 it became abundantly clear that the future of airships lay over the sea. On 1 January 1914 the army

airships were transferred to the Naval Wing, RFC under Commander Masterman, Major Maitland being second in command. Somewhere about midsummer all the airship officers of the RFC were transferred to the newly formed RNAS. I was given command of the Parseval, and Lieutenant W. Hicks, RN, eventually took over the Astra-Torres, which had originally been commanded by Commander N. Usborne, RN.

The most interesting feature of *No. 4* was that she had variable pitch propellers. These were of laminated steel and consisted of overlapping plates, held together with copper rivets and reinforced at the edges. Each blade was about 20 inches (508 mm) wide and 50 inches (1,270 mm) long and each propeller had four blades. It occurred to me at once that, sooner or later, a blade must fracture and that this would probably happen in flight. In order to see whether a blade could be changed in the air we did the job in the shed without allowing the mechanic to touch the ground. No difficulty was experienced so we shipped two spare blades and left it at that. We did not attempt, as we should have done, to change the blade in actual flight.

Between taking over command and 23 July we flew just under 1,000 miles (1,609 km), a total of 35 hours, 50 minutes, exclusive of taking over flights. My number one was Lieutenant A. D. Cunningham, RN, brother of the famous admiral.

The last of these flights was made to the Grand Fleet Review in the Solent. We had been down on the previous day and had flown over the whole Review but on the great day itself the wind was so strong that we arrived over Portsdown Hills only just in time to see the salute fired.

On 23 July, *P 4*, (as she was usually called) was ordered to Kingsnorth on the Isle of Grain near Chatham and the following week was devoted to putting her into operational order. Three flights totalling five and a half hours were made. Tension built up very rapidly during the week. Sappers came to build blockhouses; sentries fired at prowlers; recognition signals were issued and lifebelts and armament supplied. Every sort of mechanical trouble plagued us. When we fitted the approved lights our lighting set broke down, and both the main engines needed a lot of work. On 1 August the General Fleet Mobilisation was ordered;

on 3 August our wireless telegraph (W/T) set arrived with Captain Lefroy, and our role was determined: we were detailed to act as portguard-ship in the outer reaches of the Thames with a beat from Kentish Knock to Barrow Deep.

On 3 August the ship carried 15 hours' fuel and six men. Our W/T set weighed 250 lb (113.39 kg) so to compensate we dropped the anchor and cable which weighed the same amount. They were quite useless anyway, and no airship ever succeeded in making its anchor or grapnel hold in an emergency.

On 4 August we were ordered to take up our positions as guardship in view of the probable opening of hostilities at midnight, but the weather deteriorated in the afternoon and when it was time to leave the shed the wind made it impossible.

On 5 August the morning was showery and squally with a moderate SSW wind, but it cleared temporarily towards evening and at 7 pm we got the ship out and proceeded to take up our allotted station. We were under orders to maintain W/T silence except for the purpose of reporting hostile activity.

By the time we reached Sheerness it was quite dark and we received a W/T message, 'P 4 report'. In view of the W/T silence order I decided to ignore the message, but as we passed a destroyer near the Nore Light Vessel we signalled her by lamp.

Our beat lay in the extreme NE corner of the estuary and was about 12 miles (19.31 km) in length running roughly NW to SE. From the Kentish Knock Light Vessel it took us nearly two hours to reach the Barrow Deep, flying at 500 ft (15.24 m), and we estimated the wind at 26 mph. We had snow squalls and rain, so having done the beat twice we decided it was not good enough and proceeded for home. As we passed along Edinburgh Deep we suddenly saw in the moonlight a flotilla of small ships in close formation heading upstream and found they were not shown on our 'dispositions.' The inference was 'enemy minelayers', an inference that was strengthened by the sound of a shot. Some weeks later this same 'sound of shot' phenomenon occurred when someone kicked a heavy cleat against the aluminium sheeting of the car. However, at the time, the double evidence convinced us and I duly made a signal to base reporting the 'invasion'. While doing this we were taking the precaution of putting both height and distance between the enemy and our vulnerable and defenceless selves. By the time we had recovered we were high up over Reculver and dawn was breaking. The violent squalls had also disappeared and it had become relatively calm. We flew home close to the Kentish shore at about 300 ft (91 m) but became aware that we were being fired on by a Territorial Division which was encamped there, in spite of the fact that we were flying a White Ensign of battleship size. No hits were scored by the soldiers.

On arrival at base we were coldly told that we had been given up for lost when we failed to reply to the message 'P 4 report'. A powder magazine at Faversham had been hit by lightning and the resulting explosion had been attributed to us. Our message reporting the 'minelayers' had not been received (we knew that) because the W/T watch on us had been cancelled. The minelayers proved to be minesweepers which had inadvertently been omitted from the disposition.

As a result of this flight so many reports reached the Admiralty of enemy airships flying up the Thames that all airship patrols were cancelled while things were sorted out. The flight on 5/6 August was the first operational flight of the war and the first all-night flight by a British airship. We were in the air for 9 hours and 10 minutes, and flew 192 miles (309 km).

*No. 3* airship was the next to go out and her beat was rather more extensive. If I remember correctly it was from North Foreland to Ostend — a bigger radius of action. Her first flight took place on 11 August and was credited in the official naval history as the first operational flight. Her captain was Lieutenant W. Hicks, RN.

On 11 August we were off again, made a landing at Dover to take on petrol and ballast, and proceeded an hour later to take on the usual patrol. The airship camp was in the charge of Captain Hetherington, and *Airship No. 19 (Delta)* under Major Waterlow and Captain Mackworth was moored there, having broken down on her first patrol. Total flying for the day was 10 hours and 5 minutes and total distance 285 miles (459 km).

On 15 August both ships went out on their allotted beats. One of *P 4*'s propeller blades fractured while we were in the air and the two-foot long broken fragment hit the envelope 'on the flat' and was subsequently seen falling into the sea. If it had hit us 'on edge' it would have torn the envelope, a contingency we had foreseen but not properly prepared for.

65▲

65  The car of Naval Airship *No. 4*, just before the ship left Kingsnorth on patrol. She was the first airship on either side during the war to make an operational flight, being taken out under the command of Flight Commander J.N. Fletcher on 5 August 1914. She was powered by two Maybach engines and her maximum speed was 42 mph. She first flew in 1913 but was reconstructed with a covered car the same year, and she was deflated in 1917.

E. R. A. Shaw, whose job it was and who had done the job in the shed, made no bones about it and started to climb out on to the propeller arm. A light casting line was secured to him by a bowline but the only thing to which we could secure the inboard end of the line was below his working position.

The first snag was that all the nuts were secured by split-pins and all the split-pins were on the wrong side of the blade and only just within reach. Having unshipped the blade it had to be manoeuvred on board, a nasty job as we were under way at 1,500 ft (457 m) doing 15 to 20 mph. Shaw came in with it and the spare blade was got out of its slot underneath the car. Putting it into place was easy enough compared to getting the broken blade out, as the bolts, nuts and split-pins could be put in the other way; but Shaw checked the weight of the new blade against its opposite number and found a difference of two grammes. In reporting this he gave an opinion that the opposite blade ought also to be changed. I objected but he stood firm and got his way. The whole job took 80 minutes. We then resumed patrol and completed a total distance of 270 miles (434.5 km) in $12\frac{1}{4}$ hours.

One of the oddest features of this Channel patrol was the fact that the destroyer flotilla leader and three destroyers lay motionless, strung out across the 22 miles (35 km) of Channel all day long. We used to 'attend' church service each morning, hovering 100 ft (30 m) above the flotilla leader. It took a long time to learn the game! Very soon after that two cruisers were torpedoed while lying-to, picking up survivors from a third.

The problem now was to find new blades for our props. All eight were suspect and the German vendors of the ship had failed to deliver a new set. An older set, sent to Vickers after being condemned, so that they could be copied, were sent down to us and returned with contumely. Pending a new supply, which never came, we carefully examined the blades we had and condemned two of them, thus leaving four blades on one side and two on the other. Two more patrols, four and a quarter hours and five and a quarter hours long, were carried out, but one engine gave trouble and the ship was barely controllable with the other, which had only the two-bladed prop. Between then and mid-September

we flew four short test flights but serious work was impossible.

During the few weeks which followed this burst of activity, I was given the job of forming the RNAS Photo-Section, which was barely under way before I was ordered to report to Tug Wilson (Admiral of the Fleet Sir A. K. Wilson, VC, RN) at the Admiralty. His wish was for photographs of Borkum and my task was to get them. The Light-Cruiser Squadron (Admiral Tyrwhitt) was at Harwich and was the vehicle for the job. Three small aircraft carriers worked with the squadron, all of them converted cross-Channel passenger ships. I was embarked with my pilot in one of them, and three attempts were made to get within range of Borkum. On two occasions high wind and rough sea forced the Admiral to cancel the operation. The third was cancelled because we sighted a Zeppelin on the extreme horizon.

The work done by HMA *No. 3* and HMA *No. 4* in those early days evidently convinced the authorities that there was some value in airships. Vickers were given the order to build two airships on the Parseval model and I was sent to Barrow to supervise the work with a view to taking command of one of them.

Meanwhile, a vast programme was sent on foot. A large number of small ships, about *Beta*'s size, was ordered and airship sheds and barracks were constructed all round the coasts from Stranraer to Mullion on the west and from Eastbourne to Peterhead on the south and east coasts. Fifty sub-lieutenants and 'snotties' were called for from the Fleet and numbers of direct-entry officers were appointed.

At Barrow I found myself in command of the new station with a watching brief over Stranraer and Llangefni in Anglesey. Side by side with the small ships, two larger models on the Astra-Torres principle were designed, the Coastal and the North Sea types for work in wider waters.

The small ships, familiarly known as 'blimps' were little brutes. To save time and expense in construction they were given an aeroplane chassis with a 60 hp Renault air-cooled engine and a tractor propeller. The magnetos were British-made and gave endless trouble, and the slow speed of the ships caused cylinder-heads to crack. It was no uncommon thing for an airship to break down completely while on patrol and to drift help-

lessly to land. To restart the engine one of the crew of three had to get down on the skid and swing by hand, a nerve-racking affair for all concerned. As we had no launches and Air-Sea-Rescue had not yet been thought of, we were extremely lucky not to lose any of these ships.

In spite of these elementary difficulties there soon grew up a great pride and a strong *esprit de corps* amongst the personnel, and much valuable work was done. Where convoy routes passed within reach, an airship would meet and escort the convoy, and there was no case of any ship being torpedoed while under airship escort. All this took time and most of the stations were hardly operational until about mid-1917. The armament carried by the smaller ships was two 65 lb (29.5 kg) bombs set for use as depth charges. To the best of my recollection this became standard for all three types. The chance of a direct kill by an airship was therefore extremely remote but by the end of hostilities, out of 27 attacks on submarines, two were credited as successful.

Aberdeen was the victualling port for the Grand Fleet at Scapa and whenever the roads were mined — which was incessantly — all traffic stopped until the sweepers could pronounce the all-clear. In consequence the fleet was more or less starved. During six weeks of continuous fine weather in 1916 I kept an airship on patrol just outside the port all night. I could see nothing at all as the water there was far too murky. Nevertheless no mines were laid during those six weeks. When the weather broke and the airship could not get out of the shed, mines were laid at once.

We were using Coastal type ships which carried a crew of five: captain, navigator, coxswain, wireless operator and engineer. The car had an engine at each end, one pushing and the other pulling. Magneto trouble was still plaguing us and it was quite usual for the engineer to have to get down on the skid and change a defective magneto. The new one then had to be timed to synchronise and the whole job took a long time. One gallant chap changed four magnetos in one flight. In winter this was indeed no joke, and it was not unknown for the ship to have to return to base with a frozen engineer crouching on the skid because he was quite incapable of climbing back into the car.

## Admiralty interlude

In 1916 I was appointed to the Admiralty Air Department, under Rear-Admiral Vaughan Lee. While I was there I met Colonel H. de Watteville, then serving in HQ Home Defences at the Horse Guards. One of his jobs was concerned with plotting Zeppelin activities over the North Sea, and he frequently showed me the night's plot. Anything from 12 to 15 airships had effectively covered the whole area. One day I took my plot to the Admiral who showed interest but explained that the soldiers were really not capable of making an accurate plot. Would I please go and get its naval counterpart? The naval captain concerned with this had his room adjoining the Chief of Staff's own room. When I knocked at the door, the officer opened it himself but would not let me enter. I showed him the soldier's plot and gave him my Admiral's message. His reaction was the same, not worth the paper it was written on, but I could not have a copy of the naval plot without the permission of the Chief of Staff.

Accordingly I knocked at the great man's door, which opened a tiny crack, just enough for me to get a glimpse of the very irate face of Admiral Oliver, later Admiral Sir H. Oliver, then Vice-Chief of Staff. 'Admiral Vaughan Lee's compliments, sir, and could he have a copy of the naval plot of last night's Zeppelin activities?' The crack remained a crack but the voice came, 'Tell Admiral Vaughan Lee, with my compliments, that aircraft have been of no use in this war, and never will be.' Bang went the door! Not until the sinking of the *Prince of Wales* and the *Repulse* in 1941 did it begin to dawn on naval authorities that this view was really disastrous.

During this short appointment we had a signal from Wormwood Scrubbs one day to say that an airship with an Italian pilot under training, had crashed on landing and had floated away with the pilot hanging head down in the wreckage. Sure enough she was easily visible from the roof. It was lunch-time and my day on duty, and I had to decide what had to be done. The hot-heads wanted to shoot it down at once. I refused, believing that it would probably come down clear of London without further damage to the pilot, who would almost certainly be killed if it was shot down in London itself. It did come down in Epping Forest and the pilot was more or less unhurt.

Years later, as Air Attaché in Rome, I met him as C-in-C, Naples. He was then Vice-Admiral Denti.

During my tour of duty at the Admiralty several Zeppelins were shot down, and it fell to me to participate in the interrogation of prisoners. One was wearing the ribbon of the Iron Cross, and in reply to my question as to how he had earned it, he told me his Zeppelin had sighted a British light cruiser squadron on a certain date which corresponded exactly with the abortive attempt on Borkum related above. As the Zeppelin was never within 30 miles (48 km) of the squadron, I could not help thinking that the decoration was cheaply earned. The incident does, however, show the great value of the Zeppelin activities during that period.

66 Willows *No. 4*, which became SS 1 (Submarine Scout), on trials at Farnborough in the autumn of 1912. Her volume was about 20,000 cu ft.

67 *Naval Airship No. 4* flying through the haze over the Fleet at the Spithead Naval Review in July 1914, shortly after taking off from Grange Field.

66▲

67▼

The Cranwell Airship Training Wing came into being early in 1916. In the same formation there was a Boys' Training Wing, and a Flying Training School. Air Commodore J. Luce was Station Commander, and the Wing Commanders were Portal, Pierse, Sholto Douglas and myself.

Wing Commander C. M. Waterlow, who was the first CO of the Airship Training Wing was killed in an accident almost at the outset, trying to retrieve a mistake by a half-trained airship landing party, and I was posted from Longside to take his place in the late summer of 1917.

The Wing was still at that time furnished with the Maurice Farman type of SS Airship and all training flights were bedevilled by constant engine trouble. That no airship was lost was in great measure due to the magnificent work of the aircrew engineers of whom three were awarded the Air Force Medal. The pupils were all direct entry officers and the instructors were drawn from the young naval officers who had come from the Grand Fleet a year earlier.

The use of parachutes as a means of escape from damaged airships had been under consideration for some months, and Spencer parachutes had for a long time been in use in France, to enable kite-balloon observers to escape when their balloons were shot down. Airship instructors were given the opportunity to jump as a normal part of the training programme, but we never actually tried out the pupils with them on account of a disconcerting accident.

Parachutes were supplied to airship crews early in 1917. The 'chutes were packed in suitable bags fastened to the side of the envelope, and the static lines were brought to suitable places in the car so that all that was necessary was to clip it on to the harness, which was always worn, and jump.

It came to my knowledge that kite-balloon observers were being constantly killed by Fokkers while they were dangling helplessly in the air and it occurred to me that the losses might be mitigated if the air could be spilled temporarily after the parachute had opened. It did not seem impossible to rig a light line from the crown of the parachute to the observer, so that he could pull down the crown and by spilling the air increase the speed of his fall. When nearing the ground all he would have to do would be to release the spilling line. Permission

# Cranwell – Airship Training Wing I

was obtained to experiment along these lines and a series of drops, using a dummy, was initiated with the spilling line used in such a way that each successive drop was faster than the last. Two or three successful drops were carried out, but at the next drop the static line snapped and the dummy fell heavily to earth. An hour later the parachute rigger appeared in my office and reported that the parachute that had failed was the one used by me in my own live drop some weeks earlier from Parseval *No. 6*. Enthusiasm waned.

Early in 1918, or thereabouts, I was called to an interview in the Admiralty and was informed that twin-engined airships were coming into service and that the Wing would be allotted a number of these. It was also stated that a very large number of war-weary infantry officers had been transferred to the RNAS for training as airship pilots, and in consequence, the Wing's output would have to be doubled.

One remarkable incident sticks in the memory. Several airships were out with ex-infantry pupils when out of a cloudless sky a huge wind sprang up. The Meteorological Office advised that there was every likelihood of its persisting for 30 hours, so all ships were recalled. The last to land lost its trail ropes owing to defective goose-foot patches, and the pupil pilot who was doing his first solo was not quite good enough to land on his handling guys, and no blame attaches to him for that. He had on board an engineer and W/T operator with an Aldis lamp, and instructions were sent by lamp telling him exactly what he should do. The 'instruction', watched by all pupils, was to fly up-wind below the brow of the plateau on which lay the landing ground, and there switch off engines. His engineer was to flood the exhaust-pipe with Pyrene and the envelope was to be ripped as the ship cleared the brow of the plateau. All this was done exactly according to the book and the ship fell neatly into the hands of the landing party with the minimum of damage. The ambulance crept away with its tail between its legs.

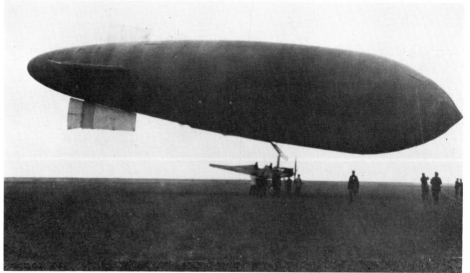

**68▲**

68 *SS 1* photographed in April 1915. She was made up from the 1913 envelope of Naval Airship *No. 2*, which had a volume of 39,000 cu ft. During her life numerous modifications were made, one of the final ones being the addition of the BE2C fuselage as her car.

Wing Commander T. R. Cave-Browne-Cave, CBE, who was connected with the RNAS from its formation, in charge of non-rigid airship design, construction and trials until 1918, eventually worked on airship research — rigid airships in particular — at the Admiralty and the

# The Genesis of the Submarine Scout (SS) Airships

Air Ministry. The following account of the evolution of the 'Submarine Scout' airships underlines the pressing need for reliable anti-submarine airships at the time. The first SS airship made its first flight in March 1915, and by 1918 several variants of the original design had been produced.

It is quite clear that the outline of the SS design had been talked out in considerable detail by Wing Commander Usborne, Flight Lieutenant Hicks and myself before the interview with Admiral of the Fleet, Lord Fisher, the First Sea Lord. Fisher summoned Masterman and Usborne to explain it in greater detail and he was sufficiently convinced to tell them to proceed at once on the understanding that the prototype flight might be achieved in a short period, which they agreed might be three weeks.

Usborne was a Commander, RN, who had specialised in torpedoes, and had many months' experience with *Airship No. 1 (Mayfly)* at Barrow. He had an exceptionally fertile mind and sound judgment, and could make his proposals appear very convincing.

Hicks was a younger naval lieutenant who had been with Usborne in each airship he had commanded, and had, as a matter of fact, the greater skill in the actual handling of an airship.

While in the navy I had followed the Specialist Long Course in Engineering Design and had then served for two years in *King Edward VII*, the flagship of what was then the Senior Fleet. This experience impressed upon me the vital necessity of reliability and economy of effort. Then followed two years in *Cornwall* in which cadets were given their first six months at sea. I then went to the staff of the Engineer-in-Chief at the Admiralty where I served two years in the Battle Cruiser Design Room and the Submarine Design Room. During this time I applied for transfer to Naval Flying, but was unsuccessful; it was not then naval policy to have engineer officers flying, but the Director of the Air Department achieved my transfer, not to seaplanes as I had hoped, but to airships. He had perhaps in mind the desirability of getting the engineering aspect of naval airships on a more reliable basis. I qualified as a balloon and airship pilot and realised at first hand how much the use of both the naval and army airships was restricted by lack of reliable machinery. When it was

decided that all airship work was to be transferred to the navy, and that Kingsnorth was to be established, we arranged for the station to have its own airship design and construction staff.

In anticipation of this we established a small nucleus at Farnborough to prepare the design of an improved airship of conventional design to be known as *Epsilon*. I realised that for the swivelling propellers which were then considered essential, really first class gear design must be adopted. We succeeded in getting Rolls-Royce to send a small party to us at Farnborough to work on this project, but unfortunately the work was halted.

## Anti-submarine airships
The experience which Usborne gained in *Astra Nos. 3* and *8*, patrolling the Dover area, convinced him that airships had great value in submarine observation, but that their life would be very short in the conditions at Dover when the Germans had reached the Belgian coast. Airships for anti-submarine duties must therefore work in less dangerous areas; they must be capable of long flights in bad weather and should largely be independent of airship sheds. If provision for this duty were to be made, the ships must be small, reliable and readily available in considerable numbers. This requirement was discussed in great detail by Usborne, Hicks and myself.

## Evolution of design
At that time, it was held by almost all airship pilots that swivelling propellers

were essential, or at any rate that engines mounted in the airship car should drive propellers mounted on gantries and driven by chains or shafts. I realised that swivelling propellers and special drives, which must be of special design, must involve great delays in manufacture and testing. All airship engines up to that time had been of special types. We therefore discussed what was the simplest form of small airship, which could use standard engines and standard construction and carry the minimum crew necessary to perform the operational functions of long patrol over the sea.

This led naturally to a two-seater aeroplane fuselage, its length and the existence of skids below the propeller providing a construction particularly convenient for rigging close under the envelope. We discussed this with F. M. Greene, Chief Engineer of the Royal Aircraft Factory, who quite naturally suggested that their own design of BE2C would be most suitable, and, as that design improved, obsolete fuselages suitable for less exacting airship requirements would become available. We therefore concluded that an aeroplane car capable of carrying two men and fitted with a standard reliable engine and airscrew was by far the simplest way of meeting the new requirement. The length of the fuselage was sufficient to make rigging to an airship envelope comparatively simple. A blower would not be necessary if we could devise a blower tube which would take the full dynamic head from the propeller stream, which would be sufficient to maintain in the envelope a pressure greater than that at the nose of the envelope under any conditions. With the bow reinforcement that was already customary, this margin would be amply sufficient. This is probably the stage we had reached when Masterman described the plan to the Director of the Air Department, Captain M. Sueter, RN.

A meeting of Masterman and Usborne with Fisher was arranged a few days in advance. There was therefore a very careful final discussion in the mess on the

69 The control car of *SS BE* was, as is indicated by her designation, a BE aeroplane fuselage. In his book *Airship Pilot No. 28* Captain T.B. Williams, AFC, mentioned that the early SS ships were 'more reliable than one would imagine, the Renault air-cooled engines giving little trouble as they were so carefully serviced by our reliable engineers.'

69▲                                                              70▼

70 *SS BE*, the prototype of the Submarine Scouts, leaving the ground at Milton Airship Station, near Pembroke, in 1916. This non-rigid was 143.5 ft (43.73 m) long and had a maximum diameter of 27.75 ft (8.45 m). Her volume was 60,000 cu ft, and she was powered by Renault engines.

71▼

71 *SS BE3*, which was built by Short Brothers. Other ships in this class were built by Armstrong Whitworth and Airships Limited. Two airships of this class were transferred to France.

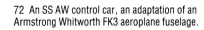
72 An SS AW control car, an adaptation of an Armstrong Whitworth FK3 aeroplane fuselage.

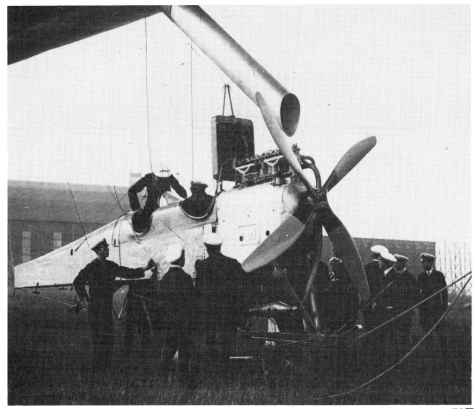
72▲

73▼

74▼

73 *SS AW40*, which flew over the German lines in France in autumn 1916. A 100 hp Rolls-Royce or Green engine was used in this class, giving a top speed of almost 50 mph. One of this class was sold to Italy.

74 An SS MF ship landing at Pulham. Twelve of these ships were constructed during 1915 and 1916. The envelope was 143.5 ft long and had a diameter of 27.9 ft. The capacity of the envelope was 60,000 cu ft. The longest flight made in one of these ships was just over 29 hours' duration.

75 The SS MF control car was adapted from the fuselage of a Maurice Farman biplane. The ships were powered by an 82 hp Rolls-Royce or Renault engines and had a maximum speed of 45 mph. The four-bladed pusher propeller can be seen at the rear of the car.

75▼

49

evening before the meeting. This was necessary so that they could put forward a proposal sufficiently complete and promising to win approval to proceed with a prototype.

## The birth of SS 1

When that approval was given at the meeting on 28 February 1915, we decided that the spare envelope which had been made at Farnborough for *Airship No. 2* should be used. Comparatively simple planes should be made and the prototype built up and tried at Kingsnorth, where we were on the point of transferring. I remember quite clearly the condition imposed by Fisher that the prototype must fly successfully within three weeks. In fact we were ready a few days within this period: Hicks carried out the first flight on 18 March 1915 and it was quite satisfactory. I understand that when Usborne saw Fisher and told him that the flight had been undertaken successfully, and how the prototype had been built up, Fisher's reaction was characteristically simple — 'Now I must have 40.'

As standard aeroplane bodies could be used, a supply of these presented little difficulty. Holt Thomas of Airships Ltd put forward an alternative proposal, that the Maurice Farman type with a pusher airscrew, which he was developing, would be preferable. We proceeded at once with the BE type. A few Maurice Farman cars were used at a later stage.

## SS 2

Out of deference to Mr E. T. Willows, the swivelling propeller enthusiast, an order for a single ship was given to him. It took a long time to complete and then depended on airscrews driven by an enormous laminated leather driving belt which was sufficiently flexible to allow the airscrews to swivel through a considerable angle. The airship was delivered and made a short trial, but was unsuitable for further development.

## Production of envelopes

The envelopes presented the greatest difficulty. We had the drawings of the envelope made at Farnborough, but the people there were fully occupied on aeroplane work and therefore quite incapable of tackling the supply of envelopes needed for the many small airships. Drawings of the new aeroplanes were prepared at Kingsnorth. Usborne

visited five firms which manufactured water-proof garments and arranged for an order to be placed with each of them for envelopes. To give some training in this new type of work, each firm was to appoint a technical representative to become a Lieutenant, RNVR and come to Kingsnorth to be instructed by us on how the envelope should be made.

The first difficulty we met was when we discovered that garment manufacturers worked wholly from patterns and did not understand the size of a number of panels. The corners of each panel were shown by holes drilled through the templates, so that a pencil mark could easily be made. Besides giving the complete sets of panel outlines on comparatively few sheets of aluminium, it did give the incidental advantage that we could make 12 sets of templates by drilling through piles of 12 aluminium sheets.

After thorough trials at Kingsnorth, the first of the new ships, *SS 1*, was sent to a patrol station at Capel near Dover. Flight Commander A. D. Cunningham was in command of the station, Flight Sub-Lieutenant Booth was captain of the ship, with Lieutenant Rope, RNVR, as engineer officer of the station. The coxswain was Warrant Officer Righton, a man of outstanding skill and enterprise.

Once several ships had been in use for some time, Capel put forward a suggestion that a modified form of car more suitable for operational purposes could be developed. This they proceeded to build with their own facilities and with very good results. This design of car was a pusher and was known as the Zero

type. It was adopted in all future airships of that size (70,000 cu ft). It was a most interesting development based on operational experience and naturally replaced the original aeroplane fuselage which had been adopted as a matter of emergency.

The engine was started by a mechanic standing in the car, looking aft at the engine. In the BE cars the only means of restarting the airscrew in flight was to climb out of the car and stand on one of the two skids, pulling the airscrew round by hand. This sounds a remarkable process, but it did prove satisfactory, because after demonstrating that it could be done, we made a practice of arranging that airship engines should always be started by their engineers in this way, even if the airship was in the shed.

In the development of these ships, and more still, perhaps in the Coastal and North Sea types which followed them, a great many new problems arose which could only be quickly and satisfactorily solved by quite new methods and devices. It is perhaps worth recording the principles we followed: a very carefully discussed definition of the requirements; a determination to make everything in the simplest possible way, after careful thought and discussion concentrated on the really essential factors; thorough tests to get conclusive results quickly; an intimate association at Kingsnorth of those who designed, built, tested and flew the airships, and carried out the widely varied experimental work, and regular visits to patrol stations to see the officers and crews of ships flying in operations.

76▲

76 An 'SS Zero' airship on convoy duty. No convoys were attacked by U-boats while under airship escort, but the Airship Service casualty figures given in the Report of the Superintendent of Airships for 10 November 1918, were: 20 officers and 34 men killed; five officers and 170 men injured; one officer and four

men missing; and two officers and three men, from *C 26*, interned.

77/78 The cars of *SS Zero 53* (top) and *SS Zero 71* (lower) at Kingsnorth in 1918. The blower to the ballonet can be seen on *SS Zero 53*.

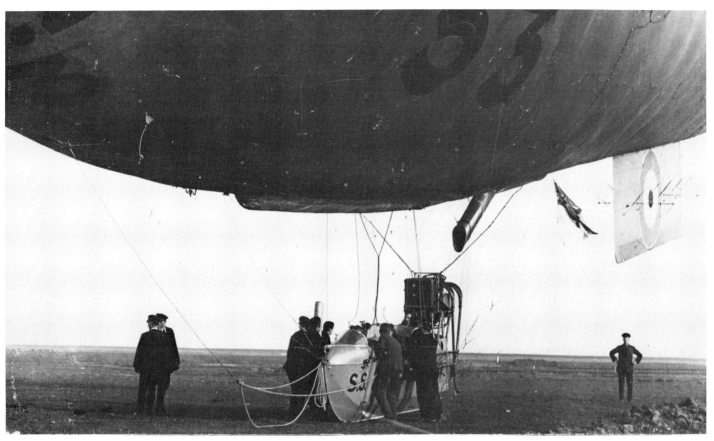

77▲

78▼

79 The control car of *SS Z 27*. The SS Zero car replaced the BE2C and Maurice Farman cars. The car was designed to float like a boat and water landings were made on numerous occasions.

79▲                                                          80▼

80 *SS Zero 37* over a ship in the English Channel. During the First World War a total of 213 non-rigid airships were constructed and another 13 were reconstructed from damaged ships and spares. This gives a figure of 226, of which 23 ships went to Britain's allies and 100 were deleted from the effective list, leaving 103 ships in commission on 1 November 1918. Of the ships lost or deflated, 37 were partially destroyed, 16 through engine failure, 16 were total losses, and *C 26* was interned in Holland.

81 *SS Z 65* landing at Longside. The reinforced sliding doors of the hangar can be clearly seen, as can the giant wind breaks to the right of the hangar.

81▼

In 1912 the Admiralty posted a number of naval officers and ratings to Farnborough to take instruction in airship work under No. 1 Squadron, RFC. The officers were Commander E. A. D. Masterman, Lieutenant Commander N. F. Usborne, Lieutenant H. L. Woodcock and Lieutenant F. L. M. Boothby. In 1913 Lieutenants W. C. Hicks and W. R. Crocker, and Engineer Lieutenant T. R. Cave-Browne-Cave joined up, and in 1914 Lieutenants E. H. Sparling, A. D. Cunningham, J. W. Ogilvie Dalgleish and R. G. Lock.

The army airships, *Beta, Gamma, Delta* and *Eta* were reinforced by the purchase, by the Admiralty, of the Astra-Torres and the Parseval airships both of which in August 1914 actually flew operationally from Kingsnorth. The small *Willows 4* was bought in 1912 and became Naval Airship *No. 2* and was used as a school ship.

The training was devoted exclusively to flying over land and no guidance was given as to the future use of airships in naval operations. Anyone who has read Air Chief Marshal Sir Philip Joubert's story of the birth and development of Coastal Command, spread over the two World Wars and the intervening years (*Birds and Fishes*, Hutchinson, 1960), will understand this omission. There was nobody who knew anything about naval airship operations and there were very few who were even thinking constructively. On the other hand there were plenty of sceptics who were thinking destructively, especially on the naval side, a phase which lasted well into the Second World War.

Both in heavier-than-air and in lighter-than-air the young pilot who had been taught to fly was posted direct to his operational unit. This policy prevailed in the airship wing until the close of hostilities. There was no alternative but to learn one's trade by practical experience.

By the end of the first year of the Second World War the young pilot went through a series of training schools before meeting the enemy. These were Primary Training School and Advanced School. At his advanced fighter training school the pupil would be switched to the type of aircraft he was eventually to use on operations. An operational research section had been formed some years before the Second World War started. But in 1916–18, the period in which airships attained their full stature, there could be

# Airship Operations 1914-18

no central guidance for reasons which will become apparent as our story develops. Each station had its own problems and each airship captain had to find his own solution to the local problems.

**The material which follows was provided by Major Struthers, DSC, AFC, and it seems desirable, at this point, to insert some general remarks on the situation. Struther's station, Mullion, was exceptionally well situated for airship operations. His work was outstanding and on more than one occasion helped to save the whole airship service from extinction. Had he, however, been working from almost any other station most of his particular genius must have been wasted as the account which follows will show.**

The first phase of naval airship operations ended towards the end of 1914. HMAs *3* and *4* (Astra and Parseval), had maintained a patrol over the narrows of the Channel during the passage of the Expeditionary Force to France and, although the results of this patrol were negative, the Admiralty publicly acknowledged the service they had given. HMA *4*, the Parseval, carried on until August 1917, when she was quite worn out and was deleted from the effective list. The two new ships HMA *6* and *7*, of the same general model, were put in hand at Barrow-in-Furness. For a variety of reasons neither of these new ships ever became really useful.

Early in 1915, as has been recorded, a sudden rebirth of the Airship Wing occurred and 50 sub-lieutenants and

'snotties' from the Grand Fleet, together with a number of direct-entry officers, of whom Struthers was one, were put into training. Stations were built at suitable places all round the coast. Those equipped with SS airships were the first to become operational and by the summer of 1915, Capel, near Dover, Polegate near Eastbourne, Anglesea, and Luce Bay (Galloway) were in use. Capel covered the narrows of the Channel, Luce Bay the narrows of the North Channel and Anglesea the approaches to Liverpool. Of these, again, Capel was directly in the track of all German submarines making passage to the Atlantic by the shortest route. The other two stations were not out of reach of the enemy submarine of that day, but they were not likely to encounter them frequently. Any submarine proceeding much beyond Polegate would have to refuel somehow or other. In none of these areas, and in fact, even at Mullion, was it really possible to see submerged objects, and Mullion was the most favourably situated for that.

The role of the airship was, then, largely negative. Its presence constituted a threat, the real extent of which was as much a mystery to the enemy submarine commander as it was to the airship captain. Large numbers of enemy submarines must have made the passage of the Straits of Dover during 1915 on their way to the Atlantic. As the submarine of that day was able to travel only 70 miles (110 km) submerged, at a speed of 4 knots, its choice was a difficult one. If it proceeded submerged by day, running the risk of nets, mines and trawlers, it could surface in the wider waters of the Channel by night to recharge batteries. If it proceeded by night on the surface in the narrows, it was forced to submerge by day by the threat of the Capel and Polegate airships. In fact Grand Admiral Dönitz in the Second World War repeatedly changed his policy and never attained a satisfactory solution. The total flying hours of the Capel airships in 1916 was impressive, over 1,144 hours, but there is no record of a sighting of a submarine, much less of an attack. The submarines got through and did their damage and returned again. The first phase of the anti-submarine campaign was not a very great success, but it must be pointed out that no surface ships were ever attacked while an airship was about.

By mid-1917 England was in sore need

82 *SS Zero 77* in flight over Kingsnorth in January 1917. The ships of this class were built between 1916 and 1918 and had a volume of 70,500 cu ft. They were 143.33 ft (43.58 m) long and 30 ft (9.14 m) in diameter. The useful lift was calculated to be 1,344 lb (609.62 kg). This class was powered by a 75 hp Rolls-Royce pusher engine, and had a maximum speed of 56 mph.

83 *C 27* making a balloon landing at Pulham after an engine breakdown. All of the 'Coastal' airships had the tri-lobed Astra-type envelope, of which a clearer idea is shown in the illustration of the *C 23A* and *C Star 1* on page 60.

82▲

83▼

of food and munitions because of the dreadful toll of merchant shipping taken by the submarines. The German Naval Staff's philosophy was justified, and only the Kaiser and the German politicians who had constantly opposed unrestricted submarine warfare had prevented this justification coming earlier. It is difficult today to realise that the submarine of 1917 was comparatively restricted in range. Approximately 200 miles (320 km) out and 200 miles home was its normal performance, which accounts for the very scanty sightings in the Scottish and Irish waters. It also accounted for the fact that the submarines' main effort was concentrated in the Western Approaches to the Channel, within 100 miles (160 km) of Lands End and in the restricted waters of the Mediterranean. The great bulk of merchant shipping passed through these waters making for Falmouth, Plymouth, Southampton and London on the one hand, and Liverpool and the Bristol Channel ports on the other. The concentration within 100 miles (160 km) of Lands End was such that any German submarine could be sure of victims; and by mid-1917 the submarine was in the ascendant.

Against this threat we had three potential defences: surface craft — destroyers, motor launches, Q ships and trawlers; aircraft — seaplanes and airships; and our own submarines. Although we had over 400 torpedo boats and torpedo boat destroyers in commission at this time we were under-equipped in every respect to deal with the menace. Moreover we lacked the experience to enable us to deal effectively with it. We suffered from misguided direction and from interdepartmental jealousy and, in particular, the sailor lacked confidence in the airman and took no steps to enable him to become more efficient. The airman had to find his own solution, but, as will be seen, suffered from a total lack of interchange of experience.

The airship captain was sent out to fly without the guidance of an intelligence report. The naval authorities did not, in the early days, co-operate in any way. Such reports as reached airship stations were not intelligently used by transmission to ships on patrol, and a case occurred of one airship captain being informed on arrival at base at the end of a long and futile patrol that a submarine attack had occurred within 15 miles

(24 km) of him. There was nothing unusual in this. Early reconnaissance reports by RFC observers in France were never believed by the Intelligence Staff at HQ: and it is an historical fact that Von Kluck refused to accept reports by his own aircraft observers that there was a gap between the French and English armies on the Marne. Had he accepted these reports Paris must have fallen.

Since 1912 the navy had been working quietly on seaplanes and airships, but without drive or conviction. The naval airship personnel had been trained by the army, which was no recommendation in the eyes of the sailor. The seaplane was quite unable to take off from or land upon anything but quite calm water and its range was about 100 miles out and home. It could not make a close examination of anything because it depended upon its speed to keep it in the air. And, with a crew of two, captain and observer, its ability to see things was not of a very high order. The smallest airship on the other hand, had a crew of three and very good all-round vision, even astern. It could fly whenever it could get out of its shed and could fly in fog and in darkness. It had, at first, no greater range than the

84 ▲

84 *SS TI* (which stands for Submarine Scout Twin) had two 75 hp Rolls-Royce engines mounted on struts above the four-seater car. The maximum speed was just over 57 mph. The length of the envelope was 165 ft (50.29 m) and the maximum diameter was 35 ft (10.66 m). The volume was 100,900 cu ft. Submarine Scouts were sometimes towed from the coast by naval vessels in order to save fuel and provide greater range.

seaplane but it could fly slowly, or even stop to examine suspicious signs without having to land on the water. Both seaplane and airship suffered from persistent mechanical troubles and neither carried any effective armament until much later.

By mid-1916 more airship stations were brought into commission and provided with larger and better airships. These were at Mullion (Lizard), Pembroke, Howden (Hull), East Fortune (Forth) and Longside (Peterhead). The mere recital of the names conjures up visions of dissimilar conditions of sea and weather. Only two of these, Mullion and Pembroke, were anywhere near the huge concentration of enemy effort. They, at least, could be sure of action. The other stations had little prospect of it.

The airships provided in 1917 were:

**SS Zero** Crew three. Duration 12 hours at full speed of 48 knots. One engine. Extreme range about 200 miles (322 km);

**Coastal** Crew five. Duration 11 hours at full speed (42 knots). Range 506 miles (814.32 km). Duration at cruising speed ($\frac{3}{4}$ full speed) 31.5 knots = $15\frac{3}{4}$ hours. Range about 543.37 miles (874.47 km);

**North Sea** This type came into service much later, but before hostilities ended. Crew ten. Duration 21 hours at a full speed of 57 miles per hour. Two engines. Extreme range about 2,000 miles (3,218.69 km).

The account that follows is concerned with the Coastal type airship exclusively.

It has already been said above that there was no information to guide the employment of airships. Each station had its own problems, dealt with them in their own way, and sat upon the results (if any). No naval or airship staff existed to sort things out and give advice. All that was known was that the submarine was there and was doing frightful damage, damage indeed that was coming within measurable distance of knocking us out. Nearly all this damage was occurring within 100 miles of Lands End, at the extreme west of the submarine's range.

The problems were to find the sub-marine, to prevent or foil its attack, and if possible to sink it. In all these problems experience had to be gained and time was very short. Experience could be bought only by constant, patient, and enduring observation. Even so, without some system of co-ordination that experience was confined to one man and his crew. Conditions were such that experience gained at one station was not available to another, a severe handicap indeed. By 1918, however, some efforts were being made to combat this. The patient and enduring observation was never, and never could have been, within the scope of the fast moving seaplane. The virtue of the airship was that it could hover over any suspicious evidence, an oil-slick, a disturbance in the water, or anything out of the ordinary, and examine it thoroughly. It could, and did, run down the track of a torpedo and bomb the source.

The first bombs supplied to airships were 16-pounders and were quite useless. They were followed by 65- and 100- and 112-pounders with a delayed-action fuse set to explode at a given depth, and these were equally ineffective. Later again 150 lb, then 250 lb, bombs with delayed-action fuses were supplied. These required extreme accuracy to have any effect.

Since the convoy was the target of the submarine, it followed that the best place to search was in the vicinity of a convoy or on its track. The slow moving convoy with its escorting airship was not unlike a flock of sheep with its sheep dog. The airship could stay with the convoy for many hours, could hand over its charge to a relieving airship, and have a very much better view of the sea than any surface vessel. Two schools of thought existed about this. The conventional naval outlook was that the bulky airship, visible from afar, gave away the convoy's position to the enemy. The airship operators' view was that the airship constituted a threat to the submarine whose captain knew that any offensive action on his part would bring quick retaliation. The naval point of view naturally predominated and it was a very long time before the naval authority could be persuaded to let the airship station commanders know when convoys were expected. Regular arrivals or departures of convoys were an invitation to disaster. They did arrive and depart at any time of the day or night, at most irregular intervals, and until the naval authority gained confidence in the airships' ability to deal with the situation a great deal of frustrating and futile patrolling had to be done. A notable exception to the irregular departures was the French convoy which left Cherbourg with coal and munitions nearly every night.

The seaplane operator's view was that the slow speed of the airship made it impossible for it to attack with any chance of success if it saw a submarine on the surface or sighted the track or the explosion of a torpedo. This view took no account of the airship's ability to wait upwind of the convoy. It was soon found that a convoy could be adequately protected by one airship correctly stationed so that, *in the unlikely event of attack*, retribution would follow within two or three minutes. The correct station depended entirely upon the direction of the wind. Assuming an airspeed of 50 knots, a wind of 30 mph, and an object to be investigated three miles away up-wind, it would take the airship nine minutes to reach its target. If the object were downwind it would take the airship two minutes. It was therefore prudent to take station relative to the convoy so that the airship was up-wind of most of its constituent ships. It was not possible to combine this with sweeping ahead of the convoy unless the convoy was heading into the wind. Given two or more airships with any convoy a sweep ahead was, of course, possible.

All this must make strange reading in the light of developments in the Second World War. The fact is that no airship was attacked by any submarine until very late in the war, and *never* when the airship was with a convoy. No British airship was brought down by a U-boat, and the only French airship that was brought down was repaired and flew again.

The submarine obviously feared the airship, over-estimating its offensive powers. No ship was ever attacked whilst under the close escort of any airship, and every attack seen by an airship crew was followed by instant retaliation, quite often with successful results.

The apparent vulnerability of the airship was soon found to be more of a legend than a fact. No German submarine captain appeared to be willing to take on an airship with gunfire, knowing that if he failed to secure a hit with one of his first shots he would be attacked as he submerged. In the Second World War this state of affairs did not persist. If an airship captain sighted a submarine on the surface up-wind his tactic was to circle out of range until he got his target down-wind of him. As he circled he called surface craft to come to his aid. In a position three miles up-wind he had the submarine in his power. If the submarine remained on the surface it would be dealt with by surface craft: if it dived the airship could bomb it, and if the bombing was immediate and accurate it could be fatal. The submarine captain did not court the dilemma and avoided being seen on the surface.

The time spent by airship captains on this kind of duty made them experts in the hunting of the submarine. It was necessary to be as constantly on patrol as the policeman on his beat. When, at last, C-in-C Plymouth gained confidence in the airship he arranged for convoy arrivals and departures to be conveyed to station commanders and for naval vessels to co-operate in every possible way.

In the end the station commander at Mullion was taken on to the staff of the C-in-C to co-ordinate all anti-submarine patrols and activities. From this arose a system which became uniform throughout the United Kingdom and the Mediterranean.

The simple beginnings of such a system were started at Mullion by the senior flying officer transmitting orders to ships in the air. Out of this arose an intelligence system whereby ships in the air got immediate information of the presence, or suspected presence, of any submarine in the area. This must now sound absurd, but the crippling fetish of secrecy under which aircraft worked, intensified by a ponderous system of transmitting intelligence data and the often bone-headed stupidity of ground staffs did nothing to help the war at sea. This saved a great deal of futile patrolling. No patrol was entirely useless, but there were limits to the amount of flying time that was possible and time spent with convoys was more useful than time spent over an apparently empty and innocent sea.

The airship suffered from two serious defects which gave constant trouble, of which the lesser of the two was the porosity of its envelope. The airship depended upon the purity of the hydrogen in the envelope for its lift, and if the hydrogen was seriously contaminated by air the useful load could be considerably diminished.

There did come a point when the mixture of air and hydrogen could become explosive but the loss of lift before this point was reached was so serious that the envelope would have to be deflated and repaired. Modern airships have envelopes of cotton or terylene with Neoprene dope (examples of more recent developments are Neoprene-coated Dacron and Tedlar plastic), which last for three to five years, even when they are continually moored out in the open, so this problem has virtually been solved. All rubberised fabric suffered from exposure to light and this trouble was quite unavoidable in those days. The other defect was mechanical. In all air-cooled engines with which SS airships were equipped, cracked cylinder-heads were so common that very few flights were completed without at least one defective cylinder. In the case of the Coastals, equipped with water-cooled engines, the magnetos made in the UK (German magnetos were very much more reliable, but obviously unobtainable) were shockingly bad. Each engine had two magnetos and cases have been recorded of all four magnetos being changed in the air. This sort of difficulty has been entirely overcome and airships have operated for years without any engine failure.

As a result of his experience Major Struthers wrote a manual on submarine hunting and allied subjects. This was published by the Admiralty and issued to all naval air stations. In compiling this work Struthers used experience gained in co-operating with our naval vessels, himself accompanying submarines on patrol or test and taking both submarine and seaplane officers with him on anti-submarine patrol. Matters such as the permanence of a torpedo-track were investigated and it was shown that the track of a cold-air torpedo was so permanent that it was well worth while to bomb the source. The hot-air torpedo, on the other hand, left no track that could be followed. The oil-slick of a submarine was found to be due to a variety of causes. Theoretically there should be nothing to show at all, but a film left by the diesel exhausts is the first and inescapable trace. The submarine's propeller-shafts and diesel exhausts are specially sealed to prevent the escape of oil but oil nearly always escapes. Lubricating oil from hydroplanes and periscopes is another source. These minute traces are not easy to find or follow and would be quite

beyond the scope of a seaplane or surface vessel to find, but they were there and could be found by the airship. Once the plates of the hull were damaged even slightly by depth-charge or bombing, oil is sure to escape. The movement of the rising line of oil inevitably gave the submarine away to an airship and, from it, it was not difficult to judge the actual position of the submerged hull.

A useful point is that no airship captain could afford to disregard his crew's reports. With a crew of five men there were five pairs of eyes on the watch, and watch could be kept all round the compass. But, and this is the important point, the man who was accustomed to an open-air life was always the first to spot the unusual.

The submarine commander had little to fear from surface craft provided he kept a good look out and behaved with reasonable prudence. The periscope is rarely seen from surface vessels as was proved time after time by our submarines creeping up to enemy vessels until the faces of men cleaning the guns were clearly visible. All this changed as soon as aircraft came on the scene. The feather of a moving periscope was often a mere slick on the water but it was not safe for the captain to assume that it was (as was generally the case) rarely seen by aircraft.

From the time when aircraft came into service nearly all torpedoing was at night and, if an airship was on the scene, no daylight torpedo attack was even attempted.

As a result of experience a very remarkable fact came to light. All too often for his safety the enemy captain revisited the scene of his attack to ascertain what damage he had succeeded in inflicting. It was sound practice for aircraft to visit and revisit the area of an attack for some hours afterwards. The chances were that the submarine would surface or at least show its periscope.

Submarine captains were found to have favourite 'billets' in which they could lie-up, resting on the bottom, to avoid detection. These billlets were 'salted' with mines.

The Airship Training Wing Cranwell devised a diagram showing the speed and turning-circle of a submarine caught in the act of diving. From this it was possible to bomb with some prospect of success. Struthers made use of this in his manual and the Admiralty used it as a wall-chart.

The narrative that follows is taken from Major J. Struthers' logs and other notes made by him at the time.

In June 1916 Mullion Air Station, Cornwall, was nearly ready to accommodate its airships and HMA *C 8*, commanded by Flight Lieutenant C. W. Dickenson, was dispatched from Kingsnorth. Unfortunately she was lost with three out of four of the crew off the Eddystone on her way down. HMA *C 9*, Flight Lieutenant J. G. Struthers, was also to have flown down, but in view of the loss of *C 8* it was decided to dispatch her by rail and road. On 1 July 1916 she made her first flight from Mullion and in the next three weeks made 17 flights of a duration varying from one to 25 hours, constantly interrupted by engine failures. This might well be called a working up period and was used by the captain both to gain personal experience and to train his crew.

Before one of these flights *C 9*'s captain arranged with the captain of HMS *Foyle* to do a joint sweep of the whole of the Western Approaches from Lands End to Ushant. The destroyer was to cruise within a wider circle swept by the airship so as to be available to deal quickly with any enemy submarine encountered. The flight lasted 25 hours and carried the airship within rifle range of the Channel Islands, which had been duly notified. An engine breakdown caused a forced landing near the destroyer and the ship was taken in tow. When the tow was quite near Mullion Harbour the gas pressure in the envelope fell so low that the envelope buckled and the crew had to be taken off by the destroyer. Subsequent investigation revealed a number of bullet holes in the envelope and it was later ascertained that *C 9* had been machine-gunned by British troops in Jersey who had not received notification of the flight.

During the same working up period the wreck of a freighter of some 10,000 tons was found in the traffic lane after the airship had already been some hours in the air. As it was an obvious danger to navigation the airship captain asked for his position by Direction Finder (D/F) and called base to ask for destroyers to be sent to sink the wreck. *C 9* then began to circle the wreck but received a signal ordering her to return to base. This was duly acknowledged, but as no surface vessels had arrived the order was not obeyed. A further message

# Mullion Air Station

was sent to base explaining the danger of quitting the wreck. Meanwhile the D/F position was received, putting the airship's position over mid-Devon owing to a mis-reading of the bearings, and yet another signal came from base ordering the ship's return. *C 9* then signalled C-in-C Plymouth direct asking that D/F Station Lizard be advised of their mistake. After a nine-hour delay destroyers arrived and sank the wreck and *C 9* returned to base. Signals were subsequently received from Admiralty, C-in-C Plymouth and Officer Commanding Channel Patrols congratulating the station on a magnificent piece of work.

To catch the submarine every device was tried. It seemed possible that one might be caught on the surface in foggy weather and on one occasion, this paid off. Flight Lieutenant Colston in a Coastal airship, saw and attacked a submarine on the surface. Most unfortunately he had been obliged to take a trainee officer as coxswain, who lost his head at the critical moment and put the ship off its course. He had caused trouble on an earlier occasion and thereafter no-one but trained and reliable personnel were allowed on operational duties.

As an example of the lack of co-operation between naval shore staffs and the flying personnel the case of the SS *Africa* must be mentioned. This valuable freighter was brought into Plymouth Sound on 11 February 1917, arriving at 1915 hrs. The boom had been closed at 1900 hrs and the Port Commandant refused to open it, directing her to return at 0700 hrs next day. At 0300 hrs she was torpedoed and became a total loss.

The following incidents from *C 9*'s log cover the period 15 March 1917 to 11 June 1917. During the whole of this period the purity of gas in the envelope was so low that no water ballast could be carried and the ship had to get off the ground heavy, like an aeroplane. Because of intense enemy activity no relaxation was possible and time could not be spared to carry out the necessary deflation and re-inflation.

On 15 March 1917 an enemy submarine was reported. Contact was made with French torpedo boat destroyers 40 miles SW of Plymouth and *C 9* began sweeping ahead of an incoming convoy which included HMS *Revenge* escorted by four torpedo boat destroyers. Between Eddystone and Plymouth the rev-counter pointer of the rear engine shot off its dial, the engine was switched off and the engineer was ordered to investigate, and reported that the engine was on fire and flames were licking the envelope. The engineer, Air Mechanic Parkes, who throughout displayed the utmost coolness and courage, was ordered to deal with the emergency, sat on the blazing engine and sprayed the envelope, the engine and himself with fire extinguishers and finally succeeded in putting out the fire. The ship returned to base on one engine. The court of enquiry found that the bolts of the after propeller had sheared, allowing the wooden propeller to revolve on its shaft so fast that the heat generated set it on fire. An application for a new pair of trousers for A/M Parkes was not regarded with favour. The duration of this flight was $6\frac{1}{4}$ hours.

On 21 March 1917 while patrolling in the Lizard-Falmouth-Bay-Eddystone-Plymouth area, airship *C 22* was sighted off Eddystone with both engines stopped. *C 9* stood by for 30 minutes reporting the situation, and adding that one of her engines had also stopped. A destroyer and two trawlers came to take off *C 22*'s crew and *C 9* then returned to base on one engine.

On 7 April 1917, while patrolling the Lizard-Wolf Rock-Scillies-Trevose Head-Eddystone-Start Point area, a W/T message was picked up that the hospital ship *Astoria* had been torpedoed near Salcombe. The ship flew overland to Fowey, and found the burning vessel 15 miles (24 km) SW of the Lizard. The subsequent search for the submarine proved unsuccessful. The duration of the flight was $10\frac{1}{2}$ hours.

On 13, 23 and 24 April and 8 May 1917, C 9 flew a total of 46½ hours unsuccessfully searching for submarines reported to be operating in the area of the Manacles-Wolf Rock-Lizard, and between Padstow and the Scillies.

During a practice bombing on a dummy submarine marked out on Bonython Moor on 11 May 1917, eight runs were made down-wind at 90 mph at 1,500 ft (457 m). One hit on the conning tower, six hits in 'danger-zone' and one miss were recorded. Practice bombing runs were also made on 14 and 15 May 1917.

During patrols from early to mid-June C 9 logged over 86 hours flying time. In the course of these patrols the torpedoed SS Christopher was escorted to Plymouth, special-value transports were escorted and sweeps were made in darkness for a French convoy. Up until 26 June C 9 had carried out 11 patrols and flown about 80 hours, mainly on escort and anti-submarine duties, but it was not until much later that she was able to claim a 'kill'.

On 29 September C 9 was patrolling the area from Looe-Eddystone-Torbay on a very foggy day. Six hours after leaving base a suspicious ripple was sighted in otherwise undisturbed water, which was investigated and a greenish sediment was seen to be churned up from below. A faint oil-track was then found moving east at 4 to 5 knots, and large circular disturbances as from a propeller were seen. Calcium flares were dropped to mark the line and trawlers were called to investigate. These agreed with the deduction made by C 9 and dropped two depth charges. C 9 dropped two 100 lb delayed-action bombs and the trawlers added six more depth charges. Oil then began to rise from one spot and all eastward movement stopped. A Dan-buoy was laid to mark the spot because no accurate position could be got from bearings because of the fog and no D/F bearings could be got on account of the nearness of the cliffs. No more bombs or depth charges were available in the forces on the spot, but two more trawlers arrived from the east and added their depth charges. Verbal exchanges between C 9 and trawlers satisfied C 9's captain that the submarine was sunk. C 9 then returned to base after being in the air 13 hours.

While escorting a west-bound convoy, on 3 October, consisting of a large mine-layer and four destroyers 20 miles (32 km) south of Plymouth a north-bound convoy consisting of a 'Devonshire' class cruiser and two American destroyers were sighted. The captain of C 9 ordered C 23A, which was in the vicinity, to take over the west-bound convoy and himself switched to the north-bound one. When this convoy was inside Eddystone and C 9 was moving westward, a huge column of water was seen to shoot up from the centre of yet a third convoy off Start Point, nearly 20 miles away. C 9 altered course 180° and proceeded down-wind at full speed. As there was a 35 mph wind blowing she probably attained a ground speed of 90 mph. It was seen that the largest ship in the convoy, a vessel of 10,000 tons, had been hit and the track of the torpedo was still visible. The end of the track was bombed with four 65 lb bombs causing a violent explosion followed by bubbles of air. An escorting trawler was signalled to proceed to the spot and use her depth charges. This was done and the trawler later reported that the submarine had been accounted for. C 9 then proceeded to base and landed in a 45 mph half-gale, with only half an hour's petrol in the tanks.

On 15 November 1917 C 9 was patrolling between Wolf Rock and Hartland Point. A message from base was received stating that C 5A had bombed a submarine between Lands End and Wolf Rock. Course was altered and the area of Lands End was carefully searched. At 1630 hrs, two explosions were seen astern and two minelayers were seen at the spot. The minelayers were unable to communicate because their Aldis lamps had failed but they fired red Verey Lights. A search revealed a line of light irridescent oil 150 yds north of the minelayers moving NNW. A flare was dropped to verify the movement of the line of oil and it became apparent that it was, in fact, proceeding from some submerged object moving at about four knots. A line of three delayed-action bombs was dropped diagonally across the track 300 ft (90 m) in front of the head of the line. All movement then stopped. The area was watched until dark, when all ships were recalled because of bad weather. On 18 November C 9 again visited the area where the submarine had been attacked. At 0730 hrs the oil patch was found to be about two miles long and at one spot was particularly thick. A trawler was instructed to buoy this spot and take a sample of the oil. C 9 then picked up a force of eight torpedoboat destroyers in line abreast proceeding west and swept ahead until 1530 hrs, when a convoy was met, and remained with the convoy until the destroyers had taken up their position and left at dusk (1630 hrs) to return to base.

On 17 December 1917, Flight-Commander Struthers handed C 9 over to Flight Lieutenant T. P. York-Moore on being posted to Kingsnorth to command NS 6. In the summer of 1918 he flew this ship on patrol from Long-side, Aberdeen, making flights of over 30 hours duration. In the autumn of 1918 the superintendent of airships, Brigadier General Maitland, sent Major Struthers out to the Mediterranean to take charge of airship operations. He spent a week in Paris, visiting French airship stations and seeing airship and other officers. After a week in Rome he was attached to the Staff of Naval Operations in command of airship anti-submarine operations. He hastened on the construction of sheds, flew to Sicily to arrange for the taking over of the Italian airship station at Marsala, then returned to Malta — afterwards visiting the French airship base at Bizerte which was commanded by Captain Tixier who had carried out a number of raids from Verdun and Epinal in the airship Fleurus from 1914–15. He also visited the Italians in Sardinia. The end of the war came and the project lapsed.

It remains to add three items of interest which do not quite fit into the purely operational record.

On 21 August 1917 the captain of C 9 sighted a long dark line on the horizon 40 miles (64 km) south of Plymouth. Thinking it might be a submarine on the surface he proceeded at full speed to attack, but on coming closer he realised that he was looking at the hull of a capsized steamer which was barely awash. Alongside was a life-boat full of water with two survivors and three dead. Surface craft were alerted and came to pick up the survivors and sink the wreck. The airship had to wait several hours for them to arrive, for had she abandoned the hull it would have taken longer for surface craft to find it, and while it was afloat it was a serious danger to navigation. This incident illustrates the superiority of the airship over the seaplane. The latter was notoriously bad at spotting unusual objects, and might well have attacked and bombed the wreck had it sighted it, and certainly could not have remained with it until surface craft arrived.

Flying in fog presented no serious problem to the airship and was regarded as advantageous since it offered the chance of surprising a submarine on the surface. Provided that the D/F stations were efficient — which was not always the case — a fix could give the captain his position if he required it. This statement needs the qualification that an airship close up against land could not expect a reliable fix. Returning to Mullion in fog, or flying over land, was quite another matter. Airship captains made a close study of the coastline so that any spot sighted could be recognised. They aimed at finding the coast anywhere between five miles (8 km) east and five miles west of Mullion Cove and then flying in, using the surf-line as a guide. On reaching Mullion Cove they would turn inland and follow the road to base. But the ground height of the base was about 200 ft (60 m) above sea level and Poldhu wireless masts stood a bare mile to the NW of the Cove. Ten miles west again was St Michael's Mount, not very high, but a nasty obstacle.

*C 9* was caught by thick fog off the Wolf Rock and flew in until she suddenly found St Michael's Mount looming up a few hundred feet away. The captain turned out to sea again and made a second careful approach but just missed the housetops at Newlyn and saw people scattering in the streets below. This was before D/F stations were in operation and things became easier once they were. Such risks would not have been justified were it not for the vital necessity of staying on patrol in all possible circumstances.

On 28 September 1917 *C 9* carried out a 13-hour patrol during which, amongst other more normal activities, she was allowed to observe a British submarine doing diving trials in Whitesand Bay. The sea was fairly calm. As the submarine submerged her dark, unpainted iron parts became invisible but her grey painted parts showed up a vivid green, and a faint track of oil was left. When the submarine was fully submerged all trace of it was lost for a few minutes. Then a slight oil trace was picked up again and followed. At 30 to 40 ft under the surface the hull was seen again and shortly afterwards the periscope broke surface.

85▲

85 The 'Coastal' airship *C 23A* out from Mullion in Cornwall on convoy duty in the Western Approaches to the British Isles. The 'Coastals' were 195 ft (59.43 m) in length and 37 ft (11.27 m) in diameter. The height from the bottom of the skids on the car to the top of the envelope was 52 ft (15.84 m). The volume was 170,000 cu ft. Two 150 hp Sunbeam engines provided the motive power in most ships while one 100 hp Berliet-Ford engine and one 200 hp Renault engine provided power in the others. The maximum speed of the 'Coastals' on trials was about 47 mph.

86 *C Star 1* was the first of a class of ten improved 'Coastal' airships produced in 1918. All ships were powered by one 110 hp Berliet-Ford engine and one 260 hp Fiat engine, but while the diameter of all the ships in the class was 49.25 ft (15 m), ships numbered *1* to *3* were 207 ft (63 m) in length and ships numbered *4* to *10* were 217 ft (66.14 m) in length. The volume was 210,000 cu ft, and the average weight of the class was 5,330 lb (2,417.64 kg).

86▼

This operational account of the 'North Sea' airships, by Air Vice-Marshal P. E. Maitland, gives a general impression of the war patrols and other activities of what were probably the most effective anti-submarine machines

# The 'North Sea' Class of Airships 1917-18

of the time. Maitland served in the RNAS from 1915 until 1918, and his account, mainly concerned with the operational roles of *NS 3*, *NS 9* and *NS 12*, takes the story to the end of hostilities on 11 November 1918.

The experience of the submarine war and the progress of non-rigid airships during 1916 showed that a larger airship than the C, or Coastal, ship was necessary: it should have a longer range and endurance, and be capable of carrying a heavier load of bombs. It was realised that the old 65 lb and 110 lb bombs were too small, and that at least a 230 lb bomb was required, to have a reasonable chance of damaging a submerged submarine. The longer range was particularly necessary in the northern North Sea on account of the distance from the Scottish coast of the routes taken by the German ocean-going U-boats on their way to the Atlantic.

The first ship, *NS 1* was built at Kingsnorth near Chatham, and made her first flight on 2 February 1917. The fifth ship passed her trials in December 1917, but both she and *NS 2* were wrecked on their delivery flights after some dozen hours flying, and the remaining three ships suffered from frequent engine defects. The envelope and engines were good, but the car, rigging and engine installations were unsatisfactory.

It was not until *NS 3* and *NS 6* and all the subsequent ships were considerably modified, from April 1918 onwards, that this type played a significant part in the anti-submarine work in the North Sea. Thereafter, until the end of the war in November, there were usually five North Sea, or NS, ships operating, based on East Fortune (near North Berwick) and Longside (near Peterhead). These airships strengthened considerably the escorts of the coastal convoys from the Tyne to the Orkneys. They took part in the special anti-submarine sweeps in co-operation with naval submarine hunting flotillas, and carried out sweeps up to a radius of 100 miles (160 km) to seaward from East Fortune and Longside.

## Technical details

The NS airship was almost twice the size of its predecessor the C and C★ airship. It had a capacity of 360,000 cu ft, was 260 ft (79.24 m) in length, its gross weight was about 12 tons, and it carried a crew of ten. It was powered originally by two Rolls Royce Eagle I engines, which gave a full speed of 60 mph. It could carry three or four 230 lb bombs, depending on the length of the flight.

Like the Coastal, or C class airship and the C★ ships, the NS was built on the French Astra-Torres system, with a cross section like the Ace of Clubs. The weight of the car and engine cabin, and the thrust of the engines, was taken by wire suspension cables which passed into the envelope at the bottom ridge and were connected by cords which spread out fan-wise to the upper ridges on either side. The airship was kept in shape by three linen curtains laced between the three ridges inside the envelope.

In addition the gas inside the envelope had to be kept at a pressure of about 25 to 30 mm of water. This was done on the ground by blowing air with a motor-driven air blower into compartments inside the envelope termed 'ballonets'. When flying, pressure was maintained by lowering a metal scoop behind the propeller which allowed air from the slip stream to be driven along a fabric tube into the ballonets. If pressure rose too high, the air in the ballonets could be let out by valves set to open automatically at a lower pressure than the gas valves.

The crew consisted of a captain and second pilot, a coxswain and second coxswain, two engineers, two wireless/telegraph (W/T) operators and two air gunners. This was sufficient to handle the ship in the air, provide lookouts and allow rest periods during ordinary conditions of flights lasting perhaps two to three days.

The captain was in charge of the airship, and with the second pilot did the navigation, maintained the height of the ship with the elevator wheel, and also kept the gas pressure inside the envelope correct. The coxswain was responsible for the rigging of the ship, and was in direct charge of the crew. He or the second coxswain steered the ship with a wheel which worked the rudders, and was seated in the front of the control car which had glass windows in front of him and so gave a good view, particularly important when bombing or landing.

The engineer worked in a cabin between the engines with sides that hinged down like a mobile coffee stall, and provided a counter on which he could do repair jobs in the air. The engineers in the modified ship could get out of their car and walk round their engines. The engineers opened their engines to the revolutions ordered by the captain on the engine room telegraph, and opened up the petrol tanks as required. The ship was capable of flying at 30 mph on one engine so that it was usually possible to stop the other when it was necessary to replace a magneto or effect repairs.

The W/T operator had a compartment and table just aft of the captain. To communicate with ships he also had an Aldis signalling lamp, and he could use semaphore at short range. Later, international code flags, which could be lowered below the car, provided a useful means of communication with foreign ships.

The air gunner acted as a look-out, and had a Lewis gun mounted at the rear of the control car. In later types he had a 1–in. Fiat gun mounted on a platform below the engines. The gun had too low a muzzle velocity, and was of little use.

The air gunner also acted as a cook and could fry or stew food in a pot or pan heated by exhaust gases from the engines. Care was necessary, however, for I lost what was possibly the first eggs and bacon ever to be cooked in the air by opening the cut-out from the exhaust too wide. It was only with difficulty that I prevented the frying pan from being blown into the propeller, which had already happened to the eggs and bacon, and the pan might well have broken the propeller and holed the envelope above.

By climbing up a wire ladder from the control car one could enter a tube and climb up through the envelope to a circular depression on top of the ship. This had also a position for a machine gun, but was never used for this purpose. But it did allow one to walk from the top of the ship to the top fin at the rear of the envelope if this had to be done.

## Working and handling an NS airship

When an airship was not flying in working hours, the crew would normally be busy with repairs and maintenance. The purity of the hydrogen had to be checked daily. After patrols the envelope had to be inspected daily for leaks and chafing. A leak detector which revealed the presence of hydrogen was used. If hydrogen was escaping air was also leaking in, and this was a greater danger that could lead eventually to the airship being able to lift less and less until it would have to be deflated and refilled with fresh hydrogen, a laborious and expensive business. With a ship in active service, deflation, overhaul and re-inflation only took place after one to one and a half years, unless some exceptional damage had been sustained. There was plenty of work for everyone. Moreover a periodic watch had to be kept on the pressure inside the envelope. If necessary, air had to be blown into the ballonets by a small petrol driven air blower connected to the ship by a canvas hose. Out of working hours this job was done by the shed gas-guard, who went round the ships in his shed topping up each when required.

As soon as an airship was ordered for a patrol, the ship's ground and flying crew got the ship ready, topping up with hydrogen and petrol if this was required, and making final adjustments. Bombs were fitted on by the armourers, and W/T gear and batteries were checked. Then the engines were run up to three-quarters power with the ship firmly held down by ring bolts in the shed's floor.

The officers meantime had collected orders, weather reports and intelligence summary, and the flying crew assembled in the ship. While this had been going on, the station buglers had been cycling round the station sounding off 'Landing Party' either of 'one watch' or 'both watches', or even, if all hands were required in an emergency 'clear lower deck'. The landing party assembled and were checked off into the various parties,

for handling guys, car party, and so on, under the control of the landing officer.

The huge shed doors were then wound open, the parties assembled round the ship, which was now 'ballasted up'. All ballast bags were removed from where they had been hooked on round the car and engine nacelles, and at the order 'hands off, ease up the guys,' everyone let go or slackened their handling guys, and the captain watched anxiously. With luck the ship would then rise slowly. Sometimes it was necessary to discard some of the load, such as a bomb, before the ship was light enough. Then the forward and after guys were manned, and, with the car party looking after the car, the cortège moved slowly out of the shed. Usually leaving the shed presented little difficulty as long as the ship was kept straight until it was completely clear of the shed. Sometimes, though, a sudden gust might catch the ship and force it against the shed doors if the landing officer and handling parties were not on the alert. Once outside the shed the ship was swung into wind as soon as possible, and the rear guys were kept slack. As long as the ship was head to wind, the wind resistance was small, and the ship could be walked without difficulty.

In gusty weather it was different, when a squall might strike the bows of the ship. If it was not swung into wind at once, then there was serious trouble. This would occur if the party on the forward windward handling guy gave ground, or because the car party were unable to move the car sideways and so allow the ship to swing.

When the ship reached the landing ground it was ballasted up again, as the trim might have been altered by such things as rain making the ship heavier, or strong sun making it lighter. The engines were then started, and at a signal from the captain, and an order from the landing officer, the car party pushed up the car, and the handling guy parties let their ropes unreeve through the loops at the end of the wire handling guys. The engines were then opened up and the ship gathered way slowly climbing steadily to patrol height. In fine weather all this was comparatively easy.

To take as heavy a load of bombs as possible, the ship often took off some 100 lb (45 kg) heavy, as this weight of petrol would be burnt in an hour or so. In this case, as the ship was leaving she would be given a cant up of some 20° by

the car party giving a hearty shove upwards as the engines opened up. Their thrust drove the ship up, while an anxious airman ran along under the tailplane to make certain that it did not hit the ground. While the ship climbed to patrolling height, usually 800 to 1,000 ft (244 to 305 m), the coxswain sitting in the bows of the car at his compass would be steering the course given to him by the navigating officer. The other officer would be controlling the height at which the ship flew by means of a wheel mounted in a fore and aft direction which worked the elevators. He would also control the pressure inside the envelope, for, as the ship rose, the atmospheric pressure outside decreased and the pressure inside the ship rose relatively. The pressure range was small: if it was too low the envelope became flabby and would lose shape, and if too high there would be an undue strain on the fabric envelope. So, the officer acting as height coxswain, had to keep a careful eye on the pressure gauges, flying pressure being about 30 mm of water. In turbulent weather the up and down currents of air made this doubly important. If pressure dropped he would work a winch to lower a scoop behind the propeller, and so blow air into either the forward or rear ballonets. If it rose too high he would open either the front or rear ballonet valves. In addition there were also two gas valves from which gas could be let out, to reduce pressure quickly, or reduce lift if the ship was too light. These valve lines were mounted on a frame, each valve control wire with a wooden block of distinctive colour and shape, to avoid error even in darkness.

In addition there was also a red coloured tape, which passed through the envelope to a rip panel at the top of the envelope, which could be pulled out if it was necessary to deflate the ship quickly. This ripped the panel out leaving a long split in the envelope, and needless to say care was taken to see that this was never pulled by mistake.

The W/T operator sat in a little compartment just behind the navigator's table, and would lower his aerial and open the W/T watch with the home station. The air gunner would be on the look-out aft and the one off duty would probably be preparing the ingredients for the next meal. The engineers, having set the engines at the revolutions indicated by the captain on the engine room telegraph, would be keeping a general eye on the engines. They could walk around either side of both engines so that petty repairs and maintenance were easy. The engineer on duty also opened the petrol tanks as required and kept a check on fuel consumption.

As soon as the sea was reached, it would be possible to make a good estimate of the direction and speed of the wind by the 'wind lanes' on the sea. When accurate navigation was necessary the wind velocity was checked every hour by slowing down and turning the ship into wind. As the air speed dropped one could see the W/T aerial weight below moving over the sea more and more slowly until at length it was stationary. A glance at the air speed indicator then gave the strength of the wind and the ship's compass heading, the direction. At the same time one could see if the airship was heavy or light by noting whether it sank or rose when steerage way was lost, and also whether it was nose or tail heavy. The navigator on duty would work out the course to steer to make the required rendezvous and the estimated time of arrival, while the crew would settle down to watch routine. The officers would scan the forward view, using binoculars if necessary, while the air gunner and crew off duty kept a watch abeam and aft. The control car of a North Sea airship was sufficiently far forward of the engines for their noise to be slight. Conversation in the car was easy, so that orders and reports could be heard readily.

Sighting a convoy was usually impressive. Often as many as 40 merchantmen of all sizes, ages and nationalities would appear out of the haze, plugging steadily along in three columns under the care of perhaps a couple of destroyers and some armed trawlers. At intervals they would alter course in a series of zigzags to throw off submarines which might be trying to work ahead of the convoy. Some ships would be spick and span from a recent overhaul in port, whilst others by their rusty hulls and salty upper works showed the marks of many months at sea.

If there was already an airship with them, the airships would probably exchange news by Aldis lamp. It would then take station patrolling across the line of advance of the convoy to put down any submarine that might be getting into position to attack the convoy. After four or five hours of this it was most welcome to hear a bustling and see the air gunner clearing the chart table and laying a meal,

perhaps of hot stew that he had cooked on the engines — a welcome change compared with the bit of chocolate and iron-hard ration biscuit that used to tide one over the six or seven hours in the open cockpit of the smaller airships, and for that matter all aeroplanes of that time. At length the patrol ended after 12 to 48 hours in the air, but all too often off the North of Scotland the ship was recalled through rising winds and so was forced to return to base.

Just before landing the ship was ballasted up. After a long flight she was probably light owing to the weight of petrol burnt, and it would be necessary to valve hydrogen and blow air into the ballonets. If the ship was heavy, water ballast was dropped. If the airship was 'down by the nose' air would be blown into the rear ballonet, and if 'down by the tail', into the front ballonet, until the ship was level and neither rose nor fell in the air when going dead slow. When all was set for landing and the landing party was ready at the snatch block, set in a large concrete slab on the landing ground, the ship was brought down on its elevating planes to a hundred feet or so from the ground and down wind of the landing party. It then flew slowly towards them. The idea was to arrive over the landing party dead into the wind and with very little forward speed so that the forward handling guy wires were dangling on the ground. The forward handling guy parties then quickly rove their ropes through the handling guy wire loops and pulled out on either bow at right angles to the ship so as to hold it into the wind. Meanwhile the car party caught the car, either to stop it hitting the ground or to pull it down if the ship tended to rise through being light.

But it did not always work out like that. To start with, when an airship is moving slowly, it has little steerage way so that it is easy for the ship to swing away from the wind at the critical moment, and then the handling party might not be able to catch or hold the guys. Similarly the airship was not easy to control on the elevators at a slow speed so that it might either come too low too soon, or else be out of reach when the ship passed the landing party. Or she might be so heavy that she lost way falling rapidly. It was worst if light for then she might start to rise rapidly and lift the men off the ground.

If the weather was squally, or the crew

inexperienced, landing low enough for the handling guys to be reached by the landing party was not attempted. Instead the ship was brought over the landing party some 80 ft (25 m) up and a heavy rope attached to the fore part of the ship, known as the trail rope, was dropped. This rope was seized by the landing party and was put through the snatch block on the ground and the airship was slowly pulled down until the handling guys could be attached and the airship brought under control.

The job of walking the airship into the hangars then started. In fine weather this was fairly straightforward. The ship was walked towards the lee entrance of the sheds, keeping the head to wind all the time. Once between the huge windscreens that projected either side of the hangar door the air usually became turbulent in strong winds. The landing officer then got the ship's head into what he thought was a suitable position, waited for a calm period, swung the ship so that it pointed into the shed, and rushed it in at the double.

When the airship only had a little clearance between the sides of the shed doors and possibly another ship inside, this could be a difficult operation, particularly if a sudden squall blew from the side as the ship was half in. Under really bad conditions a North Sea class airship could drag 500 men about, throwing them here and there like a terrier with a platoon of rats.

In fact, under these conditions, with rain or in the dark, landing an airship required a good deal of courage and devotion on the part of the landing party, and there was always a chance of the first man on the ropes being carried up before enough men were able to reach them to prevent the airship from taking charge. In fact, four deaths, one at Kingsnorth and three at Cranwell, did occur through this. Blistered hands and twisted ankles were not uncommon.

Luckily, even in Britain the wind does not always blow, but landing officers and the whole landing party had to keep alert and obey orders instantly to counter the effects of sudden gusts and squalls and shifts of wind. To the young pilot from the fleet or civil life, this was a new adventure, but for the elderly airmen who had often led a sedentary life in a small business, a very different matter, and it is to their lasting credit that the ships were rarely damaged on the ground.

## Operations

The records of the airship patrols of the 1915 to 1918 period, once held by the Air Ministry, were badly damaged by bombing in the Second World War. A careful search of the files held by the Air Historical Branch of the Air Ministry has shown that there is insufficient information to compile a complete history of the 'North Sea' class of airships. The following is an account of my own experiences with *NS 3*, *NS 9* and *NS* 12, from September 1917 to February 1919, based on my pilot's log book and my recollection of the events, supported by the little information that is now available in official records. I have omitted any mention of the seaplanes because in the northern North Sea we rarely saw them. In the confined waters of the south, the flying boats and seaplanes from Felixstowe did admirable service against submarines, performing the positive task of sinking submarines in a way we could not.

## NS 3

My first view of an NS airship was off Fraserborough in September 1917, and we, in *C 14*, were coming home after a nine hours' exercise with the Fleet, which had passed some 80 miles seaward of Longside on its way back to Scapa Flow. We envied the larger craft, the comfort of their enclosed car and the power of their engines. We knew that two of these new ships were operating from East Fortune, and we looked forward to seeing them when they refuelled at Longside that night. In the shed *NS 1* and *NS 3* looked impressively large, though they seemed to have a spider's web of rigging above the car.

Then we heard that in fact the engine installations gave continual trouble. In order to enclose the engines in a streamline 'power egg', the engines had long and heavy propeller shafts which, being lightly supported, strained the engine gears.

The two NS ships remained at Longside undergoing extensive repairs to their engine structures. Up to then I had only been faintly interested, but in December I was appointed as Second Pilot to *NS 3* under Flight-Commander J. S. Wheelwright, DSC, RNAS, and just before Christmas we flew back to East Fortune, where, to our disgust we heard that all the NS airships were to be grounded for re-designing.

Johnny Wheelwright was an artist by profession and a man of considerable originality and drive. The station's Engineer Officer, Lieutenant Commander A. S. Abell, RNVR was one of the two outstanding brothers who later proved their worth as engineers with the Bristol Aviation Company. Together, Wheelwright and Abell made plans for reconstructing the ship, and by January 1918 had obtained permission from the Admiralty to go ahead.

Briefly, the idea was to do away with the long propeller shafts and to raise the control car level with the engineer's car. This latter was mounted on a frame with an engine on either side. The control car and engineer's car were to be connected by a flexible walking way, and this was to be faired in with a light framework with canvas sides. The two cars were to form a single unit, and the crew could move about from the coxswain's position in the bow to the engineer's car aft, without too many gymnastics in the open. There was more room for the crew, and air resistance was reduced as the car was much closer to the envelope than in the original type.

Surprisingly, this proved to be possible without altering the 15 miles (24 km) of cord and suspension wires inside the airship's envelope. At the same time the petrol tanks were fitted into the underside of the envelope, being suspended from the two ridges. They were therefore inside the envelope. Many other small improvements were also made.

By the beginning of March all was completed at East Fortune and *NS 3* certainly had a more efficient look about her. On 11 March 1918, with Admiralty officials on board, we undertook her test flights most successfully, and on the following day she did an eight hours' trial flight with a full speed of more than 60 mph.

We then bombarded the Admiralty with requests for permission to start patrolling, but without result. We were aware that at Kingsnorth the official re-design was being worked on feverishly, so that when at last on 3 April permission was obtained to fly a three-quarters power duration flight over land we headed for Kingsnorth. On arrival we circled slowly over the station and waited for a crowd to gather. Our satisfaction was momentarily checked by a hissing sound which we found was caused by petrol dripping from a leaky tank on to the hot engine exhaust pipe. However,

this was put right before the engine caught fire, and in due course the landing party 'flashed' up to us asking whether we wished to land. To this we replied, 'No, we are returning to base,' and turned north again to Edinburgh.

We completed the 816 miles (1,313 km) in 22 hours which certainly constituted a record for British airships at that time. However, it was not until 17 April that we did our first convoy escort, and from 20 to 22 April completed a flight of 55 hours with various convoys, the longest flight made to date by any non-rigid airship. We would have stayed up longer had we not been recalled owing to the approach of bad weather.

The advantage of being out of the air stream behind glass, being able to walk about and talk to the crew, and of all the crew being able to rest when off duty, proved an enormous benefit and increased considerably the efficiency of the anti-submarine look-out.

It was not until 7 May that we had our first hope of success. When returning with a south bound convoy off Montrose, we sighted oil coming up from the bottom of the sea in an area in which no wreck had recently been reported. We flashed a signal to a nearby destroyer and told her that we were going to bomb an oil streak, and dropped three 230 lb bombs. The destroyer dropped depth charges on our bomb marks, and up came quantities of oil and some wreckage. They lowered a whaler and later signalled 'British Submarine'. Our consternation can be imagined, but luckily a parcel was recovered addressed to submarine *K 17* which had been lost in the North Sea earlier that year, so we had in fact only bombed a wreck!

The following day we went out and found thick fog outside the Firth of Forth. It is an eerie feeling rushing through thick fog, but in an airship, as long as one kept away from land and high enough up to clear the sea, it was a peaceful pastime, until the time came to make a land-fall again. However, after a couple of hours we gave it up and luckily found the fog clear over our base.

Next day was calm again, and off Peterhead, Wheelwright decided to try the ability of the ship to land on the water, while we hailed a trawler. Unfortunately the trawler did not appreciate that we were drifting down wind and came up astern of us. Her mast fouled our tail fin and it was only by dropping ballast and ascending suddenly that we averted a tragedy. However, we started our engines and later landed at Longside to check the damage, but luckily nothing serious had been touched and the envelope was not holed.

During the remainder of May we were busy with patrols without undue incident except that during a very heavy thunderstorm we noticed sparks some five inches long jumping across our control wires. We wondered why the long lengths of wire inside the envelope did not produce a similar discharge, and as the hydrogen was highly inflammable, we were thankful that apparently they did not. May was indeed a busy month with 97 hours flown.

In early June we started towing trials with the destroyer HMS *Vectis* as the ability to be towed at speed could be of great advantage if an airship broke down or ran short of fuel. We were making good progress and could be towed at almost 20 knots. On the last trial we came down on the sea and took two of the ship's officers in place of our own crew. We felt that we had a handy and adaptable airship.

However, on 21 June we left in the evening to escort a south bound convoy off Peterhead in the face of a very threatening weather report. By midnight it became obvious that the south-westerly wind was rising fast and that we should have a hard job to get back, so we turned for home and slowly worked our way southwards. At dawn we were near May Island at the entrance to the Firth of Forth. Home was in sight, but by now the wind was extremely squally with gusts up to 40 knots. It became more and more difficult to control both the ship and the pressure inside the envelope, owing to the violent up and down draughts. This meant pulling on valves to let the air out of the ballonets when the pressure was too high, and lowering the tubular air scoops behind the propellers when pressure dropped too low. While the captain was struggling to keep the ship at a steady height with the elevators, my job was to keep the pressure within bounds. The work of lowering the scoops when pressure dropped suddenly, and hoisting them up again with a hand winch, and hectically swinging off on the valves when pressure rose suddenly, had me dripping with sweat.

We had reached a point three miles off shore when suddenly the ship started to sink rapidly, even with the bows up and the engines at full speed. We rapidly lost our 800 ft (245 m) of height until at length the engines struck the water and the complete engine 'coffee house' and engines were ripped off and sank. In a few seconds all was quiet as we drifted with the wind. I think after the hours of severe struggle we all felt relief for at that moment there was nothing we could do.

Having shed the weight of the engines and engine car the airship rose slowly to some 500 ft (150 m) though hydrogen must have been pouring out of the tears in the envelope. I remember Wheelwright shaking hands with the coxswain, Petty Officer Hodgson, RN, and saying 'goodbye', and I could hear the clack of Davis the W/T operator trying to flash a signal to the lighthouse on his Aldis lamp. Then the ship slowly turned bows down until she was vertical and we were standing on the uprights of the car, one above the other. Then with a smack she hit the sea and it was dark.

I inadvertently said, 'Oh' and swallowed a mouthful of salt water and felt in the dark for the handle of the door which was somewhere alongside me. I had luck, opened it, dropped out and sank some depth. When I came up the whole envelope had drifted clear of me and I could see it some 10 yards away with the edge of the envelope trailing along like a giant tablecloth, while the after-part that was still inflated rose some 30 ft (9 m) giving the stern a whale-like look.

I joined the captain and second coxswain who were already on the flat part of the envelope. After a short time an air gunner popped up nearby and was hauled on too. Then there was a pause of several minutes and the W/T operator, LAC Davis came up looking very blue. He had been at his desk further aft in the car and after the ship had sunk he had some difficulty in the dark in finding the strap which lowered his window. However, he held his breath and eventually got the window open and struggled out. It was dark and the envelope covered the water for some 20 yds (183 m) with a lot of wire and wreckage below it. At last he ran short of breath and took a gasp, but luckily struck a pocket of air trapped under the envelope and got enough to hold out until he broke surface.

The two engineers were no doubt drowned when the engine car hit the sea, and the coxswain, one air gunner and one W/T operator probably got entangled in underwater wreckage. We survivors were lucky to find a portion of the envelope flat on the water as it might easily have been rising steeply from the sea, and we could not then have got a hold on the slippery rubber fabric.

It was a grim dawn with the early light on the grey sea and distant coast. Our little party collected together while the fabric slowly sank. Eventually a destroyer arrived, took off the survivors and sank the airship by gunfire — a sad ending to a good ship and a devoted crew.

## NS 9

By 28 July I had taken over as captain of a new airship *NS 9*, with Captain S. B. Harris, AFC as Second Pilot, and a new crew, but including the W/T operator of *NS 3*, LAC Davis. She had passed the trial flight, speed trials and acceptance test successfully at Kingsnorth.

Just after taking over the new ship I had a job which illustrates the varied work of an airship captain. It had been necessary for the riggers to go inside the envelope to inspect the suspensions of the petrol tanks, and in order to breathe in the hydrogen-filled space 'proto gear' was used. This was the apparatus used in mine rescues and consisted of a bag, into which one breathed through a mouthpiece, in which were chemicals to purify the air, two oxygen cylinders mounted on the back and a spring clip on the nose. The gear was not supplied to operational stations, and I had not seen one before.

I was taking a superficial interest in the work, when my coxswain came up to say that they were in a quandary. Two petty officers were trained in the use of 'proto gear', and had been working inside the envelope, but one was unwell. There was no-one else trained, and standing orders said that two people had to work together wearing 'proto gear', and 'would I? It only meant going inside and being with the Petty Officer.' There was nothing to be done but to put on a cheerful face and say 'of course'. After a quick run through the way the valves worked, I changed into a pair of rubber shoes, had the gear slung on my back, and with the nose clip, I hoped, securely on my rather short nose, was ascending the fire escape ladder for a new experience.

The gas valves were about 2 ft (0.60 m) in diameter and were at the end of a tube about 6 ft (1.80 m) in length. This was normally pushed into the

87 *NS 1*, the first of the 'North Sea' class, launched in 1917, had a gross lift of 23,313 lb (10,574.59 kg). The difference in the configuration of the cars of the ships numbered *1* to *10* and those numbered *11* to *16* was very marked. *NS 14* was sold to the United States.

88▼ 87▲

88 A close-up view of the modified car of NS3 showing the 'bumping' bags.

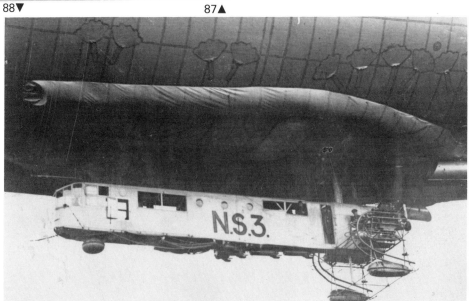

89▼

89 The crew of *NS 3* grouped by their ship.

90 *NS 6* had a volume of 360,000 cu ft. Her length was 262 ft (79.85 m) and her diameter was 51.75 ft (17.29 m). She was powered by two Fiat 260 hp engines and made 58 mph on speed trials. Her useful lift was 7,154 lb (3,245 kg).

envelope so that it was flush with the surface. If one had to get into the envelope the lacing was undone, the tube, known as a 'petticoat' tied up and the valve removed. In order to reach the valve which was some 20 ft (6 m) from the ground, a fire escape ladder was used. The procedure was for one man to go to the top of the ladder, tie up the tube near the envelope and place the tube on the top rungs of the ladder. The man in 'proto gear' then went up the ladder into the tube while a man followed him up and closed the tube behind him. The top man then untied his lashing and the 'proto gear' man climbed up the last rungs of the ladder into the envelope above him.

In practice this procedure did not seem quite so easy. Three men on the top of a fire escape ladder seemed a crowd, and when one had crept into the gloom of the tube and felt the tube being tied below, there was an awful feeling of finality about it. However, the important thing was not to fall off the ladder while climbing up the last bit of the tube into the ship. After crouching for a short time in the tube the upper lashings were removed and I went into the envelope. It was a strange experience. At first one could see little in the gloom and the light from the gas-proof electric torch seemed

to pick out nothing but a maze of cordage like a giant spider's web. It was an odd feeling that one was surrounded by highly inflammable gas that a spark could set off, and if one's nose-clip fell off and one breathed one would not last many minutes.

A nasty feeling of panic started. It seemed difficult to breathe, and if one left the vicinity of the gas valve would one ever find it again in the maze of rigging inside the envelope? Would the nose-clip stay on, and finally, would one's feet go through the envelope, for it had happened before. A moment's thought put things right. Breathing was difficult because the oxygen regulating valve was opened too wide. With that set to rights confidence soon grew. The petrol tanks could be seen hanging down in the dim light, and behind one a ballonet, a large bulge in the bottom of the envelope. I could hear the petty officer working away on the other side of the envelope, and could see the faint glow of his torch. I found a way from the outer lobes into the centre of the envelope. Here the view was rather impressive and the 90 yards of the airship gave quite a cathedral-like vista. Above, the ceiling was formed by the horizontal linen curtain laced to the top ridges, and on either side the curtains from the top ridges to

the centre line at my feet gave the impression of walls, against which one could see miles of cordage which connected the main suspension wires, which were attached to the car, to the upper ridges and which fanned to them on either side. The unbleached linen curtains made the whole thing a study in sepia.

Confidence was now fully restored and I could take a fatherly interest in all this fabric and string which made up the inside of my command. I reached the petty officer with no further difficulty, and with, I hope, the correct degree of *sang froid*. Things then seemed quite easy, and when the job was completed we returned to the valve without trouble, and so out. But it was with a sigh of relief that I finally removed the clip off my nose and breathed fresh air again.

## Rubber dinghies
At Kingsnorth I met Seaman Boy Dobbs, a very original young man who had been selected by General Maitland, Superintendent of Airships, to help him with his parachute development work. He was leaving the sheds with a mysterious package under his arms and two small oars, and on being asked what it was, he said that it was his new boat. At that time there were no rubber boats, and the only

90▼

collapsible boat I knew of was the rather cumbersome Berthon boat.

I followed him to the Medway and saw him unroll his boat, which was made of three lengths of gas hose forming an acute triangle, with a triangular piece of rubber airship fabric joined to them to form a bottom. The three tubes were blown up separately by mouth, and when blown up it made a boat whichever side hit the water.

After a short row in the Medway, in what I now realise was the ancestor of all the rubber floating rafts and rescue dinghies of the world, I was much impressed by its value for an airship, and made one for NS 9, which was later lost with NS 11 in the North Sea. The rubber dinghy was not used in the RAF again until they were adopted for the Southampton Flying Boats of the Far East Flight of 1926.

NS 9 arrived at Longside on 1 August, and the strength of airships in the northern North Sea was as follows: at East Fortune, NS 7, NS 8, C★ 1, C★ 3, C 7, R 29 and SSZ 23; at Longside, NS 4, NS 6, NS 9, NS 10, and NS 11. The airships C 7, C 10A, C 18, C★ 5, C★ 7, SSZ 58 and SSZ 65 were also based on Longside.

With the arrival of the NS airships the tempo of anti-submarine operations increased, as did the strength of airship escorts to the coastal convoys. In addition, several special operations took place in conjunction with specialised submarine hunting units.

Explosive nets were laid across the expected track of home-coming German submarines, and were watched by hydrophone-carrying surface craft, and, when possible, by airships. On the other hand the German U-boats now carried heavier guns, and when returning home were more inclined to keep on the surface.

On 31 July, C 25, commanded by Captain Hopperton, RAF, had been sunk in this way. (The Germans never claimed to have destroyed or attacked C 25, but it was the opinion at Longside that this was in fact the case. No airship was, however, attacked while with a convoy, for by so doing the U-boat would have given her own position away.) On 13 August NS 9, when patrolling off the Aberdeen coast in hazy weather, was also shot at. When visiting the engineers I noticed eight shell bursts near the tail fin, and realised that we were being fired at.

By the time I had regained the control position and got both engines running at full speed and the ship turned towards the area, the firing had stopped. No-one had been able to see the U-boat or the gun flash because of the haze.

NS 6 joined in the search, but neither airship saw any signs of the submerged submarine. On thinking it over afterwards we realised that it was one thing to surprise a U-boat surfacing, and another to approach one already on the surface with guns manned. We should have had an anxious time approaching as our 260 ft (79 m) length would be hard to miss at a range of 900 ft (275 m). We did not have an opportunity of testing that.

During September we and the other airships were busy on patrols, usually of 12 hours, and in mid-September had occasion to realise that even NS airships were not immune from all the troubles of the older ships. What occurred will give some idea of what patrolling meant.

We had been out on a long patrol to the north eastward out of sight of land, and were returning in the late afternoon. It had been a day of fresh blustering winds from the north east and the wind having backed to the south west, we were plugging back into a head wind. Our speed over the sea was obviously getting slower. Presently it became clear that unless the wind dropped we would have a very long journey home, and that there was no alternative base nearer than Norway. We hoped that our navigation errors of the past nine hours were not too great and looked forward to the time when we should sight land. We had increased speed to three-quarters power which gave an air speed of 50 mph, and we were probably making about 25 mph over the sea and less in squalls. However, at 800 ft (245 m) the air was fairly steady and the ship was handling easily except that the coxswain seemed to have difficulty in keeping the ship on course. Every time she swung off course the sea no longer moved behind us but just moved sideways. If this continued our trip homeward was going to be very long indeed.

At length the coxswain reported that the steering was getting stiffer and stiffer, and that he could hardly control the rudder. There was no alternative method of steering and it might take some time to find and rectify the fault, if it could be got at. If we let the ship get side to wind we would be drifting away from home faster than we had been approaching it

before. Luckily, in the 'spares bag' we had two small blocks and tackle known in the navy as 'Handy Billy'. By securing one to each rudder control in the cabin with a man on each, after some practice we managed to steer fairly well.

The engineer found that the bearing of the steering wheel had seized up, but fortunately he could get at it and hoped to be able to strip it down and free it in a short time. After a rather anxious period when our progress over the sea became slower and the gusts more frequent, he completed the job and we were able to dispense with our makeshift steering arrangements. By this time it was blowing hard so we increased to full speed, which used up fuel fast, and we came down to about 100 ft (30 m) over the sea in the hope that the wind might be slightly less close to the waves. Time went by slowly. The W/T operator was able to get a rough position from the D/F stations which tended to confirm our own idea of our position. Then the engineer came forward to ask which petrol tank was to be used next. This was important because it was desirable to keep the weights in the ship adjusted so that the trim was neither too nose- nor too tail-heavy. The report rubbed in that with the engines at full speed we were using petrol fast — pity that we had not filled right up with petrol, but then that would have meant one less bomb. Anyway, there was nothing we could do about it now. The urge to bother about our petrol consumption and how much we had left must be checked. After all, we were doing our best.

The next half-hour dragged by. Then to our relief the clouds above us thinned, the sea seemed less rough and the wind started to drop. Soon the sun came out and in the distance there was a faint blur on the horizon which gradually grew into the familiar landmark of Mormon Hill. Our navigation had been all right after all. The crew were all smiles again. The black cliffs of Peterhead harbour passed underneath. We were soon successfully landed and the airship back in its shed again.

Finally, on 21 September we had been out on a long patrol during which we sighted a mine drifting off Aberdeen. We had this sunk by a trawler. We were then recalled as the wind was rising rapidly from the south east. On arrival we found that C 15 and NS 10 were circling waiting to be landed, while the landing party of some 300 men were having great difficulty in controlling *C 7* which was dragging about in the eddies at the entrance of the shed. By that time the squalls were reaching 45 mph and it was clear that we should all have difficulty in getting down and in to the shed. There was no shelter in the desolate hill country in which we could have been moored, and no other station which we could reach. At last we saw that *C 7* had been ripped. With reasonable luck little damage need be done and the ship could be repaired. *C 15* was also ripped soon after landing, and an effort was then made to dock the much larger *NS 10*. This proved extremely hazardous and from the air we could see the ship swaying and plunging: one moment the car was 20 ft off the ground, and the next dashed to earth. The airmen on the handling guys were being carried off their feet, and were hanging on like grim death. This often took considerable courage even with an experienced team, in the struggle with a gale. Landing parties took great pride in it, and as Longside was in an exposed position there were often high winds, so the landing party had plenty of practice.

*NS 10* was ripped, and then it was our turn. We landed without too much difficulty, but once in the lee of the sheds the ship became unmanageable in the down draughts and back eddies. After some particularly fierce squalls when the airship envelope crashed down on the car and the 500 men were dragged hither and thither, we regretfully ripped our ship too, clear of the remains of the other three.

So ended for the moment the activities of *NS 9* and *NS 10* — a depressing sight on a rain-swept evening, with the silvery grey shapes of the four ships sprawled out on the trampled mud, and here and there the cars of the airships standing in the wreckage. However we knew that given time they could be repaired and that two new NS ships were being completed.

## NS 12

The crew of *NS 9* went down to Kingsnorth a few days later to collect a new ship, *NS 12*, and on 17 October we had completed the trial flight and acceptance trials. By the 22nd we were once more on our way to Longside. However, the Armistice was now close at hand, and we had only time for one coastal escort of 12 hours, in company with *NS 4*, *C 17*

and *C★ 7* before the Armistice was signed.

For a short time escort patrols were maintained in case submarines might be operating unaware of the news. A 43 hour flight gave us a chance of proving the comfort and efficiency of the new ship. Then as a final fling in company with *NS 11* we flew to the Norwegian coast. We flew off it for $4\frac{1}{2}$ hours and then returned: a 24 hour flight and the first British airships to fly to Scandinavia from Scotland.

In February 1919 *NS 11*, commanded by Major Warneford, made an endurance flight of 100 hours, 50 minutes. *NS 11* was, however, finally lost at sea with all hands *en route* from Pulham to Kingsnorth on 15 July. All the other airships were ordered to be deflated and sold locally in February 1919, with the exception of *NS 7* and *NS 8* which were kept on at East Fortune to train the United States naval air crews. *NS 7* was the last of the British Service non-rigids to be flown. She was based at Howden, to assist in the training of the American crew of *R 38*, and was deflated towards the end of 1920. Flight Lieutenant H. C. Irwin, who lost his life in *R 101* was her captain, with Flying Officer Bruce as second pilot. *NS 14* was purchased by the US Navy. So ended the British Service non-rigid airships, and their skilled personnel were dispersed throughout the Royal Air Force to learn new ways in 'heavier than air'.

## 'North Sea' airships
All the North Sea airships were erected and tested at Kingsnorth Airship Constructional Station.

*NS 1*. First flight made at Kingsnorth 2. 2. 17. Broken up at Kingsnorth 22. 2. 18. Commanded by Squadron Commander Robinson, then Flight Commander Mylne. 206 hours flown.

*NS 2*. Completed trials 16. 6. 17. Wrecked near Stowmarket through engine failure on delivery flight 27. 6. 17. 10 hours flown

*NS 3*. Completed trials 22. 7. 17. Flown to East Fortune in August 1917. Modified March 1918. Lost in gale off Firth of Forth 21. 6. 18. Commanded by Flight Commander Wheelwright, DSC, then Flight Commander Maitland, AFC. 323 hours flown.

*NS 4*. Completed trials 17. 9. 17. Flown to East Fortune, then modified as *NS 3*,

and transferred to Longside 17. 6. 18. Deflated at Longside 6. 2. 19. Commanded by Flight Commander Mylne (August 1918) and then by Captain Warneford, RAF and Captain Stevens, RAF. 260 hours flown.

*NS 5*. Completed trials in December 1917, and made a forced landing on her delivery flight the same month. Commanded by Squadron Commander Fuller. 14 hours flown.

*NS 6*. Completed trials 6. 6. 18. Flown to Longside. Commanded by Major Struthers, DSC, AFC, then Captain Underhill, Second Pilot Captain Jolliffe. Deflated 8. 2. 19. 397 hours flown.

*NS 7*. Completed trials 6. 6. 18. Flown to East Fortune. Commanded by Major Fuller, then Captain H. C. Irwin, AFC. Flew 204 hours during the war. Kept on for training US naval air personnel until end of 1920. Deflated at Howden.

*NS 8*. Completed trials 1. 7. 18. Flown to East Fortune. First Commander, Captain Chambers. 220 hours flown during war. Kept on for training after war.

*NS 9*. Completed trials 29. 7. 18. Flown to Longside. Ripped outside shed at Longside in SE gale 21. 9. 18. Commanded by Captain Maitland, AFC and Captain Harris, AFC. 162 hours flown.

*NS 10*. Completed trials August 1918. Flown to Longside. Ripped as *NS 9* at Longside 21. 9. 18. Commanded by Captain Montagu, DSC and Captain Jelf. 128 hours flown.

*NS 11*. Completed trials September 1918. Flown to Longside. Flights included one of 61 hours and one of 100 hours, 50 minutes including a return flight to Norway with *NS 9*. Kept on after Armistice, carrying out the world's endurance record flight in February 1919. Lost with all crew 15. 7. 19 while out from Pulham on passage to Kingsnorth. Commanded by Captain Warneford. Flew 228 hours during the war.

*NS 12*. Completed trials 17. 10. 18. Flew to Longside. Deflated Longside 12. 2. 19. Commanded by Captain Maitland, AFC then by Captain Harris, AFC.

*NS 13*. On trial 28. 10. 18.

*NS 14*. Purchased by US Navy 8. 11. 18.

*NS 15*. No information.

*NS 16*. Accepted 10. 1. 19. Arrived Howden 23. 3. 19. Flew for a short period after war, based at Howden. Deflated 16. 6. 19. Commanded by Captain Montagu, DSC, then by Captain Havers.

Squadron Leader T. P. York-Moore joined the RN Colleges at Osborne and Dartmouth during 1908–12, then he was posted to the Dreadnought Battleship HMS *Superb* of the Grand Fleet in 1913. He served as an airship captain from May 1915 to Autumn 1919, flying them in the Eastern Mediterranean, and in the Western approaches. In the early 1920s he was training motor boat crews at RAF Calshot, and was in charge of an RAF armoured car section guarding the desert air mail route from Amman to Baghdad, when he was invalided home in 1925 for six months leave. He was then in charge of armoured car training at Manston, followed by a two year engineering course at RAF Hendon. He was posted as OC Engineering and Transport to RAF Tangmere, and in 1929 as a Squadron Leader to RAF Fighter Command HQ, Uxbridge. After four months he was

# 'Up the Battle Bags!'

We are constantly being told that airships were a failure. Unless helium inflated they are highly dangerous; they are too slow either for passenger work or for war when they could be easily shot down; they cannot make headway against strong winds; and other such adverse comments are made. It is a lie; airships have not failed. Most of the critics appear never to have seen an airship, let alone piloted or flown in one. Airships are condemned owing to the loss of *R 101* and *Hindenburg*, but these critics have never made a study of airship accidents. They ignore completely the fact that the inter-war passenger Zeppelins had comfort, luxuries, reliability, and basic safety and silence far ahead of the most modern aircraft and that only *Hindenburg* killed or even injured passengers or crew members. I feel that I can speak about the use of airships as a result of first-hand experience both at home and in the Eastern Mediterranean.

I was a regular naval officer when on 15 May 1915 I was posted for work with naval airships, having served with the Grand Fleet. From May 1915 until 9 January 1919, I piloted and flew in non-rigid airships of the SS, Coastal, and C★ classes for 2,000 hours, having also qualified as a free balloon pilot, which all airship pilots and kite balloon observers had to do. During this period I piloted SS airships from Luce Bay, Kassandra (Greece) and Mudros (Dardenelles), and

Coastal and Coastal Star ships (which were much larger) from Mullion in Cornwall. Looking for new mooring out sites, I landed airships in the Governor's grounds in the Scilly Islands.

In the last ten months of the First World War, I piloted for 1,000 hours, and made frequent patrols of 12 hours' duration. In a period of nine days 108 hours were flown, and 600 hours in three months. Many other pilots of course did the same, and some were doing more than 24 hours at a stretch in the larger ships. *NS 3* for example, carried out a record flight of 54 hours, 50 minutes in April 1918 under the late Captain J. S. Wheelwright. All this was when not much was really known about flying. Engines were most unreliable and, compared to what the modern aeroplanes require, there was little weather information. Yet the airships flown by young pilots did many types of work in the face of storms, thunder and fog, and the pilots to a great extent had to judge the weather for themselves. They fully realised that the general public knew next to nothing of what they were doing.

The chief and most important task of the non-rigids was to hunt U boats, and especially to protect shipping by escorting convoys. As the work done at Mullion is dealt with elsewhere in this book I will deal with some of the experiences I had in the Near East.

When the Dardanelles campaign was being fought, it was decided to use SS airships to guard shipping against U boats, Flight Commander E. H. Sparling being in command of Airship Expedi-

granted 12 months sick leave and was retired on grounds of ill-health in 1931.

Together with Lord Ventry, and three or four airship enthusiasts, with invaluable help from RAF Cardington, they built and flew the airship *Bournemouth*. She did three flights in 1951, and eight in 1952, when lack of funds caused the project to shut down. He flew as observer and coxswain on the second flight, and pilot on the third flight in 1951. All flights were of short duration, and in 1952 the ship used a mobile mooring-mast (a 16-seat coach) with only three men as handling crew. Much useful information was obtained from these flights for future use.

With Lord Ventry, he was able to give valuable advice to Airship Developments Ltd in connection with the development of their *AD 500*, his actual experience of flying airships proving most valuable.

tionary Force No. 2 as it was termed. A portable shed was erected at Imbris, *SS 7* making the first flight there on 13 September 1915. After a short time, there was trouble with the shed, and a move was made to Mudros which was a little further from enemy bases. *SS 19* made the first ascent from Mudros on 12 March 1916.

When Gallipoli was evacuated another portable shed was erected at Kassandra in Greece, and I flew from both these bases after leaving the SS station at Luce Bay, Stranraer, picking up my ship at the construction and training station at Wormwood Scrubs. The clear waters of the Mediterranean sea were ideal for airships. Unlike heavier-than-air fixed wing craft, the airship could cruise almost at walking speed and as low as 50 ft. So it was far superior to the aeroplane where detailed and systematic searches had to be made. Nor is there the same vibration as is found in helicopters, with the result that powerful prism glasses of at least eight magnification could be used.

In addition to the routine patrols other jobs were found for us. For example at 0955 hrs on 2 July 1916 I received this signal: 'Following received from SNO to Group Captain. "HMS *Harpy* has lost a torpedo which was last seen close to, and outside Black Rock. Please direct airship to see if she can see anything of it when she returns from patrol in the morning."' The next day I left for patrol at 0425 hrs and immediately started a search for the torpedo. Within approximately 20 minutes I had found it close to the cliffs and about two to three miles from HMS *Harpy*. I reported the finding to the CO of HMS *Harpy* and also to the Airship Station by radio, and carried on patrol, landing at 0800 hrs.

At 0832 hrs a signal was received from Captain of Destroyers as follows: 'Airship has been of greatest assistance, and has saved us endless hours of trouble, very many thanks 0807.' Again at 0918 hrs a signal was received from *Harpy* as follows: 'I should like to express my greatest thanks for the extremely efficient way in which the airship found my torpedo.'

Where detailed observation is required the airship would seem to be virtually indispensable. Even the helicopter is not as good owing to the vibration and noise which hamper the crew. But even then the airships were considered useless by some of those who, though aeroplane pilots, knew nothing whatever about them. The Group Captain on one occasion devised a scheme to prove that the airships were no good.

I was still at Mudros when on 28 August 1916 I received orders to go out on patrol at 0520 hrs and report if I saw anything unusual in Mudros Harbour. In 20 minutes I had reported a layout of nine mines and asked if this was what I was meant to report on. I then carried on with my patrol landing at 0955 hrs. The quick finding of the mines proved his foolishness in underestimating the value of airships. The ship went out again with Graham, who knew nothing about all this, and he also located the mines. So Group Captain Scarlett's bluff was called! But on 15 October, when at Kassandra, the airship was able to find live mines which would have been a deadly menace to shipping. I spotted a line of nine mines from a height of 300 ft. The surface of the sea was rippled, and I could see every detail of each mine — chains, nuts, horns and so on. Three days later a signal was received from SNO Salonika: 'Thanks to the report from the Kassandra airship, nine mines have been destroyed off Panomi Point which is very creditable to the airship's crew concerned, whose names are to be forwarded to SNO Salonika.'

On 23 October 1916, ascending at 1010 hrs, I was patrolling the same area, but nearer to Salonika Harbour, when I observed from 300 to 400 ft two suspicious objects, about three feet in diameter. The surface of the sea was disturbed, and I reported to Kassandra that I considered them to be mines or large jelly fish. I brought up a couple of French mine sweeping trawlers nearby having marked the spot with calcium flares and carried on with my patrol landing at 1430 hrs. A day or two later a signal was received that two more mines had been swept up at that spot. This made a total of 11 mines, and with one mine having been swept up before, I knew that the enemy submarine had unloaded all her mines, as she only carried 12. The mines were reported as having been swept up from nearly 30 ft.

Convoys were saved from mines by the airships. For example, while I was escorting a large convoy of American troops from Mullion base, I spotted a mine floating immediately ahead of the leading ship. I semaphored and megaphoned to her CO, but she did not alter course until I fired a burst at the mine from my Lewis gun. She then took evasive action.

In fact, giving up airships we have deprived ourselves of an invaluable service which only airships can give — the mustering of convoys. On more than one occasion I have collected minesweepers and taken them to a suspected mine or object. In the same way of course convoys were assembled, using semaphore or International Signal Code, or even by speaking through a megaphone. In this manner wireless silence is possible, and surface crews with no knowledge of signalling can be contacted with ease. Noise prevents this sort of thing being done by helicopters. Very many hours are saved by using airships for this particular duty. For this task alone small airships would, of course, be invaluable, as they can do something which no other craft of any sort can perform.

Airships are also unique as they appear to be the only aircraft which can make full use of all the various anti-submarine detecting devices. I was lucky enough to have had the chance of being among the first pilots who towed hydrophones, which were the fore-runners of today's wonderful listening devices. This was at Mullion, from a Coastal airship commanded by Flight Lieutenant R. S. Montagu, who designed the first successful SS Twin airships and who alas lost his life on 24 August 1921 in *R 38*. The hydrophone was easy to tow at about 100 ft, but the instrument did not perform correctly. Still, it was the beginning.

Having discussed the modern sonar with experts, I understand that the airship would have an advantage over the helicopter as the latter cannot tow it continuously. There would be no disturbance of the surface by propeller wash, and there would be very little noise if the airship's engine is properly silenced. Far from being a failure or useless it would seem that the despised airship is really indispensable if the utmost efficiency is to be attained from our ASW forces.

It also seems quite possible that a pair of airships towing a connecting wire between them could be used for mine sweeping. As they would not pass over the mine it would not go off if it was of the acoustic or magnetic types. The airship could be made very quiet if silencers were fitted to the engines, which we did in the Mediterranean. Just at the end of the last war, some US Naval Airships did a fine job assisting Royal Naval minesweepers. They saved many from being blown up and indeed proved invaluable.

In the First World War there was, of course, no Radar, or any of the aids which modern aircraft depend upon. Yet airships, unlike aeroplanes, can operate in zero visibility, and we carried on in all weathers. The following are examples from personal experience.

I had gone on patrol from Mullion in a Coastal airship, and rounded Lands End, and from there flew to Padstow Point, North Cornwall. It was late afternoon, and I noticed that the cloud cover was descending and that it was necessary for me to return to base. I thought that I could just reach St Ives Harbour before the cloud base reached the bottom of the hills.

On crossing the coast at St Ives I considered that it would be too risky to reach Mullion by flying over the hills, and so came down to just above the telegraph poles and followed the road back to Curry Cross Roads and changed compass course to reach the aerodrome. Incidentally, at St Ives the cloud was so low that I found myself lower than a cottage at the bottom of the hill, having deviated from the road, then coming back to it again. On reaching the station, I saw the airship shed ahead, and above me. Accelerating, I managed to climb over it, and having seen the landing party came round again and landed safely.

On another occasion returning from patrol by the Scilly Islands fog prevented me from seeing the cliffs near Mullion Cove until I was almost on them. I again easily cleared them but found myself in between the six 240 ft high wireless masts at Poldhu. I slowed down my engines and lifted easily from a dangerous situation. But even the Farnborough airships in pre-1914 days flew in thick fog. Captain Waterlow, RFC, who was to die as a Wing Commander RNAS in charge of the Airship School at Cranwell on 25 July 1917, was piloting the army airship *Delta*. They were quite lost, so they came down very slowly on their swivelling propellers to find themselves over a farm at about 300 ft. They found their position by word of mouth, but were soon lost again. So they descended once again, and eventually came low enough to read a signpost on Hartford flats which showed the way to Farnborough. They then followed the road at about 50 ft and slowly worked their way back to Farnborough making a good landing. No aeroplane could ever do this sort of thing. It just cannot slow down, and, owing to the noise, the crew could not hail the ground.

When properly used on ASW work during the First and Second World Wars, naval airships certainly did not fail. They performed a task which no other aircraft could do, and this even includes helicopters. These of course are faster than modern airships by perhaps 60 mph, but even when hovering they still consume a lot of fuel, while the airship may lie too with just sufficient power to remain stationary. The duration of a helicopter would not be more than four hours while even the small 70,000 cu ft SS Zeros were up sometimes for over 30 to a little over 50 hours (*SS Z. 39* was up for 51 hours, 50 minutes, piloted by Lieutenant Bryan, 11 to 13 August 1918 from Polegate). The airship, too, is safer at low altitudes, while hovering, and also in fog. So, good as they are, the rotary winged aircraft cannot really replace the airship.

From a purely naval point of view, my own experiences have convinced me that the airship should never have been abandoned. Airships have never received the same encouragement as aeroplanes. Even small non-rigids, of the same size as the SS ships of the First World War would have a much better performance today due to the reduced weights of modern envelopes, engines and so on, and the modern airship would be a far more efficient gas holder. An SS Zero of 1918 (70,000 cu ft) would often consume up to 100,000 cu ft of gas per month (regular topping-up is required due to gas diffusion). A modern non-rigid of twice the volume and flying more than 100 hours a month might only require 1,000 cu ft in the same period. In my days too, all airship stations had to have men specially detailed for handling duties. It was quite usual for a 60,000 cu ft SS to require 20 to 30 men. An airship of modern times with a volume of 156,000 cu ft would usually only require eight to ten men. There would be no need to have additional ratings on a station for such duties.

As for the aeroplanes carrying 400 people or more on board how many survive in the event of an ordinary bad crash, let alone if fire should break out? An aeroplane with highly inflammable fuel in the wings, and engines on those wings would appear to be far more dangerous from a fire point of view than a well found hydrogen filled airship with engines in fire proof cars and a long way from the hydrogen gas. Fires in both heavier- and lighter-than-air craft are more likely to take place in the event of a crash landing; the aeroplane would touch down at well over 100 mph, the airship at zero speed. *Hindenburg* was meant for helium and if this safe gas had been available, combined with diesel engines, she would have been a virtually fire-proof ship. It is obvious then that the aeroplane is far more dangerous than even the hydrogen filled airship. I know that I would most certainly prefer the much slower, but infinitely more comfortable and basically safer airship!

Neither in peace or war has the airship failed. They have never been given the same chances as the more favoured aeroplanes. So I will end with the hope that some group of people will make their voices heard in influential places and demand that the whole airship question should be reopened and looked at sensibly. This should be done with a view to working in co-operation, and not opposition, with existing methods of transport by air and sea.

91▼

92 *C 9* on the landing ground at Mullion in 1917, having returned from a patrol. The normal landing crew is shown. The armament of two Vickers machine guns can be seen clearly, as can the 100 hp engine in the bows and the 240 hp engine in the stern. The five-man crew comprised the coxswain in the front seat, the pilot in the second seat, the observer in the third seat, the wireless operator in the fourth seat and the engineer in the fifth seat. The air scoop, which supplied air to the ballonets, is astern of the propeller. The *Eta* suspension patches can be seen on the envelope.

94 *C\* 10*, piloted by the then Flight Commander T. P. York-Moore, RN, landing at Mullion in 1918 after a patrol. It can be seen that the ship was 'light' as she is being pulled down by her landing ropes. This ship was more streamlined than the earlier Coastal ships. There were only ten C Stars built, each with a length of about 210 ft (64 m), an extreme width of 50 ft (15.24 m), and a volume of 210,000 cu ft.

93▼                                      92▲    94▼

93 *C 2* being taken into the small shed at Mullion in 1917 by a large handling party owing to a strong side wind. Corrugated sheets have been removed from the wind break. The stiffeners on the envelope's bows prevented the nose blowing in when underway.

91 No. 1 Airship Shed, Royal Naval Air Station, Mullion, in 1917. This was the first shed built at Mullion to accommodate four Coastals. Some corrugated iron sheets were removed from the wind breaks at the end of the shed to break up the wind gusts and so make it easier to get a ship in and out of the shed with a side wind.

95▼

95 *SS 23* on the landing ground at Luce Bay, Stranraer in 1915. The car is the fuselage of a BE2C aeroplane. The wireless operator is positioned in No. 1 seat, and the pilot, Flight Lieutenant T. P. York-Moore, RN, is in No. 2 seat. The third seat was specially cut into the fuselage to take an additional observer. The ship's trailing rope and grapnel can be seen hanging from the chassis directly below the third seat position. The air scoop which sent air to the ballonets in the bows and stern is fixed behind the propeller.

Roger Munck trained as a marine/naval engineer, an excellent foundation for an airship designer. He was engaged for five years upon designing Shell's large rigid airship. He became chief designer

**AD 500**

for Airship Developments, designing the *AD 500* airship. When the company merged with Thermo-Skyships, forming Airship Industries Ltd, he remained chief designer.

The *AD 500* first took shape on the drawing board in 1976 as a small non-rigid airship of 120,000 cu ft. It was originally designed to meet a need foreseen by my partner in Aerospace Developments, John Wood, as a general purpose vehicle for operations in Peru; later, we began negotiations with potential customers in Venezuela. A ship of this size was, we felt, a better investment risk for potential financiers than the vastly bigger rigid airship of the type that I had been designing for Shell International Gas. Accordingly, we decided to start small — at the time, surprisingly, an unusual concept. Also, given the choice, it was clearly more satisfactory to ease our way into a new field at a smaller size and gradually build up knowledge. However, as I became aware of the necessity to create a general purpose vehicle with adequate reserves of speed and endurance, the size of the ship gradually crept up to its present 180,000 cu ft (5,000 cu m).

While the *500* might have been relatively small ('only' about the bulk of a Boeing 747), as chief designer I was determined that whatever its role it would incorporate every possible advantage that modern materials and technology could provide, which, having spent five years in charge of the design of the Shell airship design programme, I felt that I was in as good a position as anyone to achieve. I also wanted to make the very best use of the experience and know-how built up in the earlier generations of airships and, quite apart from the substantial documentary evidence, we obtained invaluable help from some of the early airship pioneers.

A typical example of this is the use of vectored thrust in the *500*'s design — whereby the propellers (in our case ducted fans) can be tilted in the pitch plane to drive the airship upwards or downwards; it is similar in principle to the concept on which the BAe Harrier V/STOL aircraft operates. The basic concept was first employed on the Willows airships of *circa* 1910. Lord Ventry and Squadron Leader York-Moore, one of the most experienced First World War British airship pilots, were enthusiastic

advocates of the swivelling propeller system and gave us detailed information on the great advantages that this system conferred on airship operations and safety, even in its initial, relatively unsophisticated form. We in turn were able to build upon the basis of those early experiences and design a new system replacing the cumbersome hand cranked control system with a thumb switch incorporated in the control yoke, signalling to small high performance electric motors which rotated the propulsor ducts. In practice, the resulting blend of modern technology with an old concept worked perfectly first time, surprising many who had forecast major development problems.

I was determined to take advantage of the breakthrough that has been made in the use of composite materials in aircraft. Accordingly, I designed the 30 ft (9 m) long gondola as a giant one piece kevlar moulding (kevlar is an aramid fibre similar to glass and carbon fibre in its use, and somewhere between them in structural properties). In this instance my training as a naval architect was of considerable assistance and it was good to see airships once again showing the way to the aeroplane industry as so often used to be the case (duralumin and Alclad being classic examples). The use of kevlar on the gondola achieved a significant reduction in production costs and weight with very little in the way of accompanying problems. Similarly, for the tailfins we developed and patented a rather ingenious system of interlocking one piece honeycomb ribs and spars which again

reduced cost and weight while improving durability.

While we negotiated with our Venezuelan customers, design work progressed hesitantly, because of lack of funds. It was not until July 1977 that we finally managed to agree terms for the first ship and get construction underway. We were immediately faced with constructing a vast amount of special tooling — always expensive and time-consuming when using composite materials — as our objective was to build a production ship rather than a one-off prototype. This was a vital factor as we could undoubtedly have reduced costs by at least 30 per cent if the latter only had been our objective.

By March 1978 we had taken delivery of virtually all the major components such as hull, gondola, tailfins and valves and were running only about a month behind schedule and about 15 per cent over budget. Considering the very complex, advanced technology level of the project and the difficulties in bringing together components from all over Europe to one point at one time this was felt to be quite good going. However, the problems began once we moved into No. 1 Hangar at Cardington. The superstitious reader will doubtless attribute this to the *R 101* jinx which is reputed to bring bad luck to all airships built in the hangar.

Nevertheless, the first problem was with the vital valves which control gas pressure inside the hull. Originally, we had been led to believe that we would be able to use the well proven Goodyear 20 in valves but at the very last moment it became clear that this was not possible. The design of airship valves is highly specialised and we did not at the time feel at all confident about tackling it ourselves and were forced to try to find an alternative supplier of a proven valve. We tracked down a company in the UK which was manufacturing valves although these had been used mainly on barrage and meteorological balloons and it was necessary to mount these in an alternative configuration (as Lord Ventry and his colleagues had done earlier on the *Bournemouth*). However, immediately the valves were tested it became obvious that they were leaking badly from their seals and were completely unserviceable.

We eventually had to completely redesign the valves, resulting in delaying the programme four months as we were unable to inflate the envelope during this period. The only good thing to emerge was that we learnt all about airship valves the hard way and this has subsequently enabled us to design our own valves with a better performance for the new *500*. To make the best of a bad job I had some modifications carried out to part of the tailfin skin cladding to reduce weight during this delay.

We inflated the envelope towards the end of the summer. For anyone who has not seen it before — and even for those who have — the inflation of a non-rigid airship is an amazing and impressive spectacle particularly when carried out in the dead of night under the light from the headlamps of 30 cars and TV camera arclights! The achievement of a successful inflation relies on what is almost a black art — in this instance controlled masterfully by Stan White, our Chief Rigger. I remember vividly the first night watch after the inflation that I took alone with 'my' ship and the feeling when gazing at the giant white hull shimmering in the floodlights against the gloom inside the hangar.

However, such elevated feelings were soon dispelled as the months rolled on with few outward results to show in return for endless hours of late night working. In reality we were just running into that area of prototype aircraft projects where tiny details and problems seem to reduce a project to a crawl. In our case, things were made far worse by the fact that we did not have any proper workshop facilities in the hangar and had to build up our construction team from scratch. As if this were not enough, our financial position was worsening with each month's overhead bill.

Moreover, we were having to contend with increasingly severe conditions within the hangar during a winter that was the worst for many years. On one occasion we were so concerned about the water freezing in the ship's ballast tanks (not having been able to get the special anti-freeze required) that Bruce Reid, one of our team, had to spend a night watch floating night lights in the tanks to prevent ice building up and splitting them.

By the end of January 1979 we had completed many hours of engine and propulsion system running tests and I had carried out several vectored thrust vertical take-offs and landings, with the ship on loose tethers fore and aft, and had held the ship without effort in hover at 250 lb (551 kg) heavy for many minutes on end. Although we still had some typical prototype problems such as excessive friction in the control circuit and a somewhat temperamental pitch change system, the ship generally was functioning well and it was already clear to me that the vectored thrust would give us a considerable extra degree of safety. By 2 February the worst of the really bad weather had blown through and we had received our Permit to Fly from the Civil Aviation Authority (CAA). It must be said that throughout the project CAA had maintained a very close liaison with us and had always been most helpful. Accordingly they were kept closely informed of our progress and of any problems that emerged. One of the reasons for the particular interest CAA took in the project was that G-BECE was the first airship to be built to the new Section Q of British Civil Airworthiness Requirements (BCAR) — in fact, persuading CAA to write Section Q in the first place was one of the many hurdles we had to overcome in the early days.

It was abundantly clear that if we did not take off on Saturday, 3 February then in all probability we would never take-off at all as the company was under enormous financial pressure and we could only last, literally, for another few days at most without a further injection of capital, which the Venezuelans were understandably reluctant to commit without having first seen a demonstration flight. Furthermore, the weather reports indicated that the 'gap' in the weather that we needed for a first flight would be very short lived.

In these circumstances, my amazement can be imagined when I arrived at the hangar on the morning of the Great Day to find that the flight had been cancelled by our Flight Operations Department for weather reasons and that the Press had been notified to that effect. On hearing that, I immediately checked the wind conditions myself and was surprised to find that the wind strength was quite low and with every indication of remaining that way. Having got two independent, confirmatory checks, I gave instructions for the original programme to go ahead, although several hours delayed, and for the ship to be moved up on its mobile mast to the mouth of the hangar. There followed a scene of the most incredible activity and within half an hour we were at the hangar mouth. With a variable wind of about ten knots and some 'back hangar draft' we were all well within the limits of our special mobile mast, and we came out of the hangar at a run without any problem.

I think this episode illustrates a problem we tended to have with those of our staff who had come from other LTA companies where they had been involved with the conventional early, but well developed generation of airship. Somewhat understandably, they were either over optimistic and made too little allowance for the fact that parts of the *500* were of a revolutionary, and to some extent evolutionary, nature; or, as in this case, they did not take due account of those features of the ship, such as the mobile mast or vectored thrust system, which completely transformed the *500*'s capability compared to that of the ships which had preceded her.

As a result of this delay and the fact that several of our staff, thinking the programme cancelled, had not turned up, it took us until late in the afternoon to carry out handling trials on the mast and attend to the recalcitrant port pitch change system. By this time the airfield was crowded with visitors who had come to see the long awaited first flight; among them I recognised a number of extremely worried looking bank managers, Venezuelan clients, and BBC television executives.

At long last, with about an hour and a quarter to go before sunset, Ray Hall, our chief inspector, pronounced himself satisfied that the ship was ready for its first flight. Sunset we all knew was the deadline set by CAA for our test flights and so Giovanni Abratti, our pilot, John Wood, Ray Hall, Dick Cox, our electrical engineer, and myself boarded the ship. The Porsche engines fired up perfectly as usual and we started our first flight checks.

Then, about ten minutes before our last possible take-off time, Giovanni called me to say in a somewhat strained voice that our permission to take-off had been cancelled owing to the presence of a meteorological balloon nearby. Taking a very deep breath I jumped down from the gondola and was immediately met by

Ron Mason, the hangar superintendant. Ron explained that with the hydrogen-filled balloon up, we would have to move upwind to get our take-off path well clear of it — in which case we would be far too close to the road for a conventional airship take-off (which Ron had already had experience of when the Goodyear *Europa* had been at Cardington). The logic of the situation was unassailable and for a few agonising seconds I could see only the truth horrific prospect of cancelling the flight with the inevitable consequences that would ensue.

I suddenly realised that we were forgetting vectored thrust. I quickly explained that we would simply take-off vertically from the upwind site close to the road, using our vectored thrust. Ron immediately gave me the go-ahead for the amended take-off and I was literally catapulted back up into the gondola by Mick Patton our masthead man and an almost audible sigh of relief went up from around the field. In spite of his earlier reticence to use vectored thrust in initial flight testing, Giovanni Abratti, now readily agreed to the new proposal and we were moved off the mast to the new take off position. Having been weighed off at 100 lb (45 kg) heavy our crew chief gave the command 'slack the lines' and for a moment the ship stood poised on the ground.

Then with a roar of engines as Giovanni opened the throttles, the *500* rose away majestically from the ground, accompanied by a roar of applause from the crowd. We climbed away on a 45 degree flight path at a very fast climb rate and with about five degrees nose up trim in what must have been one of the most impressive airship take-offs ever. Exactly as predicted, the ship required virtually no control during this vectored thrust climb, due largely to pendulum stability and careful positioning of the propulsor ducts.

At about 500 ft (152 m) we levelled out, rather abruptly owing to the stiffness of the controls, setting up a pitch oscillation, but this quickly died out and we set course out over Shortstown heading into a magnificent sunset. The rapid ascent had caused our hull pressure to rise above normal and we accordingly valved air manually from the ballonets. We were now in steady flight and purring along at about 43 knots, close to the maximum cruise speed of a conventional *GZ-20* airship on only one quarter throttle. Even

though we were flying without the normal silencers on the engines and without any sound proofing the noise level in the cabin was really quite low and we could talk to each other down the length of the cabin with ease. Ray and I in particular were delighted with the way the ship was behaving both having noticed immediately the complete freedom from the pitch instability that is such a pronounced feature in small conventional non-rigids.

Soon it was time to return and Giovanni swung the ship round back in the direction of the hangar. We were all impressed with the way the *500* banked swiftly into the turn with no trace of the mushiness that one normally associates with airship handling. Before long we were lining up into the wind to come up to our landing point and I became aware that Giovanni was finding the controls very heavy particularly due to a nose down trim (we later traced the cause to a leaking flap valve in the ballonet control chest). I suggested he used the vectored thrust again to control his height and this immediately had the desired effect and we came in to a perfect landing.

Upon landing we were manhandled over to the mast and made fast. By this time nightfall was upon us and the whole area was lit up by the floodlamps of the TV and Press illuminating the crowds of well-wishers, and the now happy faces of bank managers, Venezuelan clients *et al*, and of course the Aerospace Developments team who had worked so hard and so long to make it all happen. Champagne was broken out and, having put the faithful G-BECE back in her shed for the night, the whole assembly retired to *The Bell* at Cotton End to celebrate in splendid style a day when everything had finally turned out right.

However, it was decided by our financial masters not to implement the original plan of re-financing the company by selling off a large portion of it via City merchant banks once we had achieved a successful first flight. We were to wait until, say, two months had elapsed and we had a Royal Navy trials lease in hand *before* we went to the City; then we would probably be able to double the selling price of our shares. Whilst this idea had a certain theoretical appeal we were very much against the new plan with its marginal funding only over the next few months, because we were all too aware of our worsening financial position, and of

the additional burdens which could be unexpectedly added to it during our test programme. However, having argued the point, we could only press on and try to get the ship through its flight test programme to Special Category Certificate of Airworthiness, basically 40 hours' flying, the point at which Royal Navy could take her over, as soon as we could safely manage it.

The Royal Navy had arranged a lease via the Department of Naval Warfare, nominally for two months but with an option on an extension, for trials evaluation of the *AD 500* in the Maritime Airborne Early Warning role, for which they would pay handsomely, an inviting prospect for us in more than financial gains. The Venezuelans considered that it would be excellent PR to wait until after the RN's evaluation, which they estimated would double share prices.

Difficulties now cropped up with our pilot regarding extra permanent ground crew and as a result we failed to fly during a spell of ideal weather which understandably upset the Venezuelans. However, an alternative pilot, Herman Peter, flew the airship while our permanent pilot was on leave. On 7 March, in weather conditions that were acceptable but certainly not ideal, we took the ship out of the hangar. By this time we had considerably lightened the flying controls and improved the ballonet air control system. The following morning, in a wind gusting 15 to 20 knots Herman took off with Godfrey Lea, Iain Reid and myself from the AD design team aboard. Once again we made a magnificent vectored thrust take-off and it was noticeable how quickly we got clear of the ground and its obstructions, once again vindicating Lord Ventry's and Squadron Leader York-Moore's advice. This time we turned immediately and set off down wind to the east, flying at some 600 ft, and really rushing along above the fields. After a while we carried out some turning trials and, satisfied, turned about for home. I had been dozing peacefully in the comfortable swivel seats in the warm cabin when Godfrey drew my attention to the fact that we were making no headway over the ground. Herman was somewhat concerned as he knew we were already flying at a speed that was close to the maximum of the ships he was used to flying. I reassured him and told him merely to give the engines more throttle as they were still only at half power, and, having seen the ship surge forward once more towards home went back to sleep again. We swept back over the fields at over 50 knots and 3,800 rpm — the engines still had another 1,200 rpm in hand — we duly came in over the ground crew at about 100 ft (30 m). Rather than risk a conventional landing with a strange ship in very gusty conditions, Herman carried out a magnificent 'flying landing' and literally dropped the ship's bow lines straight into the hands of the ground crew. Another flight had been completed, this time in very difficult conditions.

By the time the ship was docked back on its mobile mast the wind had increased to 25 knots, delaying our original plan of getting it back into the hangar to carry out the remaining work required, as the wind strength exceeded the safe limit for entering the hangar without a tail restraint system. Although, as a general principle, I wanted to avoid subjecting a brand new ship to bad conditions on the mast at such an early, unproven stage of the mooring system, we were not unduly concerned about the prospect of another day and night out on the mast — airships have frequently been left out moored for months on end without any problems, and the weather forecast did not indicate anything too alarming — in any case, we had no alternative.

As the day wore on the wind strength gradually increased and it became clear that we were unlikely to get a lull in the wind conditions before the following day. In view of the worsening weather it was agreed that we would maintain a permanent watch of three men throughout the night ahead.

I came on watch at 0800 hrs and settled down to a long, cold night in the unheated cab of the mobile mast. The watch was punctuated by visits from members of staff, who came out from their homes into the freezing wind and rain to check that all was well with the ship. In fact, she was riding what was fast becoming storm conditions magnificently, with very little in the way of the normal rolling and 'kiting' that small airships usually exhibit in such gusty conditions. In particular, Stan White, our Chief Rigger, came out and commented very favourably on the ship's behaviour, by comparison to the Goodyear *Europa* which he had previously worked on at Cardington. As the night wore on I

trudged across repeatedly to the nearby weather hut to get updates on the weather forecast and on the way back passed in the lee of the hut to admire the ship illuminated by flood lights, moving slowly and majestically to meet the rising gusts of wind and rain.

Very occasionally we operated the ground blower system to keep hull pressure up, and on two occasions trimmed the odd 150 lb (68 kg) of water ballast to compensate for the ship's weight in the downpour of rain, although the *500* seemed relatively insensitive to changes of 'lightness' and seemed quite happy anywhere in the region of neutral equilibrium to 150 lb light — a notable contrast to conventional airships which frequently have to be left light resulting in a very pronounced kiting action in which the ship is consistently well tail up with the gondola high above the ground. I well remember that on one occasion when the other two watch keepers with me were monitoring pressure readings in the gondola they passed the time playing a game of chess — a clear illustration of the stability in the ship.

By 0100 hrs, the wind had increased with really heavy gusts. I heard a loud crumpling sound from the mast head immediately around the mobile mast cab. Fearing the worst, I climbed the ladder to the top of the mast, not altogether a pleasant experience. At first I could see no visible damage but during a gust, the crumpling sound occurred again and it became apparent that some part of the ship's nose cone, a 9 ft (2.74 m) diameter glassfibre moulding secured to the bow of the hull envelope and providing the strong point for the ship's attachment to the mast, was collapsing under compressive loading during the strongest gusts — when the ship rode forward to the mast. While the nose cone was intact the ship would remain rigidly coupled to the pivotable mast head, but once the cone started to collapse the increased movement would lead to a rapidly worsening situation. I warned the other two men on watch of the emergency. The ship was ballasted slightly heavier reducing the kiting action which would aggravate the buckling of the nose cone. At about 0120 hrs, I went to call out extra staff. I also called out the RAE duty balloon crew to provide extra men, and to open the No. 1 Hangar doors in case an emergency attempt had to be made to get the ship inside.

Within 20 minutes, most of the Aerospace Developments crew and the Cardington balloon crew had arrived (a number of people could not be reached because the weather had brought down many telephone lines). For approximately half an hour men were positioned around the gondola handrail to ease the run-on loads from the cone in strong gusts, but in the prevailing conditions of 43 knot gusts, the nose cone continued to break up slowly.

With no sign of a break in the weather in the next 12 hours it was evident by now that the nose cone would fail shortly. I decided that for the ship to remain where it was would invite certain disaster, but that there was at least a chance of improving the situation by either moving it to a more sheltered position or getting it back into the hangar. Iain Reid went to reconnoitre the area behind the hangars in an attempt to find shelter for the ship in their lee, but returned to say that the ground was too soft for the mobile mast. I therefore made the decision to attempt to get the airship back into the hangar. While the wind strength was exceedingly high to attempt this, the wind direction was dead into the hangar and if we did not make the attempt the bow structure would break up within a short period of time in any case.

It was reasoned that if the mobile mast was driven extremely slowly, at less than 1 mph, there would be no added load on the cone and the ship could be manoeuvred at least into a position directly upwind of the open hangar doors. This proved to be the case and the flexibility provided by the mobile mast system permitted the operation to be carried out in gusts of Force 9, with no worsening of the situation.

The ship was manoeuvred into position head to wind behind the mobile mast, directly aligned with the hangar, with the stern approximately 240 ft (73 m) from the open hangar doors. The hangar flood lights were all switched on and the meteorological balloons inside were moved to give a clear path into the hangar. Conditions inside the hangar were calm due to the stagnation effect of being open only at one end and I have seldom seem a more frustrating sight than this haven of calm only a few hundred yards away. However, we knew that we had first to get past the enormous eddies and up-drafts around the hangar doors.

In order to pin the ship'a tail down I hitched up the stern line to my Land Rover. I told the mobile mast driver to wait for a lull and then drive 'like hell' for the hangar entrance. I would maintain station under the stern of the ship and try to keep the stern line taut. I waited until I heard the roar of the mobile mast's engine above the howling of the wind and started to drive in towards the hangar. I was just thinking to myself that we were actually going to make it when I felt the Land Rover being lifted off the ground. Fortunately, as designed, the stern line broke under the excessive load and the tail of the ship kited steeply upwards in a giant up current just in front of the hangar mouth. I ran to the mast and told them to drive back away from the hangar as quickly as possible to get the ship clear of the turbulence. However, by now it was jointly agreed that in the prevailing conditions it would be too risky to make a second attempt to get into the hangar. Shortly afterwards the nose cone collapsed completely as a rigid structure and it became apparent that a broken part of the shell had pierced the ship's hull. At 0230 hrs Stan White and I agreed that the only responsible thing to do was to deflate the ship by operating its rip-system before the ship finally broke away from the mast. Although this part of the ship's safety system had never been operated before it performed perfectly. However, during the deflation process in the gale force winds the envelope was very badly damaged in spite of all precautions. By a final irony, the nose cone failed to break completely and I had to saw through its last remains before I could finally release the envelope from the flogging it was being subjected to. My thoughts as I looked down from my wild vantage point are best left imagined.

This episode finished off Aerospace Developments financially and the fact that G-BECE turned out to be eminently repairable, and that the nose cone which failed that night was the one major component that we had not designed proved of no consequence. However, by an immensely circuitous route the old team is now back in the airship business as part of a much larger public company and a brand new production standard *500*, G–BIHN is under construction with the first flight scheduled for June 1981. Let us hope that the *500* story does have a happy ending after all.

[Indeed, on 28 September 1981, Airship Industries launched its second AD 500, now known as *Skyship 500*. This, the first production model, is only different from the prototype version in minor details.]

97 The port ducted propulsor of the *AD 500* partly swivelled. Through the employment of vectoring techniques, thrust can be delivered upwards or downwards, making the airship a V/STOL aircraft of advanced specification and comparatively low cost.

96 A view of the control car of the *AD 500*, showing the five-bladed, variable pitch, ducted propulsors, which are driven by twin air-cooled Porsche piston engines, mounted transversely inboard to the rear of the car. The propulsors are driven via Westland Lynx helicopter transmission shafts and 90 degree drive reduction gearboxes. The excellent observation facilities afforded by the design of the car are apparent.

98 *The Skyship 500* is the first production model of a new range of airships being developed by Airship Industries. This ship made its first flight from RAE Cardington at 0830 hours on Monday, 28 September 1981, and has since flown on a series of extensive trials flights. Following the assembly of one of the *500* series in the USA in 1982, it is intended to conduct a number of trials for the US Naval Underwater Systems Center to assess the viability of the ship as a maritime surveillance platform and to examine the operational deployment of AIRTASS sonar. If the trials are a success it is intended to conduct further towed array sonar trials at the US Atlantic Undersea Test and Evaluation Center at Andros Island in the Bahamas.

96◄ 97▲ 98▼

# France

French military aeronautics can be said to have begun with the formation of two companies of *aérostiers* in 1794 during the Franco-Prussian War. Under Captain Coutelle, the new Military Aerostatic Company made its first operational mission on 2 June, when an ascent was made from Maubeuge, enabling Coutelle to observe the disposition of the Austrian and Dutch troops, thus rendering valuable information to the French artillery. Shortly after this the Company was moved to Charleroi and then to Fleurus, where during the ensuing battle Coutelle ascended in his captive balloon *L'Entreprenant*, staying aloft for 10 hours, directing the French artillery and troops by means of dispatches lowered on a cord. The following year saw a notable success by Coutelle at Mainz, and a year later three more balloons were added to the Company's inventory. Coutelle, now a general, was given overall command of the Balloon Corps, which by now had increased to four companies. However, after a severe reverse at the hands of the British in Egypt, Napoleon disbanded the Corps in 1799, mainly because it lacked mobility.

The Franco-Prussian War of 1870–71, precipitated by Napoleon III's over estimation of his army's capability and Bismarck's brand of diplomacy, created the circumstances for the impressive achievement of the French aeronauts who escaped by balloon from Paris during the siege of that city. A so-called 'balloon bridge' was established, linking the city with the outside world, and by the time Paris capitulated on 28 January 1871, 66 balloons had been flown from it carrying $2\frac{1}{2}$ million letters, and 368 carrier pigeons — of which 57 returned with messages for the besieged. The lessons learned from this remarkable episode were not readily forgotten and the French Government re-established the *Ecole d'Aérostation* at Meudon, which had been closed by Napoleon Bonaparte, and it was at the Chalais-Meudon aeronautical establishment that the airship *La France* made its historic flight in 1884.

Backed financially by the politician Léon Gambetta, who was probably in

## The Historical Background

favour of the development of lighter-than-air flight because of his escape from Paris in the balloon *L'Arnand Barbès* during the siege in 1870, Charles Renard and Arthur Krebs, two army engineer officers, constructed *La France*, an airship powered by an $8\frac{1}{2}$ hp electric motor. This ship demonstrated the possibilities of *dirigible* flight to the military authorities, by completing a 'closed circuit' flight — the ship returning to its point of departure under its own power.

However, the credit for awakening more than just passing curiosity in airships must be given to the egocentric, but nonetheless admirable, Brazilian millionaire, Alberto Santos-Dumont, who was largely responsible for the development of the non-rigid airship. He constructed a total of 16 airships which were flown in and around Paris from 1898 to 1907. Santos-Dumont, although a clever mechanic, failed to understand the need for stabilising fins, but proved himself to be an able pilot, even using his airships as 'runabouts' in Paris, and in his little airship *Santos-Dumont No. 6* succeeded in winning the Deutsch Prize for making a timed circuit of the Eiffel Tower and returning to his starting point at the Aéro Club in Saint Cloud. The prize money of 125,000 francs (some £4,955 or $24,130

in 1901) was divided by Santos-Dumont, with characteristic humanity, amongst the poor of Paris and his employees.

On 14 July 1903 Santos-Dumont made a brief flight in his 'little runabout' *Santos-Dumont No. 9* in front of the President of the Republic and a number of senior army officers at the military review at Longchamps, off the Bois de Boulogne. The result of this 10 minute display was an exchange of letters with the Minister of War, General André, which led to Commandant Hirschauer, Chief of the Battalion of Balloonists in the First Regiment of Engineers, and Lieutenant Colonel Bouttiaux being appointed to examine in detail Santos-Dumont's offer of his airship fleet to France, in case of hostilities with any country except Brazil and North America. It could be said, therefore, that Santos-Dumont's experiments had spurred on an already existing interest in military aeronautics in France; indeed his prophetic remarks in his book *Dans l'air*, published in Paris in 1904, heralded an age of French military and naval aeronautics that was not to end until the last naval airship was taken out of commission in 1937. Santos-Dumont's own words are best used to describe his vision of the future use of airships:

'. . . the airship will . . . carry its navigator here and there at will, at the right height above . . . the waves. Any submarine boat, stealthily pursuing its course . . . underneath them, will be beautifully visible to him, while from a . . . warship's deck it would be quite invisible. . . . Thus, . . . the airship must become . . . the great enemy of that other twentieth-century marvel, the submarine . . .'

Going on to foretell the invention of the depth-charge, Santos-Dumont concluded that the airship

'. . . may be able to destroy the submarine boat by sending down to it . . . long arrows filled with dynamite and capable of penetrating to . . . depths underneath the waves impossible to gunnery from the decks . . . of a warship!'

99 The ninth Lebaudy semi-rigid airship made its first flight on 14 July 1910, and was bought by the *Morning Post*, a London newspaper, after which she was named. Readers subscribed to pay for it, for the British Army. She flew from Moisson in France to Farnborough on 26 October 1910 and was badly ripped on the shed while docking because she was 10 ft (3.04 m) higher than expected. As a result 'A' shed at Farnborough had to be heightened. When the ship was repaired she was taken out of her shed on 4 May 1911, but while making a trial flight crash landed across Farnborough Road and was wrecked. She never flew again.

100 *Adjudant Réau*, the French Army Astra non-rigid airship built in 1911, at Verdun in 1914. In September 1912 she made a world record endurance flight of 21 hours, 20 minutes. On 12 December 1912 she reached an altitude of 7,095 ft (2,163 m), a record for an airship. During the war she made three attempted sorties but could not gain enough height. She was 286.25 ft (87.24 m) and had a volume of 315,935 cu ft, and a diameter of 46.2 ft (14 m). She last flew at Issy on 8 August 1914.

99▲

101▼

100▲

102▼

101 *Morning Post's car* with one of the two 135 hp Panhard motors and a propeller blade visible. The envelope was 337.75 ft (102.94 m) and had a volume of 353,166 cu ft, and the maximum diameter was 39.3 ft (11.97 m). The ship had three ballonets.

102 The French Army airship *Fleurus I* at Reims. She was the first Allied airship to carry out a bombing raid, and made ten war sorties. She was taken off the effective list after the Armistice. She was 305 ft (93 m) long and 46 ft (14 m) in diameter, and had a volume of 370,755 cu ft. Two 220 hp Clément-Bayards drove her at 43 mph.

103 *Spiess*, France's only rigid airship, was built by the Zodiac company and made her first flight on 30 April 1913 at Saint-Cyr. The design of the airship was based on a patents registered in 1873 by an engineer named Joseph Spiess, but she was not built until 1911, when she was presented to the French Government. The framework was constructed from wooden fourteen-sided transverse frames joined together by hollow wooden longitudinals. The external keel was triangular in cross-section and contributed to the longitudinal rigidity of the ship. The two engine cars, each housing a 200 hp Chenu engine driving two propellers each, were suspended from the hull, set into and in line with the keel. In the photograph two of the propellers can be seen fixed by brackets to the hull. In 1913 *Spiess* was enlarged from a length of 370 ft (112.77 m) to 459 ft (139.90 m), but her diameter remained 44.5 ft (13.56 m). The modifications increased her volume from 451,968 to 579,084 cu ft. The lengthening of the ship failed to give the *Spiess* sufficient lift and she was broken up in 1914.

103▲

104▼

104 *CBVI*, the sixth airship to be built by Clement-Bayard; photographed shortly before she was sold to Russia in 1914. This ship was launched in 1913 and had a volume of 346,000 cu ft. She was powered by two C-B 120 hp engines and had a maximum speed of 33 mph.

105▼

105 *Tissandier*, the French 'Grand Cruiser' built by the Lebaudy brothers, was the twelfth airship built by the firm. She was the last of her type and was not accepted by the French Army because she could go no faster than 37 mph. *Tissandier* first flew on 12 October 1914. She had a volume of 741,510 cu ft, and was 426.5 ft (130 m) long. Power was supplied by seven 120 hp Salmson engines.

The Société Astra des Constructions Aéronautiques, a balloon manufacturing concern, was one of the most successful French airship companies. About 12 airships were built to the firm's own designs before they took over and improved on the designs of Torres Quevedo. The ships constructed to this improved design were known as Astra-Torres airships, and had a trefoil-shaped (tri-lobed) envelope. A novel feature of this design was that the rigging for the distribution of the main load was inside the envelope, therefore lowering the ship's resistance when in flight.

Towards the end of the First World War all the Astra-Torres airships were attached to the French Naval Air Service, for patrol duties in the Mediterranean and five of them, *AT 2*, *AT 3*, *AT 6*, *AT 7* and *AT 8* were sent to the North African bases at Alger-Baraki, Oran-La Senia and Bizerte-Sid Ahmed from Aubagne in the South of France. *AT 8* was subsequently lost off Tunis.

After the war the Compagnie Générale Transaérienne, which had been set up by Henri Deutsch de la Meurthe in 1908, put *AT 16* and a Zodiac cruiser into service for passenger flights. The Astra-Torres company continued building airships for the French Navy until 1920 when *AT 20* was launched — it is believed that this ship was sold to Japan.

# Airship Manu-facturers

*E 6*, an Astra-Torres ship reconstructed in 1936, was used at Rochefort for some time for training.

The French State Airship Factory at Chalais-Meudon operated until 1940, building a total of 11 airships for the army and the navy. The ships produced by this factory were employed most usefully by the navy for patrol, anti-submarine and convoy duties. The French naval airships, *CM 1* to *4*, were regarded as excellent, and were based in the Western Approaches during 1917 and 1918. The last four ships, CM 5 to 8

106▼

were never completed, with the exception of *CM 5* which was sold to America.

Airships constructed by the Lebaudy brothers were sold to many European countries, and the Lebaudy factory at Moisson also produced a number of craft for the French Government. Of the 12 ships built by the Lebaudy brothers, only six were taken over by the French Army and were used almost exclusively for training.

Clément-Bayard ceased to build complete airships in 1916, but constructed the cars of earlier Chalais-Meudon ships.

The most versatile airship builder in France must have been the Société Zodiac, which produced non-rigid, semi-rigid and rigid airships between 1908 and 1936. The Zodiac inventory consisted of military, naval, sporting and public relations ships, and a number of them were exported to other countries. Motorised kite-balloons were developed (*moto-ballons*) by the Société Zodiac and were employed with success on the manoeuvres of 1934. Three types of kite-balloon were developed, and the Type 3 variety were employed at the Front until 1940. The Armée de l'Air was supplied with 24 *moto-ballons*, one of which was used for publicity purposes after the war.

*V12*, the last French Naval airship, was built by the Société Zodiac and launched in 1936, serving until 1937.

106 *Pilatre de Rozier*, the 'Grand Cruiser' with a volume of 812,130 cu ft built by the Astra-Torres company, on trials at Issy in January 1915. As it proved impossible to maintain the pressure in her envelope, two smaller ships, *Pilatre de Rozier II* and *Alsace*, were built from her parts.

107 The French Army airship *Alsace* built by Astra-Torres from the parts of the *Pilatre de Rozier*. The photograph shows her on trials at Issy in August 1915. She was 295 ft (89.91 m) long and had a volume of 494,340 cu ft.

108 The Clement-Bayard 'Grand Cruiser' *Général Meusnier* on trails at Issy in October 1915 with M. Baudry at the controls. Pressure could not be maintained in the envelope so a number of modifications were made, including substituting a much longer car for the short one with booms shown in the photograph. Four 250 hp engines were placed at the extreme ends of the car, and the ballonets were constructed close to the ends of the envelope which was 526 ft (160.32 m) long. She was the last Clement-Bayard ship and was sold to the Russian Army, but crashed when coming down from an altitude test on 7 April 1917 and never flew again, and was not delivered.

109 The car of either *Alsace* or *Pilatre de Rozier II* showing the pylon-mounted tractor propeller. Powered by two 250 hp Chenu engines, they had speeds of 37 and 42 mph respectively. Both were destroyed in the war.

110 Balloon-airship officers at Toul in 1914. Standing, from left to right: De Kergarrieu; Poux; Lieutenant de Voucoux; (unknown); (unknown); Captain Dinochau; Lieutenant Périsée de Bédé (*Adjudant Vincenot*); Captain Tixier (*Fleurus*); M. Julliot; Captain Delagsus (*Adjudant Réau*); Captain Joux (*Adjudant Vincenot*). Seated, left to right. De Vigerous d'Arvieu; Captain Néant; Captain Izaud (station commander); Lieutenant Pacquingone (*Adjudant Vincenot*); Depoux (M. Julliot's assistant). The photograph was taken in front of the office of the commandant of the *Adjudant Vincenot*.

111 Général Etienne Joux as captain on board *Adjudant Vincenot* at Toul airship station.

107▲

108▼

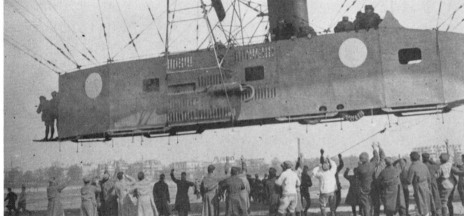

109▲

110▼

111▼

Engineer Général Joux was one of the very first French army officers to specialise in airships, and during the First World War was the most outstanding of the military pilots. After a two-year course at the Polytechnique he became a sub-lieutenant in the Engineers, and having passed out from the Engineering School at Fontainebleau (on 1 October 1909) volunteered for service with the Sapeurs Aérostiers at Versailles, qualifying for his free balloon certificate on 9 September 1909.

In 1911 he trained as an airship pilot on the Zodiac airship *Le Temps* at St Cyr, at the time Count de la Vaulx, who was then chief pilot and a director of the Société Zodiac, was then an instructor.

After qualifying as an airship pilot, Lieutenant Joux commanded *Le Temps*, and the larger Zodiac, *Captain Ferber*, and in 1912 he was put in command of the Clément Bayard Cruiser *Adjudant Vincenot*, based at Toul. He was thus able to train a very fine crew, with nearly two years to do so before the outbreak of hostilities.

Between August 1914 and October 1915, when he handed the ship over, the *Adjudant Vincenot* had carried out 29 sorties. Captain Joux was then appointed to command the big Zodiac *Champagne* at St Cyr. He flew this ship to Toul in March 1916, and together with the much smaller *Adjudant Vincenot*, took part in harrying the enemy communications in the Battle of Verdun.

Captain Joux carried out two successful sorties in *Champagne* but on 21 May while on her third sortie, the ship was shot down, making a balloon landing behind the French lines. She was salvaged and used again. He was then made Inspector of Military Airships, and carried out liaison duties with the manufacturers at Chalais-Meudon. He was also put in charge of, and had to organise a school for airship pilots at St Cyr, the old airships *Fleurus* and *Montgolfier* being used as school ships followed by the larger *Lorraine*, type *Fleurus II*.

By the summer of 1916 the army airships had to face such intense anti-aircraft fire that it became evident that their future would be with the navy, hunting U-boats, looking for mines and safeguarding convoys. A commission was formed to study the use of naval

# Engineer Général Etienne Joux

airships and kite balloons, and Captain Joux served on it. After a lot of hesitation the army airships were handed over to the navy with a number of pilots and crews in March 1917.

Captain Joux was in charge of all airship training at St Cyr, and from the summer of 1918 at Rochefort, but in November 1918, when active operations had ceased he returned to army duty, serving for a short time at Mulhouse with an Observation Balloon unit. It was then planned to use the

surrendered *LZ 120 Bodensee* on a commercial service between France and North Africa, and Captain Joux was put in charge of the planning, but nothing came of it. Then, after a period as Inspector of Civil Aerodromes, he joined the newly formed Aeronautical Engineering Service. He retired as an Engineer Général, and Director of Technical and Industrial Services on 17 October 1940, to avoid having to collaborate with the occupying power.

In July 1939, Général Joux became a Commander of the Legion of Honour, and the Aéro Club de France gave him two silver medals and one gold one for his services with airships.

The following accounts of his service in the *Le Temps*, *Captain Ferber*, *Adjudant Vincenot*, and *Champagne I* were contributed by Général Joux, and are a combination of material taken from his notes and log books. These accounts cover the majority of France's military airship operations during the First World War, and illustrate the technical experimentation with stabilising surfaces and propulsion equipment carried out at the time. The accounts indicate the bravery of the crews of the airships, when under enemy fire, while making bombing raids and reconnaissance flights over the Front Line.

| Name | Adjudant Vincenot | Le Temps | Captain Ferber | Champagne I |
|---|---|---|---|---|
| Manufacturer | Clement–Bayard | Zodiac | Zodiac | Zodiac |
| Operational | 1911–12 | 1911–13 | 1912–13 | 1916–18 |
| First flight | 6.5.11 | 15.2.11 | 6.12.11 | 21.1.16 |
| Volume, cu ft | 345,940 | 81,213 | 211,860 | 501,402 |
| Length, ft (m) | 287 (87.47) | 165 (50.29) | 249.4 (76) | 301.2 (92) |
| Diameter, ft (m) | 44.2 (13.47) | 29.6 (9) | 42.6 (13) | 52.6 (16) |
| Height, ft (m) | 74 (22.55) | — | — | 87.10 (26.54) |
| Engines | 2 × 120 hp Clement–Bayard | 1 × 165 hp Dansette–Gillet | 2 × 110 hp Dansette–Gillet | 2 × 220 hp Zodiac |
| Maximum speed, mph | 32.5 | 31 | 34.7 | 40–43 |
| Gross lift, lb | 23,529.9 | 5,522 | 14,406 | 34,095 |
| Useful lift, lb (kg) | 8,800 (3,992) | — | — | — |
| Ceiling, ft (m) | 9,735 (2,967) | — | — | 13,000 (3,963) |
| Ballonets | 2 | 2 | 2 | 2 |
| Remarks | Made 17 official flights in 1914, 12 in 1915 and 5 in 1916, over the lines | Training ship, mainly based at St Cyr. | Cruiser used for training. Not used in 1914. | Army ship taken over by French Navy in March 1918. |

Note: The above figures are taken from manufacturers' specifications The figures given in the text are quoted from operational data, and in some cases differ from the above.

# Le Temps

This airship was the first of those constructed with funds collected by the newspaper *Le Temps* after the catastrophe that befell the Lebaudy airship, *République* following the 1909 manoeuvres. It was built by the Société Zodiac, to the plans of Messrs Mallet and Spielman.

The ship was a non-rigid with a long car. The length was 166.3 ft (50.68 m) and the diameter 31.3 ft (9.54 m), the volume being 88,300 cu ft. The two ballonets had a volume of 17,650 cubic ft. The car was made of wood and was 82.5 ft (25 m) long. There was one water cooled Dansette-Gillet motor of 65 hp, driving a pair of airscrews mounted on wooden pylons. The ship's speed was between 28 and 30 mph. There was one blower, and the vertical fin and rudder were attached to the envelope. A biplane elevator, placed centrally above the car, was linked to elevating planes aft, which were not very efficient.

The trials of the ship took place at St Cyr, the private base of the Société Zodiac, the builders' crew being the pilot, the Count de la Vaulx and M. Auger, the mechanic, Lieutenant Joux, was the military receiving pilot.

The conditions stipulated that there should be one ascent to 4,290 ft (1,307 m) and one flight of five hours, for a distance of at least 87 miles (140 km), 65 miles (104.6 km) of which was to be flown at an altitude of over 2,640 ft (805 m). This inflation had been preceeded by a preliminary trial with a very porous envelope of 81,190 cu ft, with a loss of lift of 440 lb (200 kg), and the inflation with a new envelope took place on 14 June 1911.

Then began the trial flights, ending with the fourth on 4 July 1911, the duration of which was five hours, with two hours, 54 minutes above 2,640 ft (805 m), the maximum altitude being 4,399 ft (1,340 m). Aboard were Messrs de la Vaulx and Auger and myself. One of these flights was a trip to the Aerotechnical Institute of St Cyr, another a flight with a landing at St Cyr and at Issy-les-Moulineaux, and the last, a participation in the review of 14 July at St Cloud. The airship was then taken over, and I assumed the command with Adjudant Dumont as mechanic.

From this time on, there began a series of instructional flights for pupil pilots and observer officers.

On the 20th flight, which took place on 27 July 1911, the engine broke down completely when at 330 ft (100 m) above Fontenoy-le-Fleury. A landing was made in open country, and the ship was walked back to the shed. On flights 22 to 31, bomb dropping and radio experiments were carried out, and carrier pigeons were dispatched. On the 35th flight on 30 August, the blower failed, and the ship landed with a flabby envelope.

After the 39th flight on 16 August, in spite of pressing requests, no more hydrogen was available, and the ship could only be kept up to pressure by blowing air into the ballonets. Lift decreased rapidly and the airship had to be deflated.

After a fruitful series of flights at the school at St Cyr, the airship was deflated, packed up and sent to Rheims by rail. It was to be re-inflated there, so that it could be employed together with some aeroplanes for aerial reconnaissance during the manoeuvres at Verdun. But the political situation led to the government renouncing the annual *Grandes Manoeuvres* and substituting garrison manoeuvres, a mobilisation of the frontier army corps.

At Rheims, the airship was to be attached to the Aeronautical Centre commanded by a former aeronaut. In the controversy which at that time was already taking place between the supporters of airships, and those of the developing aeroplane, the commandant had already, so it would seem, secretly sided with the aeroplane.

On my arrival at Rheims I found at first no help in the way of personnel and material, and I noticed, very luckily before I began the inflation, that the portable canvas shed which had been prepared for me at Betheny was too small to hold the airship. I returned to the commandant who received me very badly, but was unable to refuse me the shed at Cormontreuil, situated about four and a half miles from the centre of Rheims. On the other hand, what he obstinately did refuse me was to transport by lorry the few soldiers I needed to complete my little team from St Cyr. These men were to sleep and eat at Rheims, and used up hours going to and fro. At the same time, the ingenious idea of experimenting with a new mobile hydrogen plant, worked by hydrolite, was decided on. This was a very clever machine invented by Captain Lelarge, which twice caught fire, but fortunately without setting fire to the airship. In spite of these incidents the airship was inflated on time and, the hydrolite plant having done its job, I was provided with a few tubes of hydrogen to maintain pressure in the airship until its departure for the base at Verdun. These tubes emptied themselves into the airship through a multiple dispenser called a *clarinette*, so that a number of tubes could be opened at the same time.

Surprising as it may seem, there was no *clarinette* at Verdun. So the commandant, who had rejoined his flying units on manoeuvres, ordered me by telegram to send him mine, on the pretext of ensuring the inflation of an airship on his return. This meant that I must leave Rheims at the earliest opportunity and whatever the weather, in an airship whose real speed did not reach 40 ft (12 m) per second.

I thus took to the air the very next day, in an increasing east-south-east wind, nearly the same speed as the airship. To reach Verdun the ship had to be steered on a course at right angles to the course made good. I had hardly reached the landing ground when a very strong rising current of air above the hill of Belleville lifted me to an altitude of 2,970 ft (905 m), from which I could only descend after an hour of prudent effort.

Now on that day no aeroplane would have dared to take to the air, and this long wait at 2,970 ft (905 m), which I would willingly have avoided, appeared to the artillery officers present in the area to be a remarkable and intentional demonstration of the unusual aptitude of an airship for making artillery observations.

It was under these conditions that several flights were made, notably the one on 17 September (45th flight) when the ship was airborne for three hours at 3,300 ft (1,000 m), and the one on 18 September (46th flight) which lasted three hours, 45 minutes, at a height of 4,230 ft (1,300 m).

Seven flights were carried out afterwards at Verdun for the training of pilots, taking photographs and so on. On 28 September 1911, the airship was deflated and stored at its Verdun base. Afterwards it was re-inflated and was commanded by other officers.

# Captain Ferber

The airship *Le Temps*, constructed by the Société Zodiac, was of the 'Scout' class. The airship *Captain Ferber*, built by the same firm under the direction of the same engineers, was of the 'Cruiser' class. The *Captain Ferber* was a non-rigid airship with a long car, 250.8 ft (76.44 m) in length, with a diameter of 41.2 ft (12.55 m). The volume was 211,860 cu ft. The car was of nickel steel and could be taken apart in five sections, and was 115.5 ft (35.2 m) in length, 6.6 ft (2 m) in height, and 3.3 ft (1 m) in width. The second and fourth sections each contained one 100 hp water-cooled Dansette-Gillet engine, each of six cylinders. Each engine drove a pair of airscrews at a normal 500 rpm. The third section of the car contained the pilot's raised control post, and a biplane elevating plane, coupled with a single elevating plane placed at the rear of the fifth section. These elevators were not very efficient, and the airship's altitude was all too often dependent, like that of a free balloon, on the gas valve and ballast. The airship was inflated by the builders at St Cyr, and left the ground for the first time on 6 December 1911. The crew numbered nine, and 880 lb (399 kg) of fuel and 2,420 lb (1,098 kg) of sand ballast were carried. By 15 February 1912, the ship had made 16 ascents. As a result of these flights Chauvière propellers were substituted for the Ratmanoff air screws, although they were 196 lb (89 kg) heavier. The speed was measured, and training flights were carried out.

The speed trial on 12 January 1912 gave the ship a full speed of just over 33 mph, and on the following day she climbed to 5,511 ft (1,680 m) and still had 363 lb (165 kg) of ballast left after landing. On 3 February a five hours' endurance flight was attempted. By some mischance the two air blowers blew in air continuously, but the height coxswain had not noticed this, and valved gas to reduce pressure. The ship started to descend, and ballast was let go forward. I realised what was happening and took over the elevators, and the airship returned to the shed without further trou-

ble. On flight number 16 on 15 February a successful endurance flight of 6 hours, 2 minutes took place. The altitude was over 4,290 ft (1,308 m), the maximum being 4,851 ft (1,478 m). About 160 miles were flown, 140 in five hours.

Having satisfied all the conditions laid down, the airship was to be handed over to a military crew, with myself in command, and Sub Lieutenant Leroy as second pilot, after a short taking-over flight. But as the airship had been ordered to take part in the Spring Review of 10 March 1912 at Vincennes, M. de la Vaulx, the Zodiac chief Pilot, seemed to want to put off this handing-over flight. I grew impatient, and assumed command on 9 March, flying it to Vincennes.

On 20 March the ship flew from St Cyr to Issy-les-Moulineaux, where it was deflated and immediately re-inflated with fresh gas to carry out a series of training and research flights. On the 30th flight, on 17 March, the ship was flown to observe the total eclipse of the sun. On board were two members of the Bureau des Longitudes, Admiral Fournier and Colonel Bourgeois. The ship took up a position 1,980 ft (603 m) above the central line. Although as already noted, the ship was difficult to control in altitude, the passage of the eclipse shadow did not affect the ship, and at 1213 hrs the observers saw the sun pass the point of the cone of the shadow.

On 21 March the ship sailed from Issy to the fortress of Toul, the crew numbering five, Commandant Alexandre and Captain Do being the passengers. The weather was very variable, stormy, with rain showers, making flying difficult and hazardous. In spite of my wish to reach my destination without unnecessary delay, Captain Do, an excellent and understanding aeronaut, planned a little detour via Villacoublay where the War Minister was carrying out an inspection. Captain Do wanted to send him his compliments, by weighted message, and he promised me that I would soon know the purpose of this procedure. I did in fact understand perfectly a few days later, when I learnt that the crew of the airship had been rewarded for the success of this flight in the person of Captain Do, nominated Chevalier of the Legion of Honour. The flight lasted 6 hours, 36 minutes, the distance covered was some 260 miles (418.43 km) and the greatest altitude attained was 4,290 ft (1,307 m).

Flying high had required, besides the

660 lb (299 kg) of petrol, 2,200 lb (998 kg) of ballast. Nothing was left on landing. Captain Do warmly supported my argument in favour of improved elevators and fins, instead of using such a quantity of ballast.

We have seen that the *Captain Ferber*, for all its good qualities, could not fly faster than 33 mph, and above all was difficult to control in altitude. In uncertain weather it used up to 660 lb (299 kg) of ballast per hour in flight. Add to this the proximity of the frontier and the particular watchfulness of the Germans, and you will see that, for every flight, I had to reserve a good quantity of ballast to make sure of returning to my base at Toul. I did not wish to expose myself to the risk of a landing in the then annexed Alsace.

On 10 May, General Joffre, Chief of the General Staff, and Colonel Hirchauer, came to Toul, in order to make a scouting flight along the frontier. Colonel Hirchauer was in command of the Military Air Service (Regiment of Aérostiers), and there were also two officers of the General Staff. The weather was hot, the rapidly falling glass foretold an approaching increase in the already established south-west wind. This was the moment, if ever there was one, to take precautions, for an accident caused by mechanical failure was always possible, which would expose me to the risk of landing Joffre and Hirchauer in Alsace!

Once the *Captain Ferber* had been ballasted up, I decided to take on board Joffre and Hirchauer, leaving the two officers on the ground. Hirchauer, very disappointed, tried for 20 minutes to make me unload some ballast or fuel. Joffre watched with amusement.

At Toul the airship continued its training flights, and took part in various manoeuvres with the 20th Army Corps. The ship flew on 21 May 1912 for the first time with the new elevating planes. These weighed 66 lb (30 kg) more than the first set, but made the airship easier to control in altitude, without however, ever making the *Captain Ferber* comparable in this respect to the *Adjudant Vincenot*. On 24 June 1912 (69th ascent) the ship was allotted to the fortress of Epinal, and flew there in 1 hour, 45 minutes, where it continued flying as before. She was deflated after the 81st flight on 14 July 1912, and was stored away at the base at Epinal. She was inflated later and continued training operations for a year.

# Adjudant Vincenot

The *Adjudant Vincenot* was the happy outcome of research by the engineer Lucien Sabathier, instigated by M. Clement-Bayard. In 1908 the Clement-Bayard factories built the mechanical part of a first airship, the *Clement-Bayard I*. In 1909 the design proposed by M. Clement-Bayard at an airship convention under the auspices of the War Ministry, was judged to be the best, and at his own expense a second airship, *Clement-Bayard II* was built, which was sent to London. The French Government then commissioned two more, *Depuy de Lôme* and *Adjudant Vincenot*. It must also be added that M. Clement-Bayard did not limit his aeronautical activities to one type of airship, or to airships alone. While the airships were being built, he put up sheds for them at Lemotte-Breuil (Compiègne) and at Issy les Moulineaux (Paris). After *Depuy de Lôme* he constructed *Montgolfier*, a very interesting small airship. M. Sabathier experimented with a new type of car, and even tried out a horizontal propeller to make the airship more manoeuvrable in altitude. The *Montgolfier* was later bought by the French Government, and made several operational ascents during the First World War, as well as a large number of instructional ascents as a school ship from 1916–18.

The *Adjudant Vincenot* had a very long car, on which were situated all the control and stabilising surfaces (none of them being on the envelope). The capacity was about 346,000 cu ft and the useful lift about 15,200 lb (6,895 kg). The two ballonets were coupled, and were at the centre of lift with a volume of 10,066 cu ft. There was a large biplane stabiliser and elevator at the centre of the car, by which elevation was controlled with great accuracy. The twin 120 hp Clement-Bayard engines gave the ship a speed of 31 mph.

The ship was much modified in July 1913. The car was cut down in length to its operative parts, and with the exception of the biplane stabiliser all the control planes were placed on the envelope. Car suspension was improved, speed was now 32.9 mph and there was a saving of weight of 880 lb (399 kg). The ship was now much more controllable. I took over the command of the ship in August 1912, and retained it until 30 October 1915.

The airship, though based at the fortress of Toul, visited the airship stations at Epinal for general training and testing searchlights, wireless and so on. Pilots and staff officer observers were put through systematic training. Visits were paid to Issy, and the airship was employed with success in the army manoeuvres of 1911 and 1913. Much of the time the ship was handicapped by the envelope which failed to keep its gas purity, pressure having to be reduced at one period from 30 to 20 mm. It was not until 1913 that a new envelope was available and the other modifications could be carried out. By August 1914 the airship had a well-trained crew, two second officers, Lieutenants Leroy and Paquignon, and Sergeant Vileroy.

## Service at the Front—seventh inflation

On 27 July 1914, when renovations were being carried out according to plan, the political situation was such that I was instructed to re-inflate the ship as soon as possible. Measures were taken immediately to obtain materials from the factory, and any improvements which might have delayed the inflation of the ship were abandoned. Congestion on the railways in August made it necessary for the materials to come by road. The airship, re-inflated, was hastily armed with two Model 1886 guns and two machine guns, against possible attack by enemy aeroplanes. The shells were not feathered, and were 155 mm in calibre, detonated by hammering a nail into a 23 second fuse. On 4 August, once Captain Gouney, a staff officer who had trained with the ship in peacetime, had joined the crew, she was ready for use. Inflation and trimming took 54 hours, and after one of these ascents, the observer officer had the heaviest part of the moveable wireless equipment taken out temporarily, in order to obtain the maximum ceiling, which on this occasion was 9,075 ft (2,766 m).

Through the staff officer observer, the ship was put under orders, first of the General Head Quarters of the Second Army, and then of the First Army, and was used on strategic and tactical reconnaissance on the army front. But because of the restrictions placed on aerial bombardments by the General-in-Command, and also because of a certain amount of hesitation by the staff officer observer, the 155 mm shells the ship carried were not used. It was only incidentally a few shells that were dropped on 23 August, on enemy camps in the forest of Vitremont, and on 9 October on the Camp des Romains which the enemy were about to occupy.

Because its speed made it difficult to provide adequate protection from enemy aircraft the ship was restricted to night flying — preferably moonlight nights. But over well-known territory, over which the ship and its observers had often flown mistakes were virtually impossible. Every billet, bivouac and forward post was clearly visible. No troop movement could escape notice; trains running without lights could not conceal the feeble but revealing glow of their engines. As for enemy reaction, there was none: a few rifle shots, which ceased the moment the enemy realised that the flashes gave their positions away; a few shells burst several miles wide of the mark, which also soon ceased, when the gunners grew tired of chasing an impossible target, and the airship returned to the shed at Toul with a few bullet holes in the envelope, not noticed until some time afterwards. Occasionally there would be a more serious tear in the envelope, usually caused by a French shell-burst. The French soldier, being rather badly informed, could not conceive of the existence of airships, other than the first Zeppelins. In general they therefore assumed our reconnaissance flares were incendiary bombs, and the low altitude of the airship on returning to its base provided the French artillery with an accurate target, which was never offered to the enemy.

In these conditions the *Adjudant Vincenot* made 17 ascents between August and October 1914, all from Toul, the most remarkable and successful of which was on 19 August, at the opening of the battle of Morhange. On this occasion the airship discovered a great concentration of men, and noticed much activity, and the extreme nervousness of the enemy in the region of Nebing-Lostroff, all of which was immediately made known to the HQ of the Second Army.

By the end of October 1914, interest was no longer centred on Lorraine or Woëvre, but on Artois. The staff officer observer returned to the army, and the airship commander asked to be allowed to take his ship to a more active theatre of the war. This permission was granted, and a portable airship shed and mobile base were set up at Crèvecoeur-le-Grand, midway between Beauvais and Amiens. After a short stay at St Cyr, the ship arrived at Crèvecoeur on 17 December. It was then immediately immobilised.

As already mentioned, our own airships had suffered more at the hands of French artillery and infantry, than from enemy fire. Repetition of these deplorable incidents caused a radical alteration in policy. An organisation was set up which would enable our airships to pass to and fro over our lines without damage, and without harming our defence against enemy aircraft. Meanwhile, however, the Commander-in-Chief had ordered the grounding of all our airships.

The crew of the *Adjudant Vincenot* profited from this enforced rest by improving its techniques and tactics. The airship, which remained inflated, was inspected and put in a state of readiness. Compass navigation was improved by means of an apparatus making use of a compass rose and a drift reader, made in the station workshops. Aachen bombs with fins were substituted for the earlier artillery Schneider shells, and a simple but effective bomb aiming device was thought out and installed. A small signalling lamp enabled the airship, when out of wireless telegraph (W/T) contact, to keep in touch with the ground. New silencers, perfected by Captain Lelarge, entirely suppressed the noise of the exhausts.

At last, on 2 April, our airships were authorised to go out again. This date, when the second period of the *Adjudant Vincenot*'s service at the front began, also marked an important development in her tactical use. To begin with, scouting flights, of less interest in this period when the fronts were becoming established, were replaced by bombing missions. Placed under the direct orders of the commanding general of the army group, the airship's commander was by and large left free to choose the most convenient target in the given atmospheric and technical circumstances. Thus, the daytime bombing flights by aeroplanes were continued in the dark by the airships, which carried a bomb load of 660 lb (300 kg) on each sortie.

However, learning from experience,

and warned by look-out posts and spies behind the lines, the enemy gradually learned to put out all tell-tale lights before the airship's approach. Also, little by little, their night-time detection of our airships improved, and they learned how to aim at them. Their fire became more accurate and prolonged, many hits being registered on each sortie.

In the end, one flew as high as possible, coming to prefer first less bright nights, and finally nights of total darkness, when flying was possible without lights. We even thought, along lines suggested by Captain Lelarge, who died early on, of putting the bomb aimer in a camouflaged cabin hanging some 3,300 ft below the airship, which would travel under cloud cover.

In particular, mention must be made of the bombardments from April to October 1915, of Valenciennes, Aulnoye, Douai, Cambrai, Tournai and so on. Important fires and explosions resulted from these missions, at the end of which it was possible to count more than a hundred holes made by enemy fire in the airship's car and envelope.

After a fruitless reconnaissance for quarries in the Marquise district, which it was hoped to use as gun sites with a view to raiding Zeebrugge, the *Adjudant Vincenot*, always with the same objective was stationed for a time in a portable shed at Arques, near St-Omer. But there it proved impossible to persuade the British authorities to work the same system of safe conducts that we had, so the airship did nothing while at St Omer. As soon as the shed at Crèvecoeur, which was being re-roofed, was ready, the airship returned there.

At the end of October the airship had been inflated for 15 months. The ripping arrangements had deteriorated, and the engines also required overhauling, so deflation was imperative and this was done at Toul. On 22 October the airship flew to Toul by day, and I handed over the command of the ship to Captain Paquignon, the Second Officer. It should be noted that after 15 months' continuous inflation the lift was still at 1,150 lb (522 kg).

## Eighth inflation, 1916
The re-inflation of the airship at Toul was postponed until the end of the winter months, which reduced the efficiency of aircraft, and at the same time halted military operations. Use was made of this

delay to stretch the envelope slightly, to perfect the electrical installations, to improve the bombing arrangements, and in a hitherto unoccupied bay in the car, to build an enclosed cabin with cupboards and a table for the commander. On re-inflation the airship had a useful lift of 8,602 lb (3,902 kg), temperature 64.5°F, pressure 29.3 in at a height above MSL of 380 ft (116 m). This was a gain of 660 lb (300 kg) above the last inflation, and the airship could now climb to 9,735 ft (2,967 m).

By now, the centre of army interest was no longer at Crèvecoeur, and because of the Battle of Verdun it was necessary for the airship to stay at Toul. It began its ascents again on 30 March 1916. Going out at the same time as the airship *Champagne* with which it shared a shed, the airship found itself faced with very powerful anti-aircraft organisation. Not a single ascent took place, but 15 to 20 guns were at once trained on the ship, which never returned to base without holes in the envelope or fuel tanks. On 1 June 1916, long immobilised above the lines by a strong head wind, it was brought down, disabled beyond repair, to the south of the trenches at Calonne, 3,120 ft (959 m) from the German lines, and there ended, with its 231st ascent, an exemplary career.

**Flight No. 169, 27 and 28 June 1914**
At the end of June 1914, a German Zeppelin established the world record for a direct flight of 34 hours, 59 minutes duration. The previous record had been made by the French airship *Adjudant Réau* in September 1912 with an ascent of 21 hours, 20 minutes. I was asked if I could beat the German record, and I was authorised to make the attempt, on condition that I made the preparations secretly, and so as not to interrupt the training of staff officer observers, I had to make the attempt during the week of 22–29 June, when no training course had been arranged. On Sunday morning the engines were stripped down for a thorough overhaul, orders were confirmed and the route studied. I had two choices. First, to fly short legs, centring on Toul for 35 hours, so as to be able to return there easily in case of damage or bad weather. This was the method of the Clement-Bayard Company in July 1911, when the *Adjudant Vincenot*, in the course of its test flights, established the original distance and duration record of

381.4 miles (614 km) in 16 hours, 30 minutes, flying the circuit, Compiègne-Soissons-Compiègne seven times. Or secondly, to establish a single closed circuit which would take 35 hours to fly given average winds, with some slight variations, the best of which could be chosen according to the circumstances prevailing during the flight. Both as a military manoeuvre and as a feat of sportsmanship this was the more interesting solution. Accordingly, the following route was mapped out: Toul-Verdun-Sedan-Mézières-Maubeuge-La Fere-Compiègne-Senlis-Paris-Versailles-Meaux-Châlons-Epinal-Belfort-Toul; with the possible variant: Châlons-Verdun-Toul, if there was a cross wind, or the engines gave trouble. This circuit, moreover, meant that there was the possibility of finding help for the airship, if necessary, at a number of airship stations: Verdun, Maubeuge, Lamotte-Breuil (near Compiègne), St Cyr (Versailles), Issy-les-Moulineaux (Paris), Camp de Châlons, Epinal and Belfort.

Another problem remained to be solved. The necessarily small crew of the airship and the trying living conditions would not allow a systematic relief of pilots and engineers. This being so, was it better for the 35 hours to comprise one day and two nights, take-off being 1800 hrs, or two days and one night, with take-off at about 0600 hrs? The first suggestion, (one day and two nights) with take-off at 1800 hrs had the advantage that the captain would be able to observe the weather throughout the whole of the day before take-off, and that his decision could then be based on his observations. Moreover, this made the piloting of the airship easier, with the calm and quiet of two nights, but it had the disadvantage that the aeronauts would take-off already very tired by a day watching the sky and tuning up the airship, so that lack of sleep would make the second night very wearing indeed. The second suggestion was therefore decided on.

On Thursday morning, 25 June, all was ready. The engines had been checked; the airship had been lightened by 198 lb (90 kg) due to the removal of the car's shock absorbers. With a light west wind, a test flight of 2 hours, 40 minutes at an altitude of 5,120 ft (1,560 m) was carried out close to Toul. Take-off was fixed for dawn on the 26th, but in the morning the sky was overcast, and there was a light ground wind of

about 18 mph. Take-off was postponed.

On the 27th, at 0600 hrs the sky was clear with a few bands of cirrus clouds to the south-west. The wind was very light and variable at all altitudes. Take-off was ordered, and the airship left Toul at 0616 hrs. On board were 594 gallons of petrol, 44 gallons of spare water, 573 lb (260 kg) of ballast, mooring-out gear and food. The altitude was fixed provisionally at 1,650 ft (503 m), 990 ft (302 m) above take-off point. Altitude would be increased as the use of fuel lightened the ship. The engines were run at the most efficient speed of 950 rpm.

To navigate the airship easily above a region which was rather turbulent at this time of day and season of the year, it would have been best to rise straight from 1,968 to 2,625 ft (600 to 800 m), but the ballast would not allow this; also the response of the airship to altitude became uncertain, so that from 0900 to 1800 hrs she was piloted by two aeronauts simultaneously, who between them worked the rudders, elevators, valves and blowers.

### 27 June
1000 hrs. Mézières. Altitude 2,130 ft (549 m). Weighted message dropped for the commandant of Toul airship station.

1250 hrs. Maubeuge. Message dropped on Maubeuge airship station.

1530 hrs. Compiègne. Altitude a little more steady.

1640 hrs. Senlis. Two radio messages despatched.

1645 hrs. Paris at an altitude of 2,620 ft (798 m). Flew over St Cyr airship base, and Issy-les-Moulineaux where news of the airship was dropped by weighted message.

1830 hrs. Charenton-le-Point. Changed course to east. With dusk a strong north wind blew up at the altitude at which the airship was flying, and slowed it down considerably. To avoid the wind the airship descended to 1,650 ft (503 m).

1915 hrs. Lagny. Since the engines had been working non-stop for 13 hours, it was decided to profit from the night, when flying was very steady, to rest the two engines turn and turn about. This would cool the bearings and the plugs could be cleaned, and so on. The airship seemed very steady, so the port engine was stopped. On one engine the airship remained almost motionless, head to wind. The chill of nightfall gradually

112▲

112 The Zodiac training airship *Le Temps* was operational from 1911 until 1914 being mainly based at St Cyr. She was eventually removed from the operational list in 1914.

made itself felt, and after some minutes the airship began to descend slowly. Five of the 13 bags of ballast were sacrificed, and as weight was being lost through the burning of petrol, the airship stabilised at 1,056 ft (322 m).

1950 hrs. Still at Lagny. The port engine was being cleaned with all plugs removed. The starboard engine suddenly began to misfire, with such strong vibration that the transmission was endangered. This had to be stopped at once. The airship was without engines for some minutes, and turned towards the south-west and began to descend. As the eight remaining bags of ballast had to be kept for landing, all the empty petrol and oil tins were thrown overboard, to the great alarm of the passers-by on the Saint-Thibaut road, who hastily took cover from unexpected bombardment. The airship attained equilibrium at an altitude of 594 ft (181 m) above MSL, 178 ft (54.25 m) from the ground.

2005 hrs. Altitude 1,650 ft (503 m). The starboard engine was stopped for five minutes to replace a broken fan belt. This stoppage allowed the ship to be ballasted up, and she was then in perfect equilibrium.

2035 hrs. The cooling effect of dusk was now at an end. The port engine was stopped in order to rest it, and also to continue the check interrupted half an hour earlier. The flight continued uneventfully on one engine. The airship was easy to control and the pilots, one by one, were able to take a short rest in the rear part of the car. The night was very dark and moonless.

### 28 June
0167 hrs. Dormans.

0225 hrs. Port engine restarted, and the starboard engine rested.

113▲

113 *Adjudant Vincenot*, constructed by Clement-Bayard for the French Army. On 27 and 28 June 1914 she established an endurance record of 35 hours, 19 minutes for non-rigids. On this occasion she was piloted by Captain Joux, who made a total of 29 operational flights in her. She was later commanded by Captain Paquignon who took her out on five operational flights.

114▼

114 The car of *Adjudant Vincenot* after reconstruction, on which the propellers can be seen, which were driven by two 120 hp Clement-Bayard engines. Her maximum speed was about 32 mph. When she was modified in 1913, the car was shortened and the planes were fixed to the envelope.

0330 hrs. Châlons-sur-Marne. The airship headed into a north wind at an altitude of 1,650 ft (503 m), remaining motionless over the town for 30 minutes. As it was by no means certain that the wind speed would decrease after sunrise, it was decided to vary the route, and to choose instead of the one provisionally planned, the new route of Vouziers-Stenay-Montmédy, etc.

0400 hrs. The record flight of the *Adjudant Réau* was broken; the airship's commander sent off a wireless message on behalf of the crew. The rising sun superheated the gas, so that the ship began to rise again, which it was allowed to do, little by little. The higher the airship went, the easier navigation became.

1525 hrs. Commercy. A wide turn around Woëvre. The descent began slowly, and more rapidly as the airship approached Toul at 1715 hours.

1715 hrs. 34 hours, 59 minutes flight. The record was broken.

1735 hrs. Uneventful landing. Petrol remaining on landing, 78 gallons. Oil remaining on landing, 30 gallons. Ballast remaining on landing, 353 lb (160 kg). The total duration of the ascent was 35 hours, 19 minutes, non-stop in a closed circuit. The distance covered was 767.2 miles (1,234.69 km) at a maximum altitude of 6,105 ft (1,860 m). The airship needed nothing beyond a general clean down after landing, and on 1 July training flights began again.

**Flight No. 231, 1 June 1916**
In accordance with orders, the airship took off from Toul on the evening of 1/2 June 1916, to bomb Damvillers railway station. In the absence of one of the regular pilots, the only officer on board was the airship's captain. On take-off the airship carried 30 bombs (660 lb/ 300 kg), 4,586 lb (2,080 kg) of ballast, 154 gallons of petrol and 17.5 gallons of oil. The wind was weak and variable at all altitudes and the barometer was low; there was a slight mist in the valleys; an east wind of 7 to 13 mph was forecast.

The ship ascended at 2040 hrs and flew by compass over Ligny-en-Barrois to remain in the authorised air corridor. From Ligny, a compass course was steered to Verdun, rising gradually to cross the front lines at the prescribed safety height of 8,250 ft (2,514.60 m). As the ship

travelled north, the ground mist became thicker and at the same time the wind rose, increasing with altitude and blowing from the west. When the airship was level with Saint-Mihiel course was altered to head for Verdun, then the lines to the north of the city were crossed. Because of the thickening of the ground mist precise identification of the target was impossible. The front could be seen clearly enough for it was lit up by flares, and on the enemy side of the lines, by lights showing quarters, billets and ammunition dumps. A mobile search-light beamed on to the airship, blinding the pilots. Two salvoes of five bombs were dropped, and the searchlight was turned off. It was not put on again until the airship had moved off some miles, but meanwhile, enemy guns had opened fire on the airship. The 20 remaining bombs were dropped at once on what appeared to be the most concentrated group of enemy artillery, thus starting a large and very persistent fire. The airship, now lightened, rose to 9,735 ft (2,967 m), where it struggled against the west wind to reach friendly territory. The estimated speed could not have been more than 12.4 mph. Enemy fire could therefore be directed more easily against the airship,

and the shells came closer and closer, until finally it was hit and began to descend.

It was decided to let the airship drop some hundreds of yards to find less wind, so that a more rapid escape from enemy fire might be made. To bring the airship into equilibrium, 220 lb (100 kg) of sand ballast and 176 lb (80 kg) of reserve water were used up. When the lines were crossed there were still 44 gallons of petrol in cans, as well as equipment, spare parts and armament, which it was intended to throw out to ease the descent. Suddenly, no doubt as the result of a more serious hit, the internal pressure in the envelope fell to zero, and the airship folded up into a kind of V, and began to fall rapidly. It was now impossible to steer the ship, and the chief engineer was ordered to declutch the propellers. Without these, the ship began to drift towards the German lines. The airship's captain then decided to speed up the descent by ceasing to drop ballast, and by valving gas, but at about 5,280 ft (1,609 m) the envelope collapsed, becoming Z-shaped. It heeled over to starboard, and the deck became vertical. The aeronauts had to cling to the port side to save themselves from falling. It was now impossible to

Camp de Châlons — Le Dirigeable Militaire " *Capitaine Ferber* " - Le Lâchez tout

retain proper command, and two of the aeronauts, misunderstanding the captain's orders, jumped by parachute, landing unhurt. Meanwhile, the chief engineer managed to stop the port engine, but could not stop the other and it caught fire just as the car plunged into the tree tops of the Senoux ravine, near Mouilly. He remained at his post and put out the fire with an extinguisher. Sergeant Legrand, however, perched at the back of the car, was thrown out by the impact and seriously injured his spine. As soon as possible he was taken to the first aid post at Mouilly, and then to Toul by car. The rest of the crew were unhurt.

The airship's commander, emerging from the wreckage, decided to destroy all the useless parts of the airship as quickly as possible so that the enemy should not know of its loss. The envelope was already badly ripped by its fall among the trees. All the gas was let out, and then it was torn into smaller pieces and spread about. The fins and planes, the frames of which were bent, were covered with branches until they could be salvaged. This operation was uninterrupted except for a few shots fired by the enemy between 0400 and 0500 hrs. Two enemy scouts, which flew over between 0700 and 0800 hrs, obviously noticed nothing for their departure was not followed by any German activity. In the course of the day the engine, rigging and instruments were salvaged and taken back to the airship station at Toul. The car, completely useless, was left where it was. The career of the *Adjudant Vincenot* was thus brought to an end with its 231st flight.

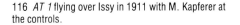

115 Captain Ferber, the Zodiac-built cruiser, photograph ascending at Camp de Châlons just after the order to 'let go' was given.

116 *AT 1* flying over Issy in 1911 with M. Kapferer at the controls.

116▲

117▼

117 *AT 1*, one of the first French Navy airships and the first Astra-Torres service airship. She was one of a class of four (*AT 1* to *AT 4*) built by Astra-Torres in 1916. Their general characteristics were the same: length 223 ft (67.97 m), diameter 44.5 ft (13.56 m), and volume 229,515 cu ft. Two 150 hp Renault engines, gave a top speed of 50 mph.

# Champagne I

In 1912, Chalais-Meudon submitted to the airship manufacturers a programme of very large non-rigid cruisers. These 'Grand Cruisers' were still not ready in 1914. Generally speaking their volume was a little over 800,000 cu ft and their envelopes had a high aspect ratio. The engines were situated inside the cars, which numbered up to three. With the exception of the Lebaudy *Tissandier*, which in any case was a write off, the construction of the others was only just under way in August 1914. Engine running promised to be difficult, and the gravest doubts existed as to whether the long envelopes with their small diameter would stand up to the torsional loads caused by tight turns. The Astra ship *Pilatre de Rozier*, which had two cars, landed after her second flight with the envelope badly distorted. The twin car Zodiac *D'Arlandes*, which was still not ready, never flew, and it was hurriedly decided to replace these ships by more orthodox and less ambitious cruisers. So the Zodiac and Astra 'Grand Cruisers' led to the birth of two airships each, with one short car, and two engines and propellers. The *Champagne* and *D'Arlandes*, sister ships, were Zodiacs.

## Envelope, flying controls and car

The airships were non-rigid, of orthodox type and had a well-designed envelope. During re-inflation in 1916, the yellow envelope fabric was replaced by dark blue, which was less visible at night. As in all Zodiac airships there was a well-designed vertical stabilising fin and a directional rudder attached to the envelope. The horizontal tail unit and elevating planes were also attached to the envelope. These were of insufficient area, an inherent shortcoming of the Zodiac airships from which I had already suffered when in command of *Le Temps* in 1911, and *Captain Ferber* in 1912. There were no planes located over the centre of the car. When flying by night or over the sea, altitude control was sufficient, but difficult by day in poor weather, making it necessary to use ballast and valve gas. The car was well conceived, and was

21.1 ft (6.43 m) in length and double-decked in the bows. On top there was a control position for the commander, pilots and bomb aimer. Below there was a closed cabin with small port holes forming a room for charts, radio and water ballast. Aft was a single deck with the two engines, blowers and petrol tanks. The bombs were at the centre of lift. Car suspension consisted of a bridge cable of large diameter girdling the car and serving as a link between the points of suspension. These were divided into four bridles of fixed sheaves. The car was slung from the bridge cable which supported it like the roadway of a suspension bridge. The advantages were that the load imposed on the car was reduced. The car retained its general shape and position when pressure fell (*see* flight of 21 May 1916). Under similar circumstances a long framed car, typical of the *Adjudant Vincenot* class, assumed a Z form, and then became displaced laterally, its deck becoming vertical (*see Adjudant Vincenot's* flight of 1 June 1916). The disadvantages were that when the ballonets were full of air and the ship pitched there was a tendency for the car to swing about the axis of two of the bridles. If the ship was flying nose down, this could be curbed by the elevators, but if she was up by the bows, control was sluggish, and the ship became uncontrollable. There was no complete remedy for this with these Zodiacs. The *D'Arlandes* for example, after a prolonged mooring out in the open had to be deflated on site, as all attempts to fly the ship back to base proved too hazardous. On my recommendation airships of this type were equipped with a machine gun platform on top of the ship, and about 60 ft (18 m) from the bow. The top gunner could communicate with the ship's captain by telegraph and lamp signalling, the telephone loudspeakers having proved unsatisfactory. The interconnecting cable had been specially developed to reduce the risk of fire when the radio was in use. The machine gunner could re-enter the car by sliding along a stout rope to which he was connected by a sliding link. He was also equipped with a parachute. Finally, an anti-flame guard had been specially designed and installed so that there was no fire danger when the top gun was being fired. I supervised the satisfactory functioning of all these systems personally, during a day flight from Toul to Epinal on board the

Astra *Pilatre de Rozier* on 9 November 1916. The gun turret reduced the ship's speed by less than $1\frac{1}{2}$ mph.

*Champagne* was 501,402 cu ft in volume; her length was 301.2 ft (92 m), diameter 52.6 ft (16 m) and height 87.10 ft (26.54 m). She had two ballonets, which gave her a maximum ceiling of approximately 14,000 ft (4,267 m), and two 220 hp Zodiac engines gave the ship a maximum speed of 42 mph. Armament consisted of one machine gun on the top platform, two other machine guns in the car with one large calibre rifle with 120 rounds of tracer ammunition. Five reconnaissance flares were also carried together with 2,860 lb (1,297 kg) of light and heavy bombs. Two dual parachutes were also carried.

*Champagne* made her first flight on 25 January 1916 at St Cyr. She was attached to the land front from 30 March 1916 to 24 February 1917, then transferred to the Naval Airship Service and was based at Corfu under Captain Larrieu. From there she carried out many anti-submarine flights. Seventeen flights were carried out in *Champagne* from January 1916 to February 1917. Flights one to eight were trial flights at St Cyr, and 9 to 15 were a combination of radio, searchlight and machine gun training flights. However, three of these flights were raids on the enemy lines. The airship which up to this time had been commanded by Captain Joux, now came under the command of Captain Larrieu, who carried out two night flights from Toul, the first on 27 December 1916 to raid the factories at Hagondange, and the second to raid Briey on 23/24 February 1917.

## Operations

The eleventh flight took place on 24/25 April 1916. The purpose of this sortie was to carry out a bombing raid over the enemy lines at Souilly. Six searchlights sought the airship as it crossed the lines. One or two in the region of Thiacourt found it and held it for about 15 minutes, during which time it was attacked by cannon fire. It was to be the same on our return. Thanks to the searchlight at Conflans going out just as we arrived, bombing was carried out without difficulty. After landing, the airship was examined for damage but did not appear to have been hit. The duration of this flight was four hours, 35 minutes at a maximum altitude of 12,540 ft (3,820 m).

The objective of the next flight on 26/27 April 1916 was a raid on Longuyon. Near Saint-Benoît the airship *Adjudant Vincenot* was observed, illuminated by three searchlights, and being heavily attacked by ground artillery. At 2200 hours our ship was simultaneously illuminated by searchlights and violently attacked by anti-aircraft fire at Marcheville. The airship had obviously been expected. The searchlights were not lit, nor did the artillery let loose until the airship was in a good position for attack. The systematic firing which followed was extremely accurate. At 2215 hrs, while over Etain, pressure inside the envelope fell suddenly: the ship had been hit. It was completely enveloped in explosions of increasing intensity. To avoid a forced descent behind the enemy lines it was imperative to turn back and gain height. We dropped 2,640 lb (1,197.48 kg) of explosives on the battery which was attacking us, rose to 13,860 ft (4,225 m) and returned, without further damage, to the shed, in spite of several guns continuing to fire at us. On landing we found that the envelope had been holed, once forward and twice aft.

**Flight No. 15, 21 May 1916**
The mission of flight No. 15 on 21 May 1916 was to liaise with the airship *Adjudant Vincenot* in the bombing of Dun-sur-Meuse and Brieulles. We crossed the lines at 2150 hrs, at 8,910 ft (2,716 m). The *Adjudant Vincenot* was sighted at Blercourt in the direction of Brieulles. It was brilliantly illuminated and under heavy fire. Our course was eastward of Brieulles, and we were soon found and lit up by 19 searchlights at once, making navigation very difficult.

The enemy launched some parachute incendiary grapeshot at us, and the ground below was brightly illuminated. We bombed Brieulles railway station accurately where we could detect the movement of rolling stock, and a big fire fed by continual explosions could be seen. Two more searchlights joined the other 19, and the adjoining batteries attacked the airship. The firing, although sustained, was unlike that of 27 April, and was far from accurate: the enemy undoubtedly assuming that the *Champagne* was at the same height as the *Adjudant Vincenot*, and fired too low. The maximum height of the explosions was 1,650 ft (505 m) below the ship which was then flying at 12,110 ft (3,690 m). The chief danger which menaced us was the incendiary buckshot through which we were compelled to navigate. We managed to avoid it and were just crossing the

lines at 2230 hrs when two isolated shots exploded just forward and aft of the ship. Pressure inside the envelope fell and the ship began to descend. We let go the emergency water, sand ballast and petrol, but fell to 6,600 ft (2,012 m) with controls set for climbing and pressure below 20 mm. The rate of descent increased and we threw overboard tools and accessories, but to no avail. At 5,940 ft (1,810 m) pressure was down to zero. The fore and aft of the envelope rose, the car canting over slightly as its bow and stern rose. We stopped the engines, and the top gunner parachuted out, fearing that he would be caught in the collapsing envelope. At 2,145 ft (654 m) the ship was extremely down by the bows, and we held on grimly. By virtue of a temperature inversion striking the night air, the descent slowed down a little and the airship landed finally on the trees of the Tilley wood, near to St Benoît and Vaux. The larger branches were snapped off, and acting like a large shock absorber, broke the descent. The ship touched down without personal injury, or too much material damage, except for the ship's commander, who had a slightly sprained ankle. We were greeted on the ground by the top gunner several minutes after. The ship was deflated on site.

From March 1918 *Champagne* was operated by the French Navy, and ended her active service later that year.

118 *Champagne* at Toul in May 1916. She was constructed, together with *D'Arlandes*, from the parts of a 'Grand Cruiser' which never flew, and was eventually taken over by the French Navy in March 1918. She was constructed by the Zodiac company, and was powered by two 220 hp Zodiac engines, which gave her a maximum speed of 42 mph. The dorsal gun position can be seen on top of the envelope, in the photograph. This platform was reached by the gunner climbing from the car and up through a canvas tube extending from the bottom to the top of the envelope.

# Italy

The following notes on Italian airships were contributed by the late Colonel Tito Tombesi for use in this book. They were translated by Wing Commander J. N. Fletcher, AFC. Colonel Tombesi's war services date from the First World War, in which he served as a second lieutenant in a medium battery. He was awarded two decorations for military valour. After a short spell of

### Early Days
The story of Italian aeronautics follows a pattern exactly similar to that of France and Great Britain, and a brief outline is related below. In 1905 an airship, *Italia 1*, designed and built by Count Almerigo da Schio at his own expense made a number of flights in and around the aerodrome, returning always successfully to its point of departure, therefore making it truly *dirigible*. The characteristics of this ship which ensured its success were the aerofoils (rudders and elevators), and the expanding envelope. In general appearance this ship nearly resembles an early British *Gamma*, but carries the aerofoils in the bows and stern of the car. Illustrations of the *Italia 1* show no ballonet.

In the next decade two competing designs were developed, the Forlanini and the P type. The designers of the P type airships were Messrs Usuelli, Crocco and Munari. This semi-rigid design became the choice of the military school, and the Forlanini was relegated to civil use.

A military balloon service had been formed in 1884, and took part in the Eritrean Campaign of 1887–88. The company had three balloons and, in four months of active service, made many ascents, observing the front line, lines of communication and troop movements.

Military airships made their first appearance in 1911 in army manoeuvres. One of the objects of the manoeuvres was to ascertain whether aircraft, both lighter- and heavier-than-air, had any useful part to play in military operations. Weather conditions were consistently adverse throughout the period. Two airships, *P 1* and *P 2*, were placed at the disposal of the chief umpire and made

# The Development of the Military Airship Service

successful reconnaissances by day and by night. In the second phase, one airship was allotted to each army and each succeeded in gaining useful information, which certainly justified the employment of airships in the imminent expedition to Tripoli in operations against the Turks.

The two airships, *P 2* and *P 3*, joined later by *P 1*, were based at Tripoli and Benghazi, and were used to find and bomb enemy concentrations, to intercept camel-trains, and to strike the principal Turk and Arab bases. On 19 March 1912, *P 3* bombed Zanzur and reconnoitred the enemy camp Suani-Beni-Adem from 4,000 ft (1,250 m). *P 2* and *P 3* were both so damaged by rifle fire that their return to base was endangered.

The following month photographic reconnaissances were carried out, and *P 2* and *P 3* made a long flight in bad weather to reconnoitre the zone in which it was planned to disembark a fresh division. *P 1*, based on Benghazi, became operational on 29 May, and remained so until 12 July, being used for incendiary bombing and night reconnaissance.

Experiments were carried out, with some success, in the detection of submarine mines and their destruction by bombing. Kite balloons were used for artillery observation, one being moored

duty in Tripolitania towards the end of the war, he returned to Italy to take a course for airship pilots, and took part in many flights in semi-rigids. He ended up as second in command of the rigid airship *Esperia* (ex-*Bodensee*). When airships were abandoned as serving no further military purpose, Colonel Tombesi converted to heavier-than-air craft.

to the hulk of a brigantine and another to a motor-driven winch. These activities, often carried out under fire, earned the commendation of the C-in-C.

### The First World War
Before the outbreak of war certain principles governing the employment of airships, based upon experience gained in Libya, had been established: it was concluded that lighter-than-air craft could be used effectively against communications, depots, HQ concentrations, and such targets as magazines, troop-trains, etc.; in effect in any zone where intense anti-aircraft opposition was not to be expected. At the onset there were four airship bases, Venice and Verona for military airships, Ferrara and Iesi for naval airships. Three semi-rigid airship types were in effective use: the M, P and V (*see* table opposite).

Every effort was made to use these ships effectively. On the night of 25/26 May 1915, *P 4* and *P 5* attempted to bomb Pola but were unable to penetrate the defences. On 27 May, *M* bombed the Trieste-Nabresina railway, the Trieste Technical Establishment and the San Marco shipyards in spite of unfavourable weather. Between May and November 1915 these ships effected 18 sorties while, on the part of the navy, *P 4*, *M 2* and *V 1* carried out a further 14. *M 4* was shot down in flames at Gorizia in 1916.

In 1917 an improved M type came into service with a maximum ceiling of 15,420 ft (4,700 m) and a useful load of 2,684 lb (1,217 kg) at 13,124 ft (4,000 m) and 7,370 lb (3,343 kg) at 6,562 ft (2,000 m). Enemy resistance, however, became more efficient, and *M 3* was so badly holed by gunfire that a forced landing away from base resulted in her entire destruction; while *M 10*, on the same night, also reported many holes in her envelope. On 23 July 1917, *M 2* was so badly shot up that she came down in the sea with the loss of three officers out of the crew of six. From February to July 1917, 18 successful sorties are recorded. In September 1917 three ships, *M 1*, *M 10* and *M 14*, made a simultaneous attack on Proseccio. *M 10* was hit, forced to land away from home and was deflated. In this incident, Lieutenant Castruccio climbed from the car into the housing under the envelope and from there to the forward ballonet. Then he crawled to the mooring-point, where he remained for one and a half hours in an attempt to trim the ship. For this gallant action he was awarded the *Medaglia d'Oro* (equivalent to the Victoria Cross). In four nights, four ships made seven sorties. In November, in spite of bad weather and increasing distances in the front line, two ships made 21 sorties, and dropped 21 tons of high explosives on targets.

In 1918, apart from continuous activity in difficult conditions, *M 11* and *M 14* were caught in fog during their return from a night action, and were forced to land away from base. Forlanini *F 5* and *F 6* came into service and were based on Milan. In one sortie they attacked the distant objective of Fucine in the Val di Sole, and dropped 882 lb (400 kg) of bombs from a height of 13,123 ft (4,000 m).

After the Armistice of 4 November 1918, the airships were used to drop flowers over liberated cities. Between the outbreak of hostilities and the Armistice, army airships made 197 sorties, and dropped 133 tons of bombs and 32 tons of manifestos. Naval airships made 1,355 scouting flights, covering a total distance of 157,000 miles (252,563 km). Seven large and 17 small naval airships were used chiefly for naval reconnaissance. In all, casualties amounted to 12 airships lost, 13 men killed and 10 captured.

## Post-war airships

Existing Italian airships of M and F types were rebuilt for passenger-carrying purposes. Mooring-mast experiments were made and a missile called a 'tele-bomb' was tried out. Flights for VIPs and photography took place. In the years preceding the North Pole flights, many small and medium-sized airships were

## Tables

In summary it can be said that Italy entered the war with the semi-rigid type of airship, which became the standard for all Italian-built airships constituting the nucleus of the Italian navy's lighter-than-air fleet during the period of hostilities. A few non-rigid airships of small cubic capacity, such as the *SS AW 27* and the *SS AWs 40* to *47*, which were purchased from Great Britain, were also in service, as were an unspecified number of motorised kite-balloons. The bombing airships were distinguished by the letters P, M, F2, V and A, according to their characteristics, and the scouting types were designated DE, PV, O and U. The increase in airship and balloon production necessitated a corresponding increase in the development of the system of aerodromes, and a total of 27 were in existence at the date of the Armistice.

The tables were compiled from official Italian navy sources, and show the development of airship and balloon construction, the causes of airship and balloon losses during the war, and the increase in the establishments at Italian aerodromes between 1915 and 1918. As a matter of interest a table showing the numbers of sorties carried out against Italian naval seagoing craft by Austrian airships is included here. Some of the official figures are at variance with each other, mainly because official navy and army statisticians differ on which facts to include in their statistics and which to exclude. Also smaller dirigibles such as the motorised kite-balloons are included, in some cases, in the figures for observation balloons and not in the ones for airships.

## Comparative data for Italian M, P and V type airships

| Class | Capacity | Length | Engines | Maximum Ceiling | Useful load at 6,562 ft (2,000 m) |
|---|---|---|---|---|---|
| M | 441,250 cu ft (12,495 cu m) | 264.04 ft (80.48 m) | Two 180 hp Itala D.1, four-blade variable pitch propellers | 12,150 ft (370 m) | 5,170 lb (2,345 kg) |
| P | 176,500 cu ft (4,988 cu m) | 203.42 ft (62.002 m) | Two 70 hp Fiat S54, four-blade variable pitch propellers | 6,880 ft (2,097 m) | 572 lb (260 kg) |
| V | 553,210 cu ft (15,665 cu m) | 287.08 ft (87.50 m) | Four 180 hp Itala D1, two-blade variable pitch propellers | 8,850 ft (2,698 m) | 3,322 ft (1,507 kg) |

## Italian airships and balloons in service from the beginning of the First World War to the time of the Armistice

| | Bombing airships | Scouting airships | Captive observation balloons | Barrage balloons |
|---|---|---|---|---|
| Ready when war began | 3 | — | 2 | — |
| Built or assigned to the Italian Navy in | | | | |
| 1915 | 1 | — | 1 | 150 |
| 1916 | 3 | 7 | 3 | — |
| 1917 | 2 | 11 | 6 | — |
| 1918 | 4 | 18 | 4 | — |
| Totals up to the Armistice | 13 | 36 | 16 | 150 |

## Italian airship and balloon losses

| Cause | Bombing airships | Scouting airships | Captive observation balloons |
|---|---|---|---|
| Lost in action | 3 | — | 2 |
| Lost by attacks on hangar | 2 | — | — |
| Lost by accident | 1 | 1 | — |
| Laid up before Armistice | 1 | 22 | 1 |
| Transferred to the Italian Army | — | 1 | — |
| Transferred from bombing to scouting service | 3 | — | — |
| Efficient at time of Armistice | 3 | 12 | 13 |

built for foreign customers, including Japan. The Norwegian Government commissioned the building of the semi-rigid airship *Norge* (airship *N1*), which, in 1926, carried Amundsen, Ellsworth and Nobile across the North Pole to Nome in Alaska, where she was dismantled.

[Testament to the trials and triumphs of the expedition can be found in the chapter on Norway in this book, in which the late Major General H. Riiser-Larsen tells his own story of the flight of *Norge* across the North Pole.]

Two years later the second polar expedition was launched, using the car of *Norge*. The ship was called *Italia*, and was manned wholly by Italian personnel under the command of Nobile, and reached the Pole. On its return it made a forced landing, and many of the crew were lost (*q.v.*). With this sad incident, the history of Italian airships ends.

**Attacks by Austrian airships on Italian naval units at sea**

| Type of vessel | 1915 | 1916 | 1917 | 1918 | Totals |
|---|---|---|---|---|---|
| Battleships and monitors | 3 | — | 13 | — | 16 |
| Scouts | 6 | — | 2 | — | 8 |
| Torpedo boats | 11 | 81 | 39 | 13 | 144 |
| Submarines | 7 | 43 | 1 | 9 | 60 |
| Auxiliaries | 3 | 15 | 7 | — | 25 |
| General totals | 30 | 139 | 62 | 22 | 253 |

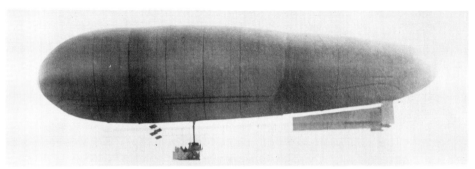

119▲

120▲

119 Messrs Usuelli and Borsalino built two semi-rigid airships, one in 1910 (volume of 135,000 cu ft), and one early in the First World War (volume of 141,200 cu ft). The first, badly damaged in 1913, was 167.35 ft (51 m) long, and had one 100 hp engine and a speed of 31 mph. The second, used for anti-submarine work, was 180.33 ft (54.96 m) long, had a useful lift of 4,136 lb (1,876 kg), and was powered by two Fiat-Colombo engines that gave it speed of 46 mph.

120 *M 1*, the prototype of the Italian semi-rigid M class, was built by the State aeronautical construction concern, the Stabilimento di Costruzioni Aeronautiche. *M 1* had a volume of 441,375 cu ft, a length of 271.25 ft (8.67 m) and a diameter of 55 ft (16.76 m). Powered by two 250 hp Fiat engines, *M 1* was launched in 1912. The two stabilising planes can be seen above the forward part of the car.

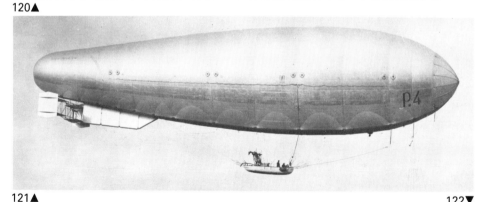

121▲                                                                    122▼

121 The Italian *P 4*, built in 1912, was one of a highly successful class of semi-rigids (*P 4* to *P 6*) built by the Stabilimento di Costruzioni Aeronautiche for the Italian Army. This class had a speed of just over 40 mph.

122 A V class non-rigid constructed by the Stabilimento di Costruzioni Aeronautiche in 1915. The ships had a speed of 51 mph, and so were regarded as particularly good night bombing aircraft. Their useful lift was 12,532 lb (5,685 kg) and weight empty 26,014 lb (11,800 kg). Only two of this class were built, *V 1* and *V 2*; the former was lost in action in 1915. The machine gun position can be seen on top of the envelope, as well as the long dorsal control surface on the tail.

# Active Italian airship personnel attached to aerodromes

| Date | Naval | | | | | Military | | | | | General total |
|---|---|---|---|---|---|---|---|---|---|---|---|
| | Officers | | Men | | Total | Officers | | Men | | Total | |
| | Pilots | Ground staff | Aircrew | Ground staff | | Pilots | Ground staff | Aircrew | Ground staff | | |
| 25 May 1915 | 6 | 1 | 14 | 225 | 246 | 3 | — | 2 | — | 5 | 251 |
| 1 January 1916 | 1 | 4 | 12 | 380 | 407 | 3 | — | 1 | — | 4 | 411 |
| 1 January 1917 | 21 | 6 | 44 | 735 | 806 | 2 | 7 | 2 | 4 | 15 | 821 |
| 1 January 1918 | 23 | 7 | 60 | 1,150 | 1,240 | 45 | 9 | 30 | 410 | 494 | 1,734 |
| 4 November 1918 | 23 | 9 | 73 | 952 | 1,057 | 66 | 20 | 54 | 1,366 | 1,506 | 2,563 |

**Note:** The figures show all pilots, flight service personnel, ground staff and establishment personnel on the official Italian lists on the dates shown in the table.

123▲

123 *M 6*, the improved M class semi-rigid built by the Stabilimento di Costruzioni Aeronautiche, like the other 19 of its type had two 180 hp Itala D 1 engines that drove her at about 42 mph. The stern of the car shows beneath the rigid keel of the ship, its scale apparent from the man standing on the shed's floor and the man in the car.

124▲

125▼

124/125 Port and starboard sides of *M 6's* car. In the top photograph the gunner is looking through the sights of his weapon, situated near the ballast sacks on the left. The pylon mounted pusher propellers and their shaft drive are particularly clear. Note how the engine exhausts point downwards towards the stern, a sensible arrangement considering the flammability of the hydrogen in the envelope.

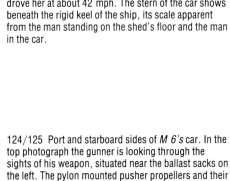

The Zeppelin *Bodensee* (*LZ 120*) was built for the German airship transport company, Deutsche Luftschiffahrts-Aktien-Gesellschaft (DELAG), and launched in 1919. She was sent to Italy in 1920 as a part of the German war reparations to the Allies, where she was renamed *Esperia* and used until 1925 by the Italian military air services, including some time as a luxury passenger airship. She was eventually broken up — an ignominious end for such

*Esperia*, (ex-*Bodensee*), was large, lovely to look upon, and luxuriously fitted to carry wealthy passengers. Having just gained my wings, I was familiar only with small semi-rigid ships, in which there was no shelter from the wind of passage, often no small inconvenience. This appointment as height cox and navigator, although filling me with pride, caused my brain to whirl and my heart to throb.

The ship was scheduled for a night flight to Tripoli. I had only just qualified as an airship officer and I was to take part, for the first time, in a long flight in a ship expressly designed for civil use, with not less than 50 passengers, senior soldiers, politicians and industrialists.

Now that the ingenuity and audacity of man has accomplished unheard-of feats of height, speed and distance, it may seem strange to talk of a flight that took place in 1925. The time is 2000 hrs. The sun dips far off in the crimsoned sea, and an incredible sky hangs over the waters and the lovely, historic Campagna Romana in which the airship shed, with its airship awaiting its captain's orders, dominates the surroundings. I am at the elevators, while an old sailor has the helm. In the after-cabin the passengers have silently taken their places, their attitude betraying the fact that most of them have never flown in such a craft. 'Start up engines,' orders the captain, and as the four engines tick over the airship leaves the ground. My eyes are glued to the statoscope whose red liquid shows the speed of ascent. In a night ascent there is a risk of inversion of temperature, and if the ship gets into a layer of warm air, the lift will diminish and ballast may have to be dropped. On this occasion nothing of the sort happened, and the ship, rising above its hangar, turned silently and swiftly towards a distant star, the only one to brighten the sky. In silent ecstasy the passengers watched the lovely spectacle.

# Colonel Tito Tombesi's First Flight as No. 1 of Esperia

The ship moved in a lunar splendour, creating in me a sense of pride and power. The strange music that reached my ears was the rumble of the engines, and the ship obeyed the least touch on its two helms. We soon reached the coast and found the sea deserted as we moved with the coast-line on our port hand. At a height of 300 m the lunar reflections on the sea's huge mirror were strangely irridescent. The crew was working in complete harmony. The navigator dropped a flare every half hour to check the drift, and on the waters the flares burned like a will-o'-the-wisp. Far ahead lights showed a mountainous land, and soon, a cluster of lights revealed Sicily. We flew past at a low height and entered into the vastness of the Mediterranean.

When my longing to qualify as an airship pilot had been satisfied, fantasy no longer amused me so much. Thinking over the thrill of a night flight in a great ship, as we ventured over open sea, I had to ask myself how it was that there were those who were openly hostile to this wonderful means of air travel, which seemed so similar to a seagoing passenger ship. Many decades of thought had gone into this marvel.

My trick at the wheel was over and, as the marvellous island of Lampedusa was lost in the luminosity of sea and sky, disappearing as it had appeared, I went to the passenger quarters. Again, nothing but sky and sea. Some of the passengers dozed, some talked and some sought information about the handling of the ship. What was the first impression? Noth-

a great airship. The following short account of Colonel Tombesi's first flight as the No. 1 on *Esperia*, on a flight from the Rome-Ciampino aerodrome to Italy's North African colony of Libya, illustrates only too well the incredibly luxurious surroundings which were enjoyed by airship passengers. The comfort offered by a passenger airship was comparable to that of a luxury liner, while its speed and range were greater than any other transport at that time.

ing heroic, because the cabin in which I was taking my short spell off duty was very similar to a Pullman car on one of the great international trains. A more exact simile would be that of travel by sea. Some life belts were to be seen, and the pale faces of a few of the passengers confirmed the impression. No thought of danger succeeded in entering any of our minds. The prevailing state of mind was that of absolute and tranquil security. All thoughts of tragedy seemed absurd even to the crew, who were aware of the weak points of a ship full of inflammable gas.

Turning from such thoughts we are struck by the fact that the horizon, in a jumble of indefinable colour, shows a yellow streak, interminable Africa! Soon, the ship like a vast eagle, came over the city of Tripoli and we heard from Africa the first sounds of urban life. For landing I resumed my post. On the outskirts of the city there was a large open, level space on which we could see detachments of troops, many wearing white turbans. In spite of the fact that these troops were quite unfamiliar with our silver monster the landing was perfect. Gently we sank to earth to be surrounded and saluted joyously. First came His Excellency the Governor of Tripoli followed by the VIPs of the colony: in all a moving event. At the edge of the field native troops were drawn up to render military honours. But the sun was shining and a problem was becoming apparent: we had forgotten that exposure to the hot African sun was not for us, since the gas would be superheated and lost. Some of the crew were already in the gangway, disregarding the fascinating and colourful spectacle in order to attend to the valves.

Some of my colleagues, profiting from the rest, had landed to smoke a cigarette. I had remained on board with the engineers for, greater than my pride in our achievement, was my sense of responsibility for the ship in case of a change of wind, which was clearly rising. It was not prudent to stay any longer, and within a few minutes passengers and crew were recalled. We were to set off again, and a sense of emotion invaded me at the admiration and greetings of the crowd of colonials, drawn together to salute us, animated by a spirit of enthusiasm and faith. This thought was of brief duration for we took off at once to the sound of 'Long Live Italy'. The silver giant was once more on its way. Soon Malta was below us. Valetta, smiling and beflagged, sheltered beside its two harbours full of ships. An aircraft carrier, possibly *Eagle*, saluted our passing with a salvo of artillery. After Malta, Marsala, Trapani and Ustica. We saw again the lovely star, spectacle of the preceding night. With indescribable emotion we sighted Na-

ples. Gaeto and Angio told us that Ciampino was near, and indeed the revolving light of our airfield showed us the way home and seemed to bestow on us its blessing. Finally Rome, city of a thousand lights. Motors throbbed, we made a slow circuit to lose height and heard the excited voices of welcome. The passengers were thrilled; 1,554 miles (2,500 km) in 24 hours.

126 *M 6* coming in to land. The forward machine gun position is just visible on the top of the envelope. *M 6* had only a bare framework to prevent the gunner falling off the ship, whereas the later M types had a canvas wind break surrounding him.

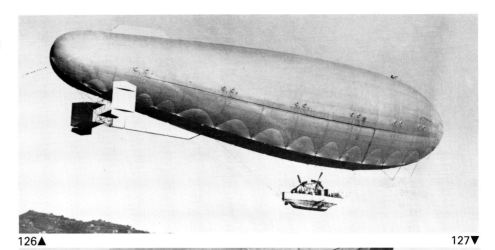

126▲                                                            127▼

127 *M 8* during a hydrogen topping up operation at her landing ground. The 12 circular objects along the side of the ship are special ports for inflating her with gas. The engine and propellers in *M 8* were placed towards the end of the car and not centrally as in *M 6*.

128/129 Two views of *M 6*. The first, from the bows, gives a good view of the battens strengthening her nose, and of the machine gunner at his position on top of the envelope. The second gives a good outline of the disposition of the control surfaces.

130 The car of *M 8* in her shed during construction. Note that the propellers are now mounted on a bracket arrangement, instead of the earlier pylons, and that the drive is now direct, instead of by the long shaft and bevel drive as in *M 6*.

128▼                            129▼                            130▼

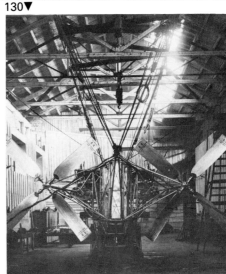

It was Colonel Tombesi's 'greatest disappointment' that through an unexplained quirk of fate he was unable to take his place as a member of the crew of the *Italia* on its fateful flight to the North Pole in 1928. Colonel Tombesi maintains that his technical knowledge

After helping in the preparations for the first polar expedition with *Norge* it was not unnatural that I should most ardently desire to take part in the expedition itself. I had made my wishes known but it proved to be impossible to include me in the crew because of the conditions imposed by Norway, which had bought the airship, and called for a mixed crew with Nobile as captain, Larsen as No. 1, and Amundsen in supreme command. All this happened in 1925–26 during which period I was No. 1 in the German airship *Bodensee*, renamed *Esperia*.

Two years later, in the early part of 1928, the second polar expedition, with the airship *Italia* and Nobile in command, set out to re-attempt the great enterprise with an all-Italian crew. At the very last moment I received an order to take command of *Mr*, the famous tiny airship, in which Nobile had flown from and landed again in the barracks which lay alongside the Air Construction Establishment in the heart of Rome. Exactly at midday, the *Mr*, with Nobile in command and his indispensable dog, Titina, left Ciampino airport and flew towards

# Italia: Disappointment and Tragedy

Rome. As he approached the barracks' square to land, Nobile asked me whether I wished to take part in the polar expedition. Without stopping to think, I accepted with alacrity. We then recalled that on the following day we were to take a party of foreign and Italian journalists in *Italia* to witness tests of a towing basket designed to set down and pick up scientists charged with important research at the Pole. After that, we were to go to the Ministry to get Minister Balbo's formal approval for the expedition.

Next day, after a sleepless night, I met

and his skill and experience as an airship pilot could have averted the disaster, had he not been left behind. The following cameo tells, in Colonel Tombesi's own words, of his involvement with the polar expeditions of the *Norge* and *Italia*.

Nobile at Ciampino. The airship, with its passengers on board, was already out of the hangar awaiting its captain. With me at his side, Nobile boarded the ship, leaving me on the ground to await his return. At that moment a dispatch rider came up and handed him a letter. The General hesitated and I drew back a few paces. After a short silence he spoke irritably, turned to the control cabin and gave orders to let go. Turning the ship's head to Ostia at first, he then quite unexpectedly made off in a northerly direction and flew to Milan, a trip of several hours. Many years have passed since this incident and, although I had the opportunity to approach the General, I have asked myself what it was in that despatch that made him forget my presence, and consequently omit me from the expedition.

The tragic end is known. Was it a good thing, or a bad, that I was omitted? I cannot help feeling that it was a bad mistake since, without presumption, if the disaster could have been avoided, I more than any member of the crew, had the necessary technical knowledge to control that ship, so very like *Esperia*.

131▼

132▼

131/132 Two views of *M 8* showing the whole underside of the ship from the bows to the tail fins, and from the tail structure to just aft of the bows. The M class, excluding the prototype *M 1*, were built in the early part of the war, mainly in 1915, and were mostly used as night bombing ships. The Italians had already used airships in the Libyan campaign, and the main alteration to the types with which she entered the First World War were in the greater capacity of the envelopes and the strengthening of the framework of the keel. However, there were no important improvements in the propulsion machinery. In naval service the P, M, F2, V and A classes were mainly used for bombing missions, while the DE, PV, O and U class were mostly valuable as scouts. Scouts had a speed of between 31 and 60 mph, and bombers had a speed range of 35 to 50 mph. With the exception of a few of the DE class, all the ships were of the Italian semi-rigid type.

The success of *Norge*'s trans-Arctic flight had fired Nobile's imagination, and he dreamed of further and more elaborate polar expeditions. The Italian Government were persuaded that the sister ship to *Norge*, due for completion in 1927, should be used for Nobile's Arctic expedition planned to take place in 1928. The airship was christened *Italia* and incorporated many improvements and modifications which were based on experience gained with her sister. The city of Milan undertook to bear the cost of the expedition, the Italian Royal Geographical Society became its sponsor, and the Italian Air Ministry, on the orders of Mussolini, facilitated the crewing and equipping of the airship. The *Città di Milano* was to be provided by the Italian Navy for use as a base vessel. Nominally on a training cruise to Spitzbergen, it was to carry all the heavy equipment, and its sailors would form the ground crew for handling the *Italia* during take-off and landing.

The *Italia*, although an identical copy of the *Norge* and having the same volume of 654,000 cu ft, had a much larger control cabin, housing radio equipment and the radio operator; the three Maybach engines, which together developed a total of 750 hp, were insulated against freezing, and the envelope was reinforced with a special encircling band strategically placed to prevent iced-up airscrews from throwing off chunks of ice which might penetrate the outer covering and damage the gas-bags inside the ship. A small car was also provided so that a member of the crew or one of the scientists could be lowered on to the ice. For navigation and wireless telegraphy the *Italia* was equipped with a solar compass, five magnetic compasses, four sextants, a radio direction-finding loop, a transmitter, an emergency transmitter and two wireless receivers.

The complexity and diversity of the scientific work to be undertaken necessitated a high degree of technical preparation, for besides a geographical study of the surface, the aim of the expedition was to cover, among other areas of research, oceanography, terrestrial magnetism, gravity, radioactivity, atmospheric electricity and polar biology. The minutest attention was paid to providing the best Arctic survival equipment, and with this in mind Nobile obtained the advice of Fritjof Nansen on the design and availability of sledges, tents, canvas boats,

# Nobile's Italia Flights

sleeping-bags and clothing. The famous Norwegian scientist Otto Sverdrup was also consulted.

Now that the expedition was almost ready to start on its polar flight, General Nobile and the crew of *Italia* were received in audience by Pope Pius XI, on 31 March 1928, who, as a keen mountaineer, had taken more than a formal interest in the affairs of the expedition. In fact, the pontiff had helped Nobile obtain meteorological data gathered by the Austrian expedition to Franz Josef Land. The Pope now presented Nobile with a large oak cross containing a scroll which was placed in a recess in the wood. Nobile was also received by the King of Italy and by Mussolini, and then set out on the first stage towards Spitzbergen, from Milan in the early hours of 15 April.

The route of *Italia* took her eastwards to Trieste and Vienna, south of the Alps, and then north west to Brno in Czechoslovakia. The weather on this flight of 1,200 miles (1,930 km) (about 30 hours, 30 minutes flying time) was exceedingly bad, and by the time that the airship had flown over the plains of Poland and landed at Stolp in Eastern Prussia, she had suffered severe damage to the framework of the upper fin. Materials for repairs were hastily sent from Italy, so that only ten days were lost, but further serious delays were caused through the reluctance of the captain of the *Città di Milano* to sail for King's Bay, which he believed to be frozen over.

Nobile started out again on 3 May,

when favourable weather reports were received, his course taking him over Stockholm and then across Finland to Vadsö in Norway, where the mooring mast he had used in 1926 was made serviceable. Here a little damage was done to the nose of the airship during mooring. Due to bad weather the *Italia* was unable to start on the next stage of her journey until two days later, but luckily after a boisterous passage in gale-force winds, she eventually reached King's Bay and was docked in the old hangar at Ålesund; a journey of 2,100 miles (3,380 km) from Stolp, on the last leg of which one of her engines broke its crankshaft. During the next four days the unserviceable engine was changed, and maintenance work done on the other engines. Most of the stores and scientific equipment had to be dragged through the snow from the *Città di Milano* moored on the edge of the ice over a mile away.

Nobile made two flights before his third and final sortie. His first flight, intended for Novaya Zemlya, was of just over eight hours duration and was aborted through bad weather. The next flight left King's Bay on 15 May and after a 60 hour flight over largely unknown territory, during which a great many valuable measurements and observations were taken, Nobile brought the *Italia* back to King's Bay on 18 May. During this flight *Italia* had covered 2,400 miles (3,862 km) to Franz Josef Land, Severnaya Zemlya and Novaya Zemlya.

There were intended to be two more flights, one to the North Pole by way of the north coast of Greenland, and the final voyage was intended to cover the greatest possible area by drifting down wind on one engine for a week with the crew reduced to 12. However, *Italia*'s next flight on 23 May proved to be her last. The *Italia* was headed up the coast to Amsterdam Island before turning on a westerly course for north Greenland. Eventually, after 12 hours, they came close to Cape Bridgman on the coast of Greenland, where the *Italia* was swung to port and course was now altered for a direct run to the Pole. They were helped by a tail wind, and flew on two engines in order to save fuel. Nobile was concerned by the strength of this following wind, for while it proved such an ally now, it would certainly present unfavourable conditions for the intended landing at the Pole, and be a force to contend with on their return to base.

The alternatives to braving the uncertainty of the return journey were to carry on with the wind behind them to Siberia or North Canada, but Finn Malmgren was in favour of taking the route back to Spitzbergen, for he was keen on completing the planned scientific programme. He predicted that the wind would change direction and that they would be helped by favourable north westerly winds on the return leg of their voyage. Nobile was persuaded by this meteorological argument and made his decision to return via the same route.

The Pole was reached at 0020 hrs on 24 May, and after the ceremony of dropping the cross and the flags of Italy and the city of Milan, Nobile turned his airship and headed into the wind for his return to King's Bay. For eight hours they battled their way through the thick damp polar fog, and after dropping from 3,000 ft to 600 ft (900 m to 183 m) so as to be able to check the drift, they forced their way on for 24 hours. The failure to run out of the stormy head-wind kept the ground speed down to less than 30 mph. Malmgren was puzzled by this and advised Nobile to increase speed in order to reach better conditions sooner. Nobile ordered the increase in speed but after some time when no advantage was apparent, he shut down one engine and throttled back the other two. Malmgren again insisted that an increase in speed would save the day, and Nobile relented against his better judgment, for he knew the effects on fuel consumption and that the strain on the framework of the airship would be severe.

Due to heavy icing the situation became critical. They were trimmed down by the stern instead of the nose and Nobile instantly ordered the running engines to be accelerated and the third to be started, hoping to lift the ship's nose and start to gain height. Speed was increased and the nose began to rise, but still the ship continued her descent. In a last attempt to save his ship Nobile stopped all engines and ordered the ballast chain to be released. All this was of no avail, for the ship hit the ice with tremendous force, the impact tearing the control car away and ripping the rear engine from the ship, killing the unfortunate mechanic who was tending the engine at the time. Considerably lightened, the hull hurtled skywards, carrying away six of the crew to certain death.

Nobile and nine of his comrades were thrown out on the ice. Remarkably, except for Nobile, the chief technician who had a broken leg, and Malmgren who suffered a badly bruised arm, the rest of the crew only received minor injuries. The nine men spent the night huddled together in a four-man tent. They were lucky in that enough survival rations for 24 days had been precipitated on to the ice with them, and the emergency radio had also miraculously escaped damage. Shortly afterwards two of the Italian crew, Mariano and Zappi, together with Malmgren, set out to find help. Two weeks after they set out Malmgren, weakened by his injuries, succumbed to mental and physical exhaustion and was left behind by his companions. The two Italians were picked up from the ice by the Russian icebreaker *Krassin* four weeks later, when with no food left, all hope of survival had been abandoned.

Twenty-eight days after the wreck of the *Italia* a Swedish skiplane piloted by Lieutenant Lundborg made a landing on the pack ice and took off Nobile, much against his will, in order that he would be able to co-ordinate the rescue attempts from the *Città di Milano*, in place of the ineffectual and constantly vacillating Captain Romagna.

After the rescue of Mariano and Zappi, the *Krassin* pressed on northwards, and in poor visibility, steamed right past the survivors' red tent. She was called back by radio messages and guided to the five survivors by a bonfire lit near the tent. They had suffered surprisingly little despite their ordeal which had lasted 48 days.

Now that all known survivors had been rescued Nobile's attention was turned to searching for the six crewmen carried off in the hull of his airship. The captain of the *Krassin* could not extend his search much further because of a shortage of coal. However, he offered to stay in the area if the Italians wished to send in seaplanes, but despite pleas from Nobile, Romagna negated the whole idea.

The tragedy of the *Italia* disaster was compounded by the loss of the explorer Roald Amundsen in a Latham biplane flying-boat, together with his old comrade Lief Dietrichson, the pilot Major René Guilbaud, along with the crew of three Frenchmen, de Cuverville, Brazy and Valette. This chivalrous attempt to rescue Nobile was used much in the publicity against him in Norway and Italy afterwards.

It is remarkable that no detailed plans for rescue were made by Nobile. However, it is also true that no formalised rescue services existed in the polar regions either, and that the uncoordinated and well-meant efforts by Italy, Norway, Sweden, France, Finland and Russia were instrumental in bringing about the initiation of such a service.

Back in Italy Nobile was treated badly by the Fascist hierarchy, being blamed by an official enquiry of negligence and causing the crash through bad management. He was forced to resign his rank and all the honours gained as a result of the success of the *Norge* expedition in 1926. He was at once offered a four-year contract by the Russians, who admired his skill and courage as an airship captain, and also wanted him for his acknowledged ability as an airship designer. During his stay in Russia Nobile designed several semi-rigid airships, including *V 6* which was launched in 1934 with a capacity of 685,000 cu ft. This airship was powered by three Osoaviakhim engines, each of 265 hp. Nobile proved that the shabby treatment meted out by his own government and his ordeal on the ice had in no way shaken his nerve, when on one of his flights he went from Moscow to Archangel in an airship of his own design. Nobile's fellow-countrymen belatedly restored his honours after the last war, and by good fortune he was to live many years as an honoured citizen in his own country.

133 *M 10* leaving her shed. Note the observation position on top of the shed above the door. The M class were 264.04 ft (80.46 m) long, 59.06 ft (17.98 m) wide, and 89.08 ft (27.12 m) high, from the bottom of the car to the top of the envelope. The volume of the envelope was 441,250 cu ft, and the useful lift was 10,890 lb (4,939.62 kg). The weight empty was 18,077 lb (81,999 kg).

134 An Italian A class non-rigid airship, probably launched in 1917. The airship is distinctive for its twin boat-shaped cars linked by a rigid walkway. The four 225 hp SPA engines, two in each car, could drive the airship at a maximum speed of 50 mph. The A class airship were 321.53 ft (97.94 m) long, 67 ft (20.42 m) in diameter, 63.97 ft (19.49 m) wide and 82.02 ft (25 m) high. The weight empty of an A class airship was 18,960 lb (8,600 kg), and the useful lift was 22,040 lb (9.997 kg).

133▲                                    134▼

135▼

135 The boat-shaped control car of an Italian A class ship in the shed. The rudder and elevator control wheels can be seen in the enclosed command position in the car.

136▲                                                137▼

136 An Italian A class ship in the foreground, showing the distinctive shape of the envelope. The ship shown at an oblique angle on the right is either an early M or P type, and has no top gun position. The M and P classes were characterised by an efficient car suspension system and had streamlined envelopes, which were divided into a number of self-contained compartments to prevent the gas surging, therefore making it difficult to keep an even keel. The other purpose of dividing the envelope into separate compartments was to prevent the total loss of gas in the event of damage. The story of *F 5*, when it landed safely after being seriously damaged in action on 4 November 1918, is a good example of this type of design working.

138▼

137 The Italian Army airship *F 5*, built in 1917 by the Forlanini Company. The ship made 22 bombing raids and was held in high regard by the Italian Airship Battalion. The two large objects under the car are landing buffers. The ship was 295.29 ft (90 m) long, 65.62 ft (20 m) wide, and 88.58 ft (27 m) high. The weight empty was 21,384 lb (9,699.61 kg) and the useful lift was 20,185 lb (9,155.76 kg).

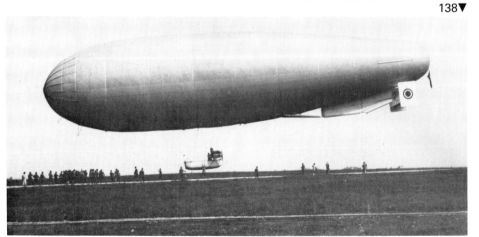

138 *O 1*, known as an 'OS' or *Osservatore* ship, landing at Ciampino. This semi-rigid ship was built by the Stabilimento di Construzioni Aeronautiche in 1918 and was used as a scout. In 1921 the ship was modified with a rigid stern on to which her fins were fixed. The result of this modification was a slight increase in speed to almost 57 mph. *O 1* was 177.66 ft (54.15 m) in length, 35.33 ft (10.76 m) in diameter, and had a volume of 123,700 cu ft. The photograph shows the ship before modification with battens on the tail to help stiffen the envelope.

139 Colonel Tito Tombesi. Behind him on the wall are plans for Forlanini-type airships.

140 A close-up of the control car of *F 5*, showing one of the four-bladed propellers on an outrigger at the rear of the car. The propellers were driven by two 240 hp Isotta Fraschini engines, and under full power the maximum speed was just over 46 mph. Note how the control car is faired on to the keel. The triple stabilising planes can be seen on the car, close up to the envelope, and the large box-kite control surfaces on the tail can also be seen. Signor Forlanini built seven airships, starting in 1908 with the *Leonardo da Vinci* and ending with *F 7*, or *Omnia Dir*, which had a blower in the keel and four air valves on the bows and stern to assist in manoeuvring. From 1915, when *F 3* was built for the Italian Navy, all Forlanini ships had an internal keel.

141 *Bodensee*, the first streamlined Zeppelin making a water landing. This airship was built for the specific purpose of small-scale passenger operations, and it was hoped that the operation of the ship would be good publicity for future undertakings. The DELAG company was revived to operate the ship, but the direction did not foresee the harshness of the Treaty of Versailles, for the *Bodensee* and the *Nordstern*, both built in 1919, were ordered to be surrendered in partial compensation for the naval Zeppelins destroyed by their crews. *Bodensee* was surrendered to Italy on 3 July 1921, and dismantled in July 1928, and *Nordstern* was surrendered to France on 13 June 1921, and dismantled in September 1926.

142 During the *Graf Zeppelin's* Arctic flight in 1931 she linked up with the Soviet icebreaker *Malygin* off Franz Joseph Land to exchange mail. In the photograph a boat from the *Malygin*, with Umberto Nobile on the right, can be seen among the ice floes off Hooker Island. Nobile took his skills to Russia when the Fascist authorities in Italy hounded him out after the failure of the *Italia* expedition. In Russia Nobile designed a number of successful semi-rigid airships.

139▲

140▼

141▼

142▼

# Norway

In this chapter Major General H. Riiser-Larsen, KCB tells of his training as an airship captain in Great Britain under General Edward Maitland, then the airship chief, and of the speculative planning of a Scandinavian airship route from London via Copenhagen, Stockholm and Oslo, and then back to London. Unfortunately, all hopes for this service foundered when Britain lost interest in airships after the *R 101* disaster.

The second part of Riiser-Larsen's story is concerned with the successful flight of the *Norge* over the Polar Sea. This expedition was a purely Norwegian affair, Nobile and his crewmen being asked to accompany it because he was the builder of the *Norge*, and they had considerable experience in flying the ship; moreover, the Norwegians, with the exception of Riiser-Larsen himself, had very little airship experience, so the Italians were essential. The success of the expedition was

## The Oslo route

One day towards the end of the winter of 1919–20 quite a short report from London appeared in an Oslo newspaper that plans were being made in the Air Ministry for an airship route between London and the Scandinavian capitals.

I knew that an airship, equipped to take passengers, was under construction at the national airship yard at Bedford. I also knew, when I read the notice, that Oslo was hardly amongst the Scandinavian capitals and that the plans concerned Copenhagen and Stockholm. My trip with the *Bodensee* had aroused my interest, so I wondered what could be done to bring Oslo into the picture, and how I could make contact and exert influence so that Norway would not be left out.

There was in fact only one thing to be done: I obtained permission, both from our own authorities and from the British, to go over and undergo training to become an airship captain. I was ordered to the airship station at Howden, near Hull, to take a course in theory and do preliminary training on board. General Maitland, Chief of the British Air Service, had his station there. At our first dinner I

## The Airship Memories of Major General Hjalmar Riiser-Larsen

claimed as a triumph for Nobile and Italy, which gave rise to much rancour between the two countries. However, in all fairness to General Nobile, he was

was, as the foreign guest, placed at the General's side and I soon turned the conversation to the airship route to Scandinavia. The intended route was London-Copenhagen-Stockholm, returning the same way. I enquired why Oslo was not included in the plan, and the General answered that it had certainly been considered but had not been chosen because of the prevailing bad weather conditions there. I immediately maintained that weather conditions at Oslo are particularly good as the town lies in a calm belt with little strong wind. I wrote the same evening to the Oslo Meteorological Institute, for a copy of Moen's tables. I translated the column headings and delivered the statistics to General Maitland who then forwarded them to the Air Ministry.

Not many days were to elapse before the General insisted I should learn to play golf, with him as instructor. This gave me an excellent opportunity to pursue my business. The General was in regular touch with the Ministry and one day during a round he mentioned that now Moen's statistics had been seen, the route London - Copenhagen - Stockholm - Oslo-

not entirely to blame for this.

The Polar expedition of the *Italia* is dealt with in the chapter on Italian airships, and it is interesting to note that Riiser-Larsen was one of those who volunteered to search for Nobile and his crew after their ship crashed on the ice. Roald Amundsen also forgot his differences with Nobile, and as a result lost his life while attempting to save his old enemy.

Hjalmar Riiser-Larsen was born in Norway in 1890 of a sea-faring family and died on 3 June 1965. He first went to sea as a deck boy at the age of 15, and in 1909 he joined the Naval School in Oslo as a Cadet. However, in 1915 he trained as an aircraft pilot, and in 1917 underwent advanced training at Cranwell and Calshot. In 1919 he made his first airship flight, in the Zeppelin *Bodensee*, and it was this experience, which aroused his interest in airships. Riiser-Larsen takes up his story after this event.

London was under consideration. I was pleased that Oslo had been included but not happy that the route had been planned that way. I knew only too well the difficulties our postal authorities had in getting our mail, coming from the continent by rail, a little quicker through Sweden to enable it to arrive in Oslo in good time for the first morning delivery. This was of particular importance to our shipowners and charterers where offers of freight were concerned. I therefore had my arguments in order for switching the route the other way round: London-Oslo - Stockholm - Copenhagen - London. The prevailing winds over the North Sea are south-westerly and are lighter in the southern part than farther north. I accordingly proposed that it would be more natural to fly London-Oslo with a strong fair wind and to make the return journey with a weaker head wind. My proposal was eventually accepted. I had achieved my object of getting the mail to Oslo first, and with this, my interest in golf ended.

## Training as an airship captain

There was no airship school at that time, so a special course was started with myself as sole pupil, and as instructor of theory, the experienced Lieutenant Butcher. Also stationed at the airport was an American airship crew under Commander Maxwell. They belonged to the American airship service and up to then had only flown American non-rigid types. They were now to be trained for service in rigid airships as America had ordered one, then under construction in England.

I took part in the daily flying programme, to obtain a foundation for further practical training at another station. Training the Americans was at that time a priority. It was typical of General Maitland to be up flying with us each morning to inspect the departure and introductory exercises, but he never stayed with us for any landing — he had too much office work to wait for that. Instead, when he saw that everything was in order he com-

manded the airship back over the airfield and jumped out by parachute. I also wanted to try this myself once, but was refused because I had first to produce the written consent of my Norwegian chief. One morning I did not go up, but stood watching the airship as it came in over the airfield at quite a good height. Suddenly I saw a man jump out, the parachute opening very nicely; a moment more, and a man, relieved of his parachute, came flapping down through the air, with arms and legs working energetically. Looking again, the parachute was still there with a man suspended from it. For the fun of the thing, the General had wriggled free from his flying suit while he hung there and had let it fall — this was what came flapping down.

I was then transferred to Pulham in Norfolk, where I was instructed by Captain Scott, the eminent airship man, and

I could not have had a better instructor. Scott was captain of an airship that made the first return flight from England to Canada. Immediately we saw each other we agreed we had met before. In 1912 when on a cadets' cruise to Ferrol in Spain, some British engineers from Vickers-Armstrong were there constructing a plant for the Spanish Navy. Scott was one of them and we cadets had been their guests in the British Club.

At Pulham, from an idea of Scott's, a mooring mast had been constructed similar to the one we erected later at Ekeberg in Oslo, for the *Norge*. Under Scott's direction, training drill was carried out daily, on departure from the mast and on mooring to it. With ordinary ground landing of an airship, the ship is first trimmed so that not a great deal of buoyancy is lost; an airship does not float in the air: she is either a little heavy and

143 The *Norge* (*N 1*) in flight. *Norge* was built in 1924 and had exactly the same dimensions, gas capacity and engines as the *Italia*. However, her weight empty was 28,660 lb (12.998 kg), and her useful lift was 18,240 lb (8,273.5 kg) — a greater weight and less useful lift than in the *Italia*.

144/145 Two views of the *Norge* landing at Pulham on 12 April 1926, piloted by Colonel Nobile, on completion of the non-stop flight from Ciampino, near Rome, in 30 hours, the first stage in the journey to Alaska via Oslo, Leningrad, Spitzbergen and the North Pole.

143▲

144▼

145▼

sinks, or is a little light and ascends. Only during flight at speed can the same altitude be maintained with the aid of elevators. When landing *to the ground*, the handling party forms up in the shape of a *V* with the tip into the wind. The ship is steered from leeward up towards the opening of the triangle, with course downwards. When the ship is in the right position the trail rope, hanging coiled in the bow, is dropped. When the end of the rope touches the ground, the ground crew at the tip of the triangle run forward and seize it. This is the most difficult part of an airship landing as the ship is now a free balloon and will either ascend or sink. The captain must let the ship drop gently by releasing a little gas while the bow rope is being hauled; he then releases two handling guys, one from each side of the bow, which are grasped by the ground staff who thereupon run out with each guy to its own side of the ship; the bow now stands in a 'crowsfoot'. The airship then sinks quite slowly, horizontally, and the remainder of the crew in the V on the ground grasp the car. It may prove necessary, immediately prior to this, to release some water ballast as the gondola must not be allowed to settle upon the ground. The airship is thereupon guided into the hangar, where a new problem arises if the wind is blowing across the entrance, making it difficult for the men on the cars and along the weather-side handling rails to prevent the envelope or hull from catching on the hangar entrance.

It was this that gave Scott his idea of the mooring mast. A wire from a winch on the ground is carried up on the inside of the mast and out on to a swivel arm at the top of the mast. This swivel arm ends in a hollow cup that fits a corresponding cone in the bow of the airship. The wire is taken through this down to the ground and pulled about 325 ft to the leeward of the mast. A shackle is then fixed to the end of the wire. Instead of an ordinary cordage bow rope, the airship has a wire one. When the airship is conveniently placed, this mooring cable is lowered, the ground crew couple the wires together, and signal to the captain when the coupling has been made. The captain then discharges a little water ballast from the bow to hold it up when the weight of the wire becomes evident. Heaving in from the ground follows and the springs are released, the ship's cone is hauled down into the hollow 'cup' of the receiving arm

and the airship is then fast. Next a gangway is lowered from the bow of the ship to the platform, and the airship, should the wind shift, floats like a vane. Gas, fuel and water connections are coupled, corresponding with the ones at the top of the mast and filling can commence, the ship's bow wire meanwhile being hauled in and coiled. Upon departure the airship is trimmed slightly light. At a signal from the captain, the mast crew slip the airship's cone, the ship ascends like a free balloon, and the engines are set in motion.

Kite balloon exercises were also carried out at Howden — an interesting experience. But unfortunately, I was accompanied by an otherwise very congenial American sergeant who had been a kite balloon man in the American Navy during the war, and he entertained me with stories of everything that could happen to us. In a kite balloon one is placed in a basket suspended by a few thin lines. The balloon is shaped like a sausage, obtaining part of its buoyancy from the kite-like effect in wind or from being towed. The sergeant mentioned how an American kite balloon, when being towed by a destroyer in the Caribbean Sea, suddenly made a hawk-like dive. The balloon straightened out just above the surface of the water, but with the jolt that ensued, the man in the basket was ejected. He survived the hawk-like dive but was now taken by a shark. This and similar stories did not make for particularly edifying entertainment.

I had now completed my training as an airship captain but there was one requirement to the rules of that time that I had not yet fulfilled, namely, a trip as pilot of a free balloon, since an airship with engines stopped is considered as a free balloon and must be manoeuvred as such. There were no ordinary free balloons in England at that time for such a purpose, but I had nothing against taking the test in a kite balloon, which is equipped as an ordinary free balloon, in the event of the mooring cable snapping.

When we were hauled down we went in for lunch but we had hardly sat down when a call came into the mess that the kite balloon had broken loose; had I been up a little longer I could have had my turn as a free balloon captain. Continuing on its own the kite balloon gradually lost gas and came down neatly a few miles to leeward of the station.

My training completed, I returned

home, to arouse interest for a route via Oslo. A Norwegian company was to be formed to erect a mooring mast at Ekeberg in Oslo, besides looking after the interests of the Norwegian section of the route. The first person I visited in Oslo was the shipowner, Mr Fred Olsen. It was the first occasion I had sat opposite this *grand seigneur* of Norwegian shipping and I remember the visit as though it were yesterday. He listened quietly while I put the case before him, and finally he said, 'This is very interesting but quite in direct competition with our line Oslo-Newcastle.' Then with a smile he added, 'If I went in for this, I would certainly be sacked as manager of my company.' Nothing emerged from our conversation but I have the suspicion that his later interest in civil flying had its origin in this meeting.

A disaster then occurred: the rigid airship *R 38*, for delivery from Great Britain to America, broke in two over the Humber at Hull during one of the trial flights. It fell in flames and the greater part of the crew perished [including Air Commodore Maitland], thus putting an end to our plans. Such accidents are caused by escaping hydrogen gas which mixes with enough air to make the gas combustible. The pure gas in the gas bags is not in itself combustible, so for fire to break out a spark must occur near the leakage. Germany used many Zeppelins for bombarding British targets during the First World War and there was very considerable difficulty in shooting these airships down in flames. At that time three kinds of projectiles had to be used in the machine guns and loaded in the order, a tracer for sighting, and then the so-called 'Pomeroy' and 'Brocks': the one had an explosive charge, the other an oxygen charge.

Some time after the accident at Hull, a second very serious airship disaster occurred, with the newly-built *R 101* which was to make a flight to Karachi, in India. During the night the ship collided with a hill in northern France and caught fire. With the exception of a few, all on board were lost. The accident made a deep impression as all of England's foremost airship experts were on board, *inter alia* General Sir Sefton Brancker, Controller General of Civil Aviation, Major Scott and quite a number of my British airship friends perished. This effectively put a stop to practical interest in airships in England.

We had to commence preparations immediately for the *Norge* expedition. The necessary capital was to be raised by means of a series of lectures, and Amundsen was engaged to speak in various European capitals. As his throat was troubling him, my wife and I accompanied him so that I could take over if he were prevented from holding a lecture. The *honorarium* was very high according to money conditions of those days — 5,000 Kroner [about £200 or $1,000 in 1925] an evening. Everything went well until we came to Berlin. The Germans had not forgotten that Amundsen had returned his German decorations in 1917 as a protest against the U-boat warfare. Moreover, about this time Hugo Eckener had started collecting funds for a new Zeppelin. In 1918 the Germans had been obliged to surrender all their Zeppelins to Britain and France. As the proceeds of Amundsen's lectures were to go to our airship expedition, it was considered disloyal for Germans to pay to listen. Amundsen was to hold his lecture in the Kroll Opera House, and at the entrance, leaflets were handed out attacking him. The place was packed and the meeting was opened by a police officer coming on the stage and announcing that plain clothes police were placed about the hall and that any attempt to demonstrate would lead to arrests. Nothing happened. After the lecture we were invited to supper at the Hotel Adlon, with Dr Streseman, the Foreign Secretary, and his wife as hosts. Dr Streseman's speech was a pearl of diplomatic tact, as was Amundsen's reply.

We took the night train to Prague, and as the train was due in at 6 am, Amundsen and I agreed we did not need to shave before we arrived at our hotel, as we took it for granted that no one would be at the station to greet us on arrival. But there we reckoned altogether wrong! The train drew alongside the platform very slowly and stopped at a red carpet just outside our compartment. There stood a row of gentlemen in top hats. We were still further surprised when we had taken our seats in the carriages that were to take us to the hotel, for the streets were packed with people — just as many along Karl Johangate in Oslo, the time we arrived home. A Czech officer told me afterwards that this was nothing to wonder at: the official office opening time in Prague was 8 am. To show the world that Czechoslovakia was ripe for independence everyone

# With Norge Across the Sea

had agreed to give the country an extra hour's work gratis by starting at 7 am. 'To do homage to Amundsen', he said, 'we only needed to get up an hour earlier.'

At the end of his tour in Europe, Amundsen went to America where he held an exhausting series of lectures that yielded a rich return. Dietrichsen took on Scandinavia and I *trawled* the rest of Europe. I returned to Czechoslovakia and held a number of fully attended lectures there, one of which I recall in particular. Bata, the prominent footwear manufacturer, had invited me to Zlin to give a lecture to the workers' children. The greater part of the lecture was translated by one of the factory welfare officers. A lecture with an interpreter is no pleasure, so in order to make some contact with the children I had had a short summary translated into Czech. A Czech speaker had taken me through my paces and I was able to speak to the children in their own language. The children understood me but it was the most fatiguing oral gymnastics I have ever experienced.

Back in Germany, the *fun* with Eckener and his airship began again. I obtained a good insight into political conditions in Germany at the time. The lectures were excellently attended in the industrial districts of West Germany, but gradually, as I neared the high seats of conservatism, places like Kassel and Hanover, the situation became precarious. I had a contract with an impresario in Berlin, who in turn had his local agents. At the more extremist centres

they had not even dared to advertise my lecture for fear of public reaction. At one place I was to hold my lecture in a gigantic building, constructed like a circus. The hall could accommodate 3,000 people but all I saw was a solitary listener here and there. I asked them all to move forward in front of the rostrum — there might have been about 60 altogether. Under such circumstances it is exhausting to hold a lecture, giving just as much as when speaking to a full house. I am glad it went off as well as it did, as I heard afterwards that my listeners were for the most part Norwegians, some of whom had travelled nearly 60 miles to be present. I then received an interesting offer from the impresario in Berlin — RM 1,000 [about £50 or $237 in 1925] per evening, *not* to hold the lecture! He would lose less by such an arrangement, and I was happy.

After the final lecture in Stettin [Szczecin] where everything was sold out, I went home to continue preparations for the *Norge* expedition. Settlement of expenses and receipts in connection with the N24 and Na5 aeroplane expedition showed a considerable surplus thanks to what had been brought in by press contracts and lectures. According to my contract I was to have a small percentage of any surplus. It amounted to about 30,000 Kroner [about £1,250 or $6,000 in 1925] which of course I passed on to the next expedition, as I considered both as one single undertaking.

Where preparations were concerned, the *Norge* expedition proved something of a job. We certainly could not, as with the flying boats, freight the airship from Rome to Spitzbergen. It had to be flown this long distance, and airship hangars were rather sparse along the route. Only one mooring mast existed — at Pulham in Norfolk. A mooring mast had to be built in Rome for training in this special manoeuvre, and masts also had to be erected at Ekeberg in Oslo, at Vadsö, and at King's Bay. It would also be necessary to accommodate the airship in a provisional hangar at Kongsfjord for a final inspection and eventual change of engines. If there is anyone to whom I would raise my hat, then it is for those fellows who in the winter of 1925–26 built the hangar, but without a roof, at King's Bay using canvas-covered timber. As Spitzbergen had become Norwegian, in accordance with the Treaty of Versailles, and had been proclaimed by the *Storting*

(Norwegian Parliament) as part of the Kingdom of Norway, all Norwegian laws became applicable to Spitzbergen as well, therefore the foundation walling would have to go down to a frost-free depth. In order to melt the frost where the foundation wall was to be cast, a small shed with a stove in it that glowed red-hot day and night had to be built, and shifted forward progressively to the next part of the foundation.

But these difficulties were child's play compared to others. When during the winter I went down to Rome, I visited the Legation to pay my respects to our minister, Mr Irgens, and I was introduced to his Legation Secretary, Mr Vangensten. I was told there was colossal interest in Italy for the expedition but that it was looked upon as an entirely Italian undertaking both as to initiative and execution, although some Norwegians with Polar experience would be on the trip. *We* had asked Nobile to take part in the expedition because, as the constructor of the airship, he would know best what emergency measures would have to be taken if any damage to the structure of the airship were revealed during the flight.

The Norwegian Minister considered I should hold a lecture and get the people to understand that the expedition was Norwegian with Italian participation, a continuation of the expedition of 1925 in fact. But then, there was the language problem: I could not give the lecture in German because that language was so hated in Italy that Norwegian tourists when conversing together in trams or buses were taken for Germans if they used the word *ja*. If I gave the lecture in French, only the so-called *cultured* person would understand me; if in English, then even fewer. I therefore proposed to hold it in Italian. 'Can you speak Italian?' asked the Minister. 'Not a word', I said, 'but I could certainly read it out loud. Only then would I be able to reach everybody.'

This was the hardest job of the whole *Norge* expedition. I wrote out the lecture in Norwegian; it was translated into Italian by Mrs Vangensten, who was Italian, from Tuscany. After I had crammed through it with her, she at last declared me good enough to commence. I wish I had kept that manuscript — it looked like something between an ordinary text and a musical score. The margin was marked to indicate when I should smile, and when to press the button for the next lantern slide.

Meanwhile the Norwegian Minister had arranged for me to give my first lecture before the Geographical Society in Rome. That I should give it in Italian without knowing the language aroused the Board's surprise and I was called in for a dress rehearsal. Perhaps the President had heard the story of Sir Ernest Shackleton who gave a lecture before the Geographical Society in Berlin, after the expedition to 88° South. Sir Ernest tried the same experiment in order to be understood, delivering his lecture in German, of which he did not understand a word. When Sir Ernest had finished, the President rose and politely asked him if he would give a short summary of the lecture in English! When I had read the first page, however, I was interrupted with the remark that it was all right.

Then came the evening when I was to hold the lecture. I have never been so frightened and nervous in all my life, and tried to calm myself with a few words from a review song that had been sung at Kongshavn Bad in Oslo, when I was a small boy:

'*Det gjör ingenting min sjel
det skyer for fedrelandets vel*'

or freely rendered:

'It doesn't matter at all, it's all
For the good of the country . . .'

The hall was packed. The entire aristocracy of Rome, led by King Victor Emanuel, was present. I had personally arranged the slides in the correct order, and instructed the attendant who was to work the apparatus in a small enclosure well down the hall, to change the slides when I pressed the button. I had instructed the attendant in French and as he replied the whole time '*Si, si, si*', I believed he had understood me. So I began the lecture with '*Maestro*' and a deep bow to the King. When I pressed the button for the first slide, to my horror one of the last pictures came up. I pressed once more and yet again, but pictures appeared that had nothing at all to do with the text. I therefore had to break off speaking, with an apology in French. I asked my wife who was sitting next to the King to go to the attendant and arrange the pictures. She told me afterwards that the attendant, for his own entertainment while waiting for the lec-

ture to begin, had taken the slides from the box, glanced at them, and then placed them around the table. I now had the correct slides and I smiled when I had to smile. According to the press, the lecture was a success.

I was requested to give the lecture at the University of Naples for a Fascist organisation. That also went well but there was a supper afterwards that did not pass off so successfully. Sitting on one side was the chief of the women fascists, a somewhat older and very beautiful Italian countess. I opened the conversation in French. Rather surprised she asked, 'Why don't you speak Italian to me?' 'For the simple reason', I replied, 'I don't know Italian.' If the eyes of the countess could have killed, this piece would never have been written. 'Sir,' she said, 'you have held an hour's lecture in perfect Italian and you now tell me you do not know our language. I will tell you why you will not talk to me in Italian but in French. It's because you consider French so much finer than Italian.' And with that she turned her back on me to talk to the gentleman on her other side. How glad I was, for the art of conversing is not my strongest forte!

After detailed discussion with Amundsen I selected the Norwegian members of the crew. For manning the rudder and the elevators we required at least four men who could take watch and watch about. Amundsen's faithful companion, Wisting, was an obvious choice, as was Lieutenant Horgen, reserve flyer of the previous year. During these discussions at Svartskog, near Oslo, Amundsen's home, I thought Amundsen's nephew Gustav Amundsen, a naval reserve commander should be considered. It must have been hard for him to see his uncle leave on his expeditions without being able to go with him, but Amundsen held to the principle that members of an expedition should not be related. On this occasion, however, he gave way but I had to stipulate that a final decision could only be taken just before departure from Spitzbergen when we saw what weight we could lift.

It was of the very greatest importance that our wireless worked well at any time, so I approached our most prominent expert in this sphere, Captain Birger Gottwaldt, who immediately declared himself willing to take on that responsibility. As radio-telegraphist, Olonkin, a Russian, was selected as a matter of course as he had been with the *Maud* expedition, but he unfortunately contracted an ear complaint and had to make way at Spitzbergen for Storm Johansen, a Norwegian. To cover our press service for which a very considerable sum was paid, Frederick Ramm, of *Tidens Tegn*, Oslo, was chosen. He had accompanied us to Spitzbergen the year before. Omdhal came as motor mechanic. Counting Amundsen and myself, there were eight Norwegians, one American, Ellsworth, and Malmgren, a Swede who was a prominent meteorologist, most useful in assisting with navigation. The chief mechanic was an Italian, Cecioni by name, a giant of a fellow, the best Nobile could have chosen. As rigger, Nobile had selected a man named Alessandrini whose agility in climbing about the airship was quite fabulous. I believe he must have been a circus acrobat in his youth. Besides taking a turn at the rudder, it was also Cecioni's job to inspect the gas valves on the top of the ship and to see they had closed properly every time we released gas. The three others who served on the Polar trip were the motor mechanics Arduino, Carotti and Pomela.

It was not only the crew, however, who were busy with preparations. A number of others were engaged as ground staff and reserves in case any member of the crew fell sick. Considerable work was done later on by Colonel Johan Hover and Commodore Sven Brun. We had also stationed Bernt Balchen at Kongsfjord where, as will be shown further on, he got the great chance of his life. In February and March the crew assembled in Rome and the training of the Norwegian members began after a brief theoretical course. On 26 March 1926 Amundsen and Ellsworth arrived in Rome and inspected all preparations, then left for Spitzbergen to superintend the preparatory arrangements there.

Then 29 March came, the great day when we took over the airship. The Italian flag was lowered and a fine silk Norwegian flag was hoisted instead, which Wisting had the honour of hoisting. The route we intended to take was from Rome to Pulham in Norfolk, and from there via Oslo to Gatchina outside Leningrad, where the most northerly hangar in Europe was situated; then on to Vadsö in northern Norway where a mooring mast had been erected, and direct to Kongsfjord where we had con-

structed a provisional hangar. A mooring mast had also been erected there in case the wind on arrival should prove strong enough to make it too risky to take the ship into the hangar. There were few airship hangars along the route should we have to seek an emergency port. I had therefore engaged a French airship captain, Mercier, as pilot across France and my old teacher, Major Scott, as pilot across England.

At last, on 10 April, we left. The intention was to have flown up, following the Rhône Valley, but according to Malmgren's weather chart the weather was not particularly fine, so we flew across the south of France and turned northward near Bordeaux. An airship station was situated at Rochefort and we would have landed there to take on more petrol if the wind had not proved so strong. We therefore continued on to Pulham where we landed with some difficulty. It was an extra pleasure for us that Crown Prince Olav was present.

Owing to a storm advancing across the Atlantic, we started again the next morning with our course already set over Yarmouth towards Kristiansand in southern Norway. On this trip I experienced something that rendered navigation difficult. The ship had two engines amidships, one on each side, and a third astern in the middle below. Our most economic speed was 80 km per hour. By economic speed is meant the largest possible action radius with a given load of petrol. We could maintain that speed with two engines at about 1,000 revolutions. The third engine was stopped and kept in reserve, as a rule the starboard engine, with the result that the port engine that was working pulled the ship over towards starboard if the coxswain did not take care to *hold* his engines. As we had fog across the North Sea I took the opportunity of getting a little sleep. Ordinarily, Nobile and I took watch and watch about as captain but I also had the responsibility of navigation throughout, so accordingly I had no real off-duty watch at all. During the night, as I had not regularly checked course, we had crept over rather to starboard and my surprise was great when we at length sighted land on that side, and I found we had come in across Jylland, just south of Limfjord in Denmark. Course was thereupon changed to Arendal, Norway and we had a fine trip in brilliant weather up to Oslo. Here the King did us the honour

of being at the landing. Because of the same storm in the Atlantic we were off again after a stay of only a few hours.

In order to be certain of having the Gulf of Finland on my starboard, I had set course for a point in south Finland. We had clouds and fog the whole night and not a glimpse of Sweden unfortunately; nor was there an opportunity of getting a wireless bearing. I was therefore somewhat confused as to our position when we caught sight of land beneath us: the churches had onion-shaped cupolas and the rivers flowed southward. I believed we were over Finland and changed course to southerly in order to get out over the Gulf of Finland, but time went on without seeing any water below. We still failed to get any wireless bearing or any sun observation as it was cloudy. At last we came to a railway line and I suggested to Nobile that we should follow it until we arrived at a railway station where we could go down low enough to read the name of the station through our binoculars. Fortunately, just before leaving Oslo I had obtained a new Russian map. The first railway station was Varga which was not shown on the old map, as various changes of name had been made following the Revolution. I found the place on the new map, a small frontier town between Estonia and Russia. The rivers running southward ran, of course, into the Bay of Riga. With our starboard engine stopped we had crept somewhat to the south during the night. We now, however, knew where we were and it was not difficult to find our way to Gatchina where we landed and got the ship into a hangar.

I had been in Leningrad and Moscow in January to arrange preparations and we were now received with all possible kindness on the part of the Russians. We had a lengthy stay here as they were not ready to receive us at Kongsfjord.

At last we left on 5 May, and moored the next morning to the mast at Vadsö. The trip was not particularly eventful apart from one episode when crossing Ladoga, the great inland sea. Because of a downward air current we began to sink very rapidly, so we put the nose upward to counteract the sinking, but before very long we were 1,000 ft (300 m) lower. There is not a great deal to say about the voyage from Vadsö to Kongsfjord. When passing the northernmost point of Bear Island I saw that the sun had shifted from the port bow to far across the starboard bow, so I went to have a look at the compass. The coxswain had kept the correct course but there must have been a very strong local deviation in the neighbourhood.

Having housed the airship in the provisional hangar I felt very relieved that everything so far had gone so well. We now had to change one of the engines. Byrd was lying up here with his Fokker machine, together with Floyd Bennet the airman, ready to start for the North Pole. The ski attachment to his 'plane, however, was not quite satisfactory and Byrd could not get into the air. Byrd asked if we had a man who could help him and I suggested to Roald Amundsen that we should let him have Bernt Balchen, to which Amundsen had no objection. Amundsen did not want to hurry on the changing of engines in order to arrive at the North Pole before Byrd — Amundsen's objective was after all what lay on the other side of the Pole. And so Bernt Balchen got his great chance — he fixed the ski arrangement and Byrd carried out his flight to the North Pole. In gratitude, Byrd took Balchen back with him to America, which proved to be the commencement of Balchen's brilliant career.

At length one morning we were ready to start, but Gustav Amundsen and one Italian mechanic had to be left out owing to the weight. I was a little nervous when the airship was being taken from the hangar as the wind drove right across it with some considerable force. But with the crew of the Norwegian warship *Heimdal* and help from men from the local coal company, everything went off well and at 0955 hrs we lifted, started the engines and went out of Kongsfjord, setting a northerly course.

Throughout the whole trip to the North Pole there was only ice, ice and still more ice. We kept to the King's bay meridian by a constant bearing on the wireless station there. As we passed our most northerly point from the previous year a telegram was received, stating that Captain Gottwaldt had been given the King's Service Gold Medal for his eminent work as the navy's radio expert for many years.

In order to determine the precise position of the point of the Pole we had so arranged our departure from Kongsfjord that, by an observation of the sun, we would get a line somewhat transverse by a bearing on Kongsfjord wireless station.

At midnight came Ellsworth's birthday which, however, was not to be of long duration [due to the International Dateline]. By the time the clock approached 0130 hours I had calculated the height the sun would have measured on the North Pole at the moment assumed. I directed my sextant in on that height. The sun was in a favourable position and so low that I could observe it from the control car. The picture of the sun approached nearer and nearer the bubble in the sextant and precisely at 0130 hrs I could say, 'Now we're there.' Amundsen dropped the Norwegian flag, Ellsworth the Stars and Stripes, and Nobile the Italian flag. We had fixed the flags to poles but not in the usual manner as they would have fallen slantwise. We had fastened them as banners so all three flags stood neatly upon the ice below. I then ordered the coxswain, 'hard left', and we took a trip round the world that lasted about two minutes.

We then set course for Point Barrow in Alaska. On passing the North Pole we had Alaska time. In Alaska the sun is due south 11 hours later than in Norway with the result that the time was suddenly 1430 hrs the previous afternoon. Only when the time was 12 o'clock again could Ellsworth celebrate his birthday afresh — not many people have had this experience!

We were now flying across a quite unknown area and everyone kept a good look out, Amundsen and Ellsworth making their notes. For myself, I was fully occupied with navigation besides relieving Nobile as captain. It was quite easy to navigate provided the weather was clear. I checked the drift as well as the speed every third minute. It was a simple operation to time the speed when the sun was transverse to us, as it was then merely a matter of using a stop-watch to measure the time the airship's shadow took to pass a particular hummock of ice. But then fog came down and wireless communications became poor. Malmgren, however, was phenomenal at drawing a weather chart with very poor or no material. During fog I had to use his chart to correct our course according to the direction of the wind and the wind force he estimated.

Then came trouble with icing. One has to be prepared for this when the temperature is around nil (Celcius) and undercooled drops of water are in the air. I also observed that icing is proportional to the

heat conductivity of the object concerned: solid ice formed on metal components; the sun compass became a single large clump of ice, and of course, it stopped; ice on the fabric that clothed the gondolas lay as a kind of rime frost; the envelope of the airship was of rubberised cloth to which, fortunately, not enough ice adhered to make any difference. Alongside the outer part of the airship were steel wires and on these ice formed thickly and broke off in large pieces. When these fell in front of the propeller they were caught up in the vortex and flung into the ship like a shot from a cannon. Alessandrini was constantly busy repairing the holes. Fortunately, the lumps of ice struck the under-part of the airship and could not do any particular damage but if holes had been made in the upper part of the gas-filled envelope, then we would have had it. The situation was extremely uncomfortable and I will never forget the noise of the reports. In consultation with Malmgren we endeavoured to change our altitude and finally escaped by going above the clouds, the top of which now lay somewhat lower.

Some excitement then arose on board when in the west, something resembling a high mountain ridge emerged through the cloud cover. We accordingly altered course westward but had not flown far before we found that this was a 'buttershore.' Course was changed to southwards again. As not many hours could be left for the coast of Alaska to appear I obtained, by solar observation, a line going north-south that intersected the coast 10 nautical miles west of Point Barrow. We had nothing to do with Point Barrow, however; we were to go down the Bering Straits so I held the same course. Gradually excitement on board grew considerably: 'Won't we soon sight land?' I had not been able to get any latitude observation for a long time. I could not be certain, therefore, how far it was to the coast, but gave a time somewhat later than I believed correct so as to avoid nervousness. At length I sighted a quite narrow brown strip far forward, but for the present I dared not say anything for the country hereabouts is quite flat and snow-covered. Only when I had become quite certain that the strip I saw was the snow-bare edge of the beach did I shout, 'Land forward.' We then flew over a small habitation that Amundsen recognised as Wainwright where he and

Omdhal had spent a winter before his unsuccessful start with *W34*.

We then set course eastward and bore down through the Bering Straits, but our difficulties now became serious. A fresh northerly wind was blowing, the clouds closed down nearer and nearer upon the sea and we had to fly through them. Time passed with no sign of clear weather. On the east side of the Bering Straits are very high mountains. I dared not continue any longer and requested Nobile to take the airship above the cloud cover if it was not too high for us.

As we had used several tons of petrol we had also had to discharge gas out of regard for the trim of the airship. There would thus be adequate space for the remaining gas to expand gradually as the barometer pressure fell with our increasing altitude. At last we were above the clouds. Land could not be seen on any

side, but fortunately the sun was in the very position I could have wished, for a good line north-south. However, it now stood so high in the sky because of our lower latitude that I could not get an observation from the gondola itself but had to get up on top of the airship. It was something of a climb up through a sausage-shaped shoulder-wide, passage that led from the keelson to the top. Inside the sausage was a ladder. I took my observation and clambered down in a hurry in order to work it out. I had by now become extremely tired because of lack of sleep; we had been in the air nearly 70 hours. I had slept for half an hour the day before when we were in the fog, and during the last 24 hours before the start from King's Bay, I had got no sleep whatever. I therefore had to ask both Gottwaldt and Horgen to check my observations. On this occasion we got a

line which, happily, lay in the centre of the Bering Straits. I did not know our position on the line but, in any case, it led clear of the land. We accordingly set course along the line and I asked Nobile to take the airship down through the clouds. As we had no idea of the barometer pressure down near the sea we could not know how wrong the altimeter was. Naturally, we had to proceed very carefully.

The situation was now far from funny. Nobile had his fox terrier Titina with him, which became infected by our nervousness, and ran up and down the control car, howling quite frightfully as though aware of some evil omen. At last we saw the sea beneath us. By now we were quite low and a fresh breeze was blowing, visibility was poor, and land could not be seen on any side. As mentioned, I did not know how far south in

146 Crew members of the *Norge*, Bjerknes, M.A. Giblett, Professor Eredia and Colonel Umberto Nobile (first, second, third and fourth from left) and Malmgren, the Swedish meteorologist (right) with Mr Johnston and Captain G.F. Meager, A.F.C., R.A.F. Retd), (third and second right), photographed at The Old House, Harleston on 13 April 1926, the day the *Norge* left Pulham for Oslo *en route* for Alaska.

146▲                                     147▼

147 *Norge* at Vadsö in Norway, before setting out for Spitzbergen. In the ship with Colonel Nobile were Captain Riiser-Larsen, Roald Amundsen and James W. Ellsworth, who had helped to finance the expedition and who was travelling as an observer only. *Norge* had started on the journey to its Arctic base from Rome on 10 April 1928, flying by way of Pulham, Oslo, Moscow and Vadsö, arriving at Green Harbour in King's Bay on 7 May. After a thorough overhaul, including changing an engine crankshaft that had broken over Norway, the ship was ready for its trans-polar flight, leaving Spitzbergen on 11 May. The Pole was reached the next day, and after an arduous flight she landed at Tellen in Alaska heavily laden with ice, only a few miles short of Nome, the scheduled landing place. This historic flight had taken the explorers over almost three and a half thousand miles of bleak Arctic wastes in 68 hours, 30 minutes.

the Bering Straits we were and I was afraid of being blown towards the Aleutian Islands. With full speed on all engines we luffed to a north-east course and, at last, by the mercy of Providence, sighted land.

We were approaching a small habitation lying on an ice-bound bay. We knew it was not Nome; it had to be placed somewhat more westerly. We would have preferred to have continued eastward to Nome where we could have obtained the help necessary for landing, and where they were ready to receive us, but by this time we could stand nothing more. When I gazed on the beach below, free from snow, I saw cavalry in crowds! I said to Amundsen we would get all the help we needed because there was at least a squadron of cavalry on the beach. Amundsen looked at me in some surprise, took the binoculars and peered below but only shook his head. I concentrated as hard as I could and looked down once more — and there were no cavalry! Thinking about this later, I realised that the horsemen I had seen were exactly the same as those in the picture I had when

we rose from Leningrad where cavalry were present at our departure. In my over-tired condition, the horses and uniforms returned as a vision upon my retina.

Then arose the question of landing. The wind was quite strong and very gusty: to land all 16 men on the ice without broken bones or worse, was a serious problem. I accordingly suggested to Nobile that we should cut away all the fabric covering the control car, keep all the engines running so that we hovered stationary above the ice, and assemble all 16 men in the control car where there was room on the outside. We would then be able to work from there both the rudder and the elevator besides the gas valves. By God's good grace, while discussing this, a complete wind-calm fell.

A number of fur clad folk had collected on the ice below. We went slowly in towards them at low altitude and dropped the bow rope, upon which those on the ice immediately went forward and seized it. To do this can be dangerous and numerous accidents have occurred in this manner. It is a most remarkable fact that those who grip a rope will not let go:

if a gust had lifted the airship, they would have followed. I seized a megaphone and in Norwegian shouted, 'Stand clear of the rope.' Whereupon Amundsen turned calmly to me and said, 'You must speak English here.' At that moment I had not realised that we were now on the other side of the globe. On looking down I saw they had dropped the rope and that I had been understood, for the person who had taken charge on the ice below among the Eskimos was a lady from Lillehammer in Norway, who was married to a local storekeeper.

Nobile neatly put *Norge* on the ice, all valves were opened fully and as the gas escaped, one after another, we could then step down. Cecioni made some long incisions in the side of the airship which then turned nicely upon its side and gradually collapsed as the gas escaped.

The journey was finished. It had taken 72 hours and Amundsen's great objective of many years had been achieved: the North West Passage, the South Pole, the North East Passage, 88°N, and now he could add that he had travelled right across the whole Polar Sea.

148 The semi-rigid *Norge* in flight, showing the keel layout of passenger and engine cars, and tail fins. The crew could gain access to most parts of the ship via the walkway which ran along the keel from bow to stern.

148▲                                         149▼

149 The shed built for the *Norge* at New Alesund, Svalbad, Norway, for use on her way to the North Pole.

150 *Norge* at Pulham, Norfolk. The photograph shows
a view of the control car and keel taken from the bows.
The two wing cars and the after engine car are also
visible.

150▲

151 A head-on view of *Norge*'s control car, while she
was flying over Ekerberg, Oslo, on her way to the North
Pole.

151▼

# Germany

This chapter was written by Captain Hans von Schiller, and tells in some detail, how the rigid Zeppelin airship, brain-child of the Graf Ferdinand von Zeppelin, developed from the frail ships of the early part of this century to the sturdy and reliable giants that were flown by the men of the German airship company, Deutsche Luftschiffahrts-Aktien-Gesellschaft (DELAG). The Zeppelin giants were luxury intercontinental passenger carriers built and flown by men whose vision of a network of international air routes far exceeded the capabilities of the time. However, the achievements of these men and their airships is a lasting monument to human endeavour: by the time the *Hindenburg* tragedy and the coming war in Europe had put paid to all further rigid

## Zeppelin: Forerunner of World Air Transport

airship operations, the Zeppelins had flown about 80,000 people over more than 1.25 million miles, and in the 30-year history of these ships, the only fatalities to passengers were when the *Hindenburg* caught fire at Lakehurst.

Captain von Schiller was the commander of the *Graf Zeppelin* on her round the world flight in 1929, and later in that year on an Arctic survey. He pioneered regular mail and passenger flights to South America, the service only being interrupted in the rainy season. Captain von Schiller gives a graphic account of the excitement of flying in these craft, and an idea of the comfort and elegance of airship travel: faster than by seagoing vessels, yet with comparable luxury.

Today, aeroplanes leave either side of the ocean every few minutes from 0001 to 2400 hrs to cross the Atlantic, carrying passengers, post and freight. However, this transoceanic transport first began a good 20 years after the end of the Second World War; previously aeroplanes were unable to make direct flights from coast to coast, although Zeppelins with passengers, post and freight were operating scheduled services to South America and other long-distance routes 20 years earlier. This fact is, regrettably, hardly known today. Who knows now that in July 1919, the British airship *R 34* made the first North Atlantic air crossing from England under the direction of Major Scott, landed in New York, changed passengers and returned? Who knows that in November 1917, the German Naval Airship *L 59* (builder's number *LZ 104*) made the 4,375-mile (7,000 km) non-stop journey under Captain-Lieutenant Bockholt to the then German East Africa with 15 tons of supplies for General von Lettow-Vorbek? Who talks today of the round-the-world flight of the *LZ 127 Graf Zeppelin*, which flew from Friedrichshafen direct to Tokyo, 6,943 miles (11,174 km) over Siberia, completing the four-stage journey in 12 days, 12 hours and 20 minutes travelling time in August to September 1929? The same Zeppelin crossed the Arctic on a

research journey in July 1931 to make a photographic survey of the route. The *Graf Zeppelin* began a regular service to Rio de Janeiro in 1931, and the *LZ 129 Hindenburg* made regular crossings of the North and South Atlantic from April 1936 to May 1937.

If one traces the history of the Zeppelin further back, one finds that as early as 1909, the world's first airline, the Deutsche Luftschiffahrts-Aktien-Gesellschaft (Delag: German Airship Traffic Company), was founded by Graf Ferdinand von Zeppelin, and by the outbreak of the First World War on 31 July 1914, had made 1,588 journeys with seven Zeppelins, carrying a total of 34,000 passengers without accident. Even in those days, a steward was provided for the 24 passengers on board, to serve meals and good wine. All this was accommodated in one long cabin, with comfortable chairs and tables placed next to the windows, which in those days could be opened! Aeroplanes could then carry only two passengers in the fuselage and a five-hour journey was the record, while Zeppelin flights could take 10 hours. From the observation windows, passengers on sightseeing trips could enjoy fine scenery in comfort: the craft generally flew at an altitude of about 600 ft (183 m) so details could easily be seen with the naked eye.

The First World War brought rapid development of both the aeroplane and Zeppelin: from the original 'fine-weather airship', an 'all-weather craft' was developed. Graf Zeppelin died in March 1917, the war by no means having suited his plans, for in 1916 he had proposed the building of large Zeppelins for transoceanic service. I still remember well a discussion with him in 1915 about these plans, confirmed in his private documents.

Immediately after the end of the war, the executor of Graf Zeppelin's will, Dr Hugo Eckener, revived the idea of airship transport, and built a small, fast craft of only 1.06 million cu ft (Knut Eckener in his book *My Zeppelins*, states that its volume was 706,200 cu ft.), the *LZ 120 Bodensee*, which travelled daily between Friedrichshafen and Berlin. It was proposed to extend this service to Stockholm, and a somewhat larger ship, the *LZ 121*, *Nordstern* was built, but before it began operating, the Allies closed down the service, and impounded the airships together with the surviving naval craft as war reparations. Among the latter was the naval airship *L 72* (*LZ 114*) which made a 118-hour journey across the Mediterranean under the French.

The United States of America received as war reparation the *ZR 111* (*LZ 126*) which we brought from Friedrichshafen

152 The *Graf Zeppelin* under construction at Friedsrichshafen, with the control car being built on to the keel, and the outer cover applied to the completed hull framework. The Luftschiffbau Zeppelin began work on *LZ 127* in 1927. Work was almost completed when Countess Hella von Brandenstein-Zeppelin christened her on 8 July 1928. She made the first of four trial flights on 18 September. Petrol was used on three and *Blaugas*, a hydrocarbon fuel similar to propane, carried in special gas bags in the lower hull, on the fourth.

152▲

to Lakehurst in October 1924 under the command of Dr Eckener. Renamed *Los Angeles* this ship served in the US Navy until 1936: in regular flight until 1932 and then used as a laboratory — it was broken up in 1940.

The voyage across the North Atlantic in 1924 attracted much attention in the States, and Eckener had dealings there with the Goodyear Tire and Rubber Company of Akron, which led to a contract for building Zeppelins.

Meanwhile the *LZ 127 Graf Zeppelin* had come into being in Friedrichshafen, an experimental long-distance craft which could accommodate 20 passengers in double cabins (often four more passengers were carried in the officers' quarters). A handsome saloon served as a lounge and dining room, where, as in the cabins, the windows could be opened. At the rear of the passenger accommodation were bathrooms and lavatories. The catering staff, assisted by electricity, provided passengers with meals comparable to those served on board a luxury liner. The cost of a single journey between Rio and Friedrichshafen was fixed at 1,500 Marks (about £73 or $356 in 1928), with a 10 per cent discount for a return.

On the first journeys, post was our greatest source of revenue. Dr Eckener introduced the lightweight air letter (now in general use) weighing only five grams and bringing us 3.80 Marks. Freight traffic also appeared, and we even received a dismantled aeroplane as freight bound for Recife de Pernambuco. A large proportion of our cargo consisted of electrical instruments and machine components. The *Hindenburg* even carried an Opel Olympia motor car to Rio. On each return journey we had up to 200 lb (90 kg) of precious stones which were later cut in Germany. A favourite freight was queen bees. As bees in Brazil quickly learned that there were no winters in the Tropics, they soon gave up collecting honey for food, so every few years, new queen bees had to be brought in from a more northerly climate.

On long-distance journeys we had three watches, as on a ship at sea. Only the captain had no watch duty to perform. There were three commanders, one for each watch, (Dipl Ing Lehmann, Captain Flemming and myself) and three men of each rank, so that each member of the crew had eight hours rest after four hours watch. The crew was relatively large, including a number of trainees on each journey, because more Zeppelins were expected to enter service.

On the first two trips to the USA we had bad luck. On the first journey in mid-October 1928 we tried to push through a dark squall in mid-Atlantic, and the airship was lifted upwards by the air currents, to an angle of 15° at the nose. The height coxswain tried to force the ship down by violently working the elevator, thus imposing too much stress on the port side fin. The stressed fabric lining of the control surface tore and flew out in tatters, which could well have caused the elevator to jam. The damage was very quickly noticed, and the ship was halted while emergency repairs were carried out. Dr Eckener's son, Dipl Ing Knut Eckener, led a group which began to climb along the aluminium struts to the control surface, which was open to the elements. After a few minutes, there was a sudden rain squall. The rain added to the weight of our now almost stationary airship, and it lost height rapidly.

Immediately a telephone order was given for everyone to get back into the ship, to avoid being blown overboard by the propellers on starting again. There was not enough time to make sure that all the party were safely back inside the ship because we were rapidly closing down on the sea. It was a difficult decision for Dr Eckener, for his son was among the repair party, but everyone returned safely. The dangerous shreds of material were cut short and the control surface patched up, but we could not continue at full speed.

The incident occurred at breakfast time. China slid off the tables, and Lady Grace Drummond Hay, on board as a reporter for an English newspaper, received cups and plates in her lap. No sooner did she learn what had happened from Dr Eckener, than she was at her typewriter again. On hearing of the damage to the fin, the US Navy immediately ordered nearby ships to make towards us, but Dr Eckener thanked them and continued westwards cautiously at reduced speed. Twenty-four hours late, we reached Lakehurst, where the crowds who had flocked there the previous day were still waiting for us. We flew over New York, which again gave us a noisy reception. The jubilation on landing was great — even a damaged airship could reach its destination. After repairs taking 12 days, we returned to Friedrichshafen.

# The First Round-The-World Flight

Dr Eckener planned a round-the-world tour for 1929, with philatelists providing the greater part of the financial backing: thousands of letters were posted at a high rate, with commemorative stamps for the world trip, and a special franking for each part of the journey. In magnificent style, William Hearst, the American newspaper magnate, offered $150,000 (about £31,000) for American coverage rights, and he sent Karl von Wiegand as reporter.

Apart from Friedrichshafen, three other landing places were used for the world trip: the naval airship base at Kasumiga Ura in Japan, the US Navy airship base near Los Angeles in California, and Lakehurst, already well known to us as the main base of the navy. At these points, gas, fuel and all necessities had to be ready — we even had a spare engine sent to Kasumiga Ura, where, as at Lakehurst, a hangar was available. This spare engine was not needed, however, and some years later we sent it to Rio de Janeiro. It remained there until the end of our service, for the engines of the Zeppelin company subsidiary Maybach Motorenbau never failed us.

In August, all preparations were complete, but meanwhile, we made a few shorter trips, to Palestine and Greece, among others, when we exceeded the depth record of the time for U-boats by descending to 160 ft (50 m) above the Dead Sea — 800 ft (244 m) below sea-level. On May 16 1929 we left Friedrichshafen late at night for an Atlantic crossing to Lakehurst, reaching the Rhône Valley shortly after midnight. A strong Mistral current of about 60 mph drew us southwards at 120 mph, but by breakfast time we were stationary above the Mediterranean sea because one of the five engines had to be stopped, due to damage. Dr Eckener calculated from the weather chart that conditions over the Atlantic were stable, and it would be possible to continue on the four remaining engines, but a few hours later, just as we reached Ibiza, another engine failed. This time we were forced to turn round.

Travelling against the Mistral of course reduced our speed considerably. Early on the 18th, we reached the mouth of the Rhône, and below us, on a northbound road, a small motor car was waiting for us. We had hardly reached it when it started off and waited for us a few miles further on. Repeating this procedure several times, we progressed slowly, at a speed of about 12 mph.

During lunch at one o'clock, as I had just taken up duty, two more engines failed within one minute of each other. We could see Valence in front of us, and had intended to turn eastward along the Rhône Valley to reach home via Geneva, out of the main current of the Mistral. Dr Eckener, who had told me of this plan a few minutes before the failure of the engines, had gone to lunch. From the sound of the reduced speed, he could tell that something had gone wrong, and immediately came to the pilot's gondola. We were no longer moving forward above the ground, but in fact drifting southwards. Eckener tried to turn eastwards along the Durance Valley to find less wind, but there the currents, although weaker, were still too gusty to make an emergency landing, which we could do under favourable conditions by mooring to a tree. Immediately after the last engine failure, we sent a radio message to Friedrichshafen, and also one to the French Air Minister, who promptly offered us either one of the French airship bases or enough troops to assist us in an emergency landing. As we could not reach the base at Orly near Paris, Eckener decided to land at Cuers Pierrefeu near Toulon, which we reached towards evening. With the wind behind us, we arrived sooner than expected. About 40 men were ready at the base, to help us land safely with only one engine, and as there was virtually no wind, we were able to take the ship into the hangar, formerly a German one, like the one at Kasumiga Ura. Both had been handed over as war reparations. We had some misgivings about entering the hangar, as the clearance between the top of the airship and the head of the entrance was only about one foot. As the ship lay in front of the hangar, a few hundred soldiers suddenly streamed out; these were the forces put at our disposal by the Air Ministry, and at a slow pace we pushed the *Graf Zeppelin* into the hangar. As the hangar doors closed and the ship was safely moored inside, we felt considerable

relief. After failure of 80 per cent of our mechanical equipment, we had still been able to reach a base without further damage or accident.

That evening we had an amusing experience. The French sailors had received us with open arms and we were given excellent accommodation — the passengers were lodged in hotels in the nearby town of Toulon. Dr Eckener called the whole crew to the passenger saloon for a few bottles of good wine. As freight for the Zoological Gardens in Chicago, we had a young female gorilla on board, which quickly became a favourite of the crew. When we assembled in the saloon, Susi the gorilla naturally had to be present as well, so she sat on my lap and ate bananas. The party was in full swing when suddenly the door opened and a gentleman in morning suit, with top hat and umbrella entered. He was a secretary at the German Legation in Paris who had flown by plane to meet the *exhausted* crew. The first thing he saw, however, was Susi on my lap, and then the laughing faces of Dr Eckener and the crew!

Five new engines were ordered from the Maybach works and sent to us by express train. After they were installed, we returned home one fine May evening a few days later.

What was the reason for the damage to our engines? Engine failure in aircraft was giving cause for concern at the time, and forced landings were sometimes necessary. It was believed that X-rays might be affecting the engines!

Leading scientists soon discovered that it was a matter of vibration stress. We had to accept part of the blame ourselves, as we had stiffened the coupling between engine and propeller, wrongly assuming that it was too flexible: the engine, once started, ran tirelessly until it stopped after landing. For the later services to South America, we had only two spare engines, one of which was kept in Rio, but never used, although the Maybach engines ran continuously for up to 100 hours.

At the end of July 1929, the *Graf Zeppelin* was again ready for service and preparations were ready for the world tour. After a journey to Lakehurst and back, we started on August 15 on a direct flight by the shortest route to Tokyo. Again, the ship was full of passengers, several thousand letters for philatelists, and freight. The Soviet Union had given permission for the flight over her territory, and a Soviet observer took part in the flight. To avoid any delay in the lengthy journey, particularly in the early stages, we closely followed the great circle route, too far away from the Russian towns of Leningrad and Moscow to fly over them. Soviet military planes met us at the Russian frontier near Narva and escorted us for some distance. In the southerly part of the Ural Mountains we flew over a pass and crossed into Siberia. Dwellings became fewer and fewer, and gigantic forests stretched out beneath us. Forest fires were often seen, making clouds of smoke beneath us. Particularly interesting was the journey over the marshlands between the rivers Ob and Yenissei, when, for a thousand miles only swamp could be seen. An immense network of lakes of all sizes allowed only sparse vegetation, dotted with birches and conifers. To enable us to provide for passengers and crew in the event of an emergency landing anywhere in unpopulated Siberia, we had brought hunting guns and shotguns with us, but no angling gear, which I then realised would have been the most useful equipment here. As we constantly had good weather and flew with a gentle wind at about 800 ft (244 m) above ground, everything could be seen even by the naked eye. From the tiny town of Verkhne Imbatsk we followed the River Yenissei downstream to its confluence with the Lower Tunguska. To left and right were enormous forests: no signs of civilisation were to be seen. We followed the Tunguska upstream reaching an area where, under an insubstantial layer of vegetable mould, the ground remains permanently frozen. In some places, rainfall had eroded away the humus so that the ice, a shining light blue, could be seen. We often saw game: deer, elk and bears, and in the rivers we recognised sturgeon jumping, which were unfortunately too far away from us to obtain caviar! The daily routine, running absolutely normally, brought no variety except for the view of this uninhabited but impressive region.

The pressmen on board were naturally interested in everything, but suffered from a lack of sensational news material. Herr Max Geisenheyner, the reporter of the Frankfurt paper, wrote, 'The greatest sensation was that there were no sensations.' Not all the journalists were so ingenious, and one of them desperately wanted to cause a sensation. He asked me to show him round the ship. We came to a small room at the end of the passenger quarters intended as a cleaning store, in which we had put our hunting equipment. I explained to him the reason for this measure, whereupon he radioed a sensational message to his editor that we were armed with machine guns. As this telegram was also received by the Soviet authorities, there was an exchange of notes between the Russian and German governments. We later made a conciliatory trip with the *Graf Zeppelin* and landed in Moscow, where we were received in a friendly manner.

The terrain became somewhat higher as we came to the Yakuten Plateau, and there, after 1,200 miles (1,930 km) without seeing human habitation, we again saw something of mankind. We could observe the inhabitants' large dwellings, like mole-hills, and it was amusing to see how these people stared at the unknown monster flying above them, until they heard the sound of the Zeppelin, when they disappeared almost headlong into their underground homes.

Our navigation had been exact, and we reached Yakutsk, lying on the River Lena which is a mile wide here. The Lena is a good 1,200 miles (1,930 km) from its mouth here, yet it already has a kind of wide delta, as it flows slowly northwards over the plain. The next noteworthy point was a small town, Nelkam, which we reached after penetrating a heavy thunderstorm. The River Vilyui lay below us, then the ground slowly rose beneath us as we found a smaller river, the Vi, whose course we followed upstream. Hills and even mountains rose around us as we came to the Stanovoi range. A Soviet officer had told us the height of the Stanovoi on our route would be up to 6,000 ft (1,829 m), but that the winding Vi valley would lead to a 3,300 ft (1,000 m) pass. It was afternoon and we had only a few hours to dusk as we reached the narrow valley, with 6,000 ft (1,829 m) mountains rising to left and right. As the valley bottom rose, we became rather uncomfortable, for the valley was so narrow that the airship could not turn round. From our echo soundings, the valley had already risen 4,500 ft (1,372 m) and as we turned another loop of the river, we suddenly saw before us an absolutely level, black horizon. To avoid losing gas unnecessarily through climbing, we stayed just below our maximum altitude of 5,400 ft (1,646 m). The weather was good and the air without turbulence, so we flew over the pass at 300 ft (91 m). Next to me stood Charles E. Rosendahl, later Admiral of the US Navy, who asked me if I intended to pick buttercups here! The land fell steeply to a narrow strip of coast. Before us lay the Sea of Okhotsk; we were over the Pacific Ocean and had smoothly overcome the last and most difficult obstacle. We reached the open sea near Port Ayan and then turned on a more southerly course. When the fuel tanks were gauged, it was found that we still had enough fuel on board to fly direct to North America, but we were expected in Japan. The weather map indicated a mild typhoon which was moving eastwards, and behind which we should find a strong north wind. And so we flew at nearly 125 mph over the Straits of Sakhalin and by morning were already above the most northerly islands of Japan.

While we had seen endless expanses of uncultivated land in Asia, now we saw multi-storey cultivation, so to speak. The smallest space was used, tiny fields lying in terraces one above the other.

In the afternoon of 19 August, we arrived over Tokyo, made a loop over Yokohama and landed at the Kasimuga Ura airship base after an uninterrupted flight of 101 hours, 49 minutes (6,943 miles; 11,174 km). A crowd of several thousands awaited us. We stayed in Japan for four days as celebration followed celebration and we were overloaded with presents, including one very fine silver goblet for Dr Eckener and the watch officers from the Emperor. We were reluctant to leave the Japanese, who had been so hospitable.

The Pacific Ocean brought us no difficulties, if we discount a 36 hour journey through fog. Fortunately the fog did not lie directly above the sea, so we were able to make cautious echo soundings, gauge the wind direction and navigate from the stars. Shortly before we reached the Californian coast we saw a ship beneath us which gave us our position by radio, but as soon as we received the message, the peaks of the mountains of San Francisco were already appearing over the horizon. As we circled the town, a salute was fired from the guns of the warships below. We then followed the coast southwards and during the night we saw the villa of the newspaper magnate, Hearst, high in the coastal mountains, and he waved to us from the illuminated terrace. On 26 August we landed after a 79 hour journey (5,972 miles; 9,611 km) at the US naval base near Los Angeles.

Unfortunately it so happened that in the afternoon (we wanted to start again that evening), because of an error in the transmission of our order, we were unable to take on enough hydrogen. As we returned after a reception in Los Angeles, it was apparent that we did not have enough lift, so Dr Eckener sent one watch (a third of the crew) by plane to Lakehurst, but even this reduction in load did not bring the desired effect. Everything which could be made dispensable was taken off, and finally the ship was 'light'; it was released from the mast and we rose to about 95 ft (29 m). But at this altitude we suffered an 'inversion' in air temperature which again increased with height: the *Graf* would not

rise any higher and indeed was slowly settling. The bottom tip of the lower rudder touched the ground but we came free again and started our journey driving upwards under power, with Knut Eckener at the elevator. Dr Eckener said to his son quite quietly, 'Hold the ship horizontal so that we can get away.' But in front of us appeared a high-voltage cable over 130 ft (40 m) high. Travelling straight towards this we were able to gain speed. Dr Eckener then ordered, 'Lift the ship gently', and the thick cables passed beneath us. 'Now get the ship level again', and immediately the nose lowered and the tail lifted, bringing the rear gondola and the underside of the ship just clear of the high-voltage cables. The whole thing seemed to us like a bad dream, but it had been accomplished.

Following the coast southwards we flew to San Diego where we turned in-

land, following the Empirian Valley, a stony desert along which runs a transcontinental railway. At El Paso we veered somewhat northerly to pass over Kansas City. Thence we continued via Chicago, Detroit and Cleveland to New York where we circled the Statue of Liberty. Although we were used to a loud reception in New York, this time the noise of the sirens was so loud that we could not make ourselves understood in the gondola. After 52 hours flight (3,014 miles; 4,850 km) we landed in Lakehurst. Dr Eckener stayed in the USA to carry out new negotiations on airship traffic, while Lehmann brought the ship back to Friedrichshafen. We had circled the world in 12 days, 12 hours and 20 minutes flying time, covering a distance of 21,100 miles (33,957 km), and we had beaten Jules Verne. This was the first round-the-world flight.

153 In the *Graf Zeppelin*'s construction hand welding was replaced by pneumatic welding, which was much more economical, precise and rapid. Two workers are seen using a pneumatic welding hammer on a duralumin main ring. The connecting point for the longitudinal girder has been welded to the ring. Between each of the main rings was a compartment for one of the 17 gas bags, which in total held a volume of 3,700,000 cu ft of hydrogen. The *Blaugas* capacity was 1,226,080 cu ft.

153▲                                        154▼

154 The *Graf Zeppelin*'s control car before completion. The rudder control wheel is on the right. The elevator control wheel is on the left; above it is the altimeter, and to the left of it a 'variometer', actually an inclinometer that informed the elevator man of the ship's up or down angle. The gas and water ballast release toggles are on the girder above the steering positions. A barograph is fixed to a window. The air and electrical thermometers by the elevator wheel, with other instruments gave remote readings of the temperatures in the gas bags, particularly important in determining the ship's lift.

155 The *Graf Zeppelin*'s completed control car from the same point as in 154 but giving a clearer view of the gas and ballast toggles. The duty crew are at their positions.

156 The *Graf Zeppelin*'s navigation room which was directly behind the pilot's room. The ladder on the left leads to the ship's lower corridor, and a door on the right leads to the communication or morse room.

## Switzerland, Spain, South America

In the autumn of 1929, the *Graf Zeppelin* made a large number of day excursions over Switzerland, on which up to 60 passengers could admire the Swiss scenery from the open windows. These journeys soon became popular: it was always an exciting experience to travel slowly at about 600 ft (183 m) above ground so that peaks like the Jungfrau, Möuch and Eiger were hidden by nearer mountains, or to fly past Interlaken into the Lauterbrunnen Valley, and then to see the finest peaks of the Bernese Oberland. Some days these trips lasted eight to ten hours, so that we were able to make the sightseeing tours even twice a day with an early and a late trip. We also undertook longer journeys — for instance to Spain, but on this flight a bearing to the shaft between the engine and propeller failed. We had a replacement shaft on board which was fitted during the flight over the Straits of Gibraltar. The journey was stopped, the propeller unscrewed and brought into the gondola, the old shaft was dismantled and brought in, the new shaft installed and the propeller replaced. The whole operation, during which we had to suspend a few routine operations, lasted only an hour and a half. During this time, Dr Eckener sat at lunch with the passengers, and not until he heard all five engines working did he mention anything of the event to them. The ability to carry out such work on an airship in flight aroused the greatest astonishment. None of the passengers had noticed anything of the manoeuvre. We also visited Holland and the Balkans that year, without however making any landings.

In April 1930 we flew to Seville, where the King and Queen of Spain visited us on board. We also visited Cardington with the *Graf* to meet our English colleagues there.

On 18 May, we made out first flight to South America with an intermediate stop at Seville. From Recife we continued south past the beautiful town of Bahia lying on a high cliff, past Victoria, another very beautiful spot in the state of Spiritu Santo, to the Sugar Loaf mountain in the Bay of Rio. Whenever we came here, as we often did later, everyone was impressed by the beauties of Rio de Janeiro. The Corcovado, on the summit of which was a gigantic statue of Christ, illuminated at night, was a wonderful and fantastic sight. The journey over the South Atlantic showed us on the first trip that the Trade Winds presented certain problems on the return journey, as also the heavy rainfall in the Doldrums. We could overcome the first problem if we flew into strong Trade Winds at a great height on the northbound journey, because the strong northeast wind at a lower altitude became a weaker east, or even southeast wind at a greater altitude. We could overcome the second problem, the considerable weight of rain on the wide top surface of the Zeppelin, by relying on our motor power to drive us upward. Thunderstorms, which we encountered in this area near the Equator, had to be crossed with the ship slack (with flabby gas-bags to avoid valving gas by rising above pressure height) which was more or less safe against lightning. We would make for a lighter part of the clouds, which could almost always be found, with the elevator only very slightly pulled to keep the ship on the level. For this operation it was necessary to have an experienced hand. We always brought trainees with us, who after they had gained the necessary experience, were available as a standby in case the regular coxswain or pilot was not able to take charge.

On the journey to Rio already mentioned, Dr Eckener proposed to return via the USA, so we travelled not direct, but to Lakehurst and thence to Friedrichshafen, with one intermediate stop at Seville.

We had a mooring mast and a temporary gas plant erected at Recife de Pernambuco the following year, when a regular service was started. The base was so equipped by our chief engineer Karl Rösch, that servicing our craft took only four hours.

155▲                    156▼

## The 'Aeroarctic' Programme

During 1930 we concentrated on journeys within Germany, excluding flights to Spitzbergen and Iceland. Our trip to Moscow, already mentioned, was made on 9 and 10 September.

1931 was known as a Polar Year, in which research was specially carried out in polar regions. The Aeroarctic, an organisation formed to carry out research in the Arctic from the air, under the chairmanship of Fritjof Nansen, chartered the *Graf Zeppelin*. When Nansen died, Dr Eckener became head of the organisation. Preparations for the expedition were made with the greatest care. The Arctic expert, Dr Med Kohl-Larson, arranged for our supplies which were sufficient to keep us in the Arctic for 18 months, in case we should lose the ship. Apart from Arctic clothing, sleeping bags, tents and spirit stoves, shotguns and angling gear were provided. For a possible march on foot there were special sledges, skiing equipment and folding boats. The crew and the scientists were divided into groups of four and given tents, provisions and so on, in convenient sacks.

The scientific equipment included electrically-controlled and automatically-loading panoramic stereo cameras of a type used for cine filming, built into the ship, 300 ft (91 m) apart, and were used for surveying. A double compass served for research into the earth's magnetism. In addition, the Russian scientist, Professor Moltchankov, had an automatic probe operated by short-wave radio, which was attached to a balloon which rose to altitudes of up to 45,000 ft (13,716 m) to give us data of air pressure, temperature and humidity. The balloon was filled with hydrogen while the ship was in motion, held down with sandbags, and released when the ship came to a halt. After about 40 seconds, a knife connected to an automatic release cut a sandbag, which fell so that the balloon could then rise. At the same time another probe was dropped by a cable from the ship to record the same information, thus obtaining a complete profile of the atmosphere.

Our navigation equipment comprised an automatic gyro pilot-compass with servo control, which functioned excellently even near to the Pole. The standby fluid compass had, as we had found on our first journeys, an excessive drag. The gyro-compass had a dial marked in tenths of a degree, so that the navigator or the auto-pilot could steer within $\frac{2}{10}°$, thus providing a much more accurate aid to navigation. We also took a sun compass with us for trial. An echo sounder invented by Professor Behm, accurately gave us our altitude, and tilt was indicated by a bubble sextant. The total weight of the special equipment was 15 tons.

The scientists, some of whom kept their instruments in their own cabins, came from Sweden, Germany, the USA and the Soviet Union. Two press observers and a cameraman also took part in the expedition. The crew was reduced to 38, excluding a Russian wireless operator.

The actual starting point of the expedition was Leningrad, where we were very warmly received by the Soviet authorities, and we arrived there after a stop at Berlin-Staaken to pick up scientists and apparatus. For the one night that we stayed there, we had a single mooring to the forward gondola permitting the ship to rotate according to the direction of the wind. The expedition started on 26 July, our route leading northwards over Lake Onega, and passing over Archangel, where the icebreakers *Lenin* and *Krassin* were anchored.

During the night we continued northwards over the Kola peninsula. Dr Eckener made a diversion because the weather map indicated a deep depression on the west side. As the relieved watch retired to bed, everyone expected the temperature to fall, and got into sleeping bags. But the temperature stayed high and the sleepers could be seen crawling one by one out of their sleeping bags because they were too warm. In the morning we saw ice, at first only in isolated floes. On the horizon, land came into sight: the islands of Franz Josef's Land, where the Soviet icebreaker *Malygin* awaited us in the bay of Hooker Island. We were expected there because a special treat had been prepared for the philatelists. We landed on the water among a few ice floes, and a boat from the *Malygin* rowed out to us and handed over the philatelists' mail while we passed

them a similar quantity of post. In the boat was General Nobile who had had an accident in his dirigible *Italia* a few years earlier. Nobile was castigated by an Italian court after his return, but this action was quite misguided because during the trial, not a single airship expert was called. It appeared that the occasion had been used to exile the anti-fascist Nobile from public life.

Professor Samoylovich who was with us on board, was a well-known Arctic explorer who knew some of the areas over which the Zeppelin was to fly, but to him the scientific organisation of our expedition seemed overdone. Samoylovich had been one of those who had rescued the crew of the *Italia* from an ice floe, with the icebreaker *Krassin*, in 1926, so a particularly warm reunion with Nobile took place, and he was certainly glad to come on board the *Graf Zeppelin*. We stayed only 20 minutes on the water but gusts of wind blew us against several ice floes, so Dr Eckener decided to make a quick start.

We began with a survey of various islands: Samoylovich knew the area particularly well, and he showed us the individual headlands, including Cape Nansen's Rest, where years ago Nansen and Johansen reached land after a trek from Franz Josef's Land. Still further north, almost on the 82nd parallel we saw two islands which Nansen had seen from a distance but had not reached: these were the Eva and Liv Islands, on the north side of which we discovered what we took to be a fantastic terminal moraine.

Most people imagine the Arctic to be a colourless wilderness of ice, but this impression is false: the ice gleams in bright colours, and often the red rock comes through. The pack and floe ice, on which greenish or yellowish algae form, gleams brightly. In summer one can see patches which have melted: little pools of fresh water which interrupt the green ice with azure blue. Neither is the Arctic dead. Countless sea-birds, seals and bears live

160 *Graf Zeppelin*'s passenger saloon with the tables set for luncheon, and decorated with fresh flowers.

161 The *Graf Zeppelin*'s passenger area/dining room during luncheon, giving an idea of the luxury. The dining room contained four tables and several comfortable armchairs.

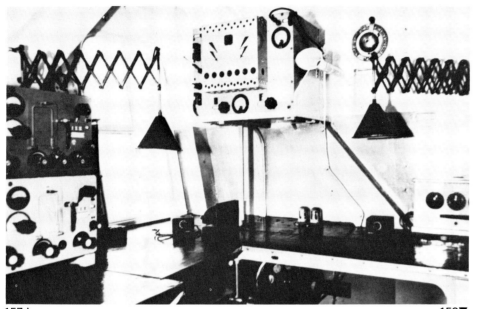

157 The *Graf Zeppelin*'s communications room showing the long wave receiver on the left, the 50 watt short wave receiver in the middle towards the top of the photograph, and another short wave receiver on the table to the right.

158 The *Graf Zeppelin*'s kitchen, in the rear of which is an electric stove, two ovens and a water container. A sink with warm and cold running water taps is on the right and surfaces for food preparation on the left. Electricity was provided by a generator powered by one of the engines.

159 On the *Graf Zeppelin* a passage led from the passenger recreation area to the rear of the ship, on each side of which were five cabins, each for two passengers. During the day they were furnished with a wide sofa which at night was converted into a second bed. The cabin contained folding chairs, folding tables at the windows, and cupboards hidden by curtains. The cabins were tastefully decorated with wallpaper.

157▲                                                   158▼

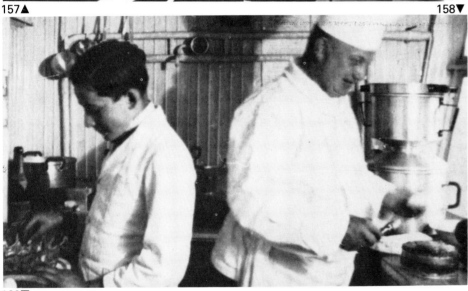

160▼                                            159▲                    161▼

there, but it was not possible to photograph them, for they rapidly took flight at the sound of our engines. I very much regret that colour film was not available at that time, for black and white pictures show less of the beauties of the Arctic than colour films. As we had sunlight for almost the whole day during the summer, we could take photographs throughout the day.

On our eastward route we had proposed to pass the 'Island of Solitude' between Franz Josef's Land and Severnaya Zemlya, where Professor Wiese, a Russian scientist, awaited mail which we were to drop him. The island is very small and level, but it was covered by fog, so that we could not let the mail down.

Out of the fog rose the mountains of the north headland of Severnaya Zemlya. We travelled up a wonderful fjord, and the photographic surveying began again. Glacier followed glacier, and often there was a drop from the glacier down the cliff face to the sea of up to 1,800 ft (550 m). The fjord was still completely covered in ice. Inland, a rare sight was to be seen. In the middle of a glacier was a pool, evidently of fresh water, on which ice was floating. We could see deep down into the clear water, as into a crater. After surveying the whole island we steered for Cape Chelyuskin, the northernmost headland of Asia, and crossed the Taimyr Peninsula. Professor Samoylovich told us only one expedition had crossed the peninsula in years, with dogs and sledges. Winter had receded more and more, and the earth was already covered in lichen, but former glacier beds could clearly be seen in the terraces, and glacial streams and moraines could be recognised. In the south-east was a range of high mountains, about which little was known. We had hoped that they would be called the Eckener or the Zeppelin Mountains, but the Soviets gave them a different name. Then below us lay Lake Taimyr, a good 120 miles (193 km) long, of great interest to geologists. It had an average depth of about 6 ft (1.82 m) and is covered with so-called *Strukturboden*, which is very rarely found.

Professor Weickmann explained this phenomena to me. It is known that the weight of water increases with a decline in temperature, but when it falls below 3° C it becomes lighter again and floats (ice, of course, floats as well). The rising water brings minute particles of the mar-shy bed with it which grow and form a honeycomb-like covering, of which we saw enormous fields beneath us.

From the southern edge of Lake Taimyr we continued to Port Dixon, where we flew over a Russian radio station, and dropped the post for Professor Wiese. A Dornier Wal (Whale) aircraft stood below on the shore, which one of the journalists mistakenly thought for a time was the plane which Amundsen lost in his search for Nobile. The Russians had a number of Wal aircraft for service in the Arctic.

Then the route veered to a more northerly direction again, and we reached the northern headland of the two islands of Novaya Zemlya. Travelling south of the coast, it was easy to see how more and more glaciers had melted. In the north of Novaya Zemlya, up to 14 glaciers stretching far inland could be seen at the same time, carrying long moraines on their back and bringing ice up to 400 ft (122 m) thick into the sea. Further south, we flew in glorious sunshine at an altitude of 5,000 ft (1,524 m) above the landscape. Professor Samoylovich told us that we had flown in a few minutes over a stretch of glacier that had taken him 14 days with dogs and sledges to cross. Now, in the heated cabin of the Zeppelin, he could make far more observations, and in comfort: the Zeppelin was the ideal ship for exploration. Between the two islands was a tortuous fjord which also had an outlet to the sea on the west. We flew over the Motochkin Islands and surveyed the south island of Novaya Zemlya. So we completed the work of our expedition. As on the outward journey, we flew over the town of Archangel with its gigantic stores of timber. The sea route to Archangel is free of ice for only a few months of the year.

As the forecast predicted a bad spell of weather, Dr Eckener decided not to land in Leningrad as originally planned, but to fly direct to Berlin, where a crowd of several thousand greeted us with admiration, but we only stayed for half an hour before returning to our home base. In one week we had covered 8,218 miles (13,225 km) and brought back valuable scientific knowledge.

## Charter flights
After four trips in Germany we flew on 18 August 1931 to England, landing near London to pick up passengers for a short tour, instigated by Lord Semphill, assisted by Lord Ventry, both of whom had already flown with us. Wing Commander Booth and Captain Meager were in charge of all handling arrangements and returned to Germany in the ship.

On 24 August we began our regular service to South America, with two further trips to Rio de Janeiro. In the spring of 1932 we made four trips to Rio. We made a break in the service for the South American rainy season, and made some trips to Germany and Holland, and again to England where we ran a charter flight round the country. By the end of August, after the rains, we made five more trips to South America.

In 1933, because of heavy passenger and freight demand from industrial concerns, we began our services to Rio in May. We made nine flights in that year, on the last of which we returned via the Amazon, Miami, Akron and Chicago. Particularly impressive was the journey over the enormous Amazon Delta whose brown waters flow far into the Atlantic. Plenty of animals were to be seen in the jungle, as well as thousands of brightly-coloured parrots and red ibis which flew off at the sound of the Zeppelin, forming blue, red and green clouds in front of us. In the jungle we could see Indian dwellings. The US Navy put its mooring mast at Miami at our disposal, where we stayed only a few hours before continuing northwards over Florida. There were heavy thunderstorms in northern Florida. After tropical temperatures in Miami, we flew into the cold season in the United States (it was already late October), so as we came in to land at Akron on October 25, the men at the base could not help us because ice prevented us from bringing the ship into the hangar. At our altitude, the temperature was below freezing point, and so, having just come from the tropics, we felt the cold acutely. The watch that was not on duty pulled everything they could reach on top of them when they went to bed, but even so they were thoroughly frozen by morning. We were all glad to have a hot bath in our hotel in Akron. From Akron we continued to Chicago to circle around the World Exhibition there.

The scheduled service began at the end of May 1934. The ship was generally commanded by Dipl Ing Lehmann; Dr Eckener himself was only on board on one flight to Buenos Aires. The service did not end until 19 December with 12 flights made that year.

## Navigation and Meteorology

Whereas we were breaking new ground when we started our long-distance voyages, we now had enough experience to cope confidently with every situation. We had a good tradition which originated with the pre-war DELAG, and had added to our number from the naval airship service. Later we had taken on younger men who were carefully selected, from the many applications for vacancies, and those who could not keep up our high standards were dismissed. The most difficult duty on board was that of elevator; not everyone could learn this skilled art. Prospective pilots either had to be qualified engineers, trained at a naval academy, or had to have captain's qualifications. The latter candidates had also to be trained in the statics and dynamics of the Zeppelin. Dr Eckener required a further intensive training period of four years on board before giving a pilot's certificate. We carried trainees on almost all our trips, which accounted for the relatively large crew.

Controlling a Zeppelin demanded a high degree of skill. In the air it was essential that the elevator-man constantly held the ship within 5° of horizontal. We had found that a tilt of 8° caused glasses to slide on a table, and that wine bottles tipped over at 10°. We used to say that the elevator-man should feel 'in his boots' if the ship was tilting and which way it would tend to tilt. Excessive application of the rudder caused the ship to shake or rock.

In landing, a Zeppelin can be regarded as an egg with a fragile shell: it must not bump the ground, for this will cause serious damage. Landing wheels or buffers could have been fitted, as on an aeroplane, but these would have added tons to the weight, and the framing would have had to be strengthened at the impact points. This would have increased the weight considerably and would certainly have been too heavy for helium gas. The larger the Zeppelins became, the greater the problem. Decisions on the control of an airship have to be taken in seconds; for example, if ballast is jetti-

soned to correct a tilt, it is easy to discharge too much, reversing the tilt. It remains to be seen whether a computer could solve these problems. Those of us who had begun with ships of 685,000 cubic feet had experience in these matters; one acquired a feeling for the condition of the ship. *Should anyone want to begin again with airships, it would be absolutely essential to build a small craft first to train upon and learn from experience.*

As to navigation during our service, this was quite primitive, though with radar and radio sounding, it has now become a far simpler procedure. We navigated in sight of the ground, and by means of a telescope which hung vertically, supplemented at night by a searchlight, we could measure drift and identify our course from the terrain. For changing our course by 45° against the wind (to avoid wasted mileage) we had our drift on two courses with which we could calculate our speed above the ground, and the intensity and the direction of the wind. For checking our location we could measure the altitude of sun and stars with a bubble-sextant.

In our time, direction-finding was still very inaccurate. I remember when on a flight to South America, one night we had seen the lights of Basle, when a dense layer of cloud drew under us. We came into a valley with 3,000 ft (914 m) high mountains on either side, and our route had to be followed exactly as we did not want to increase our altitude. After about half an hour we entered the six and a half mile-wide corridor prescribed by the French authorities, but we could see nothing of the ground. I asked by radio for a position fix, which brought a reply from two French radio stations that we were a good 13 miles westward of our course. This error seemed excessive to us, so I asked for a second reading, which placed us three miles east. At the same moment we had a sight of the ground. We were exactly on course, which we could verify from factories which we recognised. The error in the radio location was known as 'night-effect'. There was also the 'island-effect' which later fooled us as we approached the Cape Verde Islands.

Passing northwards through the Trade Winds, we often took a bearing ourselves from our German Radio Station Nauen, which was only one confirmation of our course. A further sounding was not available and we had to be satisfied with a

reading of the angle of the Pole Star. To cover long journeys in the shortest time, we relied largely upon the stars for our navigation, as on the high seas.

On the South America flight, the Trade Winds determined a large part of our route. There were several possible variations if we came north, roughly on the same latitude as Gibraltar. We could choose the shortest route up the Rhône if the Mistral currents down the Rhône Valley were not too strong. Unfortunately our narrow corridor over France was often closed to us so that we frequently had to make a diversion over Spain and even Belgium or Holland, which meant adding a good 500 miles (800 km) to the journey. Under favourable weather conditions, we kept to the south of a depression and gained speed through the westerly winds.

On the flight to North America it was similarly to our advantage to keep north of a depression, as it was to keep to the south on the return journey to make the most of the following wind. A Zeppelin was by no means a jet plane with a speed of 600 miles an hour. When the latter flies against a 70 mph wind, it can still fly at 530 mph. With our maximum speed of 75 mph, we had to rely heavily on meteorological navigation.

The most difficult manoeuvre was landing. A ship with a length of 775 ft (236 m) — the *Hindenburg* and the *LZ 130* were in fact 808 ft (246 m) long — and a flying weight of 125 tons (250 tons) demanded much practice. At sea every large ship is brought to the quay by a tug, but we had to land with a third dimension — the height — without the aid of a tug. We did very often manage, if we knew that we were free from turbulent wind, to bring the ship right into the hands of the ground crew without a bump on the ground.

Until the beginning of the 1920s, navigation on Zeppelins was most primitive, but we developed new instruments. The gyro-compass, its inventor Professor Anschütz believed, would tip over in the airship and be useless to us, so lengthy argument was necessary before Professor Anschütz was convinced enough to make a trial. As I came by express train to Friedrichshafen with a normal gyro-compass, I was laughed at, for the compass alone weighed half a ton, but I calculated that Dr Dürr would be able to reduce the weight considerably with aluminium alloy and plastics. Professor

Anschütz sent two of his engineers to Friedrichshafen, the compass was completely dismantled and everything was replaced where possible with lighter material. Even the original weight had brought us an advantage, for on our first voyage over the Atlantic we had lost 75 miles due to straying from our route — more than we had originally planned for, and for every 35 miles (56 km) or an hour's journey we needed 0.45 tons of fuel. With the $\frac{1}{10}°$ gyro-compass dial, accurate steering was possible. In fact Dr Dürr was able to reduce the weight of the compass to such an extent that all the equipment on the *Hindenburg*, which included four repeaters, weighed only 250 lb (113 kg). Nowadays every large plane has a gyro-compass, and an automatic pilot, which we also built in the early days. To give another example of the many experiments in the great laboratory that was the Zeppelin, we could mention the bubble-sextant. Like old friends, we find some of our experimental equipment now a standard installation in aeroplanes.

It was difficult, especially in the First World War when our radio stations were often not working, to ascertain our altitude by barometer. This was particularly important when air pressure was falling. Our first method of measuring altitude above ground level from the Zeppelin was to drop a standard type of bottle overboard and measure the time taken to fall with a stop-watch. In the early 1920s we made experiments with an echo sounder built by Professor A. Behm, which brought good results. At the same time Professor Mieses, an Austrian, made trials with a balloon at Friedrichshafen, of a system which measured the electrical field.

Probably Graf Zeppelin's greatest contribution to aviation and indeed wider fields of technology was the lightweight construction which he developed for airships. In the Count's diary which is still extant, we find under the heading for 25 April 1874 the first sketches for his 'balloon vehicle'. Even this first design was so thoroughly thought out that later construction did not require one *basic* modification, but the time was not ripe for building until two decades after these sketches were made. In the diary is a newspaper cutting from 1895 with the following information:

Aluminium in 1885 cost 1,000 Marks
in 1888 20 Marks
And now has
fallen in price to 4 Marks per kg

At last a metal was available to the Count with which he could make a start on his lightweight frame construction. Today aluminium is no longer a precious metal and is used for all kinds of utensils, and construction of ships, buildings, aircraft and engines, to name only a few examples. The cradle of lightweight construction was Friedrichshafen.

Graf Zeppelin, himself primarily interested in building aircraft, sponsored Dornier metal construction in his Zeppelin concern. Professor Cl. Dornier was originally in the experimental section of the airship works, but after he had tackled the problem of building airships he applied his experience to the first all-metal aircraft construction.

By 1896 the Verein Deutscher Ingenieure (Institute of German Engineers) had recognised the importance of aerodynamic and aerostatic principles evolved in airship construction, and their application to other branches of technology.

162▲

163▼

162 The *Graf Zeppelin's* rear engine car with the ground crew holding on to the hand rails after the ship has landed. The *Graf*, as she became known, had 550 hp Maybach VL-II engines, and flew at a maximum of 69.5 mph on her trials. Her actual top speed was 79.6 mph, and she had a cruising speed of 68 mph.

163 The *Graf Zeppelin* over the Engelberger Valley during its flight to Switzerland in 1929. This rare and remarkable photograph shows the sleek form of the *Graf* outlined against the majestic ruggedness of the Swiss Alps, contrasting the giant creations of man and nature in breath-taking circumstances.

# The South Atlantic Postal Service

The year 1934 brought us many successes and a working liaison with the Deutsche Lufthansa (German Airline), which planned a direct postal service across the South Atlantic. As the aircraft of that time could not cross the ocean without an intermediate landing, two ships the *Westfalen* and *Schwabenland* (formerly of the Australia Line) were provided, and each was equipped with a catapult. Dornier flying boats were launched from these. The post was despatched by a fast plane, the Heinkel Blitz, via Lisbon or Seville to the Canary Islands (Gando on Gran Canaria) and beyond, at first to Natal and later to Bathurst on the African coast. Outside the harbour lay a catapult ship which launched the flying boat which flew to Fernando Noronha, an island not far from Brazil. The second catapult ship was based here and the post was flown from there to Natal in north Brazil. A further flight by Junkers seaplane followed to Rio de Janeiro. In the course of time this route was extended to Santiago de Chile. A Ju 52/3m flew over the Andes.

The flight started every fortnight. On alternate weeks, the *Graf Zeppelin* handled the post, picking up the sacks by rope from a lorry at Gando while flying slowly, and taking them to Recife de Pernambuco, while every second week the seaplane flew over the South Atlantic. This method of postal delivery worked well, for it enabled a letter to Santiago or Valparaiso to be posted in Berlin and a reply to be received in seven days.

Almost every year it was necessary for the catapult ship to be taken in dock for cleaning the hull. The ships were in the tropics and rarely in motion, thus encouraging marine growth. The cleaning lasted about four weeks, during which time the Zeppelin, based at Recife, took over the service between South America and Africa. However, we did not land in Africa, but dropped the mail by parachute, picking up by rope as mentioned earlier.

The number of scheduled flights to South America rose from year to year. Although the journey to the coasts was an experience, not only for the passengers but also for ourselves in the crew, there was also something to be seen over the ocean. Sometimes we saw one of the sailing ships that at that time still carried wheat from Sydney to Liverpool. It was always a wonderful sight when we circled these sailing ships in the Zeppelin. Once, a little north of the Equator, we saw six of these beautiful ships below us at the same time, although they could not see each other. On one journey, I saw a large whale, north of the Cape Verde Islands, spouting a mighty fountain in the air. We stopped our journey and descended to 300 ft (91 m) over the whale, which would not be disturbed. Nearby we saw what may have been a female and her offspring.

Dr Eckener had been in command on all our long journeys until 1931, when he handed over to Dipl Ing Lehmann. Captain Flemming died in February 1935, and in the same year Dipl Ing Lehmann became head of the newly-founded Deutsche Zeppelin Reederei (DZR: German Zeppelin Shipping Company). This was connected with the *Lufthansa* airline, and we were no longer a purely private concern, as the DELAG had been. Command of the *Graf Zeppelin* was handed over to me as the last of the older generation. Meanwhile a further generation of pilots had worked its way up. There was Captain A. Wittemann who came from DELAG, and Captain Max Pruss, with whom I had been in the Zeppelin service since October 1914. Pruss had been elevator-man in the crew of Freiherr von Buttlar and was probably the best that the service ever had.

Under Dr Eckener's command we visited Buenos Aires on our third trip in 1934, but Dr Eckener decided not to make a regular journey there on account of the frequent *Pamperos* winds. Altogether, the *Graf Zeppelin* was at Rio de Janeiro 12 times in 1934, while the following year we made 16 of these trips. For this achievement I was awarded the Harmon Trophy and the title of World Champion of Airship Navigation for 1935 by the *Ligue Internationale des Aviateurs*. Dr Eckener was given this honour in 1929 and Captain Lehmann in 1934.

We learned much from our experiences in the first year, particularly towards a faster servicing of the craft at the mast in Recife. Whereas in 1930 we needed two whole days for servicing, our chief engineer, Karl Rösch developed a new technique which reduced our stay in Recife to four hours. By 1935, when we were able to use a new airship base at Santa Cruz near Rio, Recife became an intermediate stop. At the new base we had a mobile mooring mast which ran on rails, enabling us to take on supplies outside the hangar.

To haul the ship towards the hangar, we had an electric capstan which automatically cut out at a predetermined pressure. But we had not reckoned with the snares of tropical moisture. On one manoeuvre, the cutout failed, so that the rings suspending the gondolas were overstressed. It was, of course, the main ring which broke, suspending the rear gondolas. As the wind turned and increased, we drew the ship into the hangar to carry out the repair, and since replacements were not available, we had to make do with a massive wooden construction around the broken ring, weighing several hundred pounds. We arrived safely at Rio and Recife, but we then had to be prepared for strong, gusty winds over the Spanish coast and above Belgium and Holland. I decided on an intermediate stop at Seville, where we took on extra fuel in order to be prepared. We crossed Spain towards Badajoz, but it became very turbulent, so Chief Engineer Beuerle asked me to look at the broken ring which was beginning to fail again. Small piles of sawdust could be seen on the timber. The question now was, how long could we carry on without the risk of another breakage. Herr Beuerle thought that it would last for at least 24 hours after we left the winds, so I decided to turn round and make for the shortest and quietest way home. This route took us along the Rhône Valley which, however, the French Government did not normally make available to us. A radio call to the French Minister of Aviation, in which I explained our predicament, was answered within 20 minutes. We were allowed up the Rhône Valley as we requested, and arrived at Friedrichshafen that evening without further damage. But there was a sequel: strictly speaking, I should have made the communication through the German Air Ministry. But as it was Saturday lunchtime and I assumed that very few staff would be available, I had decided to make the call direct to the French Minister. I did not under any circumstances want to take the risk of losing time. After landing came the message from Berlin: I was asked why in this case I had not returned over the Appennines and Vienna. To this I could reply that the Appennines were too high and thunder storms were forecast over Yugoslavia and the northern Alps.

On another occasion we were moored at the mast because a strong cross-wind made it impossible to reach the hangar. The rear gondola rested on a rail truck so that the airship could rotate around the mast. The truck itself must have weighed two tons, in addition to which we had three tons of water ballast on the wagon, while the ship then weighed at least a ton. A sharp side-wind caught the horizontal control-surface and lifted the airship with the truck into the air. At a height of about 30 ft (9 m), the overload-link of the fastening broke and the truck fell to the ground. Fortunately all the posts on the ship were manned. Our elevator-man, Richard Müller, immediately realised what had happened and gave the order 'hard down', bringing the airship close to the ground until it gently landed. The truck was then attached in a makeshift manner to the gondola. A little later the winds returned. One of the crew stationed at the top of the mast reported to us in the command gondola that an important part of the anchor cone had sheared, and that there was a danger that the cone could not open. A few men were immediately sent up with a strong cable to make the cone secure. Now we were safely moored fore and aft, but we could not have set off very quickly in an emergency. Fortunately the wind subsided and turned in the direction of the hangar, so that we could enter. Richard Müller repaired the broken cone for us in 36 hours' continuous work (meals were brought to his workbench) without sleep. As we were ready to start next evening after dark, I told him to take a rest, but he stood at the helm and would not be moved. With such a crew we were able to combat every contingency.

These days we often read in the press that an airship has the advantage that it can land in any small field. This is certainly true in some respects, but when heavy loads have to be taken on or off, a field is not adequate. Even with a mooring mast it is hardly possible to trans-ship heavy loads. The airship constantly moves round with the wind, so that a revolving platform the length of the airship, to move with the wind is really necessary. Rapid loading gear is essential to equalise a reduction or increase in weight within seconds. A hangar is much better for such activities.

We always tried to fly to time, particularly with our arrivals over Rio, when promptly at 1400 hours we would round the Sugar Loaf Mountain, a popular event in Rio. A local watchmaker advertised in the Rio press with the following caption beneath an illustration of a Zeppelin:

Punctual like the Zeppelin?
Do you wish that your watch was the same?
Then bring it to me!
*Antonio Perreira*, Watchmaker

In the late autumn of 1935 we were again operating a shuttle service between Recife and Bathurst, with Dipl Ing Lehmann on board. We had dropped our post over Africa, had taken over the post for South America and were halfway over the Ocean when we heard by radio from Recife that revolution had broken out and that we could not land there. We intended to keep to our timetable under all circumstances. A direct return to Friedrichshafen was out of the question, as it would have meant a broken journey, but we did not have enough fuel to reach Rio, so Lehmann decided to wait. We flew, with only two engines to save fuel, towards Recife, knowing that the revolution there would be short. At Recife we were asked not to come into sight. Our landing field had been selected by the revolutionaries as a battlefield, so we kept flying out of sight up and down the coast never closer than 60 nautical miles to the south of Recife. How often we went back and forth I do not remember any more, but we soon knew every village. We were pleased to see a peasant girl in a red dress taking clothes to wash in a stream. She waved to us each time we passed. By now we had been over 90 hours in the air, and our Chief Steward, Kubis, reported that our provisions were slowly running out. At the northern limit of our shuttle-service back and forth we saw a cargo-boat of the Hamburg-America Line, and we sent a radio message asking if we could be given any provisions. The captain of the ship thought it was a joke on our part, but agreed. He knew that we were only 60 nautical miles from the landing-place, but we said that we wanted enough for three days. The freighter turned into the wind and we came up slowly from behind at a low altitude, dropping a line weighted down with an empty beer bottle which could be seen when it landed on the water. We steered the Zeppelin so that the line hung alongside the ship. The line was taken up on to the ship, and we then hauled up the line with the provisions loaded into a net. Lehmann sent his thanks by radio and added, 'Now we can easily survive the revolution'. The prompt answer came, 'Where is the revolution, then?' as they had not heard of this occurrence.

Dr Eckener was on board on one trip in the autumn of 1934 when we flew again on a triangular route over North America. We came along following the South American coast over the huge Amazon Delta. From the mouth of the Orinoco we went northwards, flying over the three Guianas and along the islands, above the tropical winds and Haiti to Miami in Florida, where the US Navy placed their anchor mast at our disposal. It was tropically hot there and we only stayed a short while, just long enough to take on our provisions. In the evening we started off again, in front of us the swamps of Florida over which towered dark thunder clouds, through which we travelled. The temperature dropped sharply, and when we arrived at Akron the following evening we could not land because of the icy ground, so we had to stay in the air. Coming from the tropics it seemed terribly cold, for we could not heat the crew's quarters during the journey. We put on every stitch of clothing we had, and still froze, but the following morning the ice had disappeared and we could enter the large hangar. A hot bath in the hotel was the first necessity to warm us up. From Akron we made a return trip to Chicago where there was a World Fair. We made a short landing to change passengers, then back to Akron and from there to Lakehurst before returning to Friedrichshafen.

164 The crew of the *Graf Zeppelin* standing beneath the ship in the shed at Friedrichshafen prior to the Arctic flight in 1931. Dr Hugo Eckener can be seen in the centre of the group, wearing a dark suit. The idea for the Arctic flight was embodied in the aims of the International Association for Exploring the Arctic by Means of Airships (Aeroarctic for short) which was founded by Fritjof Nansen. Dr Eckener was elected president of this organisation when Nansen died in 1930.

164▲                                                           165▼

165 An unusual view of the *Graf Zeppelin*, showing the ship from underneath. The ship was 775 ft (236.22 m) long and 100 ft (30.48 m) in diameter. The height of the ship from the bottom of the buffer on the car to the top of the envelope was 147 ft (44.80 m).

166 The *Graf Zeppelin* at Recife. Her silvery appearance was a result of the last coat of *cellon*, a solution of cellulose acetate in acetone ('dope') to which was added pulverised aluminium. The thick cotton fabric covering the framework was impregnated with a flame-proof chemical, then given several coats of *cellon* before the final silver grey coat to protect the fabric against the sun's ultra-violet rays, and reflect heat, preventing the lifting gas from superheating. To minimise friction, the hull was polished with sand paper.

167 A tail view of the *Graf Zeppelin*, showing the cruciform fin structure. The tail cone was large enough to accommodate a gas bag. The fins were supported by two sets of cruciform girders passing through the structure of the ship from one into the other. The fins had no external bracing and were of cantilever design. The rudders and elevators were operated by either electrically powered controls or manually. As in the *Akron* and *Macon*, the *Graf* had an auxiliary steering position in the lower fin.

166▼                                                           167▼

# The Hindenburg

In the year 1936 we saw great progress with the building of the new *LZ 129, Hindenburg*. In place of the earlier experimental craft we now had a dream ship of 7 million cubic feet — twice as large as the *Graf Zeppelin*. The new ship had four engines with a total of 4,200 hp, compared with 2,650 hp of the *Graf Zeppelin*. Its speed was 83 mph, whereas that of the *Graf* was only 75 mph. The passenger accommodation was separate from the control gondola, and was arranged inside the ship itself. As we intended the ship to be filled with helium, it would have been the safest mode of transport, but unfortunately the US Government would not let us have any helium.

On the upper deck port side was a dining room to take 50 passengers in one sitting, together with the commander and another officer. The starboard side was reached by a wide corridor, and here there was a splendid lounge which even had a grand piano. Professor Wilhelm Kempff once gave a recital during a flight. Ahead of the lounge was a quiet-room for reading or writing, and along both sides was a promenade deck. One could enjoy the view from here, and the windows could be opened! Within the ship were the double cabins for 50 passengers, each with two beds, wardrobe, hot and cold running water and air conditioning. The cross gangway formed a roomy staircase hall leading to the main deck. On the port side were the shower baths and lavatories. Beneath the dining room was a large electrically-equipped kitchen and pantry, which also connected with the crew and officers' dining rooms. On the starboard side were a bar and smoking room, which could only be reached through a fireproof door. The walls of the dining room, lounge, reading room and bar were lined with Japanese silk and were decorated with delightful paintings. In the dining room could be seen some of the important places on the journey, while in the lounge was a decorative map of the world in the style of Merian, showing the route of our greatest flights. In the reading room was a series of paintings depicting the development of

the postal services, from a relay-runner to the Heinkel Blitz.

The crew quarters were located on both sides of the main deck, abaft the passenger accommodation, generally with four men to a cabin. The control gondola of the *Hindenburg* was considerably shorter and comprised the command cabin, the navigator's cabin and a small mess. Access to the main deck was at the rear of the gondola. Unlike the earlier airships, the wireless cabin was not in the control gondola but on the main deck immediately above. The *Hindenburg* would cover 10,000 miles (16,093 km) without a stop, having 65 tons of diesel oil on board.

By mid-March 1936 the new Zeppelin was complete. On this occasion we had abandoned the Maybach engines, driven by a petrol-mixture or gas (*Blaugas*), which had served us well, and used diesel engines built by the Daimler firm, which had built engines for our very first Zeppelins at the beginning of the century. As a new type of engine was necessary for our purposes, it had to be painstakingly tested for endurance. Dr Eckener, after trials with the new ship, proposed a 72-hour journey with all engines working at full capacity. The timetable was arranged and it was planned to leave for Rio on 1 April, the flight already being fully booked, but the government stepped in. Elections were to be held on 27 March and the Propaganda Minister demanded that both Zeppelins should make a tour on the 26th and 27th. Dr Eckener protested strongly because of his trial programme, but his objections were overruled, so both ships started off early on 26 March. I was already in the air and saw the *Hindenburg* jolted by a gust of wind as it came out of the hangar. The ship drove forward over Friedrichshafen towards Lake Constance, apparently without control of the rudder. The jolt had twisted the lower stabilising fin, jamming both rudders. After a few minutes, however, it could be seen that the ship was following the rudder again, but the damage was too great to make a long journey, and Dipl Ing Lehmann decided to land and carry out repairs. Lehmann sent me alone on the first part of the tour. Dr Eckener, who was present at the start that morning, let slip a few uncomplimentary words on the purpose of the tour, and as a result, he fell out of favour with the Ministry of Propaganda. He was not mentioned in the press again.

In the *Graf Zeppelin* I completed the first part of the tour which was over Silesia. That evening I learned that the *Hindenburg* was in the air again. The weather was most difficult, with dense low cloud, so Lehmann and I decided to make our journey north at different altitudes to avoid the risk of collision. At 1000 hrs next morning we saw each other again over Königsberg, as we circled round East Prussia. In the afternoon we flew westwards and were due to meet over the Alster in Hamburg. That night Lehmann stayed over the North Sea to carry out sounding tests, while I stayed further south. Next morning we heard on the radio that the *Hindenburg* was over Bremen. We followed it to Osnabruck and through the Rhineland. That afternoon Lehmann let me go while he stayed with the *Hindenburg* at Frankfurt.

Although the *Hindenburg*'s journey did not satisfy our programme of trials, the date of our South American trip was too close to make any further trials, so the ship started off on 1 April and arrived at Rio without incident. No landing was made at Recife as there was enough fuel for the through journey. On the return journey, however, after the African coast had been passed, one of the engines had to be stopped because of a defect, while another showed signs of minor damage. So the *Hindenburg* returned to Frankfurt on only 50 per cent of its engines. Modifications were immediately made by the manufacturers, and so on the later journeys the engines ran without any failures.

After this flight to South America, the *Hindenburg* started regular flights over the North Atlantic. Ten trips were made, almost always fully booked. Travelling westwards the longest journey time was 78 hours, 30 minutes; the shortest journey took 52 hours, 49 minutes, while in the other direction the longest took 61 hours, 5 minutes, and the shortest, 42 hours, 52 minutes. In the autumn of 1936 a weekly Zeppelin service to Rio began operating, with both ships flying alternately, due to pass just south of the Cape Verde Islands. Fourteen journeys were made by the *Graf Zeppelin* and seven by the *Hindenburg* during 1936.

A sister-ship of the *Hindenburg* was under construction, the *LZ 130*, which we hoped to place in service in the autumn of 1937. I took part in the first trip of the *Hindenburg* to Rio in March 1937 to gain experience of handling a large ship (I was to be commander of the *LZ 130*), and to test trainee navigating staff while they were working. Compared with the *Graf Zeppelin* this journey was most impressive. The astounding spaciousness and the high standard of service were a great step forward — one could even smoke on board, although only in the smoking room. This pleasure was denied on the *Graf*. Only on the American helium-filled blimps was smoking allowed, and the first time I had smoked my pipe on board was on the

*Puritan* which met us on our world tour at Los Angeles in 1929, when I was invited to make a short flight on board. Every passenger was astounded by the comfort of the new ship. The worst weather could be endured without seasickness; there were comfortable cabins and even a promenade deck, while the catering was as good as on an ocean liner. The journey was a real holiday in itself.

Dipl Ing Lehmann asked me to accompany him on the first flight of the *Hindenburg* to the USA in 1937, as he

wanted to continue the talks started by Dr Eckener many years earlier on a world airway system — he had been in England for the same purpose in February. He asked me to go with him to America at the beginning of May to take part in the talks. For purely private reasons, I asked Lehmann if I might follow on the next trip as I had an engagement on the 13 February to which he agreed.

Now I had enough time at the end of April and the beginning of May to make a journey with the *Graf Zeppelin* to carry

168▲

168 The *Hindenburg* first flew on 4 March 1936 and made a further 62 flights, of which 37 were ocean crossings. She was the last airship to cross the Atlantic and did this three years before the first fare-paying aeroplane passengers. Four Daimler-Benz engines gave a normal cruising speed of 78 mph.

169 The *Hindenburg*'s dining saloon. Weight was of paramount importance but the luxurious splendour of an ocean liner was maintained.

169▼

170▼

170 *Graf Zeppelin II*'s sleeping accommodation. After the *Hindenburg*'s destruction, it was hoped that America would allow the export of safe helium and the *Graf Zeppelin II* was modified with smaller quarters for 40 passengers. However, America refused, perceiving the war potential of a helium-filled Zeppelin. In fact, although she never carried fare-paying passengers, she made 30 ascents inflated with hydrogen on a number of which she was equipped with electronic gear by the *Luftwaffe* and taken on spying missions over Russia and England. She was dynamited in her shed in spring 1940.

171 The *Graf Zeppelin II*'s port wing car, housing a 1,200 hp Daimler-Benz diesel engine. Mechanics could enter the engine car in flight to carry out routine maintenance.

171▼

A simplified cutaway drawing of *LZ 129, Hindenburg*
illustrating a section of the ship showing four main
transverse frames and six intermediate rings. The
forward part of the ship is to the right of the drawing. A
gas-bag is shown in position together with the wire
bracing, which helped to maintain the shape of the bag
and prevent surging of the lifting gas, and also
maintain the rigidity of the ship. The cotton fabric
panels of the outer cover, depicted at the top left of the
drawing, were attached to the hull and laced together
by cords, and the gaps between the panels were sealed
with canvas strips. The outer cover was coated with
several applications of dope, the last of which
contained powdered aluminium to reflect the heat of
the sun. The dope was then polished with fine
sandpaper to reduce air resistance. The spaces
between the 'squares' created by the transverse frames
and longitudinal girders were braced by a series of
diagonal wires which were designed to take some of
the loads and stresses. (For the sake of clarity the wire
cross-bracing is not shown in detail in the drawing.)
The main keel structure, which ran from stem to stern,
provided the longitudinal rigidity, and housed the fuel
and water tanks and ballast containers. The main
walkway, or catwalk, ran the length of the keel at the
very bottom of the whole structure. At various
intervals, ladders from the main walkway ascended to
the central catwalk, which ran through the centre of
the gas-bag. The vertical air shaft running through a
gas-bag is also illustrated, which could be entered by a
hatch at the lower end of the central catwalk, as is the
transverse air pipe adjacent to the vertical shaft.

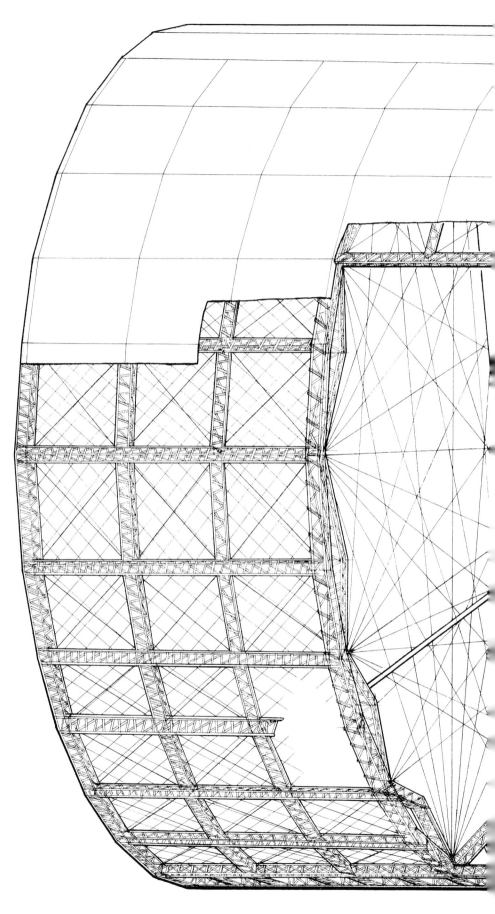

134

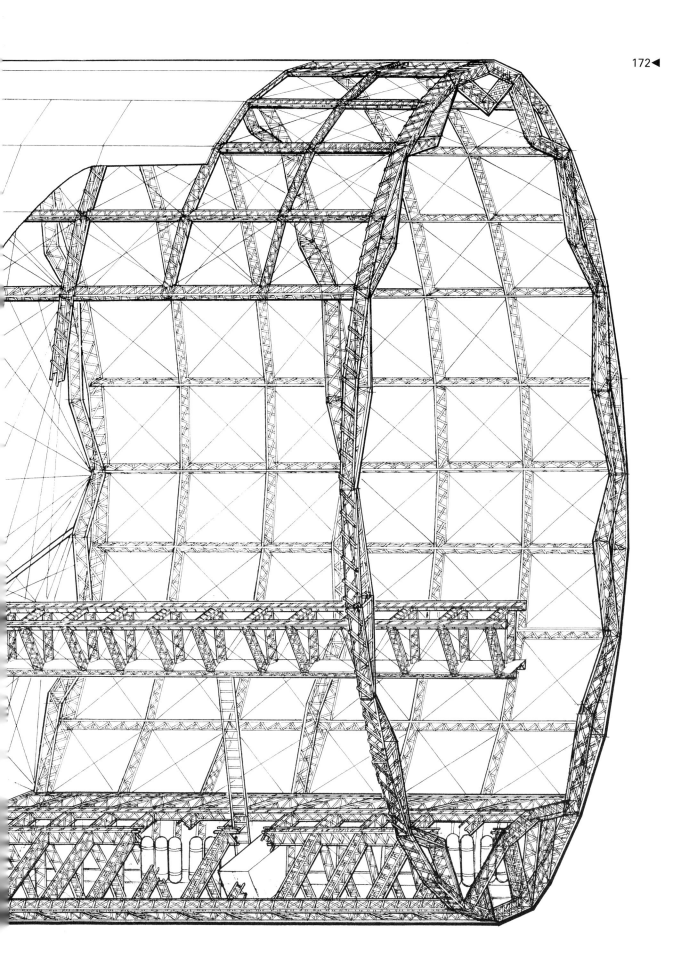

similar trials to those I had made on the *Hindenburg*. Everything went well and we were on our return journey south of the Cape Verde Islands. I had followed the course of the *Hindenburg* with interest and had spoken by radio-telephone with Lehmann who told me that they had met much wind and thunder, and that they would arrive at Lakehurst a good 12 hours late. Late that evening one of our radio operators reported receiving a message from the *Hindenburg*: 'arr Lakehurst'. This meant that the anchor cable had been lowered and that the aerial cable had been hauled up. We climbed up above Trade Winds to make our journey easier. During the night our radio cabin was busy and had no time to take press reports as was our custom, while I needed weather reports of the course ahead which lay northwards along the Portuguese coast. We had mail on board, so we also had to be in communication with the airport at Gando. In the early morning of 7 May we were over the Canary Islands to drop our mail by parachutes, so many parachutes that we needed a full 45 minutes to drop the sacks as near the landing point as possible. I went into the saloon for a cup of coffee, where there were already a few passengers who had watched the manoeuvre despite the early hour. Suddenly the door opened and Freund, our Radio Inspector stood there, white as chalk. He signed to me to come out quickly. In the radio cabin he gave me a message from our station in Rio (Deutsche Zeppelin Reederei: German Zeppelin Lines) to Frankfurt, which read, 'Local press reports *Hindenburg* exploded in air no survivors'. As a little earlier we had received a similar report from the same source that the *Graf Zeppelin* had been struck by lightning and that a list of missing persons had been issued in which I was reported as dead, my reaction was to laugh. Freund gave me a second message from Frankfurt to Rio which merely read 'Regret report confirmed'.

This news, I thought, could not be passed on to the passengers immediately, since it could easily have led to panic. Accordingly, I instructed the radio operators not to allow anyone into the wireless cabin, and that no radio messages should be given to passengers before I had seen them. Finally I asked them to obtain as many press reports as they could so that we could find out as much as possible about the catastrophe. I also told the Chief Steward not to allow passengers into the control gondola or the body.

What could be the cause of this dreadful accident? My first thoughts were of sabotage, perhaps a bomb. Perhaps just such another was on our ship! Of members of the crew, I could have no suspicions. No one except the crew was allowed to board the ship at landing bases without my permission, and the crew kept a constant watch. But a time-bomb could be on board, perhaps concealed under the cargo, so it seemed to me necessary to inspect our cargo. For this operation I would have to have witnesses to confirm the manner in which the inspection was carried out. I chose Chief Officer Hans Ladwig and Leading Engineer Grözinger. Grözinger had a son who was on board the *Hindenburg* as cook, and other members of the crew had relations on that ship, including Radio Inspector Freund's brother, who was a cabin boy, so I asked the two officers not to pass anything of the accident on to the rest of the crew. We checked every piece of freight although we knew most of the senders, but nothing was to be found.

My thoughts kept returning to the *Hindenburg* accident, but as captain, I could not let it be noticed and took my meals with the passengers who wondered why I was so quiet. Every time on a trip as we reached our destination, the spirits of the passengers rose, and this time they were surprised that I could not join in. Even the Navigating Officer told me later that he wondered how things would be later on, seeing me so nervous at the beginning of the season. At midday we flew over the Gironde to France. I posted a notice in the crew's and officers' messes in which I informed the men of the accident in greater detail. I also wrote that it would be the best tribute to our comrades lost in the accident if we made our next flight according to the timetable.

Towards evening we flew over Basle into Germany. Flags were flying everywhere at half-mast, people in the street stood still as they watched us fly past, and there were none of the cheerful waves to which we were so accustomed. Shortly before reaching Lake Constance, I requested by radio that the landing field should be cordoned off, as I wanted to prevent passengers from hearing the news from outside, and I also asked that immigration and customs control should not start until a few minutes after the landing. A crowd of several thousand surrounded the field, this time in silence, whereas generally there was music and cheering. I must admit that this landing was most difficult for me.

As the ship was safely in the hands of the ground crew, I stayed in my cabin where all the passengers were assembled and apologised for bringing them this sad news, but that it was best for them that they should be told after their journey was over. Anyone who wanted to leave immediately could do so and passport and customs control would be available, but none of the passengers did leave the ship. We entered the hangar, and our voyage was safely concluded.

My first question was of Dr Eckener's whereabouts. I was told that he was sailing to the USA on the liner *Bremen* of the Norddeutsche Lloyd, with Dr Dürr the chief designer, to try to determine the cause of the accident with the Enquiry Commission. I was able to reach Dr Eckener on board the vessel by a radio call through Cherbourg, to tell him of the safe arrival of the *Graf Zeppelin* and to report that we were ready to start on our next journey according to timetable on the following Tuesday, being fully booked. But Dr Eckener replied that in future flights could only be with helium. Even though we had been flying for years with hydrogen, we would not be allowed to do so any more. This was the sad end of our Zeppelin traffic.

The cause of the accident is not known to this day. The remnants of the ship at Lakehurst were scrupulously examined, but the many studies carried out by scientists failed to provide any conclusive evidence of the cause of the explosion. One thing can be said: had the *Hindenburg* been filled with helium instead of hydrogen, as originally intended but refused by the US Government, there would have been no loss of life on 6 May 1937 at Lakehurst. In contrast to the present-day air disasters which generally result in a 100 per cent loss of life, of the 97 people who were on board the *Hindenburg* as it burst into flames 130 ft (40 m) in the air, 62 survived.

Meanwhile the *LZ 130* was still under construction at Friedrichshafen. Dr Eckener tried to obtain helium for the ship from the USA but this was finally refused. The reason given was that there might be war! Eckener replied that it seemed to him like going to a war in which he did not believe with a mediaeval sword, but the refusal was confirmed.

# End of the Zeppelins and a Look at the Future

As passenger traffic was now out of the question, we were given permission to carry out further tests on the *LZ 130* filled with hydrogen, at least for its trials. Some of the problems of operation with helium had yet to be solved, in particular that of equipment to combat condensation from the exhaust of our engines. Dr Eckener piloted the ship himself on its first flight, after which I took over until handing charge to Captain Samt in 1939, shortly before leaving the Deutsche Zeppelin Reederei.

Attempts to produce helium in Germany did not result in sufficient quantities and the cost was too high. When the Second World War came, on the orders of Hermann Göring the last two Zeppelins (*Graf Zeppelin* and the *LZ 130*) were broken up and the hangars demolished. The erection yards at Friedrichshafen were destroyed during the war.

Graf Ferdinand von Zeppelin wrote in the 1870s of his first idea of a balloon craft, that 'this new means of transport would bring distant nations closer together.' This intention of linking the peoples of the world was realised conspicuously with the airship traffic.

The Second World War again brought a speedy development of aircraft. Long distances and oceans could be crossed safely and with heavy loads. As Eckener once observed, we Zeppelin flyers were the last romantics. A Zeppelin flight was a voyage, not a race across the world at rocket tempo. But who cares now for the beauties of nature during a flight? On two long journeys in a modern aeroplane to Japan and Buenos Aires which I made since the war, I watched the passengers during the fantastic play of colour at sunset. They read magazines or otherwise occupied themselves until I pointed the sunset out to them; they looked for a moment and then returned to their earlier activity. Very few showed any pleasure in this event.

These reminiscences lead to the question of whether large airships will ever be built again. Technically this is quite feasible, but it must be made clear that it is a long time since the last Zeppelin was built at Friedrichshafen. It would be difficult to achieve the same high standards again, even if experience from the LZ craft were used. There is of course no yard in Europe where building could begin. If new materials were to be used, costly experiments would have to be carried out first, and several problems would have to be solved before starting. All this would involve considerable cost. Helium is heavier than hydrogen, the lift being 0.0113 lb/cu ft less, so to have the same carrying capacity, the ship would either have to be larger or of lighter construction. It should be said from our experience that the speed of the Zeppelins was inadequate, and should be at least 84 mph for greater safety. Every increase in speed demands a stronger, and therefore heavier framework for the ship. One should add that the larger the ship, the more difficult it is to land. Years of experience are necessary to achieve this. Before the opening of an airship service it is therefore necessary to build a smaller craft to test and to train crews.

It would be outside the scope of this essay to discuss in detail the problems which have yet to be solved, but some facts should be mentioned. An increase in speed involves extra weight of the airship as well as the engines, and the extra fuel consumption (assuming petrol or diesel fuel) is a cubic progression. This appears to be a vicious circle unless new ways can be found. If we ignore present-day economics and assume that a patron could be found who was willing to finance new experiments, perhaps there is scope in atomic science, though still in its infancy, for a revival of airship travel. Whereas only recently the weight of equipment to produce one horsepower of atomic energy was 200 lb (91 kg), this weight has now been halved for rocket propulsion. When one realises that the first petrol engine to be used on a Zeppelin weighed 55 lb (25 kg) per unit horsepower and that one can reckon with only 2 lb (0.90 kg), perhaps there is hope for atomic power in the future. There is the considerable advantage that the weight of nuclear fuel is very little, so that the loss of weight with consumption hardly needs to be calculated. Water replacement equipment would not be necessary as with liquid fuel, nor would it be necessary to take on more gas. Even a nuclear reactor weighing 60 tons could be carried, although the framework of the ship would have to be strong.

Whereas we formerly had to fly with a large crew because almost all control was by hand, it would be possible today to save manpower by using modern electrical equipment. A substantial saving in weight would thereby be effected, for not only the weight of 150 lb (68 kg) per person but also bed, table and provisions had to be carried. On the *Graf Zeppelin* and the *Hindenburg* the weight of a passenger including everything necessary for a trip to Rio was 550–600 lb (249–272 kg), and that of the crew somewhat less. A reduction in the crew could save tons.

Projects for airships are frequently reported in the press today, but a large proportion of these schemes are Utopian. Neither a vacuum-filled nor a hot-air balloon will ever bring success.

It must be borne in mind that no rigid airships have been built since 1938 and none have flown since 1939; no new building or flying techniques have been developed since then, and there are no builders left. During the 1950s a German firm made a proposal to re-open an airship service to South America. A feasibility study was made but the company turned the scheme down because it appeared to be uneconomic. When Dr Eckener planned his world services in the 1930s, there were no commercial aeroplanes that could fly across oceans. At that time it was intended to operate services over the whole world with 16 Zeppelins, keeping four more in reserve. If we think of the future we would hardly be able to achieve this number. Cruises of the kind now offered by travel agents would probably be too expensive for most people.

Dr Eckener once wrote of the Zeppelin that, with its elegant shape, it would become an idol of mankind, but that it would be a purely peaceful mode of transport, but there is no place for it in the unsettled times of today. Not until there is lasting peace in the world and prosperity increases will there be a place for the silver fish of the sky.

We, the second generation of Zeppelin flyers stood on the shoulders of our predecessors, whose experience we were able to use. We were able to open a world service under the direction of Dr Eckener and, until the day of Lakehurst, carry almost 80,000 passengers over more than 1.25 million miles. May later generations be so protected from accidents!

# United States of America

## Early US Naval Airships

The US Naval Airship Service, which operated from 1917 to 1962, did a fine job in both world wars. After the Second World War they developed a type of large non-rigid airship which broke all previous endurance records. The ships were nearly all designed and built by the Goodyear company of Akron, who have constructed two large rigid ships, one semi-rigid, and over 300 non-rigids.

Although the British invented the mooring mast, and the late Major Scott's design was employed, the US forces and Goodyear have carried out many improvements, and by towing an airship in and out of a shed, while the ship is still on the mast, they have made it possible to launch airships in cross winds of up to 20 mph, and in winds of over 40 mph blowing up or down the sheds. They have also proved that airships can remain moored out on a mast for over a year at a time.

It was the success of the British and Allied naval airships in the First World War that persuaded the US Navy to follow suit. By 1918 16 'B' class airships had been commissioned, and were based on the east coast of the USA. Working entirely from sheds these airships flew 13,600 hours and covered some 300,000 square miles. When an airship was about no surface craft were attacked by U-boats, and no ships were blown up by mines. Although one or two airships broke down, there were no losses to the crews.

Between the wars, the US Navy maintained a few non-rigid ships which were mainly used for training purposes, the big rigids *Shenandoah*, *Akron* and *Macon* being the main operational craft, the two latter being aircraft carriers as well as fleet scouts. All were lost in accidents and by the summer of 1935 the only rigid left was the *Los Angeles* (*ZR 3*) which was then being used only for mooring experiments.

When the USA entered the Second World War the navy had 10 airships: the ex-army *TC 13*, *TC 14* and four 'K' class ships, which were the only vessels large enough for extended operations; three 'L' class and one 'G' class ships, which were used for training. At the operational peak there were 168 airships in commission, consisting of 134 'K' class, four larger airships of the 'M' class, which were mainly designed for use in the tropics where high temperatures reduced the lift. In addition there were 22 'L' class ships and eight 'G' ships, which were larger; these ships were employed for advanced training, and experimental work of all kinds. From an operational point of view these airships were no longer confined to permanent stations and sheds, but could operate for months at a time on an expeditionary basis, using mooring masts, therefore increasing their value as military aircraft immeasurably.

By the end of the war there were 1,500 airship pilots, 3,000 crewmen and 7,200 ground personnel. The area patrolled totalled about 3,000,000 square miles and 89,000 surface craft were escorted without loss, although no less than 532 ships were sunk in US coastal waters when no airships were about. A total of 550,000 hours was flown, and 55,900 operational flights were made. The Airship Service always had 87 per cent of their airships ready for action, which was a record for service aircraft. This imposing record is the testimonial of the US Navy airships that found themselves centred over North, Central and South America, Europe and North Africa. A total of 125 operational airships, attached to 15 squadrons organised under five wings, had patrolled a vast area off the coasts of four continents from 1942 until VE Day 1945.

After the war, the US Navy continued to employ non-rigid airships for maritime patrol and anti-submarine duties, and in the 1950s several classes of 'long duration' ASW ships were brought into service. In the second half of the 1950s Goodyear built two classes of large strategic early warning radar airships, which operated until they were replaced by aeroplanes in 1962. However, the US Navy and Goodyear have shown renewed interest in constructing and operating updated versions of the wartime 'K' class for fishery protection and other naval and coastguard roles. So it would seem that the story of US naval airships is not yet over.

Much of the information on specific airship operations recorded in the following pages comes from the men who flew the airships, and full information on these sources is given in the acknowledgements at the beginning of this book and in the bibliography.

In 1915 the US Navy decided to experiment with airships, and James F. Boyle, Don Douglas and Jerome Huhnsaker, of the Connecticut Aircraft Company, were employed to design 'Dirigible, Naval, No. 1' (*DN–1*), official designation *A 1*.

The envelope of *DN–1* was constructed at the naval shipyard at Portsmouth, New Hampshire, in an open shed in which a submarine was also under construction. The car of the ship was built at the shipyard of Fred Lawley in Neponset, Massachusetts, where swivelling propellers for the 140 hp Sturtevant engine were tried out.

When completed, *DN–1* was taken to Pensacola in Florida, where a floating hangar had been built. On the day of her maiden flight the ship was hauled out of the hangar, and instead of taking to the air, began to settle in the water, lower and lower, until Jimmy Shade, the pilot, invited the onlookers aboard for 'the first submerged flight of the *DN–1*'. This was the fault of the swivelling propellers, for they had not been allowed for in the original calculations and, therefore, they made the ship overweight.

The ship was rescued and changes were made to lighten her, and Hans Otto Stagel, the company pilot, took her offshore for her qualifying trials. *DN–1* only just made her hand-over speed of 35 mph, and then proceeded to do some manoeuvres which drew applause from the spectators: flying along then dipping down on to the water and rising again. It turned out that the pilot had to dip down to scoop up pails of water to pour over the transmission on which a bronze bearing had melted. After only two more flights the *DN–1* was grounded because of unsatisfactory performance. The total cost of the ship had been $45,000.

New designs ('B') were soon developed on similar lines to existing British SS airships, but in constructing the new class of ships, the builders encountered problems with the fabric of the envelope, which taught them to ensure that the material was properly manufactured with a left and a right bias: when the first 'B' ship was inflated the tail twisted around 45° putting all the control surfaces well out of alignment. This was soon put right by relocating all the tail surfaces.

The balloon fabric used at this time was made from two plies of cloth, rubberized on the outside, inside and in between the two layers. The inside ply was laid straight, while the outside ply was laid on the bias; which prevented the spreading of tears. The main film of rubber, which prevented gas leakage, was in between the two layers of cloth, and was protected from weathering by the outer layer of cloth, which also protected the inner layer of the fabric which took all the loads. A coating of aluminium powder was put on the outer surface of the fabric, and helped to protect the rubber from the sun's infra-red rays.

Sixteen 'B' ships were built: nine by Goodyear, five by Goodrich and two by the Connecticut Aircraft Company. The cars and engines were built by the Curtiss Aeroplane Company. One of the Goodyear-built ships acquired a pinkish colour because of chemical reaction in the rubber coating, and from then on was referred to fondly as *The Pink Lady*. Jimmy Shade, who had flown in the *DN–1*, decided to drop a bag of sand on his house to frighten his wife in *revenge* for some domestic upset. He took *The Pink Lady* up and dropped a 30 lb (13.60 kg) bag of sand, missing his own house, but badly damaging the one next door. Needless to say Mr Shade was dismissed from the service for this act.

### The first coastal patrol airship

In view of the experience in airships accumulated by the time America entered the First World War, Goodyear was given the major role in producing coastal patrol airships for the navy. At this time no suitable construction sheds were available, and while arrangements were being made for one to be built, the first US coastal patrol airship was being assembled at a fairground in Chicago. This ship was *D–2*, the first of the 'B' class.

The first and actual flight test was carried out at night on a run from Chicago to Akron, with Ralph H. Upson as pilot and H. T. Kraft as co-pilot and engineer. During or after inflation the envelope accumulated a considerable quantity of air in the lifting gas, about ten per cent, which decreased the lift by about 500 lb (227 kg). The condition of the gas presented such a serious problem that it looked as if the flight would have to be cancelled. However, after due consideration nearly 200 lb (90 kg) of unnecessary equipment was taken off to lighten the ship. Conditions at the start made it impossible to carry any ballast, but almost 100 gallons (378 L) of reserve fuel and an extra five gallons (19 L) of oil were carried, and served the same purpose as ballast during the flight.

Take-off was made just after midnight and after some trouble with the rudder controls, which was soon put right, course was set for Akron, flying at 1,400 to 2,000 ft (427 to 610 m) above sea level. Several of the cylinders on the engine started to misfire and eventually stalled. A downward draught of air nearly forced the ship to the ground but all the reserve oil and some petrol were thrown out, so lightening the ship. The problem with the engines was caused by fouling from accumulated oil while running at slow speed (800 rpm) and was soon remedied by keeping the revolutions above 1,000, which gave an estimated air speed of between 25 and 30 miles per hour.

Throughout the flight the air scoop behind the propellers worked as planned, but some trouble was experienced with the rear ballonet, which was larger than the other and caused a surplus of air to accumulate at that end of the ship. This imbalance made the ship difficult to control. Then because of a combination of engine failure and rough weather the ship was forced down west of Akron. The anchor was dropped but failed to hold and the ship came to rest against some trees, receiving minor damage to the envelope, fin structure and landing gear.

By this one-day test flight, the practicability of the design had been proved and much more valuable experience gained than would have been possible in a series of short flights. Therefore, this flight in 1917 marked the practical beginnings of airship operations in the USA

In January 1917, as relations with Germany were becoming strained, 16 'B' class airships were ordered, which was much more than the building resources of the navy could cope with, but by allocating the production of cars and engines to the Curtiss Aeroplane Company, nine airships to the Goodyear Company, five to the Goodrich Company, and two to the Connecticut Aircraft Company, delivery of all craft was made between July 1917 and June 1918.

'B' ships had a volume of 84,000 cu ft, a length of 163 ft (49.68 m) and a maximum diameter of 31.5 ft (9.60 m). Power was provided by a single 100 hp Curtiss engine which gave a top speed of 47 mph and a cruising speed of 35 mph.

The ships were stationed in pairs along the coast between Chatham and Pensacola for the duration of the war, and although some were lost, no fatalities were suffered by the crews. During this period some 13,600 hours of flying time was logged, covering over 300,000 miles (136,077 km).

While on patrol off the Highland Light on 19 July 1918, one of the ships from Chatham lost its rudder, and was kept in the air by free ballooning, with the occasional use of the engine, until the next day, when the envelope lost its pressure and the fins fell into a vertical position. The ship then went down into the sea where she floated for 24 hours. Eventually a Swedish cargo vessel came alongside and with the help of morning superheat, the crew were able to lift the ship off the water and land it on the deck of the vessel!

139

173 *H 1*, really a motorised kite-balloon, was built in 1922 by Goodyear for the US Navy. The H class was designed to be towed at 70 mph, and a blower was needed to keep up the envelope pressure. In the photograph the blower can be seen lowered behind the 50 hp Lawrence engine at the rear of the car. The maximum speed attained by *H 1* under its own power was 45 mph. The envelope was 94.8 ft (28.89 m) long and the volume at one hundred per cent inflation was 43,030 cu ft.

174▼                                          173▲

174 *C 5* of the US Navy's C class was built, together with 15 sister ships, in 1918, production being divided between the firms of Goodyear and Goodrich. The ships were mainly employed for anti-submarine warfare, but a few were handed over to the US Army which operated about 30 non-rigid airships between 1919 and the early 1930s. *C 5* is famous for its attempted trans-Atlantic flight from Newfoundland. The first part of its journey, from Monbank Point, NY, was started on 14 May 1919, but the second and last leg of the flight had to be abandoned, leaving the honour of the first lighter-than-air crossing of the Atlantic to the British rigid airship *R 34*.

175▼

175 *C 3* about to leave the ground at the US Naval Air Station at Cape May, NJ. C class ships had a length of 196 ft (59.74 m), a diameter of 42 ft (12.80 m), and were 54 ft (16.45 m) high. The gas volume was 181,000 cu ft.

176▲

177▼

176 The US Navy non-rigid airship *C 1* being prepared for take-off at Rockway Beach, New York, for her 1,500-mile (2,778 km) flight to Key West, Florida. Note the large ground crew needed, even for a relatively small airship. Helium was successfully tested in *C 7* during a five-hour experimental flight on 5 December 1921.

177/178 The car of *C 5* just before the ship takes to the air. The blowers can be seen in the raised position, and in the underside of the envelope, just forward of the nose of the car, an air valve to one of the ballonets can be seen. In the lower photograph the blowers are lowered behind the two-bladed pusher propellers. Note that only one bomb is in place on the two-place rack towards the rear of the car. This C class ship has not been identified. It is interesting to compare the different radiator and exhaust systems in each car.

178▼

On 26 July 1917 the US Army-Navy Airship Board considered a proposal by the Bureau of Mines to undertake the experimental production of helium, which was approved, and an allocation of $100,000 was recommended for the construction of a small plant for this purpose. This was the beginning of the helium production programme in the United States. Largely at British insistence the programme was expanded and two separate experimental plants were constructed at Fort Worth, Texas. By the time the Armistice was signed these plants had produced 150,000 cubic feet of helium, some of which was in cylinders ready for shipment to Europe.

By 26 September 1917 Lieutenant Louis H. Maxfield, commander of the Naval Air Detachment at Akron, reported the qualification of 11 students, including himself, as lighter-than-air pilots and requested their designation as Naval Aviators (Dirigibles). These were the first men trained specifically as airship pilots, and seven of them were immediately given assignments overseas, departing for France on 9 November, to join Lieutenant Maxfield at Rochefort. Then some of the men went on to duties at Paimboeuf, while others were posted to lighter-than-air patrol stations along the Atlantic coast.

The initial training programme was undertaken by Goodyear on contract to the US Navy, but gradually it took over more responsibility for the instruction and upkeep of the men training as airship pilots, but throughout the war the main training and lighter-than-air base was at Akron, although some pilots did graduate from other stations.

*AT–13* was acquired from the French Navy on 1 March 1918 and made her first flight under American control at Paimboeuf on 3 March. On 1 October 1918,

# The First World War and After

after escorting a convoy through her patrol area, she turned to meet another convoy, and while on the way to the rendezvous zone two shots were fired at a rock for target practice. On the second shot the firing spring broke, putting the only gun out of action and therefore reducing her offensive capability to bombs. At 1430 hrs the convoy was sighted and *AT–13* made the usual circle overhead. Then a heading was made to pass between two storms which were approaching from the north and the north east. Shortly afterwards a suspicious object was sighted to the north, and while still a mile away it was positively identified as a submarine, which soon opened fire on the airship. Thirteen shells burst near *AT–13* but she suffered no damage.

The airship gave chase in order to get into bombing position but the head wind was so strong that the submarine could not be overtaken. The convoy was informed of the situation by signals via

radio and Aldis lamp, and the chase continued until dark, but to no avail for the submarine vanished in the gloom.

Although *AT–13* was unable to get to grips with the submarine, she was able to drive it off, thus confirming the extent to which the naval aeronauts met the challenge of their first test in combat. But more importantly the airship presented a real threat to the submarine commander and kept him from his appointed task.

With the signing of the Armistice, the hostilities came to a close, but anti-submarine patrols were flown until 13 December 1918, in order to make certain that all U-boats had left the high seas. During America's 19 months of involvement in the war the strength of her naval aviation arm had grown to a force of 6,716 officers and 30,693 enlisted men in navy units, and 282 officers and 2,180 men in Marine Corps units, with 2,107 aeroplanes, 15 airships and 215 kite and free balloons on hand. Of these 18,000 officers and men were sent abroad to form the US Naval Air Force Foreign Service.

Although the lighter-than-air service achieved its first successes during the war, preparations were made to demobilise many of its members, and the school at Akron was prepared for abandonment.

From 1919 until 1937 the US Army operated over 30 airships including several motorised kite-balloons. In the early 1920s some of these ships were taken over from the US Navy, and one ship, the *RN 1*, was an ex-French Navy Zodiac. When the army ceased lighter-than-air operations in 1937 all remaining airships were handed over to the navy, which had continued with airships after the war, although by the start of the Second World War the service was so run down that only 10 ships were available.

179▼

179 USS *Shenandoah*, the *ZR-1* (1923–25) was the first rigid airship of the US Naval Airship Service. The ship was basically a facsimile of a late First World War German design, which was broken down in England, and was fabricated from plans drawn up from the *L 49* at the naval aircraft factory in Philadelphia and assembled at the Naval Air Station at Lakehurst, New Jersey, where she was commissioned into navy service on 4 September 1923.

The American monopoly of helium and the possibility of a Pacific war were contributory factors to the persistent attempts to develop the rigid airship as a naval scout, long after the Germans and British had abandoned it as a military weapon. Therefore, in 1919, after much preliminary work, the American Secretary of the Navy authorised plans for the construction of ZR 1, the *Shenandoah*, and ZR 2, the British *R 38*. The *R 38* was the first to fly and provision was made for the training of US Navy personnel in Britain where the airship had been built. The *R 38* did not reach America for she crashed into the River Humber after breaking in two over Hull on a trial flight on 24 August 1924, and out of a crew of 49, of which 16 were Americans, only five men survived. This tragedy deprived Britain and America of their most experienced airship men, and left a lasting distrust of British designs as a legacy of the disaster.

For the design of the *Shenandoah*, the US Navy Department turned to German models, but with variations proposed by C. I. R. Campbell, the constructor of *R 38*, and the famous warship designer, Professor William Hovgaard, who was employed as consultant to Charles P. Burgess of the Bureau of Construction and Repair. The design was finally approved by the Secretary of the Navy on 31 October 1921, and all parts of the ship were fabricated at the Naval Aircraft Factory at Philadelphia and moved to Lakehurst by road for assembly. The first ring was hoisted into place on 24 April 1922 and by 13 August the airship was almost complete, floating in the hangar.

*Shenandoah* made her first flight on 4 September 1923 as the first rigid airship to be inflated with helium. (The first flight of a helium inflated airship was made by the US Navy non-rigid *C 7* on 5 December 1921.)

*Shenandoah* was used mainly on an experimental basis to iron out the problems associated with the use of helium lifting gas. In particular, all sorts of experiments were made to increase or decrease the lift of the ship through superheating or supercooling, in order to conserve the helium, which in 1922 cost $120.22 per thousand cubic feet as opposed to $2 to $3 per thousand cubic feet for hydrogen.

Mooring-out experiments were also conducted, for the naval authorities

# American Rigid Airships

deemed it good airship practice to avoid having their ships 'grounded' by crosswinds while still in their sheds. Therefore, *Shenandoah* was kept moored to the mast as much as was practicable. As well as the 160 ft (48.76 m) high mast at Lakehurst and similar ones at Detroit, 'semi-portable' field masts were erected at Fort Worth, San Diego, Camp Lewis in Washington State, Guantanamo Bay in Cuba and Ewa in Hawaii. Also, a special triangular mast was erected on the stern of the naval tanker USS *Patoka*.

The *Shenandoah*'s greatest achievement, proving her inflation with helium and her water recovery apparatus, was the trans-continental flight from the east to the west coast of America. With Admiral Moffett on board the airship departed from Lakehurst on 7 October 1924 for San Diego, stopping after 37 hours at Fort Worth. The next stage of the journey was the most difficult, taking the ship 37 hours, 44 minutes to complete. *Shenandoah* remained at San Diego for five days in order that repairs could be made to girders damaged while landing with an inexperienced ground crew in attendance. Then from 16 to 18 October a flight lasting some 58 hours was made up the Pacific coast, with a return flight of 47 hours being made back to San Diego from 19 to 21 October. The return flight to Lakehurst proved more strenuous than the westward flight, but after stopping at Fort Worth to take on fuel and helium, the ship landed at Lakehurst just before midnight on 25 October, after spending 235 hours, 1 minute in the air.

After spending some time in the shed

because of the shortage of helium, the *Shenandoah* made a series of publicity flights followed by scouting exercises with the US fleet. Then on 2 September 1925 the airship left the mast at Lakehurst for a flight to the mid-west, which included landing at Scott Field near St Louis, Minneapolis and Detroit. Early in the morning of 3 September *Shenandoah* was caught in a squall of unusual severity and was broken in two in the vicinity of Ava in Ohio. The ship disintegrated rapidly and fell to the ground, one half, with some helium still in the gas cells, drifted down slowly, landing with fourteen survivors, while four more were in the part of the tail section torn off as this part of the ship was dragged through some trees.

The bow section, containing seven men, including the then Lieutenant Commander Charles E. Rosendahl, ascended to about 10,000 ft (3,048 m), before Rosendahl was able to bring it down to the ground by valving gas.

Of the 43 crew members on board the *Shenandoah*, 29 survived as a direct result of the use of helium, for if hydrogen had been used, the ship would in all probability have exploded in flames as she broke up.

As a result of the loss of the *Shenandoah* a total re-evaluation of structure of rigid airships, with regard to 'unusual' aerodynamic loads, was made by the American airship designers, and future airships were built with much stronger hulls and with a lower fineness ratio. Also the new designs incorporated the control car and engines within the hull structure.

The *Shenandoah* tragedy left one rigid airship on the navy list: the ZR 3 *Los Angeles* (builder's number *LZ 126*). This ship was built for the US Navy by the Luftschiffbau Zeppelin Company of Friedrichshafen as part of Germany's war reparations. The German Navy Zeppelins *L 65* and *L 14* were to have been allotted to America, but were instead wrecked by their crews in the North Sea bases in emulation of the scuttling of the German High Seas Fleet at Scapa Flow.

The first flight of *LZ 126* was made on 27 August 1924, and four subsequent flights were made during September that same year, ostensibly to test the endurance of the ship on long voyages before it was handed over to the US Navy, but in reality, deliberately planned as propaganda flights for the revival of rigid airships in Germany!

180 US Navy airships *J 4* and *L 1* over Barngate Bay, New Jersey on 30 September 1939. The L class were training ships of which seven of the 22 ships built were originally Goodyear publicity craft. *J 4* was passed to the US Army after the loss of the *Macon*, but when the Army Airship Service was closed down in 1937 she reverted to navy control.

181 The *Shenandoah* in her hangar at Lakehurst shortly after completion. The ship was 680.25 ft in length (207.34 m) and 78.66 ft (23.97 m) in diameter, and had a volume of 2,235,000 cu ft. From January to June 1924 she was rebuilt, reducing her useful lift from 53,600 lb (24,312.55 kg) to 47,500 lb (21,545.63 kg). One of her seven Packard engines was also removed, reducing the total horse power by 300 to 1,500, and her maximum speed from 68.4 to 62 mph.

180▲                                    181▼

182▼

182 The *Shenandoah* moored to the mast of the converted fuel tanker USS *Patoka*. The yaw booms for steadying the airship's nose at the base of the mast protruded out on either side of the vessel. The first mooring to the *Patoka* was made in August 1924, and as a result a number of modifications were made to the mooring gear and the most suitable technique for approaching the mast was established. This pioneering experiment was successful in that it enabled the airship to work with the fleet on exercises for extended periods, being replenished from the mast rather than having to return to a shore base for fuel, ballast and other logistic requirements. The smoke from *Patoka's* funnel caused one of the few major problems when the *Shenandoah* was moored to the mast, by filling the airship's control car with dense black smoke, a problem only solved by keeping all windows in the control car shut when the smoke blew towards the airship.

183 The wrecked front section of the *Shenandoah* near Sharon, Ohio, after the ship broke up on 3 September 1925. A contributing factor to this tragedy must have been the many rigorous flights and the amount of exceptionally severe accidents suffered by the ship during her two-year existence, which must have weakened her structure to a considerable degree. Shortly after the tragedy, and before the nose section, containing Lieutenant Commander Charles Rosendahl and a few other lucky crewmen free-ballooned to the ground, souvenir hunters and the morbidly curious swarmed over the area to rip pieces off the ship and stare at the wreckage. Some sources estimate that over 10,000 people descended on the site of the accident by mid-morning, causing confusion and congestion on the roads leading to the area.

183▲                                                                184▼

184 *ZMC 2*'s eight radially disposed control surfaces. This unconventional fin arrangement gave good control but did not prevent her from being slightly unstable, the main reason why she was unpopular among US Navy pilots, for she caused air sickness. With two 220 hp Wright Whirlwind engines, the *ZMC 2* was able to reach a maximum of 70 mph on her speed trials.

185 The rigid airship *Los Angeles* and the non-rigid *J 2* flying over the light cruiser USS *Raleigh* during fleet manoeuvres off Atlantic City on 11 October 1930. The black wall of cloud is not a gathering storm but a smoke screen laid to cover the movements of one of the 'sides' during the exercise.

186 The interior of the *Los Angeles*, *ZR 3*. The light-weight construction of the furnishings and the comfort provided are remarkable by modern standards.

185▼                                                                186▼

The delivery flight to America began on 12 October, with a crew of 27, and three US Navy officers and an Army officer included among the passengers. *LZ 126* was flown across France, passing north of Cape Finisterre and flying on to the Azores, and then passing Boston before flying over New York to eventually land at Lakehurst at 0937 hrs on the 15th. The trans-Atlantic flight had covered 5,000 miles (8,046 km) in 81 hours, actual flying time.

*LZ 126* now became *ZR 3*, and on 25 November 1924 she was christened as the *Los Angeles* by the wife of President Coolidge at Anacosta Naval Air Station. The airship, now commissioned into the US Navy, began a career lasting almost eight years, during which she made 328 flights and logged 4,092 hours, 41 minutes flying time.

The main value of the *Los Angeles* was in the training facilities she provided for flight and ground personnel in rigid airship handling, and in being a platform for experiments in connection with the design and operation of the *Akron* and *Macon*: the next generation of rigid airships. Although some work had already been done in the operation of aeroplanes from airships by the Germans, the British and the US Army, the main early development of picking up and releasing heavier-than-air machines from an airship's 'trapeze' was carried out with the *Los Angeles*. The first 'hook-on' aeroplane was a Vought NO-1 and subsequently Consolidated N2Y aircraft were used. The last hook-on to *Los Angeles* was made by a Curtiss XF9C-1 on 26 October 1931.

The US Navy was restricted to use the *Los Angeles* in a 'civil role' by an agreement concluded with the Allies before the ship was built, but after seven years permission was finally received for her to be used in exercises with the US fleet. During this period she flew 14,500 miles (23,335 km) in 272 hours flying time and was away from her base at Lakehurst for 27 days. At first the *Los Angeles* flew to Guantanamo Bay and then, after mooring to the expeditionary mast there, she flew to Dulce Bay off Costa Rica where she moored to the USS *Patoka*'s mast. Then from 7 to 22 February 1922 she operated entirely from the *Patoka*, alternating between Dulce Bay and Panama Bay, and replenishing fuel, food and water while at the mast of her sea-going base.

Although the *Los Angeles* was tech-nically 'shot down' on the manoeuvres, proving her vulnerability in tactical encounters, the evaluation of her performance neither confirmed nor disproved the military usefulness of rigid airships. Indeed, what was proved was that the scouting techniques of 1914 had been superseded by the capabilities of new and faster war machines. Had the *Los Angeles* been given a strategic role the evaluation of the manoeuvres might have proved a little more positive.

On 30 June 1932, the *Los Angeles* was decommissioned as an economy measure, and yet for over seven years she was kept at Lakehurst for mooring experiments. Eventually came the inevitable, and the *Los Angeles* was dismantled for scrap, between December 1939 and 3 January 1940.

## The Metalclad airship

Development work began on the Metal-clad airship, *ZMC-2*, in 1921, and after consideration of the design proposals in lengthy committee hearings, the US Bureau of Aeronautics was given an appropriation of $300,000 for its construction in 1926. Tests on several full-size structural parts of the ship were carried out by the manufacturing company, the Development Corporation (later to change its name to the Metalclad Airship Corporation) in 1927 and 1928, and on 1 March 1928 the Bureau of Aeronautics authorised the company to begin construction.

In order that construction could go ahead with reasonable speed, an automatic riveter, capable of inserting 5,000 rivets per hour, was designed by Edward J. Hill, the engineer in charge of construction. The reason for this machine was that the 'alclad' metal sheets had to be lap-jointed with three staggered rows of rivets, and well over three and a half million of these aluminium wire rivets were to be used to complete the job.

The ship was constructed from a series of rigid circular transverse frames and a small number of longitudinal members, which provided the support for all the weight loads. All parts of the internal framework were covered with a thin coating of duralumin. The metal envelope, which took all tensile and sheer stresses, was fabricated from a laminated 'sandwich' of duralumin, protected from corrosion on either side by a thin layer of aluminium. This combination of materials was known as alclad.

Eight radically disposed surfaces comprised the fin arrangement, which although an unconventional pattern, still gave good stability and control. It would seem that this high degree of control was essential for the ship proved longitudinally unstable, due to her low fineness ratio of 2.83 to 1. This lack of stability caused air sickness on many occasions, and it is therefore easy to see why the *ZMC-2* was not popular among airship pilots. However, in fairness to the ship's designers it is important to note that the lack of stability was not inherent in the general concept, and for a prototype the ship proved herself successful to a high degree, remaining in service for 12 years.

In March 1928 the construction of *ZMC-2* began when the first rivet was driven in the bow section, and by February 1929, the two halves of the hull, which had been built separately, were joined together. During June and July the engines were installed, the control car attached to the hull and all instruments and control lines fixed in place.

The first flight was made on 19 August and lasted for 19 minutes, 55 seconds. On 25 August a cross-country flight was made from the airship works in Detroit to Cleveland, then on 12 September *ZMC-2* made a flight of 600 miles (965.60 km) from Detroit to Lakehurst. Her high-speed trials were made over New York and then out over the Atlantic and back to Lakehurst, and the final tests required by the navy contract were completed on 25 September 1929. *ZMC-2* completed each trial successfully on the first attempt and with a safe margin over her contract requirements.

Some authorities regard the *ZMC-2* as a pressure airship, but this surely is wrong for the internal structure of the ship places her fairly and squarely in the camp of the rigid airships. Douglas H. Robinson, in his book *Giants in the Sky*, says that the Metalclad concept owes little to the rigid, metal-covered, *Metallballon*, built by Schwarz, which made its first flight on 3 November 1897. However, it is fairly certain that the *Metallballon* owes much to an earlier design by the Russian scientist Konstantine E. Tsiolkovski, whose paper describing an 'all-metal aerostat', was translated into French, German and English in 1892 and aroused great interest in Western European aviation circles. It would also seem from the evidence presented by the construction of the American State Aircraft Company's metal airship *City of Glendale*, between 1927 and 1931, that Tsiolkovski's ideas were still in currency, for certain aspects of his original concept were incorporated in that airship. For example, according to Tsiolkovski, the 'all-metal aerostat' was to have been covered with a corrugated skin which he claimed would 'stretch' altering the cubic capacity of the ship according to its altitude. The *City of Glendale* also had a hull made from corrugated sections of duralumin, but there is little evidence to indicate why the hull was constructed like this. For the record it is interesting to note that the *City of Glendale* had a volume of 330,000 cu ft, a length of

212 ft (64.61 m) and a diameter of 58 ft (17.67 m). The ship was to be powered by a steam turbine engine driving a fan at the nose of the ship which was supposed to create a vacuum which would draw the ship forward! The ship made two tethered balloon ascents, without a power plant, in 1929 and 1931, and as these were failures she was dismantled.

*ZMC–2* had a successful career spanning 12 years, making 752 flights and logging 2,256.5 hours flying time. The ship was in continuous operation for most of her life up until 1938, after which she only completed five hours' flying before she was scrapped in 1941. During an overhaul in 1935 *ZMC–2* was found to be in 'excellent condition with no serious

deterioration of the alclad material noticeable', but towards the end of her life the ship was found to suffer from gas leakage as the bituminous compound used to coat her seams internally was found to be dried out and cracking.

The safe operation of the helium inflated *ZMC–2* prompted the Airship Development Company to propose several larger designs, including Metalclad airships for passenger and freight transport, but despite the soundness of the projects no funds for further construction of Metalclad airships were forthcoming. The reason for this decision can safely be assumed to be a greater commitment to the fabric-covered Zeppelin-type airship in the Bureau of Aeronautics.

## General characteristics and performance data of *ZMC–2*

**Length** 149.5 ft (45.56 m)
**Diameter** 52.8 ft (16 m)
**Fineness ratio** 2.83 : 1
**Volume** 202,200 cu ft
**Ballonet displacement:**
   **front** 22,600 cu ft
   **rear** 28,000 cu ft
**Ratio of ballonet volume to hull volume** 25%
**Thickness of skin** 0.0095 in
**Length of car** 21 ft (6.40 m)
**Width of car** 6.5 ft (1.98 m)
**Air valves** 3
**Gas valves** 2
**Fins** 8
**Fin area** 440 sq ft
**Elevator area** 190 sq ft
**Rudder area** 95 sq ft
**Automatic rudder area** 95 sq ft
**Engines** Two 220 hp Wright Whirlwind J–5, giving 440 hp at 1,800 rpm
**Propeller diameter (all metal)** 9.2 ft (2.80 m)
**Gross lift at 100% inflation with 92% pure helium at 60°F, 29.92 inches Hg** 12,212 lb (5,540 kg)
**Weight empty** 9,115 lb (4,135 kg)
**Useful load** 3,127 lb (1,418 kg)
**Range at cruising speed (with 250 gallons of fuel)** 680 miles (1,094 km)
**Maximum still air range** 1,000 miles (1,609 km)
**Cruising speed at 200 hp** 50–52 mph
**Maximum speed at 440 hp** 62–70 mph
**Ceiling** 9,000 ft (2,743 m)

187▲

The information in the table is taken from documents prepared by the Metalclad Airship Corporation to promote their projected 100-ton commercial airship. The useful load is broken down as follows: crew (3), 600 lb (272 kg); fuel (200 gall), 1,200 lb (544 kg); oil (25 gall), 200 lb (90.71 kg); ballast (50 gall), 420 lb (190.5 kg); passengers and cargo 707 lb, (320.68 kg).

187 *ZMC 2*, was often referred to as the 'Tin Bubble'. After a long and useful career she made her last flight on 19 August 1939 and was scrapped in 1941. The *ZMC 2* is generally thought of as a rigid airship because there was an internal framework over which the metal envelope was constructed, but she had some of the characteristics of a pressure airship, and must be regarded as a successful hybrid.

188 *Los Angeles, ZR 3* (LZ 126), was built at Friedrichshafen and launched on 27 August 1924. After a successful career she was decommissioned on 30 June 1932, and was dismantled in December 1939.

189  A completed main ring for the *Akron* being hoisted into position at the Goodyear-Zeppelin airdock in Ohio. The two structures breaking the symmetry inside the ring are the girders for the keel walkways.

190  The *Los Angeles* landing on the USS *Saratoga* (CV 3) on 27 January 1928. The carrier's handling crew can be seen holding toggle ropes connected to a line from the airship. The two lines angled over from the airship and fastened to either side of the *Saratoga's* flight deck are helping to keep *Los Angeles* bows steady. The airship is being kept headed into the wind by her engines, which are still running, keeping the propellers turning at the required number of revolutions for the operation. The *Los Angeles* was 656.6 ft (200 m) long and had a volume of 2,470,700 cu ft. Five Maybach VL-1 engines produced a total of 2,000 hp and gave the ship a maximum speed of almost 80 mph on trials, but her service maximum was about 68 mph.

191  The nose of the *Akron* inside her airdock, partially covered with the untreated outer fabric. Note that the seams between the pieces of cloth have not yet been covered. The material for the outer cover was a cotton cloth, coated with four applications of clear dope, and two applications of dope mixed with aluminium pigment. The weight of the fabric after this treatment was 5.5 ounces per square yard, and the total weight of the outer cover after treatment was 11,300 lb (5,125.59 kg). The area of the outer cover was 33,000 sq yds.

188▲                                                189▼

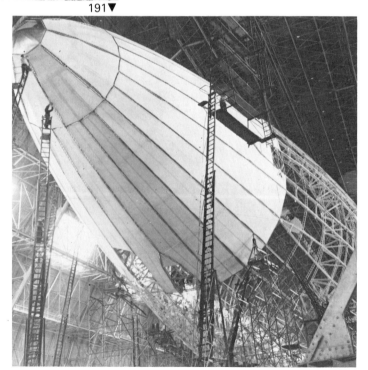

190▼                                                191▼

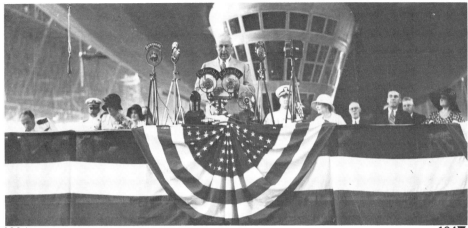

192▲

193▲

194▼

195▼

196▼

195 A Consolidated NZY-1 trainer suspended below the *Akron* on the hook-on trapeze, during early launching tests.

196 The Consolidated NZY-1 trainer, pictured left, immediately after release from the trapeze as it falls away from the airship with its propeller spinning before picking up airspeed.

192 When Mrs Herbert Hoover christened *ZRS 4*, *Akron* on 8 August 1931, more than half a million people were reported to be present. By all accounts the occasion was made pleasant by the forecast of the *Akron Beacon-Journal*, for a hot and rainless day, being, for once, correct. However, the day was made less auspicious by the five high school brass bands that were competing for sympathetic listeners in the hostile acoustic conditions of the airdock. The few lines of doggerel sung by the city's schools' combined 'glee' clubs was only surpassed by the spectacle of Mrs Hoover pulling a red, white and blue cord, visible on the left of the photograph, which released 48 pigeons, loaned by members of the Akron Racing and Homing Pigeon Club. In the field outside the airdock the crowds were amused by US Navy and Army aerobatic teams, while the fairground atmosphere was completed by the souvenir and popcorn salesmen.

193 One of *Akron*'s swivelling propellers, which, because of the reversibility of the engines could be turned to deliver thrust either forward, astern, up or down. There were few differences in the construction, equipment and appearance of the *Akron* and *Macon*. However, while the *Macon*'s radiators were in streamlined housings along the hull, the *Akron*'s were fixed on the leading edge of the propeller outrigger. The power from the engines was geared down so that the propellers could be turned at a maximum of 925 rpm. The propeller diameter arc was 16.33 ft (4.97 m), and the maximum upward thrust with the propellers tilted was 6,000 lb (2,720 kg), and the maximum downward thrust was 8,000 lb (3,628 kg).

194 During an attempt to moor the *Akron* at Camp Kearny, near San Diego in California, on 11 May 1932, the ship's helium had superheated making her light, and when the command to value off helium was given, some of the emergency ballast bags unaccountably discharged themselves, making the ship uncontrollably light. The ground crew were ordered to let go the handling lines, but three of them held on to their lines and were carried aloft by the ship. The composite photograph shows Apprentice Seaman C.M. Cowart dangling high above the Californian countryside as he makes himself fast to the line, and in the second photograph from the left he can be seen perched in a tangle of toggles in the mooring line as the *Akron*'s crew slowly winch him up to safety. The two unfortunate recruits who were unable to improve their holds on the lines can be seen in the photograph second from the right, just before they fell to their deaths. The last photograph shows Cowart pictured aboard the airship looking none-the-worse for his two-hour ordeal.

## Flying aircraft carriers

Despite official and public prejudice against the rigid airship, on the one hand caused by the tragic loss of life resulting from the *ZR 1* and *ZR 2* tragedies, and on the other hand by the innate anti-airship feelings of some ultra-conservative senior navy personnel, two more rigid airships were built for the US Navy. These were the USS *Akron* and the USS *Macon* (*ZRS 4* and *ZRS 5*), launched in September 1931 and April 1933 respectively.

The reasons for America's rigid airship programme are tied in with the complexities of the political situation in the Pacific region during the inter-war years. In general, American involvement with the British left the Atlantic Ocean reasonably secure, but the growing aggressiveness of Japan and her expansionist ambitions posed a considerable threat to peace. American concern about Japanese imperialism, and the need to protect the Pacific coast from surprise attack, underlined the navy's deficiency in cruisers, which precluded comprehensive scouting requirements being met by the fleet. This pressing requirement led to plans being drawn up for a squadron of airships to operate on reconnaissance missions ahead of the fleet.

*ZRS 4* and *ZRS 5* were conceived as Bureau of Aeronautics projects in March 1924, formally proposed to the Secretary of the Navy in November 1925 and finally approved by the 69th Congress in June 1926. Competitive bids were called for by the Navy Department, and the Goodyear-Zeppelin presentation of three alternative designs were accepted as the only serious contenders. However, a second design competition was announced as a result of proposals being made by the American Brown-Boveri Electric Corporation, but their project, presented with the aid of drawings made by Dr Schütte of the Schütte-Lanz company, was not accepted, and the contract went to the Goodyear-Zeppelin Company.

The contract, for two airships to be built for a total of $7,825,000, was signed on 6 October 1928. The first ship was to be built for $5,375,000 and the second one for $2,450,000. It was reasoned that the second airship would be cheaper to build because of experience gained while building the first, which justified the disparity in the building costs.

Before construction could begin a spe-cially large hangar, called an airdock, was built at Akron. The hangar was completed in 1929, and today is still regarded as the largest structure in the world without internal support. The hangar is 1,300 ft (396.24 m) long, 300 ft (91.44 m) wide and 200 ft (61 m) high. It also has special semi-circular doors weighing 600 tons each, which are fastened by a steel pin 17 in (43.2 cm) in diameter and 6 ft (1.83 m) long. By 1933 mooring sites had been established at Lakehurst, Sunnyvale, Parris Island, Miami, Guantanamo, San Diego, Fort Lewis and Hawaii, and the navy were investigating the possibility of erecting a mooring mast in the Panama Canal Zone. As has already been mentioned, the ex-oiler USS *Patoka* had been equipped as a floating airship tender, the *Shenandoah* and the *Los Angeles* already having spent time moored to her mast.

Construction of *ZRS 4* began officially on 7 November 1929 when Admiral Moffet drove a golden rivet into the first main ring to be erected. The construction practice that was adopted followed closely the methods evolved by the German Zeppelin builders, in that the individual main frames, built on the hangar floor, were numbered from forward to aft of the rudder post, which was marked as frame zero. All of the frames were numbered according to their metric distance from frame zero, the first main frame being numbered 17.5 to indicate that it was that distance in metres (57.41 feet) forward of frame zero. Three intermediate rings were placed between each pair of 'deep ring' main frames, and all the rings were connected by the girders of the three keels and the main longitudinal members. The rectangular space between the frame and the longitudinal girders was braced with six lengths of steel wire. The internal engine rooms, only made possible by the use of safe helium lifting gas, were completed, power plants (eight Maybach VL–IIs) and propeller outriggers installed, and the control car and fins built on.

The duralumin framework was covered by 99,000 square feet of rectangular cotton panels, to which five coats of dope were applied, the last two coats being a mixture of dope and aluminium pigment to reflect the rays of the sun and therefore minimize the heating effect of the sun on the helium lifting gas. However, clear dope was used on the strakes over the lateral keels to allow for internal illumination of the hull.

The 12 gas cells were distributed, one to each bay between a pair of main frames, the volume of the largest cell being 900,000 cubic feet. Each bay had a bracing structure within the main rings to prevent the gas cell surging. This feature was a requirement specified by the Bureau of Aeronautics as an 'elastic bulkhead'. The gas cells were lighter and cheaper than ones previously made from gold beaters' skin, being made from cotton fabric impregnated with a synthetic compound of gelatin-latex to make them gas proof.

### General characteristics and performance data of *Akron* and *Macon*

**Length** 785 ft (239.26 m)
**Diameter** 132.9 ft (40.5 m)
**Height** 146.5 ft (44.65 m)
**Fineness ratio** 5.91:1
**Volume** 6,500,000 cu ft
**Gas cell volume (largest of 12)** 900,000 cu ft
**Gas valves per cell** 3
**Area of vertical tail surface** 7,200 sq ft
**Area of horizontal tail surface** 7,100 sq ft
**Engines** Eight 560 hp Maybach VL–II
**Propeller diameter** 16.33 ft (4.97 m)
**Maximum propeller rpm** 925
**Maximum propeller thrust upwards** 6,000 lb (2,721.5 kg)
**Maximum propeller thrust downwards** 8,000 lb (3,628 kg)
**Gross lift** 403,000 lb (182,798 kg)
**Weight, empty** 242,356 lb (109,931 kg)
**Useful load** 160,644 lb (72,867 kg)
**Maximum fuel capacity** 126,000 lb (57,153 kg)
**Normal fuel load** 110,000 lb (49,895 kg)
**Maximum oil capacity** 12,000 lb (5,443 kg)
**Normal oil load** 2,400 lb (1,090 kg)
**Normal ballast load** 20,000 lb (9,070 kg)
**Range at cruising speed of 55 knots** 5,940 N-miles (11,000 km)
**Range at standard speed of 65 knots** 4,855 N-miles (8,990 km)
**Range at 46 knots (158 hours' endurance)** 7,268 N-miles (13,460 km)
**Maximum speed** 75.6 knots
**Ceiling** 6,900 ft (2,103 m)

The powerplants consisted of eight 560 hp Maybach VL–II, 12-cylinder engines, giving a total horsepower of 4,480 with each engine running at 1,600 rpm. The engines were carried inboard, driving the propellers, which were fixed on outrigger constructions. The reversibility of the engines allowed the propellers to deliver thrust either forward or astern, and by swivelling the propellers vertical thrust could be delivered for manoeuvring either up or down. The propeller was 16.33 ft (4.97 m) in diameter and operated at a maximum revolutions per minute of 925, delivering a maximum upward thrust of 6,000 lb (2,721.5 kg) and a maximum downward thrust of 8,000 lb (3,628.7 kg). Two Westinghouse 8-KW, 110-volt direct current generators were installed, as well as two Universal Lighting Company 30 hp petrol engines which were used as prime movers for the generators.

*Akron* and *Macon* were set apart from earlier rigid airships by their unique ability to carry five aeroplanes, of which four were housed in the hangar abaft the control car and one was carried on the trapeze ready to be launched. From 1929 to 1935 17 aeroplanes were modified for flight with the airships; these consisted of one Vought UO–1 spotter plane, six Consolidated NZY trainers, eight Curtiss F9C Sparrowhawk fighters and two XJW–1 utility machines. If the rigid airship programme had continued after the accidents to the two airships, a utility tanker aircraft would probably have been developed for in-flight refuelling of the 'parasite' aeroplanes.

The concept developed for the most efficient use of the 'hook-on' aeroplanes was to improve the airship's scouting ability by extending its possible 'field of vision'. This was achieved by using a technique whereby the aeroplanes were launched from the airship, when on manoeuvres with the fleet, and flew at twice the speed of the mother ship, in vectoring tracks which diverged from the lighter-than-air carrier's course at 60°. By using this 60°–60° search system the aeroplanes maintained a constant bearing on the airship, and by executing a 120° turn at any point on their divergent tracks would return to the airship in the same amount of time as had been taken for the outward journey. This formula for operating aeroplanes beyond the airship's horizon and providing a safe base for the plane to return to had the disadvantage of committing all aircraft concerned to a fixed speed and course throughout the operation, but for the time at which it was developed it was a remarkable achievement.

197 The *Akron* flying over the mobile stub mast at Akron, Ohio. The four dark bands of square patches partly around the circumference of the hull from the propeller outriggers upwards, are the condensers of the water-recovery apparatus. The water recovered from the engine exhausts helped to maintain relative equilibrium by compensating for the loss of weight as fuel was used, eliminating the need to valve off the helium lifting gas.

197▲                                                    198▼

198 The *Macon* in flight on 7 July 1933, two weeks after she was commissioned, practising hook-on operations with two of her Curtiss fighters, which can be seen below the ship pulling up to the trapeze. The pilot in the first aeroplane is Lieutenant D. Ward Harrigan, and the pilot in the second aeroplane, below and behind the other, is Lieutenant Frederick N. Kivette. The *Macon* was christened on 11 March 1933, before making her first flight on 21 April. Her commissioning took place on 23 June. Before she was lost on 12 February 1935, she made 54 flights, logging 1,798.2 hours, flying time.

## The Skyhook Aeroplanes

One Vought UO-1 fleet observation aeroplane, Bureau of Aeronautics serial number (BuNo) 6615, was modified in 1928 and used in initial trapeze experiments with the *Los Angeles* at Lakehurst until 1931. A Prüfling glider weighing 196 lb (89 kg) was procured from the American Motorless Aviation Company, under a contract dated 2 January 1930, for operation with the *Los Angeles*. Only two flights were made from the airship and the glider crashed at Akron Municipal Airport in 1931 when its towline failed to release. Six Consolidated N2Y-1s, BuNos 8600–8605, were procured and modified in 1930 and used at Lakehurst with *Los Angeles* and *Akron* until special hook-on aeroplanes were designed. Two Waco UBF sport aircraft were bought and redesignated XJW-1, with BuNos 9521 and 9522, because the Navy had no aircraft with similar performance small enough to pass through the *Macon's* hangar opening. The single Curtiss XF9C-1 prototype, BuNo 8731, designed as a small aircraft carrier fighter, which flew on 12 February 1931, was used as an expedient high-performance hook-on aeroplane. Initiated by Curtiss, the XF9C-2 prototype airship 'parasite' fighter (BuNo 9264) was identical to the XF9C-1, except for detail improvements and a 400 hp instead of a 421 hp Wright R-975-C engine. Gross weight increased from 2,502 lb (1,135 kg) to 2,770 lb (1,256.5 kg); maximum speed remained 176 mph. It was delivered in December 1931. Six F9C-2 Sparrowhawk production models, BuNos 9056–9061, were built and delivered on 3 May 1932. The XF9C-1 and -2 were modified to F9C-2 standard. Five could be carried in the hangars of the *Macon* and *Akron*. Four were lost with the *Macon* but none with the *Akron*. Designs existed for a utility tanker aeroplane and for a small, low-wing monoplane, with retractable landing gear, but these two outstanding designs never left the drawing board. Four other hook-on projects, for use with the projected ZRCV rigid airship, and one for operation with a non-rigid airship, came to nothing. However, 'parasite' aircraft operations were tried out during the early 1950s, but with heavier-than-air craft as the mother ship.

## Specifications

### Chance Vought UO-1
**Span** 34 ft 1 in (10.61 m)
**Length** 22 ft 1 in (6.95 m)
**Gross weight** 2,230 lb (1,011.5 kg)
**Engine** 180 hp Wright E-3
**Maximum speed** 120 mph

### Consolidated N2Y-1
**Span** 28 ft 0 in (8.53 m)
**Length** 21 ft 5 in (6.52 m)
**Gross weight** 1,637 lb (742.5 kg)
**Engine** 115 hp Kinner K-5
**Maximum speed** 108 mph

### Waco XJW-1
**Span** 29 ft 6 in (8.99 m)
**Length** 20 ft 8 in (6.29 m)
**Gross weight** 2,355 lb (1,068 kg)
**Engine** 210 hp Continental R-670-98
**Maximum speed** 128 mph

### Curtiss F9C-2
**Span** 25 ft 6 in (7.77 m)
**Length** 20 ft 1 in (6.34 m)
**Gross weight** 2,770 lb (1,256.5 kg)
**Engine** 438 hp Wright R-97-E3
**Maximum speed** 176 mph

The *Akron* was christened on 8 August 1931 and made her first flight on 25 September before being commissioned into service with the navy on 27 October. In this airship the US Navy at last had a large rigid airship designed specifically for operating with the surface fleet. However, many operational and material difficulties were experienced during the first year of operation. *Akron* took part in a number of fleet exercises, demonstrating her value by launching her aeroplanes in conditions that kept the surface carriers' aircraft on deck. In particular she covered over 3,000 miles (4,828 km) in three days, through very bad weather conditions, during a scouting exercise between Cape Lookout, North Carolina and the Bahamas, in which her performance and technical abilities were proved

199 A Vought UO-1, flown by Chief Aviation Pilot J. O'Brien, climbs up to the trapeze on the *Los Angeles* during an experimental hook-on flight. The carriage of fighters by airships was not a new concept. Both the British and the Germans experimented with 'parasite' fighters in the First World War; a Sopwith Camel was successfully dropped from the British rigid *R 23* in 1918, and in 1926 two Gloster Grebes were launched from the British *R 33* at 2,000 ft (610 m). The US Army used a Sperry Messenger with the non-rigid airships *D 3* and *TC 3* in 1923 and 1924.

200 An XF9C-1, piloted by Lieutenant Howard L. Young, approaching the *Akron's* trapeze on 3 May 1932, the first time that aeroplanes were operated from her.

201 The XF9C-1 hooked to the trapeze. Young is reaching out to guide one of the stabilising arms of the trapeze mechanism into the 'jaw' of a steadying point on the aeroplane's wings. With the XF9C-1 wobbling on its sky-hook it often took 15 minutes to lock the steadying arms into place. This process required the aeroplane and yoke to be cranked up to the end of the trapeze.

202 The XF9C-1 ready to be swung into the *Akron*, the yoke of the trapeze now locked in the claw of the 'third pole' in the centre of the trapeze. The steadying points on the wings are engaged to the stabilising arms. All is now secure, but the engine is kept idling until the XF9C-1 reaches the hangar door.

203 The XF9C-1 passing through the hangar door, its engine now switched off. It will be hoisted up to the roof of the hangar and transferred from the yoke of the trapeze to a 'trolley' on the overhead monorail system, and winched to one of four storage and service points.

199▼

in a remarkable fashion for a prototype aircraft. During this exercise the *Akron* went through snow conditions which no aeroplane could have survived, carrying more than eight tons of ice dynamically with little effect on her performance.

On 3 April 1933, the *Akron* set out for a flight along the New England coast to help in calibrating radio direction finding stations. No really bad weather conditions were forecast but towards evening, although a cold front was approaching from the west, and a thunderstorm, which was developing over Washington, was moving north-east. On the evening of the 4th the ship was caught in this low pressure disturbance and was repeatedly buffeted about, falling and rising rapidly, until the lower fin struck the sea with such force that the lower rudder controls

200▲

201▲                          202▼

203▼

were carried away. The ship rose into the air once more before finally coming down into the sea tail first.

The crash was sighted by Captain Karl Dalldorf from the bridge of the German motorship *Phoebus*, who altered course and launched his lifeboats to search for survivors. Four men were found clinging to wreckage and were taken aboard the tanker. Lieutenant Commander Herbert V. Wiley, Moody E. Erwin, aviation metalsmith second class, and Richard E. Deal, boatswain's mate second class, were the *Akron's* only survivors out of a crew of 76. The fourth man taken from the water, Robert W. Copeland, the airship's chief radioman, never recovered consciousness and died on board the German ship.

It was in an atmosphere of considerable gloom that the *Macon* was launched to make her first flight three weeks after the loss of her sister ship. With the exception of a number of relatively minor differences the *Macon* was an almost exact reproduction of her sister. Among changes were improvements on the prototype, such as the streamlining of the radiators and propeller outriggers, and the controllable pitch three-bladed propellers, but despite plans to enlarge her, the ship was in essence the same. However, one big difference was that during the *Macon's* career she was not beset by the intrigues and fits of McCarthyistic xenophobia which troubled the *Akron* in her early days and marred the rest of her life.

*Macon* made her first flight on 21 April 1933 and after successfully completing her trial tests she was commissioned into navy service on 23 June, to begin a career spanning 22 months. During this time she took part in fleet exercises and made a number of public relations flights. The tactical scouting role set for the *Macon* during exercises with the fleet gave inconclusive results as to her military usefulness, but her vulnerability when operating in close proximity to 'enemy' carriers proved conclusively that the airship should not have been set this task. This was something that the airship men knew, but on the other hand, it was not appreciated by senior naval officers and the opponents of the airship who regarded the *Macon's* performance as a failure. Had the *Macon* been used in a strategic scouting role during these fleet exercises, a mode of operation to which she was properly suited, the conclusions

reached on her performance might have been different. In later operations the *Macon* was able to prove the worth of her hook-on aeroplanes, employing them in several ways for search operations. The over-the-horizon 60–60° system, mentioned above, was used and sometimes modified by having the aeroplanes rendezvous with the airship at a predetermined point; but the most simple method of operation was developed whereby two aeroplanes flew on station ahead, straddling the airship's track or flying a 60°–60° pattern across it; and lastly, the planes were navigated from the airship by radio.

The end of America's rigid airship era came with the crash of the *Macon* on 12 February 1935, in which, fortunately, only two lives were lost out of a crew of 83. The disaster occurred when the *Macon* concluded an exercise with the fleet and about six hours later was struck by a violent gust of wind while off Point Sur on her way to Sunnyvale. The force of the gust carried away the upper fin, causing part of Ring 17.5 and some of the upper structure to disintegrate and puncture several gas cells, with an immediate loss of helium. Ballast and fuel tanks were ordered to be dropped and with the engines still running, the ship was forced up to 4,850 ft (1,478.28 m), which was 2,050 ft (625 m) above her pressure height. The ship had now lost so much helium that she was no longer able to stay in the air and at 1739 hours she plunged into the sea. A marked difference between the *Akron* and *Macon* disasters was that whereas the great loss of life on the former ship was caused by a sad lack of life saving equipment and the extreme cold of the water, the *Macon* at least had adequate life saving gear in the form of rubber rafts and life jackets, and the water was warm.

In her life *Akron* made 73 flights in 1,695.8 hours of flying time, while the *Macon* only flew on 54 occasions, logging 1,798.2 hours in flight.

In the short period in which rigid airships were operated by the US Navy, they failed to prove of significant value in naval warfare. The airships were given unsuitable roles and used in unrealistic trials, which were neither exhaustive nor conclusive, but the die was cast and the era of rigid airships came to a close in the United States, and the hopes for a squadron of ten naval rigid airships came to nothing.

204▲

204 The *Akron* on the expeditionary mooring mast at Sunnyvale, California, in 1932, before flying to Lakehurst.

205 The observation car, or spy basket, of the *Akron* and *Macon*, seen on 29 January 1932, in the configuration in which it made its only 'flight' from the *Akron* on 29 April 1932. It proved dangerously unstable, so she was never used with the *Akron* again. Alterations cured the problems. After unmanned tests from the *Macon*, it was used with its first passenger, Lieutenant Commander Jene Kenworthy, on 27 September 1934. It was used extensively by the *Macon* after this, but never in fleet exercises, being an obsolete concept.

206 The framework of the *Macon*'s hull being erected in the Goodyear-Zeppelin airdock. The main frame number 170 has just been lifted into place, ready to be joined to frame 147.5, the next main frame aft, by the longitudinal and keel girders. An intermediate frame is under construction on the floor on the left, and, on the right, main frame 187.5 is on the jigs. The nose section is under construction towards the stern on the left. Following Zeppelin construction practice, the rudder post, frame zero, acted as a starting point from which the transverse frames were numbered forward and aft according to their metric distance from frame zero, the first of 12 main frames being 17.5. Three intermediate rings (33 in all) were positioned between each pair of main frames; all the ring elements were joined by the three keel girders and the main longitudinal members.

206▼

207▼

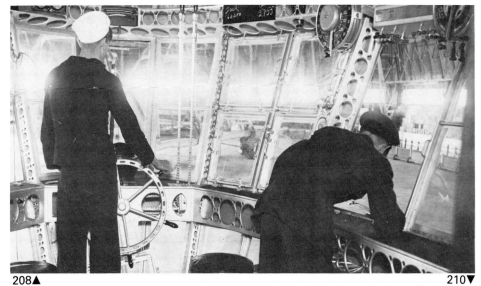

208▲

209▲

210▼

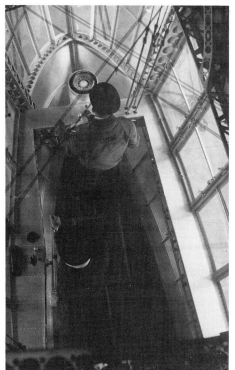

211▼

207 One of the *Macon*'s fins taking shape on the floor of the Goodyear-Zeppelin airdock. The fins would have to be covered with cotton fabric, and then doped, before being lifted into place on the tail of the airship. Each of the three upper fin structures weighed 2,700 lb (1,224.69 kg). The axial length of each fin and its movable control surface was 119.76 ft (36.5 m), and their length, from the leading edge root to the rudder pintles was 104.99 ft (32 m). The area of the vertical tail surfaces was 7,200 sq ft, and that of the horizontal tail surfaces was 7,100 sq ft. At the junction of each fin with the hull the maximum thickness was 11.48 ft (3.49 m). The lower fin contained an auxiliary steering position.

208 The fore part of the *Macon*'s control car, showing the rudderman at the wheel on the navigating bridge. Directly in front of the wheel, between the rudderman's arm and body, is a magnetic compass; above the wheel is the clinometer, and slightly to its right is the box containing the gauges which give the static condition of the ship while moored. On the same horizontal girder, but coming around to the right is a small blackboard on which the total fuel and barometric reading at take-off are chalked up; and further to the right is the mooring telegraph, while another telegraph is in the extreme top right corner of the photograph. In the deck of the control car there is a port for a drift meter, with its cover removed. The seats were for the officers conning the ruddermen. The airship is inside the Akron airdock, with one of the officers leaning out of the control car, giving instructions to the ground crew. One of the windows has been removed, the frame leaning against the front of the car beneath the rudder wheel. Note the chains leading out and up from the rudder wheel to the control wires.

209 Inside the *Macon*'s control car, with an officer at the elevator wheel, which governs the up and down direction of the ship. The gas valve controls can be seen behind the elevator man, while instruments, including an altimeter and an inclinometer, indicating the ship's rate of climb or dive, are apparent in front of the wheel.

210 The *Macon*'s communication officer, Lieutenant H.N. Coulter, working at the chart table in the navigator's area in the control car, with the navigation bridge behind him.

211 This photograph, taken on 20 April 1933, gives a bird's eye view of the emergency control position in the leading edge of the *Macon*'s lower fin. There is an elevator wheel on the left side and a control wheel forward. Apart from the ship's compass in the binnacle, forward of the ruddermen, there were few instruments in the auxiliary control position.

212 A Curtiss F9C-2, piloted by Lieutenant D. Ward Harrigan, hooking on to the improved trapeze mechanism of the *Macon*. This modification eliminated the steadying arms and the 'third pole', and substituted a 'saddle', which was a padded yoke, lowered over the fuselage to stop the aeroplane from wobbling. A 'fork' device was lowered immediately after hook-on to centre the sky-hook on the yoke. These modifications lightened the ship by 300 lb (136 kg), but the most important aspect of the new trapeze system was that the delay in getting the parasite aeroplane into the hangar for refueling was now cut from 15 to a bare few minutes.

213▼            212▲

213 The *Macon* cruising by the vast Goodyear-Zeppelin airdock in Ohio. This hangar was specially built for the US Navy's *ZRS4/ZRS5* programme, and was completed in 1929. The structure is 1,175 ft (358.14 m) long, 325 ft (99 m) wide, and 211 ft (64.31 m) high. The airdock was last used in the early 1960s to house the US Navy's ZPG-3W airborne early warning airships, but Goodyear Aerospace started work on renovating the structure in 1976, in preparation for the construction of what the company term 'airships of any significant size' in the future. In repairing the roof, 8,700 corrugated metal panels will replace old ones over about one third of the surface. After the panels are in place, the entire structure will be coated with 10,000 gallons of asphalt primer.

214▼

214 Graduating exercises being carried out from *G 1* at the Parachute Material School at Lakehurst Naval Air Station on 27 July 1937. *G 1* is the ex-*Defender* (built in 1929) used by Goodyear for commercial operations. When first built she had a volume of 178,000 cu ft, and as the navy *G 1* she had a new envelope of 196,000 cu ft fitted in September 1935. As the *Defender* she was 190 ft (57.91 m) long and 45 ft (13.71 m) in diameter, and her two 220 hp Continental engines gave her a speed of over 63 mph. Ten more ships of this class were ordered but numbers *9, 10* and *11* were cancelled.

215 *L 8* being walked to the airdock at Akron on 2 September 1942. This ship was one of a training class of 22, of which seven were originally Goodyear publicity ships. The 'L' class was 150 ft (45.72 m) long, had a diameter of 46 ft (14 m), and held 123,000 cu ft of helium. Two 145 hp Warner engines enabled the ships to fly at about 63 mph. Note the large semi-circular doors of the airdock, which were designed aerodynamically to reduce the wind currents and eddies which make the handling of the large lighter-than-air craft difficult and dangerous.

216 An 'M' class airship in company with a US Navy submarine. In 1943 22 'M' class ships were on order but only four were completed because of an improvement in the U-boat situation. 'M' class ships were 287 ft (87.47 m) long, 66 ft (20 m) in diameter, and had a volume of 625,000 cu ft. The two 500 hp Pratt & Whitney engines enabled the class to reach a maximum speed of 79 mph.

217 A part of the Goodyear 'K'-ship assembly line, showing two rows of cars at various stages of construction. The nearest cars only have the framework of the engine outriggers in place, while the cars in the background have the structure covered, while in the furthest an engine can be seen installed.

218 An envelope of a 'K'-ship being deflated after inspection at Lakehurst. The envelope was inflated with air and deflated by withdrawing the air through the non-collapsible lines, whose ends had been placed well inside the gas valve openings. The volume of the envelopes of *K 14* to *K 135* was 425,000 cu ft. The 13 ships built before 1943 had various capacities. In the far part of the shed several tail fins can be seen ready for attachment to the envelope.

215▲      216▼

217▼

218▼

At the time of the Japanese attack on Pearl Harbor the US Navy had 10 operational airships of which only six were capable of extended patrol duties. However, although a non-rigid airship programme had been endorsed by the General Board of the Navy, no definite provisions for lighter-than-air craft were made until Congress included a clause in the '10,000 Plane Program' of 15 June 1940 enabling the procurement of 48 airships. Yet when Hitler declared war on the United States of America in December 1941, the airship organisation was still on paper, with no fleet airship unit in service.

The restatement of the naval policy recommended by the General Board in February 1937 and reaffirmed in October 1939 was again considered sound by the King–Fulton report on airships to the Secretary of the Navy on 12 February 1940. This report by Rear Admiral Ernest J. King and Captain Garland Fulton recommended that non-rigid airships should be built and maintained in numbers and classes adequate for coastal patrol and other essential naval purposes, and as mentioned above the recommendation was embodied in the '10,000 Plane Program', authorized under Public Law 635 of the 76th Congress. By 25 October 1940 the Secretary of the Navy had approved the non-rigid airship programme, and on 9 January 1941 the General Board gave its affirmation for five Atlantic and three Pacific coast lighter-than-air stations to be put in operation during 1942 and 1943. The whole Second World War airship build-up finally received its seal of approval when H.R. Stark, Chief of Naval Operations, reported on 12 December 1941 that, 'The President has directed execution of the full non-rigid airship program.' On 16 June 1942 authorisation of an increase to 200 of the airship fleet was made under Public Law 612 of the 77th Congress.

Starting practically from the basis provided for in the legislation mentioned above, an adequate airship building programme for operational and training ships was inaugurated. A huge increase in trained personnel was also necessary and a large scale training programme was established at the bases at Moffett Field in California and at Lakehurst in New Jersey. During the war 1,400 airship pilots and 3,000 crewmen were trained at these bases, at first in free balloons and then in training airships. In 1941 there

# The Second World War Airship Squadrons

were only 100 pilots and 100 crewmen but by 1944 these were increased to 1,500 and 3,000 respectively. Administrative and ground staff were also increased, from 30 officers and 200 enlisted men in 1941 to 706 officers and 7,200 men in 1945.

The first steps in establishing operational bases were made with the commissioning of Airship Squadron ZP–12, with four ships, at Lakehurst on 2 January 1942, and Airship Squadron ZP–32, also with four ships, at Moffett Field on 31 January. The other squadrons that were established are indicated in the table set out below, together with their main operating bases.

**Airship squadron ZP–14**
The Second World War airship squadron

## Fleet Airship Wing One (Headquarters, Lakehurst, New Jersey)

| Squadron | No. of airships | Main operational base |
|---|---|---|
| ZP–11 | 8 | South Weymouth, Massachusetts |
| ZP–12 | 8 | Lakehurst, New Jersey |
| ZP–24 | 8 | Weeksville, North Carolina |
| ZP–15 | 8 | Glynco, Georgia |

**Other bases** ZP–11: Argentia and Sidney (Detachment 14 ferry stations), Yarmouth, Bar Harbor, Brunswick. ZP–12: Cape May. ZP–24: Patuxent. ZP–15: Charleston.

## Fleet Airship Wing Two (Headquarters, Richmond, Florida)

| Squadron | No. of airships | Main operational base |
|---|---|---|
| ZP–21 | 15 | Richmond, Florida |
| ZP–22 | 4 | Houma, Louisiana |
| ZP–23 | 4 | Vernam Field, Jamaica, British West Indies |

**Other bases** ZP–21: Banana River, Key West, San Julian, Isle of Pines, Guantanamo. ZP–22: Brownsville, Hitchcock. ZP–23: Barranquilla, Mandinga, La Chorrera.

## Fleet Airship Wing Five (Headquarters, Trinidad, British West Indies)

| Squadron | No. of airships | Main operational base |
|---|---|---|
| ZP–51 | 8 | Carlsen Field, Trinidad |

**Other bases** ZP–51: San Juan, Atkinson Field (British Guiana), Zandery Field and Paramaribo (Dutch Guiana).

## Fleet Airship Wing Four (Headquarters, Recife, Brazil)

| Squadron | No. of airships | Main operational base |
|---|---|---|
| ZP–41 | 8 | São Luiz, Brazil |
| ZP–42 | 8 | Maceió, Brazil |

**Other bases** ZP–41: Amapa, Igarapé Assu, Fortaleza. ZP–42: Recife, Ipicanga, Caravellas, Vitoria, Santa Cruz.

## Airship Utility Squadron One (Headquarters, Meacham Field, Key West, Florida)

| Squadron | Detachments | No. of airships | Type of airships |
|---|---|---|---|
| ZP–1 | 1–3+HQ | 8 | 6 'G'-ships, 2 'K'-ships |

**Bases** NAS South Weymouth, Massachusetts; Fisher's Island, New York; Naval Mine Warfare Test Station, Solomons, Maryland; Naval Proving Ground, Dahlgren, Virginia.

**Functions** Photographic calibration, torpedo recovery, etc, for fleet and shore units, relieving other squadrons of all utility obligations; to administer airship anti-submarine training detachment, Atlantic Fleet.

## Fleet Airship Wing Three (Headquarters, Moffett Field, California)

| Squadron | No. of airships | Main operational base |
|---|---|---|
| ZP–31 | 12 | Santa Ana, California |
| ZP–32 | 12 | Moffett Field, California |
| ZP–33 | 8 | Tillamook, Oregon |

**Other bases** ZP–31: Lompoc, Del Mar, Abilene (ferry stop). ZP–32: Eureka, Watsonville. ZP–33: Quillayute, Shelton, Astoria, North Bend.

## Squadron 14 — North Africa (Headquarters, Port Lyautey, French Morocco)

| Squadron | No. of airships | Main operational base |
|---|---|---|
| ZP–14 | 6 | Port Lyautey, French Morocco |

**Other bases** Terceira (ferry mast) (Azores); Cuèrs (France); Venice, Pisa, Cagliari (Italy); Gibraltar; Oran (ferry) (Algeria); Bizerte (Tunisia); Malta.

## Armament carried on US Navy airships during the Second World War

| Class | 'K'-ships (K–3 to K–135) | 'M'-ships (M–1 to M–4) |
|---|---|---|
| Depth charges | 4 x 325 lb (147.41 kg) Two internally in a bomb hatch forward of the landing gear; two externally, one on each side of the car below the lower outriggers | 8 x 325 lb (147.41 kg) Four internally in the bomb-bay in the forward section of the car; four internally in the bomb bay in the aft section of the car |
| Machine guns | 1 x 30 cal (1 x 50 cal in later ships) Extreme forward upper section of the car (on later ships a portable Browning automatic rifle was carried for firing out of the aft door or windows) | 1 × 50 cal Forward end of the keel blister on the car mid-section |

ZP–14 was originally commissioned in 1942, and in the spring of 1944 it was the first airship squadron to be ordered overseas. The wartime base was to be at Port Lyautey in French Morocco, about 90 miles (145 km) south of Gibraltar. The six 'K'-type airships to form the squadron were flown to Morocco from Lakehurst via South Weymouth in Massachusetts, Newfoundland and the Azores, and the majority of the 18 airship crews were sent ahead by surface vessels to prepare for the arrival of the six 'K' ships. When the airships arrived at Port Lyautey US aeroplanes were patrolling the Straits of the Gibraltar on a 24-hour basis equipped with magnetic airborne detection equipment, which had to be flown close to the water in order to detect submarines below the surface. However, at night the aeroplanes were unable to fly less than 50 ft (15.24 m) from the surface, so the 'K' ships took over all night patrols; from the spring of 1944 until VE Day a year later, the airships patrolled the straits in pairs — every night! The Commanding Officer at the time was Captain E. J. Sullivan.

Some difficulties were encountered while setting up the new airship bases, in particular carrying out airship operations while the Seabees (CB = US Navy construction battalion engaged in building naval shore facilities in combat zones)

were completing an airfield. In this particular case the blasting that the Seabees were doing sent several large stones through the envelope of one of the airships, and after a quick patch-up job the helium purity inside the envelope was found to have dropped from 90 to 40 per cent; for the next six months the portable helium plant was kept in almost constant operation. In another case, an airship taking off from the still unfinished airfield struck a huge pile of rubble, ripping off the entire bottom of the car. The pilot, who was having trouble keeping the ship up in the air, thought that he had a hole in the envelope, but he was found to be weighed down by about 500 lb (225 kg) of rubble that he had scooped up in the car. Later measurements were taken of the car and sent to Lakehurst, where a new bottom was built; the section was sent back to Port Lyautey and welded on to the car while the ship was riding at the mast. An idea of the time it took to prepare an airship for patrol was given in a lecture to the Wingfoot Lighter-than-air Society by Lieutenant Commander Walter Bjerre, one time Commanding Officer of Akron's Naval Airship Squadron ZP–651, who was a pilot with *ZP–14* during the Second World War. He mentioned how it took four months to assemble the equipment required to erect an airship in

the old airship hangar at Cuèrs, near Toulon, and how Hank Nettling and Tom Ewing had the ship flying in only 28 days.

Late in 1944 airship bases were established around the Mediterranean, at Cuèrs, and in Gibraltar, Sardinia, Pisa, Venice, Malta, Oran and Port Lyautey. Airships from these bases were mainly employed for visual spotting of mines for Royal Navy minesweepers, markedly reducing the casualty rate in these ships. All of the major harbours in the Adriatic Sea between Venice and Trieste were heavily sown with German mines, and the airships were responsible for saving many lives aboard the minesweeping vessels by spotting and pointing out the deadly mines to the surface vessels.

The increasing rate of shipping losses to U-boats in the approaches to Britain, despite heavy concentrations of aeroplanes and surface vessels, belatedly prompted the Allies to request that a squadron of non-rigid airships be based in the south west of England to complement the anti-submarine effort. However, VE Day came while this airship squadron was being prepared for active duty, and the four airships destined for Britain never left the USA.

Only one airship was lost directly through enemy action during the war. This was the *K–74* which was on patrol during the night of 18 July 1943 in the Caribbean. Although the airship's crew had been briefed that no submarines were in her assigned patrol area at the time, a U-boat was detected by radar and the airship engaged the submarine immediately. After momentarily silencing the U-boat's guns during an exchange of fire, *K–74* was badly hit by the submarine's guns and slowly brought down into the sea. Her bombs failed to release while she was directly over the enemy while in bombing position. *K—74* floated on the surface for many hours and all of her crew but one were rescued by surface vessels the next day.

In addition to their escort and other duties, the airship squadron were instrumental in finding and saving hundreds of survivors from torpedoed ships. A special technique was developed for lowering food and medical supplies to survivors, and generally airships stood by until surface craft could be directed to the area, but direct rescues were also made.

159

Squadron ZP–14 was decommissioned in the autumn of 1945 and was sent back to the United States. After the war many of the airship crews were employed by various concerns in flying advertising airships. For example the Douglas Leigh Company operated three 'K' airships from Lakehurst for MGM, Tidewater Oil Company and the giant Ford concern, flying over Philadelphia, New York and Washington. In addition these ships also operated from the mast at Milwaukee and Rochester. Also one 'L'-ship flew for Wonder Bread and another flew advertising for Mobilgas.

219 A three-quarter view of the car of a 'K'-ship from the rear. One of the 425 hp Pratt & Whitney engines can be seen on the streamlined outrigger. The top speed of a 'K'-ship was 77 mph. Tubes of helium can be seen stacked up along the side of the shed to the right of the car.

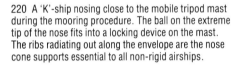219▲ 220▼

220 A 'K'-ship nosing close to the mobile tripod mast during the mooring procedure. The ball on the extreme tip of the nose fits into a locking device on the mast. The ribs radiating out along the envelope are the nose cone supports essential to all non-rigid airships.

The greatest problem facing the lighter-than-air organization at the end of the Second World War, was that not one positive 'kill' of an enemy submarine was credited to the airship service. Despite this, the wartime record of the lighter-than-air wings was magnificent, but it still remained that while the record was imposing, it was so in a negative sense. The heroes of the day emerged in charge of the reconstruction of the forces of the future. Thus, without any positive submarine kills to their credit, the airship men had no representation on the figurative council of heroes. Nevertheless, these men were dedicated and convinced that their craft had the potential to make a contribution to post-war anti-submarine warfare, in view of the tasks that were looming ahead as the East and West settled down to the cold war.

When the Second World War ended there had been five airship wings in com-

# US Navy Airships 1945-62

mission, and by the end of 1946 all the wings had been decommissioned, but two squadrons of 'K'-ships remained operational — one on the East coast at Lakehurst and one on the West coast at Santa Ana in California.

The first steps towards a reconstruction programme were taken in April 1946 when a class of lighter-than-air students was convened at Lakehurst. Pilot training remained at Lakehurst until 1954 when the Airship Training Unit at Glynco was commissioned, and trained some 400 naval aviators in lighter-than-air piloting.

With the advent of the Korean War, the American defence 'recession' ended, and lighter-than-air sections of the defence forces joined in the new expansion programme. The upswing continued and airships were in demand for a multitude of differing tasks, until the post-war peak was reached when Airship Airborne Early Warning Squadron One was commissioned on 3 January 1956.

221 The crew of a 'K'-ship at their stations in the control car. Crews of between eight and ten were normal.

221▲

222▼

222 The interior of a 'K'-ship's car, looking aft.

## New development programmes

On 30 June 1946 there were two anti-submarine squadrons, a research and development, and a training activity, with 16 operational airships between them. However, by 1957 the post-war operational peak was reached with the following units functioning: ZP–1, six airships, NAF Weeksville; ZP–2, six airships, NAS Glynco; ZP–3, four airships, NAS Lakehurst; ZP–4, six airships, NAF Weeksville; VX–11, four airships, NAS Lakehurst; Airship Test and Developments, two airships, NAS Lakehurst; Naval Air Development Unit, Research and Development, three airships, NAS South Weymouth; NARTU, four airships, NAS Lakehurst; Reserve Training, West Coast, one airship, NAS Oakland; ZW–1, four airships, NAS Lakehurst; and Airship Training Unit, four airships, NAS Glynco.

At this time the airship was making a worthwhile contribution to US anti-submarine warfare *readiness* in the Atlantic Fleet and a significant contribution to CONAD forces. It is clear that the Navy Department aided the growth and transition of lighter-than-air from the depleted post-war forces to the ASW airship fleet of the post-war years, particularly when hardware development and some of the accomplishments are reviewed in retrospect. Although the navy's airship fleet never attained the size of the war-time force, the size of the individual airship followed a reciprocal pattern. Several factors lie behind this growth. First, the electronic equipment required for anti-submarine warfare includes electronic counter measures (ECM), magnetic airborne detection, *i.e.* magnetic anomaly detection (MAD), towed sonar and so forth. Airborne early warning (AEW) functions required more lifting power to compensate for the large antenna of the radar. Long time on-station capabilities made increased crew facilities and in-flight refuelling necessary.

The post-war ZP2K/3K programme cost the US Navy $12,000,000 for what was a magnificent and capable airship, flown in the fleet until 1955 when the last one was decommissioned. The next class of airship was a result of the crash programme started during the Korean War era. This was a modernized 'K' type, the ZPG–4 of which 15 were commissioned at a cost of $40,000,000. Also known as the ZSG–4, they were flown until 1959 when all were decommissioned and

scrapped.

The final programme in the 'K' series was the ZS2G–1, that was also developed on a crash basis during the Korean War, and was able to sustain operations of long duration, which was the principal advantage of the design. The last of these airships were delivered to the Navy just when the service entered the 'keep the state of the art alive' phase of American post-war lighter-than-air history. A total of 18 of the ZS2G–1 airships were commissioned, at a cost to the navy of $54,000,000. By 1960 all but one ship had been scrapped.

The first of the patrol ASW airships was known as the NAN–1. This experimental ship was followed by the ZPG–2 programme. The ZPG–2 ships became known as the 'work-horses' of the US Navy ASW lighter-than-air squadrons, and were intended for anti-submarine patrols in collaboration with surface ships. This programme, with 12 commissioned ZPG–2 airships, cost $64,000,000.

When the Navy was assigned an air defence committment by the Joint Chiefs of Staff, the ZPG–2W airship was developed. Essentially, this was a modification of the ZPG–2 design in that certain ASW equipment was removed and AEW electronics were substituted. Five were commissioned at a cost of $23,000,000.

In the last airship programme the well-known ZPG–3W airships were developed. These were the world's largest non-rigid airships. The ZPG–3W was designed exclusively for AEW missions of long duration, and of the four ships built one was lost in a tragic accident in 1960. The four airships cost the US Navy $54,000,000. Large as this sum is, it is certain that these AEW ships were relatively cheaper than some of the other programmes because the '3W' class was funded under a new system whereby ground support, spares and so forth, were included in the cost envelope for the entire programme. The last '3W' airship was taken out of service in 1962.

## Support equipment

At the end of the Second World War, it was determined that an in-flight refuelling at sea capability was required, which was achieved through the development of the carrier landing technique. Carrier landings were practised extensively from the first landing of the *K–29* on board the *Altamara* in 1944 until 1956. The prin-

cipal drawback of carrier landing was that it committed the carrier to a fixed course, which any carrier captain was reluctant to do in submarine infested waters. Therefore, a better means of at-sea in-flight refuelling had to be developed.

The first method to be developed was the hose method, whereby the airship refuelled, by a method similar to at-sea refuelling in surface ships. This method provided much more flexibility than did the carrier deck system, but it had drawbacks too, in as much as special equipment was required and great skill in airship handling was demanded during the refuelling operation.

The initial idea of the bag method, which became the most successful mode of refuelling, was fathered by Captain E. J. Sullivan when he was commodore of the wing in 1953. This method sidestepped the ticklish task of hovering above a surface craft and maintaining station during the refuelling operation. It also eliminated the need for a specially equipped ship. Using this method fuel cells could be picked up from land, from the surface of the sea, or almost any surface over which the airship can be flown. This system not only applied to refuelling but also offered a system compatible for delivery, engagement, and recovery of objects other than fuel cells, such as sonobuoys, sonar devices, mines, replenishment packages, and air-sea rescue equipment.

One of the most significant developments in airship collateral equipment since the war was the mechanization of ground-handling procedures — accomplished by use of a team of mechanical 'mules'. These mules consisted of two large specially-rigged trucks which held the airship's yaw lines taut. Formerly, large groups of men were required to hold these lines until the airship was attached to the mast or was ready to take off. Forty men was the minimum the navy permitted to handle a 'K' ship, and if it had not been for the mules at least a hundred men would have been needed to handle the '3W' ships. The '3W' airships were, in fact, easily handled by a mere handful of men — less than ten.

Mooring masts also underwent considerable development after 1945, resulting in the type V mast for a '3W', which weighed 122,000 lb (55,340 kg), carried its own electrical power unit, and was therefore able to supply electricity to moored airships, and was nearly fully automatic in its operation.

The air transportable mooring mast, in simple terms known as the 'stick mast', was developed after 1955, and the chief advantage offered by this mast was its light weight, and the ease of transportation which gave great flexibility in emergency deployments.

Snow removal has long been a problem to airships, since even a thin covering spread over the envelope can create a large weight problem. However, snow removal masts were developed to help diminish this problem. An old mast with an extended tower, equipped with high-pressure water hoses, was moved to the snow-laden airship, and the 'top men' then directed the nozzles to wash away the snow.

The one piece of equipment that is unique to the airship alone is the towed sonar system. While modern helicopters can be deployed with dunking sonar, the airship is the only airborne craft capable of towing a variable depth sonar. This piece of equipment is most significant in ASW. The airship, using its winch, is able to drop the sonar 'fish' into the ocean and trail it behind it below the surface of the sea. This type of sonar has many advantages over those carried by surface craft: the equipment can be lowered to various depths to get the best sounding; rough seas do not hinder it; the towing airship does not create a propeller disturbance such as surface ships do at high speed; and the airship, while conducting a sonar search, is still in a better position to carry on a visual search.

223▲

224▲

223 A 'K'-ship shown in profile. The ships of this class were 251.7 ft (76.71 m) long and 57.8 ft (17.61 m) in diameter.

224 A 'K'-ship lowering emergency supplies to the survivors of a shipwreck in January 1943. During the Second World War airships were instrumental in locating many survivors of ships sunk by enemy action, and quickly leading surface rescue craft to them.

225 A 'K'-ship landing on the deck of the carrier USS *Yorktown* (CV-10) to pick up some passengers.

225▼

226▲

227▲

226 A depth-charge attack on a U-boat by a US Navy destroyer and the airship *K 58*. Another 'K'-ship can be seen in the distance. In the early days of the war the airships were handicapped by crude equipment and ordnance but as the number of airships increased and their armament improved, submarines almost completely avoided airship-patrolled areas.

227 A 'K'-ship flying over a convoy in the Atlantic on 23 July 1943. Not one of the thousands of ships escorted by airships during the war was lost, and the reliability of the airships was so great that by the end of the war they had amassed an 87 per cent availability record, reflecting the low maintenance required to keep the ship aloft.

228 *U-858* surrendering off Cape May, New Jersey, after being escorted by a destroyer escort for 1,000 miles (1,852 km). A boarding party from USS *ATR-57* is being put aboard the U-boat as a 'K' class airship flies above providing cover.

229 *N 1*, launched in 1951, the prototype of the 'N' class which was re-designated as the ZPG2 class, landing after a flight from Akron. A 'K'-ship can be seen moored in the background. *N 1* had two 700 hp Wright Cyclone inboard engines, arranged so that one engine could drive both propellers if necessary. This was the first ship to have an 'X' fin arrangement, known better as 'ruddervators'. The ship was 324 ft (78.75 m) in length, 71 ft (21.64 m) in diameter, and had a volume of 825,000 cu ft.

228▲

229▼

164

230 A ZS2G class airship about to start a take-off run at Lakehurst. This class was intended for long duration anti-submarine warfare patrols. The first was launched in 1954. Their envelopes were 285 ft (86.86 m) long, 68 ft (20.72 m) in diameter, and had a volume of 670,000 cu ft. Power was supplied by two 800 hp Curtiss Wright engines. A noticeable feature of the 'ZS2G' ships was the curious inverted 'Y' fin arrangement.

230▲                                    231▼

231 A ZPG-2 airship from Squadron ZP-3, Lakehurst, hovering over the aircraft carrier USS *Leyte* (CVA-32), prior to a new refuelling-at-sea operation that dispensed with the fuel hose. Instead fuel was raised in a special bag by means of a winch in the airships. The envelope's length was 343 ft (104.59 m), the diameter was 75 ft (22.80 m), and the volume was 1,011,000 cu ft. Two 800 hp Wright engines provided power; one engine could drive both propellers for cruising at under 46 mph.

232 A ZPG-2W airship in flight. Five of these airborne early warning ships were built in 1955. The envelope was 343 ft (104.54 m) long and had a capacity of 1,011,000 cu ft. Both 800 hp Wright engines were placed inboard, and gave the ships a maximum speed of 80 mph.

233 The crew of a ZPG-3W airship installing a spare testing wheel under the centre of the car during evaluation procedures. Working on the wheel, from left to right, can be seen AM/1 Taggart, AM/C Moore, W/O Melaughlin, and AD/1 Turtelot, with Lieutenant Commander Krueger supervising in the background.

232▼                                    233▼

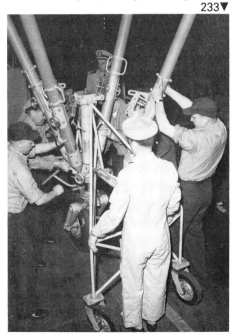

## Record breaking airships

Several well-publicised flights were carried out which were significant in demonstrating one of the airship's principal attributes — long endurance. In 1946 the old *XM-1* made a flight of 170.3 hours duration under the command of Lieutenant Walton. In 1954 a ZPG airship, commanded by the then Commander Marion H. Eppes, broke all previous endurance records by remaining in flight for 200 hours, 12 minutes. This record was broken in March 1957 by a ZPG-2 commanded by Commander Jack R. Hunt — Commander Hunt's ZPG-2 left the mast at NAS South Weymouth on the evening of 4 March 1957, and 11 days and 9,448 miles (13,222 km) later it landed at Key West in Florida. This ship's 264 hours, 14 minutes and 18 seconds of flight time had not only shattered the previous endurance record, but the airship had also broken the distance record established by the *Graf Zeppelin*. The airship had, in addition, made the first non-stop round trip flight over the Atlantic between the United States, Europe and Africa. The 1958 Arctic flight commonly referred to as the 'snowbird hop', of a ZPG-2 attached to the Naval Air Development Unit, also proved that geographic barriers were down as far as non-rigid lighter-than-air craft were concerned.

The Naval Air Development Unit's primary objective at this time was to determine the all-weather capability of airships, and before Commander Hunt was assigned to South Weymouth there were nine 'airship all-weather flights', the most productive of which were Lieutenant Charles A. Mill's icing-study flights during the winter of 1955–1956. For the first three months of this programme, the group studied previous tests on the icing characteristics of airships, working with NACA in Cleveland to determine the various meteorological effects that could be expected during the experimental flights. Also, test flights were made in Lockheed Constellations to see how these aeroplanes behaved under icing conditions. After this a ZPG-2 airship, nicknamed *The Snowbird*, was specially configured for the study with electrically heated propellers, special anti-icing paint on the fins, closed-circuit television with the camera mounted on the tail, 13 cine cameras mounted at strategic points around the ship, and meters to measure ice accretion and temperature.

The experimental programme was divided into three phases, with *The Snowbird* under the captaincy of Commander Hunt. In the first phase weekly flights were made in the course of which the ship made a 30-hour flight during the worst weather predicted for each week, and remained on-station, 50 miles (80 km) out to sea, for 24 hours. In one flight 4,000 lb (1,815 kg) of ice was accumulated on the ship in almost three hours, and the ship still worked satisfactorily.

A 10-day on-station demonstration was conducted for the second phase, together with ZW-1, the early warning squadron at Lakehurst. The ships were to make a total of ten flights between them, patrolling on-station 200 miles (322 km) out at sea, each ship 24 hours on-station, with a total flight time of 36 hours. This part of the test was carried out in January 1957 during the worst weather New England had experienced for 75 years. Eleven flights were made in the ten days; the extra one was made because strong winds caused one watch to be shortened, for by the time the ship reached the patrol area only 8,000 lb (3,630 kg) of fuel was left — the same amount as in the tanks of the ship being relieved.

The third phase consisted of an 'extended' flight for which a consideration was that it should not be made into a stunt but it should *prove* to those sceptics in the navy who were not aware of the operational capabilities of airships, that these craft could be operated with a full electronic load, fly across the Atlantic, and (if necessary) land, and return to base. The calculated flight time for taking off from South Weymouth and flying the Great Circle route to the Azores, depending on the prevailing wind conditions, varied from 40 to 120 hours; and when the flight route was determined, the airship was outfitted for an operational flight, except for the inclusion of an auxiliary power unit to start the engines in case of failure. It was also planned to have a portable mast carried in a Constellation which would fly slightly ahead of the airship at all times.

Approval for the flight was obtained from nine admirals, but permission from the tenth, Admiral Burke, only came while they were surveying possible emergency landing places on the Atlantic route. A crew was selected on the basis of their performance during the earlier all-weather flights, and a test flight made.

At 1830 hrs on Monday, 4 March *The Snowbird* took off. The watches were arranged for six hours' duration during the day, and three hours at night — seven men on and seven men off watch. Flying at 500 ft (152.40 m), with a good tail wind the ship averaged between 70 and 75 knots ground speed, but by the third day strong headwinds soon reduced the ground speed to about 10 knots. However, information on wind conditions at various points around the ship was obtained from the Constellation, and a new course was set, taking them within sight of Portugal by that evening.

By midnight they were crossing the Straits of Gibraltar, when a check revealed that only 9,000 lb (4,080 kg) of fuel was left. But weather conditions were such that it was determined to return across the Atlantic without stopping to refuel. They then proceeded south along the coast of Africa to Cape Jube, a Foreign Legion outpost on the edge of the Sahara. After heading out to sea, the real navigation started, for they were not to see land for three days — celestial navigation was used at night and the daytime ground speed was determined by calculating the speed of the airship's shadow on the water.

On the seventh day, they were 1,500 miles (2,414 km) from Puerto Rico, and the ship was becoming light so water ballast from the sea was picked up to avoid valving helium. On the ninth day a message was received from the Chief of Naval Operations ordering them to land at Key West. Two days later they were informed by radio that *The Snowbird* had broken the *Graf Zeppelin*'s 1929 distance record of 6,980 miles (11,233 km) without refuelling. The airship landed at Key West at about 1845 hrs, in front of an official reception complete with admirals, rear-admirals and a military band, in recognition of the achievements of the crew.

## Winter ASW operations

By 30 June 1960 the lighter-than-air force was reduced to two fleet squadrons, which amounted to about one-third of the operational airships flying in 1958. The future of naval airships looked uncertain and to prove that they should be continued in the inventory of ASW weapons tests were devised. In this connection, ZP-3, during the winter of 1959, conducted an operation that was unparalleled by any aviation patrol unit

234▲  235▲

234 The car of a ZPG-3W airship before it is joined on to the envelope. The car was suspended by cables connected to a catenary curtain inside the envelope. Fabric was then faired down from the envelope and joined on to the streamlined section of the car.

235 The ZPG-3W car and envelope during the mating process. The three discs on the underside of the envelope are air-spill ports for the ballonets.

236 The completed ZPG-3W ready for take-off. The ZPG-3W airship carried a multiplicity of electronics gear, some of which can be seen on the fore part of the car.

236▲                     237▼                            238▼

237 An intermediate and major check routine being carried out by technicians on the electronics panel of a ZPG-3W airship. From left to right the technicians working at the panel are AE/2 Woolfe, AE/2 Cook, AE/1 Benuet and ATC Frundenberg.

238 A view of the navigation table in the control car of a ZPG-3W.

in peace or war. ZP–3 was assigned the task of assisting in the development and evaluation of a new system of submarine detection. This operation began on 15 September 1959 and was completed on 31 March 1960, requiring sustained on-station flights of over 40 hours duration through some of the most severe winter weather ever recorded off the Atlantic coast: sleet, snow, freezing rain, dense fog, gale-force winds, and severe turbulence were common-place. These months of mid-winter were selected deliberately because had the operation taken place in May or June, the desired effect, on officialdom, would not have been achieved.

Phase I of the operation, which lasted from 15 September until 31 January, was a training phase. Phase II, when the operation began in earnest on 1 February 1960, continued through to 31 March 1960. During this period *ZP–3* was committed to maintain an airship continuously on station; a total committment of 1,440 'on-station' hours. Despite the extremes of adverse weather encountered, *ZP–3*, with the able assistance of *ZW–1*, generated more flight time than in any similar period of history — a total of 1,644 flying hours were required. Airships, manned by five flight crews, maintained on-station coverage for 1,277 hours out of the required total, which provided for a coverage factor of 88.6 per cent — a feat unprecedented in the history of airships.

For 25 per cent of the 60 days of the operation, whole gale winds existed in the area. During this period the crews flew an average rate of 164.7 hours per month. Airship utilization was the greatest in history, being 205.9 hours per month. The designed endurance of the ZPG–2 class was adequately proved. The ships were designed for 55 hours unrefuelled endurance in ASW configuration, and three particular flights not only reached this, but also exceeded it. The first ship of ZP–3, piloted by Chief Aviation Pilot Brewster, remained airborne for 65.6 hours. The second ship, piloted by Lieutenant Commander Suchicki, landed 73.1 hours after take-off. These flights were topped by an almost unbelievable performance for a ZPG–2, when, under the leadership of Lieutenant Commander Lundi Moore, a record of almost 100 airborne hours was achieved. After Moore had spent some 80 hours airborne a relief ship was launched, which developed a minor 'casualty' and returned to base. The Commanding Officer sent a message to Moore informing him of the situation and asking him to conserve fuel. (A ZPG–2 normally burned about 250 lb (115 kg) of fuel per hour.) The reply from the ship was, 'Now burning 55 pounds per hour. Do you have any suggestions for further fuel economy?' The airship landed after being airborne for 95.5 hours.

During this operation diversions were required to be made on two occasions, because of adverse weather, one to Bermuda and the other to South Weymouth. In-flight refuelling with the bag method, in heavy winds and blowing snow, became routine. The Coast Guard Station at Cape May, New Jersey, and Barngate Beach were utilized as refuelling platforms, adequately demonstrating the value of the bag refuelling method.

At the completion of the exercise ZP–3 received a 'well-done' message from Vice-Admiral Taylor, then Commander Anti-submarine Development Force, Atlantic. The Commander's message read: 'The completion of Phase Two of my OPORDER marks another page in our book of knowledge of anti-submarine warfare. We need not wait for the results of a final evaluation to know that your performance, often under extremely adverse weather conditions, over a long period of time was most outstanding. A sincere well done to you and all who made this performance possible.'

239 An internal drawing of a ZPG-3W showing details of the forward and aft ballonets, the catenary curtains and suspension cables, the AEW radar antenna, the height finding radar, and the access shaft to its compartment at the top of the ship.

240 The internal arrangement of the crew's quarters and flight decks of a ZPG-3W. A drawing of the platform on the top of the envelope is shown on the right.

241 A ZPG-3W from beneath the stern, giving a clear view of the 'X' fin or 'ruddervator' configuration.

239▼

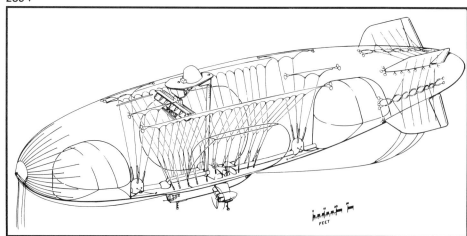

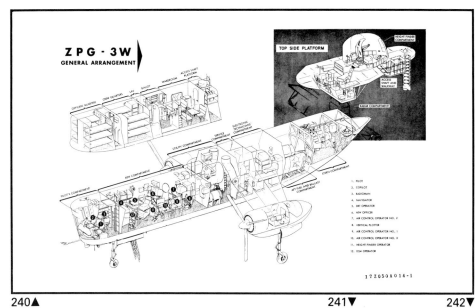

242 Outline drawing of the ZPG-3W class showing the airship in front and side elevation, with a front view of the car and engines.

243 A ZPG-3W early warning radar ship in flight. Four of these craft were built in 1958, each with a volume of 1,516,300 cu ft. The length of the envelope was 403 ft (122.83 m), the diameter 85 ft (25.90 m), and the height of the ship from the bottom of the car to the top of the radar compartment on top of the envelope was 118 ft (35.96 m). Power was supplied by two Curtiss Wright engines, each producing 1,500 hp. The top speed was about 80 mph. The ZPG-3W ships were the largest non-rigid airships ever built, and the last US Navy airships to fly.

240▲      241▼      242▼

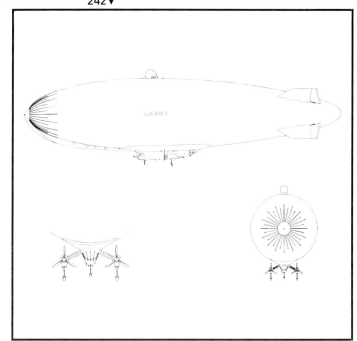

243▼

# The Present and Future of Airships

The Goodyear public relations airships, at present flying in the United States and Europe, have done much to reinstate the idea of the airship with the public as a safe and effective transport medium. Goodyear currently operates four non-rigid airships, *America*, *Columbia IV* and *Mayflower*, all based in the United States, and *Europa*, which was built at Cardington and operates throughout Western Europe from its base at Capena in Italy. The latest *Mayflower* was constructed in 1978 and is slightly larger than its predecessor, which was launched in 1976. Goodyear have constructed 261 airships under contract for the US Navy and Army; the remaining 43 were commercial airships, of which the first was the *Pilgrim*, launched in 1925. Goodyear's newest commercial airship, *Enterprise*, is the 304th to be built by the company.

Like its sisters, *Mayflower* has a gross volume of 202,700 cu ft and an envelope surface of 21,600 sq ft; The envelope is made of two-ply Neoprene-coated Dacron and is filled with helium. Four-colour display panels 105 ft (32 m) long and 24.5 ft (7.47 m) high are fixed on either side of the envelope, and flash static or animated messages which can be read at one mile when the airship is cruising at a height of 1,000 ft (305 m). These sign panels are powered by a turbojet mounted in a removable pod on the undersurface of the control car. The control car has accommodation for the pilot and six passengers, and has a simple non-retractable landing wheel mounted beneath it. It is powered by two 210 hp Continental IO-360-D flat-six engines each driving a Hartzell two-bladed metal reversible-pitch pusher propeller.

## Potential roles and markets

However, Goodyear's latest lighter-than-air technology ambition certainly transcends the purely public relations aspect of airship operations. With its eye now firmly fixed on future markets, the company is strongly in favour of developing large airships for use as airport passenger shuttles, flying cranes, and coastal patrol craft. The company has studied these and several other projects for the US National Aeronautics and Space Administration (NASA) and US Navy, and as a result of work done in 1975 has proposed that a government funded up-rated version of the non-rigid ZPG 3W airborne early warning (AEW) airship should be flown as a test-bed for the various applications so far proposed for airships. Morris B. Jobe, then president of Goodyear Aerospace, speaking from Akron in 1975 said that there was a world-wide need for an economical, environmentally sound, go-anywhere mode of transportation that could be filled by the airship. He went on to say that the ZPG 3W design 'exists and is proven' and that Goodyear would modernize it by removing all military equipment and utilizing new propulsion and materials technology for the test-bed airship.

Another Goodyear executive, Fred Nebiker, manager of airship programmes at Akron, later stated that the use of airships for coast guard duties was feasible because of the international extension of coastal boundaries to the 200-mile (370 km) limit, which has in a sense created 'millions of square miles of new ocean for the nations of the world to patrol'. Goodyear base their arguments for a new generation of coastal patrol airships on the evidence of reliability presented by the record of the US Navy airship service during and after the Second World War. Goodyear and some elements in the USN are convinced that airships built using recent improvements in materials and propulsion technology would be more effective than their forerunners. A good indicator of the future of airships in the USA was given by Vice Admiral Malcolm W. Eagle, executive director of the US Naval Air Museum, when he said that 'lighter-than air was an important part of naval history and will be an integral part of the future', when speaking at a meeting of airship veterans at Pensacola, Florida in mid-1980. It is of interest to note that at the same meeting Rear Admiral Carl J. Seiberlich (USN, Retd) gave a presentation on current USN lighter-than-air projects.

A British-based company, Airship Developments (formerly Aerospace Developments), run by a team of enthusiastic businessmen and designers, could well challenge Goodyear in future competition for world markets for the airship. This new company has researched, designed and built the first British home-produced commercial airship since 1929 when the non-rigid *AD1* flew on advertising flights round Newcastle, excluding, of course, the large rigids that were being constructed at about the same time. The *AD 500* design has substantial constructional and operational advantages over existing and previous airships. For example, the integration of vectored thrust capability into the design allows the ship to take-off heavy and, therefore, extends its endurance, and also significantly improves manoeuvrability and provides a VTOL capability. Other factors affecting performance are the low permeability of the envelope material and the full fit of advanced avionics and navigational aids.

As the *AD 500* and its derivatives will provide quiet, stable platforms of great endurance capability, the applications envisaged cover a number of roles in the civil and military spheres. Minesweeping, anti-submarine warfare (ASW), AEW and coastal patrol are just a few of the military applications envisaged, whilst the ability to hover and manoeuvre at low to zero speeds makes the airship suitable for interception and interrogation duties, such as fisheries protection, oil rig surveillance and air-sea rescue missions. Sight-seeing, tourism, freight carrying and aerial advertising are just a few of the other applications, but surely the most interesting ones must be the scientific and surveying roles. A report by the Aero-Mechanical Programs department of Goodyear, in 1971, describes the use of airborne sensing equipment flown aboard one of their airships, which included an isolated nose-probe acoustic sensor, a steerable acoustic sensor, stereo acoustic sensors, a directional acoustic sensor, a remotely controlled television camera, an infra-red covert illuminator, an acoustic gradient array, low-light level and daytime television cameras, a remote trailing sensor, and an aft-looking sensor. The value of airships for carrying this type of delicate equipment is indicated in a report by the US Geological Survey, in

which it was stated that test equipment can be located virtually anywhere on an airship, and that acoustic and infra-red devices can be isolated from engine noise and heat. It is interesting to note that acceleration in the cabin of a Goodyear airship during powered flight is less than $\frac{1}{40}$ g (acceleration of gravity) with a vibration frequency range of 10 to 1,000 hertz (Hz); figures for the *AD 500* are comparable. This indicates that an airship is a suitable carrier for delicate scientific instruments and that it provides the paramount fundamental consideration of platform stability, and can, should it be considered necessary, provide the environment free of vibration and long-period oscillations required for photogrammetry and other remote-sensing missions.

244 Anthony Smith's little non-rigid airship, *Santos Dumont* flying in front of the old Royal Airship Works at Cardington in August 1975.

245 The British non-rigid airship *Bournemouth* on her belly transporter mast, a converted bus, in September 1952 at Cardington. She has her second set of de Havilland fins. The Eta patches are noticeable. She was designed by a team of old airshipmen headed by Jack Beckford Ball, including Lord Ventry, Squadron Leader T. P. York Moore, coxswains Gerry Long and Freddy Twinn, rigger Deverell, and engineers Arthur Bell and Joe Binks.

246 *Güldenring*, ex-USN *L19*, was enlarged from 123,000 cu ft to 158,895 cu ft in 1958.

247 *Güldenring*'s name was changed to *Underberg* when she was modified in 1956.

244▲

245▲

246▼

247▼

248 *Trumpf II* was built in 1956 and only made 26 flights totalling 43 hours before she was damaged by high winds while riding at the mast at Stuttgart in 1957. She was not flown again. This ship, built by the Ballonfabrik Augsburg, made its first flight on 24 November 1956.

249▼          248▲

249 *Trumpf III* was the first really successful post-war German airship. She was built by Ballonfabrik and Metallwerk and made her first flight on 17 July 1958. She was the first German airship to be inflated with helium gas.

250▼          251▼

250 The West German advertising airship, *Schwab*, which until 1961 was flying under the name of *Underberg*. Note that the registration code, D-LAVO, remains unchanged. She was sold to Japanese owners in 1968.

251 A close-up view of the stern of the car of *Trumpf III*, showing the two 180 hp Warner Scarab engines.

252 *WDL 1*, also known as *Wicküler* and *Der Fliegende Musketier*, was the first airship to be built by Herr T. Wüllenkemper of Westdeutsche Luftwerbung, at Mulheim Airport. In the photograph the ship can be seen taxiing along the runway before take-off.

252▼

In a recent marketing survey Airship Developments predicted that a potential total of 868 airships could be sold for civil and military surveillance roles to Great Britain, Europe, Japan, Australia, the United States, Africa, South East Asia, and the Middle East. Airship Developments also indicate that the world market may be as high as 1,000 when activities such as port safety and fire watching are taken into consideration. These figures were extrapolated from world-wide operational requirements during the decade spanning 1980 to 1990, and the company believes that its share of the market would be at least 150 airships. Five types of airship have been proposed by the company, with payload capabilities of 0.5, 2, 5, 10 and 20–25 tons respectively. However, Airship Developments is concentrating its efforts on the *AD 500* for the moment.

## Heavy-lift airships

As mentioned, Goodyear were considering developing lighter-than-air flying cranes, which the company envisage as hybrid heavy-lift airships, obtaining power, part of the lift and all of the forward motion from four Sikorsky CH-54B helicopters, harnessed on a star-shaped frame attached to the envelope, and controlled in parallel from a single cockpit by a digital fly-by-wire control system. This concept was first proposed by the Piasecki Aircraft Corporation, formed in 1955 by Frank Piasecki, formerly chairman of the board and president of the Piasecki Helicopter Corporation (now part of the Boeing Vertol Company). Goodyear's early feasibility studies on this airship were conducted for NASA's Ames Research Center, and during the first phase of the study Goodyear, together with Boeing Vertol, performed parametric investigations of a greater number of missions and classes of airship than the brief called for. However, in the next phase of the study some of the most promising concepts were looked at in greater detail, and a model was designed, built and tested in the Ames wind-tunnel by Nielson Engineering and Research Company of California. As a result of the studies Goodyear recommended construction of flight research vehicles in heavy-lift and conventional configurations. Airships in the latter mode were considered for long-endurance anti-submarine warfare, sea control, including airborne early warning, and sono-

buoy delivery, amongst numerous other applications. Goodyear are devoting considerable resources to researching and developing the airship, so that the re-emergence of that company as the prime producer of airships on the American continent would seem inevitable.

In France Aérospatiale has also investigated the possibilities of a hybrid heavy-lift airship, and an indivisible load-carrier was studied in Britain by Airfloat Transport in 1971, but the most exciting development in Britain, so far, is the Skyship project of the Isle of Man-based company Airship Industries. This company, formerly Thermo-Skyships, tested a research model at Cardington in April 1975, and has now joined forces with Airship Developments.

The projected dimensions of Airship Industries' Skyship are 168 ft (51.2 m) wide with a maximum thickness of 120 ft

## General characteristics and performance data of project *Skyship R 40*

**Length**  600 ft (182.88 m)
**Diameter**  120 ft (36.57 m)
**Fineness ratio**  5.0 : 1
**Volume (hull)**  4,540,000 cu ft
**Volume (gas bags)**  4,220,000 cu ft
**Hull surface area**  174,395 sq ft
**Fin area (four)**  8,900 sq ft
**Engines**  Two Pratt & Whitney PT6A-50 turboprops, each giving 1,120 shp at 2,120 rpm (take-off power) and 900 shp at 1,020 rpm (continuous cruise power)
**Weight empty (estimated)**  112,500 lb (51,030 kg)
**Aerostatic lift at pressure altitude** 228,082 lb (103,456 kg)
**Useful load**  138,390 lb (62,773 kg)
**Maximum vertical take-off weight** 250,890 lb (113,802 kg)
**Payload: 500-mile still air range**  58 tons
  **2,000-mile still air range**  45 tons
  **2,500-mile still air range**  40 tons
**Total disposable load**  60 tons
**Cruising speed at reduced power** 77.55 mph
**Maximum level speed at maximum continuous power**  109.69 mph
**Designed diving speed**  119.10 mph
**Still air range at 57.57 mph**  12,000 + miles (19,310 + km)

(Refers only to Airship Industries' ellipsoidal rigid airships for Redcoat Cargo Airlines.)

(36.57 m), and the estimated weight would be about 60 tons. Four turboprops would enable the airship to travel at a cruising speed of 86 mph (138 km/h). Airship Industries also have plans for larger Skyships, and one idea is for a circular craft with a disposable lift of 400 tons, but the preferred shape is for a symmetrical lenticular form 700 ft (213.36 m) in diameter with a maximum thickness of 208 ft (63.39 m). The design for the proposed airship is unique in that hot air as well as helium provide the lift, and closing down the supply of hot air to the balloon compartment in the centre of the envelope means that the Skyship becomes less buoyant, loses lift and descends. It is also claimed that the Skyship would be able to continue flying, using dynamic flight, if for any reason there was a sudden loss of lifting gas.

## Projects

The idea of combining the principles of aerostatic and aerodynamic flight was first demonstrated effectively by the Aereon Corporation of Princeton, New Jersey, in 1965 when the company flew a remarkable triple-hulled airship named *Aereon III*. Since then Aereon has built and tested a 27.6 ft (8.4 m) long flight model of a new hybrid research vehicle which was intended to prove the company's concept for a 'lifting-body airship'. A study was carried out for the USN on the endurance potential of what William McE. Miller, Aereon's president, calls an aerobody-type vehicle. By 1977 Aereon had developed the concept and has proposed a 'Dynairship' (an acronym for dynamic-lift airship) 400 ft (122 m) in length for use as a 'very long endurance' craft by the USN. A number of other designs were also forwarded, and the company is trying to raise funds to develop its project further.

Hot-air airships, built by Cameron Balloons and Thunder Balloons in Britain, and Raven Industries in the United States, are probably more suitable for leisure activities and advertising than any other type of employment. These airships dubbed as thermal airships, have been recommended for a variety of tasks, including military logistic-load carriers, but their slow speeds of between 17 to 25 mph make them vulnerable to moderate winds and therefore ineffective as serious contenders for any role that would require high reliability and an endurance of more than a few hours. The hot-air airship is no more than a motorised hot-air balloon and as such is best suited as a craft for sporting purposes. The *Albatross* made by B. J. Bowland in the United States, is a good example of this type of craft as a source of fun, but unfortunately for those with an eye for the aesthetic qualities of fine lines and proportion, the first generation of hot-air airships, being dumpy and a little lumpy, must look a little like ugly ducklings. However, Thunder Balloons' two prototype models and the production model have much cleaner lines than some of the hot-air airships yet flown. The production model has a total volume of 70,000 cubic feet and is capable of a top speed of 25 knots. The company only envisages that its hot-air airship will be used for advertising and sporting activities.

Among some of the projected airships the Ames Research Center's hybrid Megalifter and the curious Aerocrane of All-American Industries can be regarded as exotic ideas that could only be developed with vast government aid, and so must be regarded as developments for the distant future. Professor Francis Morse of Boston University has produced a design for a nuclear-powered airship with twice the volume of the *Hindenburg* and a conventional airship configuration. This project is also in the category of the ones mentioned above and therefore will have to depend on large-scale government funding to be developed. But it would seem that the present escalating costs of hydrocarbon fuels will soon make the use of small nuclear reactors to generate energy for propulsion more attractive.

The present revival of interest in the airship has produced a new generation of enthusiasts who have built small airships in Australia, Britain, Germany, Japan and the United States. A list of some of the most interesting home-builts is given in the table accompanying the text.

**Russian airship progress**

Technical developments in Russia are of perennial interest in the West, particularly if a military flavour is present. It is therefore of no surprise to find that a great deal of interest has been expressed in the progress of lighter-than-air technology in that country. From 1909 to 1914 six Russian-designed airships were built and another two were constructed from designs based on the French Lebaudy and Zodiac ships. Non-rigid ships were also bought from France, Germany and Britain, but it was General Nobile's expertise that provided Russia with the semi-rigid airships constructed during the so called 'Red Airship Programme'. At least one of these airships was still in existence at the end of the Second World War. The Russians did not use any airships for military purposes during the Second World War, but during the First World War the army used a number of airships for reconnaissance or bombing purposes with varying degrees of success. At the beginning of the war the Czarist *Stavka* (Staff of Supreme Command) considered the airship the most important means of strategic reconnaissance, and during the early part of the war Russian airships successfully completed a number of short and long-range missions. Several of the Imperial Army's airships were lost to artillery and small arms fire and were not replaced, and a number of airship sheds were destroyed by enemy action. But the most damaging blow to the army airship service was the capture of the Sosnovits factory which produced pressure cylinders for hydrogen gas, and the general situation became even bleaker when the shortage of materials for the production of hydrogen became acute in 1916.

A number of non-rigid and semi-rigid airships were in use for passenger carrying and experimental purposes in the interwar years and during the 1960s a band of airship enthusiasts produced several small non-rigid airships. Since then numerous reports have emerged from the Soviet Union indicating that a considerable amount of effort has been put into researching new materials and new techniques for building airships. Several reports suggest that a semi-monocoque rigid airship with a length of 275 ft (84 m) was constructed by the Kiev Design Bureau, but so far no convincing evidence has been produced to indicate that this machine was actually flown or that it even existed at all. It is known that a few small non-rigid airships similar to the Zodiac Moto-Balloons have been produced for forestry work and fire observation duties, and it is possible that these airships may still be in service at present. However, a vociferous airship lobby is still at work in the Soviet Union and may yet be successful in persuading the authorities to re-introduce the airship for use in Siberia, whose vast tracts of tundra, broken terrain and hilly enforested areas precludes most types of transport. Recent press reports indicate that a small passenger airship, operating on the same principle as the tethered kite-balloons used for timber haulage in Siberia's Taiga region, is being experimented with in the Soviet Union. However, the statement's validity and the scheme's practicality are open to doubt.

253 The car of *WDL 1*, showing the good all-round vision afforded to the crew. In front of the car one of the air valves can be seen.

254 *WDL 1* viewed from the bows to the rear. The configuration of the two 180 hp Rolls-Royce engines can be seen. This ship made its first flight on 12 August 1972 piloted by Herr K. Hess.

255▼                    254▲

255 The Fuji Air Research organisation's model 503 Aero-Ship, is one of a series of radio-controlled research airships built for a number of Japanese commercial concerns. Cameras or other specialised equipment can be carried in a compartment in the front of the car. Number eight in this series of airships was sold to the Taisei Construction Company.

256▼

256 *WDL 1* was sold to the Orient Lease Company of Tokyo, and can be seen in the photograph as the *Flying Dragon*. The ship is flying over a shellfish farm, and is displaying the bright decorations painted on it by the Japanese artist Taro Okamoto, whose signature can be seen on the tail.

175

257 This small remotely piloted airship was built by Development Sciences Inc., of California, in 1977, and is one of a series of craft the company is designing for 'urban surveillance'. The small airship would mainly be used to monitor traffic but other uses are envisaged. Note the camera in the plastic bubble under the nose.

261 One of Goodyear's airships on station over a Sea Sentry 12–24 oil boom. The US Naval Sea System Command ordered 21 of these booms from the Goodyear Aerospace Corporation, at a cost of $1 million. Each boom is 1,000 ft (305 m) long, and is for oil spill containment.

258▼                          257▲

258 Goodyear's *Columbia III* is one of a fleet of three non-rigid airships operated in the United States for publicity purposes. The ship is 192 ft (58.52 m) long, 45.92 ft (14 m) in diameter, and has a volume of 202,700 cu ft.

259 *Europa* was built at Cardington in 1972, and was the first airship to be flown there since the *Bournemouth* in 1951–52.

259▼                          260▼

260 *America*, sister ship to *Columbia III*, was named after the yacht *America*, for which the America cup sailing race was named after the inaugural race in 1851.

261▲

262▲

263▲

265▼

264▲

262 Peter Buckley of Teddington, Middlesex, was the twenty-third airship pilot in the world when he joined Goodyear's European lighter-than-air team in 1975. He is seen at the controls of the *Europa*, of which he was the fifth pilot.

263 The mayor of Pompano Beach, Florida, christening the *Enterprise*. The *Enterprise* is similar to Goodyear's other airships, and replaces the *Mayflower* which was destroyed on the ground in a storm in *Iowa* in July 1979.

264 The *America* circling near its home base at Houston in Texas in 1979, with its night sign flashing an appeal for Americans to save petrol. The Goodyear airships fly for a week on the amount of fuel it takes for a Jumbo jet to taxi from an airport terminal to its take-off point!

265 The Piasecki *Heli-Stat* in model form. This concept for a helicopter powered heavy-lift airship is now being researched by Goodyear.

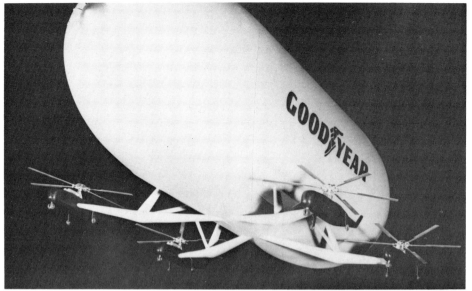

266▲

267▲

266 A model of an early Goodyear proposal for an airship in combination with four US Army CH-54B helicopters. The combined lift of the 2.6 million cubic feet of helium in the envelope, and the power of the rotors, would give the airship a lifting capacity of 75 tons.

267 Socialist realism in the form of a model of the semi-rigid *Pravda* erected on a special statue in Sverdlov Square, Moscow, in 1931, to celebrate 'Dirigible Day'. *Pravda* was one of the Nobile airships built as a result of the Soviet 1934–1935 programme by the Dirigible Construction Trust.

268▲                                                      269▼

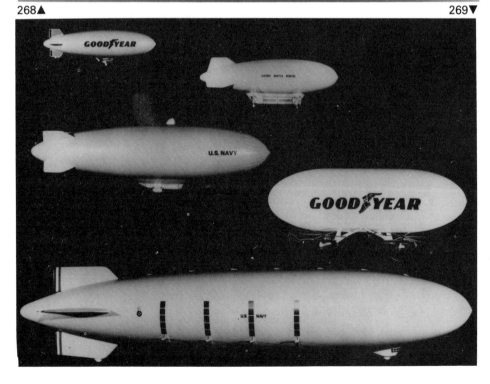

268 The latest proposal for a heavy-lift airship from Goodyear dates from 1979, but instead of employing actual helicopters, the airship would employ helicopter-like rotors for part of the lift and conventional propellers for forward motion. It is envisaged that an airship of this type could lift up to 160 tons. A Goodyear executive addressing a US Senate sub-committee in 1979 said that the company estimated that it would take over two years, and $15 million, to complete technical verification of the project and then another three years, and $70 million to get the project airborne.

269 A comparison of the sizes of various airships proposed and built by Goodyear. From top to bottom: one of the publicity airships, flying today; a proposed 428,500 cu ft airport shuttle which could carry 80 passengers; a ZPG-3W ship; the heavy-lifter; and the *Akron*, largest of them all.

270 The Russian airship *USSR-V6* (in Cyrillic *B 6*), *Osaviakhim* which was designed by General Nobile and first flew in 1934.

270▲            271▼

271 *USSR L-157*, a projected Russian giant non-rigid airship that would be used for transporting fish protein products from a trawler factory ship to a land base. Little has been heard of this project or any of the other Russian ideas for new airships since they were first given voice in the early 1970s.

272▼

272 *USSR L-200* is an idea, probably emanating from the Kiev Design Bureau, which envisages a twin-hulled airship that can be used as a heavy lifter or for transporting oil or gas line pipes to remote areas of the Soviet Union.

273▼

273 The triple-hulled *Aereon III* which was an experimental airship that could fly using a combination of static and dynamic lift.

274 Test mating of semi-completed car of the *TX-1, Silver Hawk*, to the envelope in April 1975.

275 *STARship*, the prototype hot-air, or thermal, airship built in the United States by Raven Industries Inc., in 1975. No further development has been undertaken.

276 *Silver Hawk*, the experimental semi-rigid airship built by the Tucker Airship Company, almost completed, in August 1978.

274▲                275▼                276▼

277▼

277 An artist's impression of the passenger variant of the metalclad *R. 30* designed by Wren Skyships. The skin material for this ship will be the aluminium alloy Alelad 2024–T3, with a thickness range of .010 to .025 in.

278 Brian Boland's hot-air airship *The Albatross* on 21 May 1977.

282 The latest airship to join Goodyear's publicity fleet is the new *Enterprise*, which replaces the *Mayflower*. Note the two blowers to the ship's ballonets.

278▲

279▲

280▼

281▼

282▼

279 One of the improved hot-air airships produced by Cameron Balloons in the United Kingdom. These ships have been produced for a number of customers and are used mainly for advertising purposes.

280 A production model *D 96* Cameron hot-air airship sold to Sultan Carpets of Australia.

281 Test flying of a prototype one-fifth scale model of the Thunder Balloons hot-air airship in one of the sheds at Cardington. This project, termed a hot airship, was conceived as an airship with a pressurised envelope, having a cruising speed of 25–35 knots, with a payload of a pilot and two passengers. Normal instrumentation carried in the car would be an altimeter, a pyrometer, a variometer and a pitch monitor. The total weight of the envelope, car, engine and propulsion fan would be 730 lb (331 kg). With 280 lb (127 kg) of fuel on board the airship would be capable of carrying a pilot and one passenger, together having an estimated weight of 170 lb (77 kg), making the total flight weight 1,180 lb (535.29 kg). With an envelope capacity of 65,000 cu ft, and an operational temperature of 100° to 110° centigrade, the gross lift to 3,000 ft (900 m) would be 1,200 lb (553.38 kg). A ground crew of four, including the pilot, is needed to handle the airship.

## A SELECTION OF PRIVATE AIRSHIP PROJECTS FROM 1956 TO THE PRESENT

| Name | Company | Country | Launched | Volume, cu ft | Length, ft (m) |
|------|---------|---------|----------|---------------|----------------|
| Ardath | Maintainer Pty Ltd | Australia | 1977 | 22,385 | 88(26.82) |
| Güldenring (ex-L19) | Goodyear/Ballonfabrik | Germany | 1947 | 123,000 | 150(45.72) |
| Trumpf II | Ballonfabrik Augsburg | Germany | 1956 | 189,728 | 188.1(57.33) |
| Trumpf III | Ballonfabrik/Metallwerk | Germany | 1958 | 158,895 | 159.3(48.55) |
| WDL 1 (serial No. 100) | Westdeutsche Luftwerbung | Germany | 1972 | 211,888 | 180.5(55.01) |
| WDL 1 (serial No. 101) | Westdeutsche Luftwerbung | Germany | 1972 | 211,888 | 180.5(55.01) |
| Fuji Model 500 Aero-ship | Fuji Manufacturing Co Ltd | Japan | 1974 | — | 26.25(8) |
| — | Hammars Group | Sweden | 1979 | 140,000 | — |
| AD 500 | Airship Developments Ltd | UK | 1979 | 181,160 | 164.04(50) |
| Bournemouth | Airship Club | UK | 1951 | 45,000 | 108(32.91) |
| Cameron D96 | Cameron Balloons Ltd | UK | 1973 | 96,000 | 100(30.48) |
| Chitty Bang Bang | M. Brighton | UK | 1967 | 37,000 | 112(34.13) |
| Gloster | — | UK | (1974) | 25,000 | 82(25) |
| R 30 | Wren Skyships Ltd | UK | (1985) | 1,000,000 | 334(103) |
| R 30 | Wren Skyships Ltd | UK | — | 1,000,000 | 334(103) |
| Santos Dumont | A. Smith | UK | 1974 | 33,000 | 76(23.11) |
| Sky Ship | Airship Industries | UK | 1975 | — | — |
| Thunder Hot Airship | Thunder Balloons Ltd | UK | 1980 | 70,000 | 125(38.10) |
| Aereon III | Aereon Corporation | USA | 1965 | 40,000 | 85(25.90) |
| Aereon 26 | Aereon Corporation | USA | 1970 | — | 27.6(8.41) |
| Albatross | Brian J. Boland | USA | 1975 | 140,000 | 112(34.14) |
| BG-1, Dolphin | B and G Airships | USA | (1976) | 37,983 | 97.25(29.64) |
| Conrad | Conrad Airship Corporation | USA | (1977) | 250,000 | — |

| Engines | Max Speed, mph | Project Status |
|---|---|---|
| 2 × 45 hp Xenoah G50B | 48 | A helium-filled non-rigid airship for which the advertising rights have been acquired by W. D. & H. O. Wills. It is also intended for shark spotting and other surveillance duties. |
| 2 × 145 hp Warner | 63 | Launched in 1947 as the US Navy airship *L19* and became *Underberg* in 1956. Enlarged to 158,895 cubic feet in 1958 and became *Güldenring*. When she became the *Schwab* in 1961 her overall length was 160.01 ft (48.78 m). Sold to a Japanese concern on 24 April 1968, she was re-named *Flying Dragon*; wrecked because of mooring mast failure on 4 April 1969. |
| 1 × 215 hp Franklin | 48.4 | Made 26 flights in which she logged 43 flying hours. Deflated after her mooring mast collapsed in high winds at Stuttgart in 1957, and not flown again. *Trumpf I*, a Parseval-Natz airship was first flown in 1928 and made 1,200 flights. |
| 2 × 180 hp Warner Scarab | 68 | The first German airship to be inflated with helium. Flown as the *Braun Sixtant* in 1969, and then taken over by WDL in 1970. |
| 2 × 180 hp Rolls-Royce | 62 | Named the *Flying Musketeer* and then renamed *Wicküler*. Designed as an advertising airship. |
| 2 × 180 hp Rolls-Royce | 62 | The envelope was damaged when her inflatable hangar collapsed during a storm in 1972, but before this event the ship survived winds gusting at over 100 mph. After repairs she was bought by the Orient Lease Company of Japan and was operated near Tokyo. |
| 2 × 1.3 hp ENYA 60 IIIB | 50 | A radio-controlled research airship, of which about 12 others are believed to have been built. |
| — | 17.27 | Hot-air airship which can carry three people. The speed given is for still air operation only. |
| 2 × 200 hp Porsche | 71 | This, the prototype, was damaged during a gale in March 1979; a new ship flew in 1981. Airship Developments intend to construct and market a series of airships ranging in size from 181,160 to 1.76 million cubic feet in volume. |
| 1 × 60 hp Salmson | 27 | The *Bournemouth* was a one-off airship built and designed by Lord Ventry and a few veteran airship men. Only eight flights were made because of a shortage of funds, the last one being on 16 August 1952. |
| 1 × 45 hp Volkswagen | 17 | The world's first hot-air airship, which was a prototype for a series of improved versions that have been sold to customers in Australia, Belgium, France, the Netherlands, Sweden and the UK. A new single-seater model is under development. |
| 1 × 40 hp Volkswagen | — | This, the first British airship to be inflated with helium, was a replica of a Lebaudy airship, and was made for the film *Chitty Chitty Bang Bang*. |
| 2 × 26 hp Hirth F10-A1B | — | It is not clear whether this airship ever flew. |
| 2 × 1,645 hp<br>2 × 500 hp | 116 | Projected metalclad cargo/passenger and military logistics ship. |
| 4 × 1,645 hp | 133 | Projected metalclad cargo/passenger and military logistics ship. |
| 2 × 20 hp Wankel-type | 30 | An interesting private venture. The pressure height is approximately 6,000 feet (1,825 m) and the weight empty is about 1,020 lb (481 kg). |
| Electric motors | — | A test model for the future series of lenticular-shaped airships proposed for passenger and cargo carrying, of which full details are given in the text. The model was 9.5 ft (2.89 m) high at the centre and had a payload capacity of 40 lb (18.14 kg). The gross lift was 215 lb (97.52 kg). |
| 1 × 496 cc Honda CX500 | 29 | A one-fifth scale radio model, and another test model, have been flown successfully. The production model mentioned in the table is the first of a series of sporting and advertising hot-air airships for customers in Britain and overseas. This airship design is unique in that it incorporates an envelope pressurisation system that operates from an extended main drive shaft. The total weight of the airship and its component parts is 1,180 lb (535.29 kg). Normal loading allows for one pilot and one passenger. |
| 1 × 70 hp Solar Titan | 65 | A triple-hulled hybrid airship combining aerostatic and aerodynamic lift. Flew successfully on a number of occasions, but was not developed because of lack of finance. |
| 1 × 90 hp McCulloch | 127 | Hybrid research model employing a rigid framework and embodying certain characteristics of *Aereon III*. See text for details of Aereon's projected long endurance hybrids. |
| 1 × 40 hp Rockwell | — | Hot-air airship constructed for private use. |
| 1 × 80 hp Barker CE 2000 | 34 | Semi-rigid airship with accommodation for a crew of two. Reported to be under construction in 1976–77. |
| 2 × 130 hp Evinrude,<br>1 × 150 hp Mercury | 40 | Rigid lentoid-shaped airship with a circular platform, which will provide accommodation for a pilot and seven passengers. |

| Name | Company | Country | Launched | Volume, cu ft | Length, ft (m) |
|------|---------|---------|----------|---------------|----------------|
| *America* | Goodyear Aerospace Corporation | USA | 1969 | 202,700 | 192(58.52) |
| *Columbia II* | Goodyear Aerospace Corporation | USA | 1963 | 147,000 | 157(47.85) |
| *Columbia III* | Goodyear Aerospace Corporation | USA | 1969 | 202,700 | 192(58.52) |
| *Columbia IV* | Goodyear Aerospace Corporation | USA | 1975 | 202,700 | 192(58.52) |
| *Enterprise* | Goodyear Aerospace Corporation | USA | 1980 | — | — |
| *Europa* | Goodyear Aerospace Corporation | USA | 1972 | 202,700 | 192(58.52) |
| *Mayflower III* | Goodyear Aerospace Corporation | USA | 1959 | 132,500 | 150(45.72) |
| *Mayflower IV* | Goodyear Aerospace Corporation | USA | 1976 | 147,300 | 160(48.77) |
| *Mayflower V* | Goodyear Aerospace Corporation | USA | 1978 | — | 192.5(58.67) |
| *HX-1* | Hov-Air-Ship Inc | USA | 1978 | — | 19(5.79) |
| *Silver Hawk (TX-1)* | Tucker Airship Company | USA | (1979) | 20,500 | 91(27.74) |
| *STAR-ship* | Raven Industries Inc | USA | 1975 | 138,435 | 120.1(36.60) |
| *RPMB* | Developmental Sciences Inc | USA | 1974 | — | 16(4.87) |
| *RPMB* | Developmental Sciences Inc | USA | 1977 | 900 | 26(7.92) |
| — | World Balloons Inc/George Stokes Balloons | USA | 1979 | — | — |
| *D1* | Kiev Design Bureau | USSR | 1969 | 953,495 | 175.6(84) |
| *Izvestia* | Urals Engineering Group | USSR | 1965 | — | 82(25) |
| *LL1* | — | USSR | 1964 | — | 165(50.29) |

## Revival?

It seems that the advantages of the airship have captivated the imaginations of people throughout the world, and that as environmental considerations, particularly noise and air pollution, militate in favour of it, governments may yet have to bow to the pressure of public opinion. However, what makes the airship an increasingly attractive proposition is the dramatic increase in fuel costs over the past few years, making the conservation of fuel of paramount importance for the economic operation of aircraft. A comparison of the fuel consumption of an Airship Industries Skyship with a Boeing 747 over a route, which for certain reasons the Skyship has to travel over a greater distance, shows that the Skyship uses about a quarter of the fuel of the Boeing. Comparisons with a Boeing 707 show that it uses less than half as much fuel, and with a Britannia the fuel used is just under a third less. It is these and other factors that present the modern airship as a viable and attractive proposition to air freight companies. Redcoat Cargo Airlines, who intend to operate airships by 1984, indicate that at present day costs the use of airships would reduce freight charges by 25 per cent. But another reason just as important as the reduction in freight costs is the greater cargo capacity of the airship. For example a Britannia can carry 17.5 tonnes of cargo in 110 cubic metres of available space, while the Skyship can carry 40 tonnes in 1,000 cubic metres. The superior useful load/fuel consumption performance indicated here is clear.

It would be fatuous to consider that the use of helium instead of hydrogen for lift, strong light-weight structural materials, computer assistance in design calculations, and the employment of modern avionics equipment would make the airship completely fail-safe. Similar considerations applying to the safe operation of any ship or aeroplane would also apply to the airship. However, the airship of the future could use modern devices for guidance, control and bad weather avoidance, therefore reducing the risk factor considerably. The large modern airship

| Engines | Max Speed, mph, | Project Status |
|---|---|---|
| 2 × 210 hp Continental | 50 | Car of former navy airship *L-8* used on this ship. |
| 2 × 175 hp Continental | 57 | Envelope replaced in 1969. |
| 2 × 210 hp Continental | 50 | Car of *Enterprise* used (ex-navy *L-16*). |
| 2 × 210 hp Continental | 50 | Replacement for *Columbia III*. |
| — | — | Goodyear's latest airship. |
| 2 × 210 hp Continental | 50 | Built at Cardington. |
| 2 × 175 hp Continental | 61 | Sister ship to *Columbia II*. |
| 2 × 154 hp Continental GO-300-F | 50 | Normal operational altitude 1,000–3,000 ft (305–915 m). |
| 2 × 210 hp Continental IO-360-D | 50 | Ceiling 7,500 ft (2,285 m). Endurance at cruising speed of 30–40 mph is about ten hours. |
| 110 v electrical power source | — | Remotely controlled test model for a 75,000 cubic foot capacity full-scale airship. A private venture but tests were conducted on the model by the US Navy in 1978 and 1979. |
| 1 × 120 hp | 55 | First of a series of three prototype airships of semi-rigid and non-rigid construction. *TX-1* is a semi-rigid of modular construction, breaking down into 12 portable units. |
| 1 × 65 hp Volkswagen | 25 | Hot-air airship prototype for future models, but design problems precluded development. |
| 1 × .25 hp model aeroplane engine | 20 | The RPMB (Remotely Piloted Mini Blimp) is a demonstration model for a series of remotely controlled surveillance airships, of which several have been constructed. |
| 1 × — | 30 | A much larger type of RPMB with a maximum diameter of 9 ft (2.74 m) has recently been produced. |
| 1 × Lycoming 235 | — | Hot-air airship with a pressurised envelope. Produced for Busch Gardens in New Mexico. |
| 1 × turboprop | 124 | A semi-monocoque rigid, helium-inflated airship which, according to Soviet press reports was first flown in 1969. Little information on the *D1* has been forthcoming from Soviet sources since 1974 and so far little evidence has been made available to substantiate the performance figures given earlier. |
| — | — | Probably also known as *Ural 1* and 'Bimbat'. Constructed and designed by an engineering group under the leadership of David Bimbat for the Gorky Film Studios. Used for filming and for experimental forestry work. Non-rigid. |
| 2 | 62 | Reported to be designed in 1962 by V. Murytshev and O. Antonov for forestry work. Can carry a crew of five. Non-rigid. |

would undoubtedly be equipped with an extensive array of radio, computer and satellite navigation aids upon which to draw for vital up-to-the minute information, and automatic picture transmission consoles could give wide-area real-time weather displays transmitted from spacecraft, which would also be capable of furnishing highly accurate positional data. It is obvious that the airship has more space available than an aeroplane for the installation of sophisticated meteorological and computing devices, so it is clear that the airship could be better equipped than its heavier-than-air sister. The computing installations could have an additional monitoring function if coupled to sensors placed at strategic points throughout the airship, and in this mode the stresses existing within the structure of the airship could be continuously monitored to provide warning of incipient high stress concentrations.

When the *Hindenburg* burst into flames at Lakehurst on 6 May 1937 the first fare-paying passengers in over 28 years of passenger carrying operations were killed. The *Hindenburg* carried a total of 97 crewmen and passengers; of the 35 fatalities 13 were passengers and 22 were members of the crew. Thus, of the total number on board 36 per cent were killed, but of the passengers 80 per cent survived. Conversely when a modern airliner crashes the result is most usually a total loss of passengers and crew. As a result of the loss of the *Hindenburg* a whole era of technological experience was thrown away, and yet it seems possible that with the present interest in airships the real age of the airship has yet to begin. NASA's endeavours, particularly the interest of some of its engineers in the use of an airship to transport Space Shuttle components, especially the Orbiter Vehicle, could have far reaching consequences for the future development of the airship. What developments will take place in the next decades remain to be seen, but what is certain is that what is happening now is not so much a renaissance of the airship but rather a new epoch of lighter-than-air technology.

# Glossary of Airship Terminology

**Aeronaut:** One who operates or travels in a balloon or airship.

**Aeronautics:** Science or practice of aerial navigation.

**Aerostatics:** Branch of pneumatics dealing with the equilibrium and pressure of air and gaseous fluids, and of solid bodies immersed in them.

**Aerostation:** Part of aerial navigation treating with the practice of raising and guiding balloons in the air.

**Airdock:** Name coined by Goodyear for the giant hangar built for the construction of the *Akron* and *Macon*.

**Air scoops:** Tubular scoops, hanging behind a non-rigid airship's propellers, through which air is forced into the ballonets in order to 'trim' the ship, making it heavier or lighter, fore or aft, as needed.

**Alclad:** Combination of materials fabricated for the construction of the envelope of the *ZMC–2*, consisting of a laminated sandwich of duralumin, protected from corrosion on either side by a thin layer of aluminium.

**Ballast:** Droppable ballast carried, water for rigid airships, and either sand or water for non-rigids and balloons. Dropping ballast enables a ship to ascend, or to compensate for gas loss or increased loads.

**Ballonet:** Air-filled compartment of variable volume within an airship, kept under pressure by the use of air scoops or blowers, to control trim, ascent and descent, and maintain the correct pressure in the envelope, despite changes in the volume of the lifting gas.

*Blaugas:* Hydrocarbon fuel gas, similar to propane and having the same specific gravity as air, carried in gas-bags in the *Graf Zeppelin* and used as fuel for her engines.

**Blimp:** Generic term for non-rigid airships, and which supposedly derives from the sound made by striking the envelope.

**Blowers:** Power units used for pumping air into the ballonets.

**Catenary curtains:** Fabric curtains sewn to the top inside surface of the envelope of a pressure airship, to which are attached a system of load-bearing rigging cables supporting the car.

**Ceiling:** Maximum altitude an aircraft can attain depending on prevailing weather conditions, barometric pressure, air temperature, and the useful load.

**Control car:** Compartment on board an airship containing the instrumentation and controls for the safe operation of the ship.

**Cover:** Fabric panels, laced to the framework of a rigid airship, the lacing and adjoining panels, covered with strips of fabric glued in place, and the whole painted with several coats of dope.

**Dirigible:** Early term for an airship, from the French word *dirigeable*, meaning capable of being guided, directed or steered.

**Docking rails:** Ground handling equipment used to run German rigids into and out of their sheds. Wheeled trucks (*laufkatze*), serving as fastening points for tackle attached to the ship, ran on the rails, preventing lateral movement in gusting winds.

**Duralumin:** Light aluminium alloy, containing copper, magnesium, manganese, iron and silicon, comparable in strength and hardness to soft steel.

**Dynamic lift:** Force derived by flying an airship at a negative, or positive, angle in order to compensate for any degree of lightness or heaviness.

**Elevators:** Movable horizontal planes, usually on an airship's tail fin structure, used to control ascent or descent.

**Engine car:** Nacelle attached to the hull of a rigid airship, containing an engine(s).

**Envelope:** Gas-bag of a pressure airship.

**Eta patch:** Suspension patches fixed to the envelope, and retaining D-rings through which were passed the rigging cables attached to the control car. By placing these patches at strategic points on the envelope the weight of the car would be evenly distributed along its length.

**Fins:** Vertical and horizontal stabilising surfaces attached to the tail of an airship, at the rear of which are fixed the movable control surfaces.

**Gas-bags:** Gas containers for the lifting gas, held in place by a system of wire and cord netting in a rigid airship. Rubberised cotton fabric was used for the gas-bags in early rigids, but was superseded by gold beaters' skin (six layers being used) in 1911. In 1914 'skinned fabric' bags, consisting of two or three layers of gold beaters' skin glued to cotton fabric, were used. Cotton was substituted by silk in 1918. The bags in the *Akron* and *Macon* were made from a synthetic gelatin-latex film, and a similar material was used for those in the *Hindenburg*.

**Girders:** Light-weight, high-strength girders, triangular in cross-section, used for constructing the transverse rings and longitudinal members that made up the framework of a rigid airship. The Zeppelin Company used rolled duralumin channels, while the girders of the Schütte-Lanz ships were fabricated from aspen plywood.

**Gold beaters' skin:** Outer membrane covering the *caecum* of cattle, used because of its light weight and gas-tightness, to line the inside of gas-bags.

**Gondola:** Name for the car suspended below an airship.

**Gross lift:** Total lift of the gas contained in an airship, under standard barometric and other conditions, equal to the weight of air displaced less the weight of the lifting gas.

**Helium:** Second lightest element known, being odourless and non-flammable; found in small, and varying, percentages in northern Texas, Kansas, Colorado, the North Sea, the Sahara, and in Dutch and Soviet natural gas fields. Helium is calculated to weigh 63 lb per 1,000 cu ft, and is a totally safe lifting medium, but with only 93 per cent of the lifting force of hydrogen.

**Hydrogen:** Diatomic gas, being the lightest substance known, having a specific gravity of about one-fourteenth of that of air. It is not only highly flammable, but is also explosive when contaminated by as little as six per cent of air. Hydrogen is computed to weigh 68 lb per 1,000 cu ft and is seven per cent lighter than helium.

**Inclinometer:** Instrument, used by the elevatorman, registering the angle of the ship.

**Intermediate rings:** Structural components of a rigid airship, without transverse wire bracing, placed between the main rings, to reduce bending loads in the longitudinal girders.

**Keel:** Longitudinal girder fitted to the underside of the envelope of a semi-rigid airship. Also, the triangular, in cross-section, corridor, composed of two longitudinals and an apex girder, running from the bows to the stern along the underside of a rigid airship.

**Longitudinals:** Main structural members running along the length of a rigid airship. Intermediate longitudinals were girders, extending from the bows almost to the stern, designed mainly to support the outer cover.

**Main rings:** Main transverse structural components of a rigid airship, braced with a system of radial and chord wires, in most designs intended to withstand the forces exerted by the lifting gas and the combined weight of the ship and its load.

**Nose cone:** Rigid structure attached to the nose of a non-rigid airship, on the tip of which is a steel ball designed to lock into a portable mooring mast. The larger nose area is stiffened by battens radiating from the nose back along the envelope.

**Non-rigid airship:** Pressure airship comprising an envelope made of a gas-tight fabric, the streamlined shape of which is maintained by the internal pressure of the lifting gas and the expansion or contraction of the ballonets inside it, and from which a single control car is suspended.

**Observation car:** Small streamlined nacelle lowered about half a mile below a rigid airship and connected by telephone with the control car to enable an observer to communicate directions to the airship concealed in the clouds above. Used only by the German Army airships between 1914 and 1917, when it was known as *Spähkorb* (sub-cloud car). Also used to a limited extent on the *Akron* and *Macon*.

**Pressure airship:** Term applied to non-rigid and semi-rigid airships referring to the fact that the envelope shape is maintained by gas pressure.

**Pressure height:** Maximum altitude at which an airship can fly before decreasing atmospheric pressure allows the lifting gas to expand, causing automatic safety valves to open.

**Rigid airship:** Airship having a covered rigid structure, consisting of a series of polygonal transverse frames to which longitudinal girders were attached. Inside the ship a number of gas-bags, located between the transverse frames, provided buoyancy.

**Rip panel:** Detachable panel which can be torn from the envelope of a pressure airship, to deflate it in an emergency.

**Rudder:** Device on the tail of an airship, consisting of movable vertical surfaces, specifically for steering the ship to port or starboard.

**'Ruddervators':** Radially disposed stabilising and control surfaces, which served as a combination of rudders and elevators, on US Navy non-rigid airships having 'X' and 'Y' fin configurations. The *ZMC–2* had an unconventional arrangement of eight fins.

**Semi-rigid airship:** Pressure airship having, in some cases flexible, keel structure running the length of the envelope, and either suspended below it or faired into its underside. All loads are supported by the keel, and engines, car(s), etc., are attached to it.

**Shed:** Hangar designed to house one, or several, airships.

**Static lift:** Lift provided by the buoyancy of the lifting gas. As the ship ascends, the weight of the air it displaces becomes less as the atmosphere gets thinner, and so the lift diminishes.

**Supercooling:** Increase in the density of the lifting gas and, therefore, a reduction in buoyancy, usually caused by the airship flying at night or through cold layers of air.

**Superheating:** Expansion of the lifting gas, accompanied by an increase in buoyancy, due to its temperature rising above that of the surrounding atmosphere, and usually, to the sun's heat being trapped inside the hull.

**Suspension ropes:** Rigging in the form of ropes, or cables, acting as supports for the control car in a non-rigid airship.

**Trim:** Attitude of an airship in flight, whether on an even keel, when the ship is 'in trim', or when inclined down by the stern, or bows, and the ship is 'out of trim'.

**Useful lift:** Lift of an airship calculated by deducting the fixed weights of the structure and permanent fixtures from the gross lift.

**Useful load:** Disposable load equal in weight to the useful lift, and includes fuel, ballast, cargo, crew and passengers.

**Vectored thrust:** Variable, or directionable, thrust delivered from rotatable (swivelling) power units, enabling an airship to take off with heavier- or land with lighter-than-neutral buoyancy. Vectored thrust was first employed by the Welsh airship pioneer Ernest Thompson Willows on the six airships he built between 1905 and 1915.

**Water recovery apparatus:** *Akron* and *Macon* were fitted with condensers to recover water from the engine exhaust gases, in order to avoid valving helium to maintain the ship's static condition, as the ship became lighter through fuel consumption.

**'Weighed off':** Practice of adjusting the static condition of an airship, before flight, or landing, by releasing gas or ballast to bring the ship into equilibrium. Also termed 'ballasting-up'.

**Weight empty:** Combined fixed weight of the structure and permanent installations on an airship.

# Select Bibliography

The following lists are not intended to be a complete record, but rather a concise guide to some of the best sources of information on the development and history of airship aeronautics. For ease of reference the bibliography is divided into a selection of some of the official documents consulted and a selection of published material. The latter category covers technical research papers and brochures, descriptive of services or products, issued by manufacturers and other commercial organisations, and the former category covers journals, periodicals and books, including some annuals. An indication of the principal documentary sources, apart from the authors' collections, can be found by referring to the list of acknowledgements at the beginning of this book, where mention is made of those who provided much of the primary material from which this book is compiled.

## Official documents

Commissariato Generale per L'Aeronautica Dirigibili e Aerostati. Battaglione Dirigibilisti, Sezione Fotografica. Rome, *c*. 1910–1921. (A photograph album)

*German Rigid Airships.* Admiralty War Staff Intelligence Division. London, February 1917

*Handbook on S.S. Type Airships.* Admiralty Air Department. Wormwood Scrubs, January 1917

*Handbook on the 'Coastal and C Star' Airships.*
Admiralty. London, 3 May 1918

*Investigation of Dirigible Disasters. Hearings Before a Joint Committee to Investigate Dirigible Disasters. Seventy-third Congress. May 22 to June 6, 1933.* US Government Printing Office, Washington, 1933

Knight, R. W. *The Hindenburg Accident. A Comparative Digest of the Investigations and Findings, With the American and Translated German Reports Included.* Department of Commerce, Bureau of Air Commerce Safety and Planning Division, Report No 11, August 1938

*Rigid Airships and Mooring Gear, 1917–1918.* Admiralty and Vickers Ltd. London, 1917–1918

*The Italian Navy in the World War, 1915–1918: Facts & Figures.* Office of the Chief of Staff of the Royal Italian Navy (Historical Section). Provveditorato Generale Della Stato Libreria, 1927 — Anno V

*'They Were Dependable' — Airship Operation in World War II.* US Naval Air Station, Lakehurst, NJ, 1946

Van Wyen, Adrian O. *Naval Aviation in World War I.* Chief of Naval Operations. Washington, DC, 1969

## Research Papers and Manufacturers' Publicity Material

*Airship R 100.* Howden, 1928

Colvocoresses, Alden P. *Remote Sensing Platforms.* US Geological Survey Circular 693. Reston, VA, 1974

*First Flight of US Thermal Airship Raven.* Raven Industries Inc., Sioux Falls, 1975

*Goodyear, Commercial Airships. Brief Summary of Operations, 1925–1942, 1946–1969, and 1969–1973.* Airship Operations Engineering, Goodyear Tire & Rubber Company, Wingfoot Lake Division. September 1970 and June 1974 respectively

*Helium, The Element of Extremes.* Air Products. Bracknell, *c.* 1975

Hoagland, John H. and Weinent, Lois D. *Soviet Press Commentary on Dirigibles.* Research Memorandum, Wellesley, March 1974

Hyde, F. W. *Airships Reborn.* Paper read before The Society of Engineers. London, 6 December 1971

*Hydrogen Generator.* Johnson Matthey Metals Ltd, London, *c.* 1976

McLeish, R. D. 'Airships: Have They a Future?' *Advance 11.* The University of Manchester Institute of Science and Technology. Manchester, December 1971

Pritchard, J. Laurence, Captain. Editor, Aeronautical Reprints. *Proceedings of The Royal Aeronautical Society*
Baker, J. F. *Secondary Stresses in Airship Hull Structures.* 1927
Cave-Browne-Cave, T. R. L., Wing-Commander. *The Machinery Installation of Airship R 101.* 1929
*Safety from Fire in Airships.* 1927
Chitty, L. and Southwell, R. V. *A Contribution to the Analysis of Primary Stresses in the Hull of a Rigid Airship.* 1931
Fritsche, Carl B. *The Metalclad Airship.* 1930
Lyon, Hilda M. *The Strength of Transverse Frames of Rigid Airships.* 1930
Richmond, V. C., Lieutenant Colonel
*R 101* Roxbee Cox, Harold. *The External Forces on an Airship Structure, with Special Reference to the Requirements of Rigid Airship Design*
Scott, G. H., Major. *Handling and Mooring of Airships*

*Profile.* Goodyear Aerospace. Akron, Spring 1977

*Skyship.* Skyship Research and Development Ltd. London, *c.* 1974

Stinton, D. *Airship Possibilities and Problems.* The Institution of Civil Engineers, London, 16 December 1971

*The Airfloat Project. Proceedings of a One Day Symposium, September 20th 1971.* Multi-Science Publishing Company Ltd. London, 1972

*The Thunder Hot Airship.* Thunder Balloons Ltd. London, 1979.

*TX-1 Semi-rigid Airship Program.* Tucker Airship Company. Los Angeles, 1975

*WDL Airship Information.* Westdeutsche Luftwerbung. Essen-Mulheim, *c.* 1974

## Journals and periodicals

'A New Floating Crane!' *ICHCA Monthly Journal.* London, March 1972

*The Aerostat.* Journal of the British Balloon and Airship Club. London

*Buoyant Flight.* The Bulletin of the Lighter-Than-Air Society (formerly Wingfoot LTA Society). Akron

*Aerostation*, Vols 1–3. Journal of the Association of Balloon and Airship Constructors, USA, 1973–76

Allen, Roy. 'UK Evidence of the Practicalities of the Aerostat.' *Fairplay International Shipping Journal.* London, 24 August 1972

Allward, Maurice. 'Goodyear Airship *Europa*'. *Air Pictorial*, Vol. 39 No. 3. Windsor, March 1977

Boyes, Jane. 'Airships — The Missing Link.' *Containerisation and Unit Transportation.* London, April 1972

'Bring Back the Airship.' *Engineering*, 29 November 1968

Clarke, I. F. 'The othello Syndrome.' *History Today*, Vol. XV, No. 8. London, August 1965

Elson, Benjamin M. 'Hybrid Heavy-Lift Airships Under Study.' *Aviation Week & Space Technology.* 21 June 1976

Fritsche, Carl B. 'The Metalclad Airship.' *The Aeroplane*, Vol. XL, No. 20. London, 20 May 1931 (in the same issue see also 'On the Development of Airships' and 'The Debate on Airship Policy'.)

'Cargo Airship Concept — No Longer a Pipe-Dream.' *Freight Management*, Vol. V, No. 51. London, April 1971

George, I. A. 'Flying the Goodyear Airship.' *Pilot*, Vol. 10, No. 7. Claygate, July 1976

'Goodyear Studies Airship Concepts Under NASA Contract.' *Aerospace Daily.* 7 June 1976

Davey, C. J. T., Major. 'Freighter Airships: Is There a Defence Role?' *Journal of the Royal United Services Institute for Defence Studies.* London, March 1974

Dörpinghous, Rolf. 'Comeback der Luftschiffe.' *Aerokurier*, Vol. 1, 1973

Dudley, C. A. 'Time to take up market gardening?', *Lloyd's Log*, April 1980

Horne, Alistair. 'By Balloon from Paris.' *History Today*, Vol. XIII, No. 7. London, July 1963

'Hot Ship'. *Flight International.* No. 3541, Vol. III. London, 22 January 1977

Klass, Philip J. 'Balloon Design Advances Spurred.' *Aviation Week & Space Technology*, 15 January 1973

Koleśnik, Eugène M. 'Is there a Maritime Role for the Airship?' *Journal of the Royal United Services Institute for Defence Studies.* London, March 1982

Levitt, Ben B., Commander. 'The Rigid Airship in the Sea Control Mission.' *United States Naval Institute Proceedings*, Vol. 103. Annapolis, January 1977

Miller, W. McE., Jr, *et al.* 'The Lifting-Body-Airship: A Future Delivery System For Remote Area Logistics.' *Canadian Aeronautics and Space Journal*, Vol. 22, No. 1. January/February 1976

Morisset, Jacques. '*Dirigeables: Nouvelles Formules à L'Etude.*' Air et Cosmos, No. 563. Paris, 1975

Mowforth, Edwin, Dr. 'The Low Technology Airship.' *New Scientist*, Vol. 63, No. 907. London, 25 July 1974

Mutschall, Vladimir. 'Status of the Airship in the USSR.' *Foreign Science Bulletin*, Vol. 1, No. 10. Aerospace Technology Division, Library of Congress. Washington, DC, October 1965

'NASA Researchers See Large Cargo Transport Program.' *Aerospace Daily*, 26 May 1976

'Nulli Secundus.' *RAE News*, Vol. 20, No. 10. Farnborough, October 1967

Parry, Don. 'Return of the Airship?' *Aerospace Review*, Vol. 1, No. 3. London, March/April 1971

'Past and Present at Cardington.' *RAE News*, Vol. 26, No. 10. Farnborough, October 1973

Pusey, Harry H. 'Air Cargo in 1981.' *ICHCA Monthly Journal.* London, October 1971

Rea, Alberto. 'Dirigibili Italiani Nella Grande Guerra'. *Rivista Aeronautica*, Vol. 1. Rome, January 1969

Stehling, Kurt R. 'A Renaissance of the Airship?' *Interavia*, Vol. XXX. Geneva, September 1975

Rynish, M. J. Cargo Airships — a plan for the future. *ICHCA Monthly Journal.* London, October 1971

'Skyship model demonstrated.' *Flight International.* London, 24 April 1975

'Sir George Cayley's Navigable Balloon.' *Mechanics Magazine*, No. 708, 4 March 1837

*The Airship*, Vol. 1, No. 1 — Vol. 6, No. 22, July–September 1939, and Vol. 7, No. 1–No. 6 (new series), 1948–49

Turpin, Brian J. 'More Gas and Goodyear.' *Aeroplane Monthly*, Vol. 1, No. 8. London, December 1973

'Technical Aspects of the Loss of the USS Shenandoah.' *Journal of the American Society of Naval Engineers*, Vol. XXXVIII, No. 3, August 1926

'The Airship and the Ocean Liner. Where the Lighter-than-Air Machine Scores.' *RAE News*, Vol. 30, No. 4. Farnborough, April 1977

Ventry, Lord. 'Airships.' *The Aeroplane.* London, 23 February 1945

*Warship International*, No. 2, June 1970

Wilson, Michael. 'Britain's Export Airship.' *Flight International*, No. 3540, Vol. III. London, 15 January 1977

Wilson, Michael. 'British Airships for Venezuela.' *Flight International*, No. 3502, Vol. 109. London, 1 May 1976

**Books**

Abbott, Patrick. *Airship: The Story of R 34 and the First East-West Crossing of the Atlantic by Air.* Adams & Dart, London, 1973

Amundsen, Roald and Ellsworth, Lincoln. *The First Flight Across the Polar Sea.* Hutchinson. London, 1927

Arnesen, Odd. *The Polar Adventure: The Italian tragedy seen at close quarters.* Victor Gollancz. London, 1929

Bacon, Admiral Sir Reginald. *The Dover Patrol*, 1915–1917. Hutchinson & Co. London, 1919

Beaubois, Henry and Demand, Carlo. *Airships: An Illustrated History.* Macdonald and Jane's. London, 1973

Berget, Alphonse. *The Conquest of the Air.* William Heinemann. London, 1909

Bethuys, G. *Les Aérostiers Militaires.* H. Lecène et H. Oudin, 1889

Blakemore, Thos L. and Watters Pagon, W. *Pressure Airships.* Ronald Press, 1927

Bouttiaux, Général. *La Navigation par Ballons Dirigeables.* Librairie Ch. Delegrain

*Braunbeck's Sport Lexikon.* Verlag Gustav Braunbeck. Berlin, 1910–1913

De Brossard, Captain. *Lachez Tout.* France Empire.

Burgess, Charles P. *Airship Design.* 1927

Colliva, Giuliano. *Uomini E Aerei. Nella Storia Dell'Aeronautica Militare Italiana.* Bramante Editrice. Milan 1973

De Forest Chandler, Charles and Diehl, Walter S. *Balloon and Airship Gases.* 1926

Dollfus, Charles. *En Ballon.* Paris, 1962

Dollfus, Charles and Bouche, Henri. *Histoire de L'Aéronautique.* L'Illustration. Paris, 1942

Duz, Pyotr A. *The History of Aeronautics and Aviation in the USSR, 1914–1918.* State Scientific – Technical Publishing House, Oborongiz. Moscow, 1960

Eckener, Hugo, Dr *Count Zeppelin, The Man and his Work.* Massie, 1938

Eckener, Hugo. *My Zeppelins.* Putnam. London, 1958

Étève, A. Général. *Avant Les Cocardes.* Charles-Lavauzell

Fisher, John. *Airlift 1870. The Balloon and Pigeon Post in the Siege of Paris.* Max Parrish. London, 1965

De Forge, L. Sazerac, Capitaine. *La Conquête de l'Air en Dirigeable.* Berger-Levrault. Paris, 1910

Gamble, Snowden. *The Story of a North Sea Air Station.* Neville Spearman, 1967

Gibbs-Smith, C. H. *Sir George Cayley, 1773–1857* HMSO. London, 1968

Glaisher, James, Camille Flammarion, W. de Fonvielle and Gaston Tissandier. *Travels in the Air.* Richard Bentley & Son, 1871

Grierson, John. *Challenge to the Poles. Highlights of Arctic and Antarctic Aviation.* G. T. Foulis. London, 1964

Hartcup, Guy. *The Achievement of the Airship.* David & Charles. Newton Abbot, 1974

Hearne, R. P. *Zeppelins and Super-Zeppelins.* John Lane, The Bodley Head. London, 1916

Henderson, Ernest F. *Germany's Fighting Machine.* The Bobbs-Merrill Company. Indianapolis, 1914

Higham, Robin. *The British Rigid Airship, 1908–1931: A Study in Weapons Policy.* G. T. Foulis & Company Ltd. London, 1961

Hogg, Ian V. *Anti-Aircraft: A History of Air Defence.* Macdonald and Jane's. London, 1978

Hook, Thom. *Shenandoah Saga.* Air Show Publishers. Annapolis, Md, 1973

Hovgaard, William. *Modern History of Warships.* London 1920. Reprinted 1971

Hyth, Viscount and Leyland, John. *The Naval Annual, 1913–14.* William Clowes. London

Jameson, William, Rear Admiral. *The Most Formidable Thing. The Story of the Submarine from its Earliest Days to the End of World War I.* Rupert Hart-Davis Ltd. London, 1965

*Jane's All The World's Aircraft.* Jane's Yearbooks. London, 1909 to date

Jellicoe of Scapa, Admiral Viscount, GCB, OM, GCVO. *The Grand Fleet, 1914–16: Its Creation, Development and Work.* Cassell and Company. London, 1919

Jobe, J. *The Romance of Ballooning: The Story of the Early Aeronauts.* The Viking Press. New York, 1971

Jones, H. A. *The War in the Air. Official History of the War.* Oxford, 1937

Jones, Neville. *The Origins of Strategic Bombing: A Study of the Development of British Air Strategic Thought and Practice up to 1918.* William Kimber. London, 1973

Joubert, Philip, Air Chief Marshal Sir. *Birds and Fishes.* Hutchinson. London, 1960

Joux, Etienne, Engineer Général. *Un Dirigeable Militaire, 1911–1916.* Edition Blondel de la Rougery. Paris, 1931

Koleśnik, Eugène M. 'Future Trends.' *Jane's Freight Containers.* Jane's Yearbooks. London, 1970–1978

Kollman, Franz. *Das Zeppelinluftschiff: Seine Entwicklung Tätigkeit und Keistungen.* Verlag von M. Krayn. Berlin 1924

Lehmann, Ernest A., Captain and Mingos, Howard. *The Zeppelins.* G. P. Putnam's Sons. London 1927

Lehmann, Ernst A., Captain *Zeppelin.* Longmans, Green and Co. London, 1937

Levitt, E. H. *The Rigid Airship.* Sir Isaac Pitman & Sons. London, 1925

Liddell Hart, B. H. *History of the First World War.* Cassell and Co. Ltd. London, 1970

Litchfield, P. W. and Allen, Hugh. *Why has America no Rigid Airships?* First published 1945 and reprinted with additional material by 7C's Press, Inc. Riverside, CT, 1976

Luschnath, H. *Zeppelin–Weltfahrten.* Bilderstelle Lohse. Dresden, 1933

Maitland, E. M., Air Commodore. *R 34.* Hodder and Stoughton. London, 1920

Matt, Paul R. *United States Navy and Marine Corps Fighters, 1918–1962.* Harleyford Publications. Letchworth, 1962

Meager, George F., Captain. *My Airship Flights 1915–1930.* William Kimber. London, 1970

Morpurgo, J. E. *Barnes Wallis: A Biography.* Longman. London, 1972

McKinty, Alec. *The Father of British Airships: A Biography of E. T. Willows.* William Kimber. London, 1972

McPhee, John. *The Deltoid Pumpkin Seed.* Farrar, Straus and Giroux. New York, 1973

Nobile, Umberto, General. *My Polar Flights, An Account of the Voyages of the Airships Italia and Norge.* Frederick Muller. London, 1961

Nobile, Umberto, General. *With Italia to the North Pole.* George Allen & Unwin. London, 1930

D'Orcy, Ladislas. *D'Orcy's Airship*

*Manual: An International Register of Airships with a Compendium of the Airship's Elementary Mechanics.* The Century Co. New York, 1917

Orlovins, Dr Heinz, and Schulz, Ing. Richard. *Die Deutsche Luftfahrt Jahrbuch, 1937.* Naturkunde und Technik, Verlag Fritz Knapp. Frankfurt

Poirier, J. *Les Bombardeurs de Paris, 1914–1918.* 1930

Pratt, H. I. *Commercial Airships.* Nelson. London, 1920

Queck, Ulrich. 'Luftschiffahrt in Vergangenheit und Zukunft.' *Flieger-Jahrbuch, 1969.* Transpress VEB Verlag. Berlin, 1968

Raleigh, W. A., Sir and Jones, H. A. *The War in the Air* (official history). HMSO. London, 1928–35

Rawlinson, A. *The Defence of London, 1915–1918.* Andrew Melrose Ltd. London, 1923

Riiser–Larsen, H. J. *Femti År For Kongen.* Gyldendal Norsk Forlag, 1957

Robertson, Bruce. *Sopwith — The Man and His Aircraft.* Air Review Ltd. Letchworth, 1970

Robinson, Douglas H. *Giants in the Sky: A History of the Rigid Airship.* G. T. Foulis & Co Ltd. Henley-on-Thames, 1971

Robinson, Douglas H. *The LZ 129, Hindenburg.* Arco Publishing. New York, 1964

Robinson, Douglas H. *The Zeppelin in Combat: A History of the German Naval Airship Division, 1912–1918.* G. T. Foulis & Co Ltd. Henley-on-Thames, 1962

Role, Maurice. *L'Étrange Histoire des Zeppelins.* Editions France–Empire. Paris, 1972

Rosendahl, C. E., Lieutenant Commander. *Up Ship.* Dodd, Mead & Co. New York, 1932

Rosendahl, C. E., Lieutenant Commander. *What About The Airship.* Charles Scribner's Sons. New York, 1938

Roskill, S. W., Captain. *The Naval Air Service.* Vol. 1, 1908–1918. Navy Records Society, 1969

Santos–Dumont, Alberto. *My Airships: The Story of My Life.* Dover Publications. New York, 1973. Published in French as *Dans l'air* by Charpentier et Fasquelle in 1904, and the translation published in English by Grant Richards in London, 1904

Saunders, Hilary St George. *Per Ardua: The Rise of British Air Power, 1911–1939.* Oxford University Press. London, 1944

Shute, Nevil. *Slide Rule: The Autobiography of an Engineer.* William Heinemann. London, 1954

Sinclair, J. A., Captain. *Airships in Peace and War.* Richard & Cowan Ltd. London, 1934

Smith, Richard K. *The Airships Akron & Macon: Flying Aircraft Carriers of the United States Navy.* United States Naval Institute. Annapolis, Md, 1965

Tapper, Oliver. *Armstrong Whitworth Aircraft Since 1913.* Putnam. London, 1973

Upson, Ralph H. and de Frost–Chandler, Charles. *Free and Captive Balloons.* 1926

Ventry, Lord and Koleśnik, Eugène M. *Airship Development.* Jane's Pocket Book 7. Macdonald and Jane's. London, 1976

Voyer, Hirschauer, Colonel. *Les Ballons Dirigeables.* Berger–Levrault

Walker, Percy B. *Early Aviation at Farnborough. The History of the Royal Aircraft Establishment.* Vol. 1: *Balloons, Kites and Airships.* Macdonald & Co. (Publishers) Ltd. London, 1971

Warner, Edward P. *Aerostatics.* 1926

Whale, G. *British Airships Past, Present and Future.* John Lane, The Bodley Head. London, 1919

Williams, T. B., Captain. *Airship Pilot No. 28.* William Kimber. London, 1974

# Index

Page numbers in **bold** type refer to illustrations.

192